Table of Contents

Chapter One

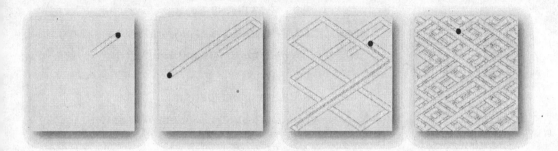

Elements of Programming

OUR GOAL IN THIS CHAPTER IS to convince you that writing a program is easier than writing a piece of text, such as a paragraph or essay. Writing prose is difficult: we spend many years in school to learn how to do it. By contrast, just a few building blocks suffice to enable us to write programs that can help solve all sorts of fascinating, but otherwise unapproachable, problems. In this chapter, we take you through these building blocks, get you started on programming in Java, and study a variety of interesting programs. You will be able to express yourself (by writing programs) within just a few weeks. Like the ability to write prose, the ability to program is a lifetime skill that you can continually refine well into the future.

In this book, you will learn the Java programming language. This task will be much easier for you than, for example, learning a foreign language. Indeed, programming languages are characterized by no more than a few dozen vocabulary words and rules of grammar. Much of the material that we cover in this book could be expressed in the C or C++ languages, or any of several other modern programming languages. But we describe everything specifically in Java so that you can get started creating and running programs right away. On the one hand, we will focus on learning to program, as opposed to learning details about Java. On the other hand, part of the challenge of programming is knowing which details are relevant in a given situation. Java is widely used, so learning to program in this language will enable you to write programs on many computers (your own, for example). Also, learning to program in Java will make it easy for you learn other languages, including lower-level languages such as C and specialized languages such as MATLAB.

1.1 Your First Program

IN THIS SECTION, OUR PLAN IS to lead you into the world of Java programming by taking you through the basic steps required to get a simple program running. The Java system is a collection of applications, not unlike many of the other applications that you are accustomed to using (such as your word processor, email program, and internet browser). As with any application, you need to be sure that Java is properly installed on your computer. It comes preloaded on many computers, or you can download it easily. You also need a text editor and a terminal application. Your first task is to find the instructions for installing such a Java programming environment on *your* computer by visiting

```
http://www.cs.princeton.edu/IntroProgramming
```

We refer to this site as the *booksite*. It contains an extensive amount of supplementary information about the material in this book for your reference and use. You will find it useful to have your browser open to this site while programming.

Programming in Java   To introduce you to developing Java programs, we break the process down into three steps. To program in Java, you need to:

- *Create* a program by typing it into a file named, say, MyCode.java.
- *Compile* it by typing javac MyCode.java in a terminal window.
- *Run* (or *execute*) it by typing java MyCode in the terminal window.

In the first step, you start with a blank screen and end with a sequence of typed characters on the screen, just as when you write an email message or a paper. Programmers use the term *code* to refer to program text and the term *coding* to refer to the act of creating and editing the code. In the second step, you use a system application that *compiles* your program (translates it into a form more suitable for the computer) and puts the result in a file named MyCode.class. In the third step, you transfer control of the computer from the system to your program (which returns control back to the system when finished). Many systems have several different ways to create, compile, and execute programs. We choose the sequence described here because it is the simplest to describe and use for simple programs.

Creating a program. A Java program is nothing more than a sequence of characters, like a paragraph or a poem, stored in a file with a `.java` extension. To create one, therefore, you need only define that sequence of characters, in the same way as you do for email or any other computer application. You can use any *text editor* for this task, or you can use one of the more sophisticated program development environments described on the booksite. Such environments are overkill for the sorts of programs we consider in this book, but they are not difficult to use, have many useful features, and are widely used by professionals.

Compiling a program. At first, it might seem that Java is designed to be best understood by the computer. To the contrary, the language is designed to be best understood by the programmer (that's you). The computer's language is far more primitive than Java. A *compiler* is an application that translates a program from the Java language to a language more suitable for executing on the computer. The compiler takes a file with a `.java` extension as input (your program) and produces a file with the same name but with a `.class` extension (the computer-language version). To use your Java compiler, type in a terminal window the `javac` command followed by the file name of the program you want to compile.

Executing a program. Once you compile the program, you can run it. This is the exciting part, where your program takes control of your computer (within the constraints of what the Java system allows). It is perhaps more accurate to say that your computer follows your instructions. It is even more accurate to say that a part of the Java system known as the *Java Virtual Machine* (the *JVM*, for short) directs your computer to follow your instructions. To use the JVM to execute your program, type the `java` command followed by the program name in a terminal window.

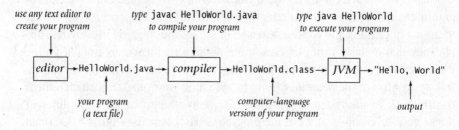

Developing a Java program

Program 1.1.1   Hello, World

```
public class HelloWorld
{
   public static void main(String[] args)
   {
      System.out.print("Hello, World");
      System.out.println();
   }
}
```

This code is a Java program that accomplishes a simple task. It is traditionally a beginner's first program. The box below shows what happens when you compile and execute the program. The terminal application gives a command prompt (% in this book) and executes the commands that you type (javac and then java in the example below). The result in this case is that the program prints a message in the terminal window (the third line).

```
% javac HelloWorld.java
% java HelloWorld
Hello, World
```

PROGRAM 1.1.1 IS AN EXAMPLE OF a complete Java program. Its name is HelloWorld, which means that its code resides in a file named HelloWorld.java (by convention in Java). The program's sole action is to print a message back to the terminal window. For continuity, we will use some standard Java terms to describe the program, but we will not define them until later in the book: PROGRAM 1.1.1 consists of a single *class* named HelloWorld that has a single *method* named main(). This method uses two other methods named System.out.print() and System.out.println() to do the job. (When referring to a method in the text, we use () after the name to distinguish it from other kinds of names.) Until SECTION 2.1, where we learn about classes that define multiple methods, all of our classes will have this same structure. For the time being, you can think of "class" as meaning "program."

The first line of a method specifies its name and other information; the rest is a sequence of *statements* enclosed in braces and each followed by a semicolon. For the time being, you can think of "programming" as meaning "specifying a class name and a sequence of statements for its main() method." In the next two sections, you will learn many different kinds of statements that you can use to make programs. For the moment, we will just use statements for printing to the terminal like the ones in HelloWorld.

When you type java followed by a class name in your terminal application, the system calls the main() method that you defined in that class, and executes its statements in order, one by one. Thus, typing java HelloWorld causes the system to call on the main() method in PROGRAM 1.1.1 and execute its two statements. The first statement calls on System.out.print() to print in the terminal window the message between the quotation marks, and the second statement calls on System.out.println() to terminate the line.

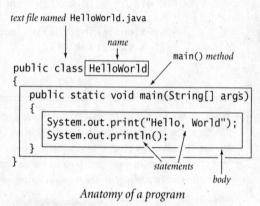

Anatomy of a program

Since the 1970s, it has been a tradition that a beginning programmer's first program should print "Hello, World". So, you should type the code in PROGRAM 1.1.1 into a file, compile it, and execute it. By doing so, you will be following in the footsteps of countless others who have learned how to program. Also, you will be checking that you have a usable editor and terminal application. At first, accomplishing the task of printing something out in a terminal window might not seem very interesting; upon reflection, however, you will see that one of the most basic functions that we need from a program is its ability to tell us what it is doing.

For the time being, all our program code will be just like PROGRAM 1.1.1, except with a different sequence of statements in main(). Thus, you do not need to start with a blank page to write a program. Instead, you can

• Copy HelloWorld.java into a new file having a new program name of your choice, followed by .java.

• Replace HelloWorld on the first line with the new program name.

• Replace the System.out.print() and System.out.println() statements with a different sequence of statements (each ending with a semicolon).

Your program is characterized by its sequence of statements and its name. Each Java program must reside in a file whose name matches the one after the word class on the first line, and it also must have a .java extension.

Program 1.1.2   *Using a command-line argument*

```
public class UseArgument
{
    public static void main(String[] args)
    {
        System.out.print("Hi, ");
        System.out.print(args[0]);
        System.out.println(". How are you?");
    }
}
```

This program shows the way in which we can control the actions of our programs: by providing an argument on the command line. Doing so allows us to tailor the behavior of our programs.

```
% javac UseArgument.java
% java UseArgument Alice
Hi, Alice. How are you?
% java UseArgument Bob
Hi, Bob. How are you?
```

Errors. It is easy to blur the distinction among editing, compiling, and executing programs. You should keep them separate in your mind when you are learning to program, to better understand the effects of the errors that inevitably arise. You can find several examples of errors in the Q&A at the end of this section. You can fix or avoid most errors by carefully examining the program as you create it, the same way you fix spelling and grammatical errors when you compose an email message. Some errors, known as *compile-time* errors, are caught when you compile the program, because they prevent the compiler from doing the translation. Other errors, known as *run-time* errors, do not show up until you execute the program. In general, errors in programs, also commonly known as *bugs*, are the bane of a programmer's existence: the error messages can be confusing or misleading, and the source of the error can be very hard to find. One of the first skills that you will learn is to identify errors; you will also learn to be sufficiently careful when coding, to avoid making many of them in the first place.

Input and Output   Typically, we want to provide *input* to our programs: data that they can process to produce a result. The simplest way to provide input data is illustrated in UseArgument (PROGRAM 1.1.2). Whenever UseArgument is executed, it reads the *command-line argument* that you type after the program name and prints it back out to the terminal as part of the message. The result of executing this program depends on what we type after the program name. After compiling the program once, we can run it for different command-line arguments and get different printed results. We will discuss in more detail the mechanism that we use to pass arguments to our programs later, in SECTION 2.1. In the meantime, you can use args[0] within your program's body to represent the string that you type on the command line when it is executed, just as in UseArgument.

Again, accomplishing the task of getting a program to write back out what we type in to it may not seem interesting at first, but upon reflection you will realize that another basic function of a program is its ability to respond to basic information from the user to control what the program does. The simple model that UseArgument represents will suffice to allow us to consider Java's basic programming mechanism and to address all sorts of interesting computational problems.

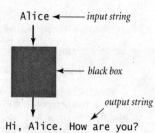

A bird's-eye view of a Java program

Stepping back, we can see that UseArgument does neither more nor less than implement a function that maps a string of characters (the argument) into another string of characters (the message printed back to the terminal). When using it, we might think of our Java program as a black box that converts our input string to some output string. This model is attractive because it is not only simple but also sufficiently general to allow completion, in principle, of any computational task. For example, the Java compiler itself is nothing more than a program that takes one string of characters as input (a .java file) and produces another string of characters as output (the corresponding .class file). Later, we will be able to write programs that accomplish a variety of interesting tasks (though we stop short of programs as complicated as a compiler). For the moment, we live with various limitations on the size and type of the input and output to our programs; in SECTION 1.5, we will see how to incorporate more sophisticated mechanisms for program input and output. In particular, we can work with arbitrarily long input and output strings and other types of data such as sound and pictures.

Q&A

Q. Why Java?

A. The programs that we are writing are very similar to their counterparts in several other languages, so our choice of language is not crucial. We use Java because it is widely available, embraces a full set of modern abstractions, and has a variety of automatic checks for mistakes in programs, so it is suitable for learning to program. There is no perfect language, and you certainly will be programming in other languages in the future.

Q. Do I really have to type in the programs in the book to try them out? I believe that you ran them and that they produce the indicated output.

A. Everyone should type in and run `HelloWorld`. Your understanding will be greatly magnified if you also run `UseArgument`, try it on various inputs, and modify it to test different ideas of your own. To save some typing, you can find all of the code in this book (and much more) on the booksite. This site also has information about installing and running Java on your computer, answers to selected exercises, web links, and other extra information that you may find useful or interesting.

Q. What is the meaning of the words `public`, `static` and `void`?

A. These keywords specify certain properties of `main()` that you will learn about later in the book. For the moment, we just include these keywords in the code (because they are required) but do not refer to them in the text.

Q. What is the meaning of the `//`, `/*`, and `*/` character sequences in the code?

A. They denote *comments*, which are ignored by the compiler. A comment is either text in between `/*` and `*/` or at the end of a line after `//`. As with most online code, the code on the booksite is liberally annotated with comments that explain what it does; we use fewer comments in code in this book because the accompanying text and figures provide the explanation.

Q. What are Java's rules regarding tabs, spaces, and newline characters?

A. Such characters are known as *whitespace* characters. Java compilers consider all whitespace in program text to be equivalent. For example, we could write `Hel-`

loWorld as follows:

```
public class HelloWorld { public static void main ( String []
args) { System.out.print("Hello, World")          ; System.out.
println() ;} }
```

But we do normally adhere to spacing and indenting conventions when we write Java programs, just as we always indent paragraphs and lines consistently when we write prose or poetry.

Q. What are the rules regarding quotation marks?

A. Material inside quotation marks is an exception to the rule defined in the previous question: things within quotes are taken literally so that you can precisely specify what gets printed. If you put any number of successive spaces within the quotes, you get that number of spaces in the output. If you accidentally omit a quotation mark, the compiler may get very confused, because it needs that mark to distinguish between characters in the string and other parts of the program.

Q. What happens when you omit a brace or misspell one of the words, like public or static or void or main?

A. It depends upon precisely what you do. Such errors are called *syntax errors* and are usually caught by the compiler. For example, if you make a program Bad that is exactly the same as HelloWorld except that you omit the line containing the first left brace (and change the program name from HelloWorld to Bad), you get the following helpful message:

```
% javac Bad.java
Bad.java:2: '{' expected
   public static void main(String[] args)
   ^
1 error
```

From this message, you might correctly surmise that you need to insert a left brace. But the compiler may not be able to tell you exactly what mistake you made, so the error message may be hard to understand. For example, if you omit the second left brace instead of the first one, you get the following messages:

```
% javac Bad.java
Bad.java:4: ';' expected
        System.out.print("Hello, World");
                                         ^
Bad.java:7: 'class' or 'interface' expected
}
^
Bad.java:8: 'class' or 'interface' expected
^
3 errors
```

One way to get used to such messages is to intentionally introduce mistakes into a simple program and then see what happens. Whatever the error message says, you should treat the compiler as a friend, for it is just trying to tell you that something is wrong with your program.

Q. Can a program use more than one command-line argument?

A. Yes, you can use many arguments, though we normally use just a few. Note that the count starts at 0, so you refer to the first argument as args[0], the second one as args[1], the third one as args[2], and so forth.

Q. What Java methods are available for me to use?

A. There are literally thousands of them. We introduce them to you in a deliberate fashion (starting in the next section) to avoid overwhelming you with choices.

Q. When I ran UseArgument, I got a strange error message. What's the problem?

A. Most likely, you forgot to include a command-line argument:

```
% java UseArgument
Hi, Exception in thread "main"
java.lang.ArrayIndexOutOfBoundsException: 0
        at UseArgument.main(UseArgument.java:6)
```

The JVM is complaining that you ran the program but did not type an argument as promised. You will learn more details about array indices in SECTION 1.4. Remember this error message: you are likely to see it again. Even experienced programmers forget to type arguments on occasion.

Exercises

1.1.1   Write a program that prints the Hello, World message 10 times.

1.1.2   Describe what happens if you omit the following in HelloWorld.java:
  a. public
  b. static
  c. void
  d. args

1.1.3   Describe what happens if you misspell (by, say, omitting the second letter) the following in HelloWorld.java:
  a. public
  b. static
  c. void
  d. args

1.1.4   Describe what happens if you try to execute UseArgument with each of the following command lines:
  a. java UseArgument java
  b. java UseArgument @!&^%
  c. java UseArgument 1234
  d. java UseArgument.java Bob
  e. java UseArgument Alice Bob

1.1.5   Modify UseArgument.java to make a program UseThree.java that takes three names and prints out a proper sentence with the names in the reverse of the order given, so that, for example, java UseThree Alice Bob Carol gives Hi Carol, Bob, and Alice.

1.2 Built-in Types of Data

WHEN PROGRAMMING IN JAVA, YOU MUST always be aware of the type of data that your program is processing. The programs in SECTION 1.1 process strings of characters, many of the programs in this section process numbers, and we consider numerous other types later in the book. Understanding the distinctions among them is so important that we formally define the idea: a *data type* is a *set of values* and a *set of operations* defined on those values. You are familiar with various types of numbers, such as integers and real numbers, and with operations defined on them, such as addition and multiplication. In mathematics, we are accustomed to thinking of sets of numbers as being infinite; in computer programs we have to work with a finite number of possibilities. Each operation that we perform is well-defined *only* for the finite set of values in an associated data type.

1.2.1	String concatenation example
1.2.2	Integer multiplication and division
1.2.3	Quadratic formula
1.2.4	Leap year
1.2.5	Casting to get a random integer

Programs in this section

There are eight *primitive* types of data in Java, mostly for different kinds of numbers. Of the eight primitive types, we most often use these: `int` for integers; `double` for real numbers; and `boolean` for true-false values. There are other types of data available in Java libraries: for example, the programs in SECTION 1.1 use the type `String` for strings of characters. Java treats the `String` type differently from other types because its usage for input and output is essential. Accordingly, it shares some characteristics of the primitive types: for example, some of its operations are built in to the Java language. For clarity, we refer to primitive types and `String` collectively as *built-in* types. For the time being, we concentrate on programs that are based on computing with built-in types. Later, you will learn about Java library data types and building your own data types. Indeed, programming in Java is often centered on building data types, as you shall see in CHAPTER 3.

After defining basic terms, we consider several sample programs and code fragments that illustrate the use of different types of data. These code fragments do not do much real computing, but you will soon see similar code in longer programs. Understanding data types (values and operations on them) is an essential step in beginning to program. It sets the stage for us to begin working with more intricate programs in the next section. Every program that you write will use code like the tiny fragments shown in this section.

type	set of values	common operators	sample literal values
int	integers	+ - * / %	99 -12 2147483647
double	floating-point numbers	+ - * /	3.14 -2.5 6.022e23
boolean	boolean values	&& || !	true false
char	characters		'A' '1' '%' '\n'
String	sequences of characters	+	"AB" Hello" "2.5"

Basic built-in data types

Definitions   To talk about data types, we need to introduce some terminology. To do so, we start with the following code fragment:

```
int a, b, c;
a = 1234;
b = 99;
c = a + b;
```

The first line is a *declaration* that declares the names of three *variables* to be the *identifiers* a, b, and c and their type to be int. The next three lines are *assignment statements* that change the values of the variables, using the *literals* 1234 and 99, and the *expression* a + b, with the end result that c has the value 1333.

Identifiers. We use identifiers to name variables (and many other things) in Java. An identifier is a sequence of letters, digits, _, and $, the first of which is not a digit. The sequences of characters abc, Ab$, abc123, and a_b are all legal Java identifiers, but Ab*, 1abc, and a+b are not. Identifiers are case-sensitive, so Ab, ab, and AB are all different names. You cannot use certain *reserved words*—such as public, static, int, double, and so forth—to name variables.

Literals. A literal is a source-code representation of a data-type value. We use strings of digits like 1234 or 99 to define int literal values, and add a decimal point as in 3.14159 or 2.71828 to define double literal values. To specify a boolean value, we use the keywords true or false, and to specify a String, we use a sequence of characters enclosed in quotes, such as "Hello, World". We will consider other kinds of literals as we consider each data type in more detail.

Variables. A variable is a name that we use to refer to a data-type value. We use variables to keep track of changing values as a computation unfolds. For example, we use the variable n in many programs to count things. We create a variable in a *declaration* that specifies its type and gives it a name. We compute with it by using the name in an *expression* that uses operations defined for its type. Each variable always stores one of the permissible data-type values.

Declaration statements. A declaration statement associates a variable name with a type at compile time. Java requires us to use declarations to specify the names and types of variables. By doing so, we are being explicit about any computation that we are specifying. Java is said to be a *strongly-typed* language, because the Java compiler can check for consistency at compile time (for example, it does not permit us to add a String to a double). This situation is precisely analogous to making sure that quantities have the proper units in a sci-

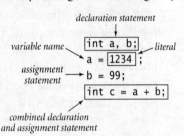

entific application (for example, it does not make sense to add a quantity measured in inches to another measured in pounds). Declarations can appear anywhere before a variable is first used—most often, we put them *at* the point of first use.

Using a primitive data type

Assignment statements. An assignment statement associates a data-type value with a variable. When we write c = a + b in Java, we are not expressing mathematical equality, but are instead expressing an action: set the value of the variable c to be the value of a plus the value of b. It is true that c is mathematically equal to a + b immediately after the assignment statement has been executed, but the point of the statement is to change the value of c (if necessary). The left-hand side of an assignment statement must be a single variable; the right-hand side can be an arbitrary *expression* that produces values of the type. For example, we can say discriminant = b*b - 4*a*c in Java, but we cannot say a + b = b + a or 1 = a. In short, *the meaning of = is decidedly not the same as in mathematical equations.* For example, a = b is certainly not the same as b = a, and while the value of c is the value of a plus the value of b after c = a + b has been executed, that may cease to be the case if subsequent statements change the values of any of the variables.

Initialization. In a simple declaration, the initial value of the variable is undefined. For economy, we can combine a declaration with an assignment statement to provide an initial value for the variable.

Tracing changes in variable values. As a final check on your understanding of the purpose of assignment statements, convince yourself that the following code *exchanges* the values of a and b (assume that a and b are int variables):

```
int t = a;
a = b;
b = t;
```

To do so, use a time-honored method of examining program behavior: study a table of the variable values after each statement (such a table is known as a *trace*).

	a	b	t
int a, b;	*undefined*	*undefined*	
a = 1234;	1234	*undefined*	
b = 99;	1234	99	
int t = a;	1234	99	1234
a = b;	99	99	1234
b = t;	99	1234	1234

Your first trace

Expressions. An expression is a literal, a variable, or a sequence of operations on literals and/or variables that produces a value. For primitive types, expressions look just like mathematical formulas, which are based on familiar symbols or *operators* that specify data-type operations to be performed on one or more *operands*. Each operand can be any expression. Most of the operators that we use are *binary operators* that take exactly two operands, such as x + 1 or y / 2. An expression that is enclosed in parentheses is another expression with the same value. For example, we can write 4 * (x - 3) or 4*x - 12 on the right-hand side of an assignment statement and the compiler will understand what we mean.

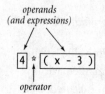

operands (and expressions)

operator

Anatomy of an expression

Precedence. Such expressions are shorthand for specifying a sequence of computations: in what order should they be performed? Java has natural and well-defined *precedence* rules (see the booksite) that fully specify this order. For arithmetic operations, multiplication and division are performed before addition and subtraction, so that a-b*c and a-(b*c) represent the same sequence of operations. When arithmetic operators have the same precedence, the order is determined by *left-associativity*, so that a-b-c and (a-b)-c represent the same sequence of operations. You can use parentheses to override the rules, so you should not need to worry about the details of precedence for most of the programs that you write. (Some of the programs that you *read* might depend subtly on precedence rules, but we avoid such programs in this book.)

Converting strings to primitive values for command-line arguments. Java provides the library methods that we need to convert the strings that we type as command-line arguments into numeric values for primitive types. We use the Java library methods `Integer.parseInt()` and `Double.parseDouble()` for this purpose. For example, typing `Integer.parseInt("123")` in program text yields the literal value 123 (typing 123 has the same effect) and the code `Integer. parseInt(args[0])` produces the same result as the literal value typed as a string on the command line. You will see several examples of this usage in the programs in this section.

Converting primitive type values to strings for output. As mentioned at the beginning of this section, the Java built-in `String` type obeys special rules. One of these special rules is that you can easily convert any type of data to a `String`: whenever we use the + operator with a `String` as one of its operands, Java automatically converts the other to a `String`, producing as a result the `String` formed from the characters of the first operand followed by the characters of the second operand. For example, the result of these two code fragments

```
String a = "1234";          String a = "1234";
String b = 99;              int b = 99;
String c = a + b;           String c = a + b;
```

are both the same: they assign to c the value "123499". We use this automatic conversion liberally to form `String` values for `System.out.print()` and `System. out.println()` for output. For example, we can write statements like this one:

```
System.out.println(a + " + " + b + " = " + c);
```

If a, b, and c are `int` variables with the values 1234, 99, and 1333, respectively, then this statement prints out the string 1234 + 99 = 1333.

WITH THESE MECHANISMS, OUR VIEW OF each Java program as a black box that takes string arguments and produces string results is still valid, but we can now interpret those strings as numbers and use them as the basis for meaningful computation. Next, we consider these details for the basic built-in types that you will use most often (strings, integers, floating-point numbers, and true–false values), along with sample code illustrating their use. To understand how to use a data type, you need to know not just its defined set of values, but also which operations you can perform, the language mechanism for invoking the operations, and the conventions for specifying literal values.

Characters and Strings

Characters and Strings   A char is an alphanumeric character or symbol, like the ones that you type. There are 2^{16} different possible character values, but we usually restrict attention to the ones that represent letters, numbers, symbols, and whitespace characters such as tab and newline. Literals for char are characters enclosed in single quotes; for example, 'a' represents the letter a. For tab, newline, backslash, single quote and double quote, we use the special *escape sequences* '\t', '\n', '\\', '\'', and '\"', respectively. The characters are encoded as 16-bit integers using an encoding scheme known as Unicode, and there are escape sequences for specifying special characters not found on your keyboard (see the booksite). We usually do not perform any operations directly on characters other than assigning values to variables.

values	sequences of characters
typical literals	"Hello," "1 " " " * "
operation	concatenate
operator	+

Java's built-in String data type

A String is a sequence of characters. A literal String is a sequence of characters within double quotes, such as "Hello, World". The String data type is *not* a primitive type, but Java sometimes treats it like one. For example, the *concatenation* operator (+) that we just considered is built in to the language as a binary operator in the same way as familiar operations on numbers.

The concatenation operation (along with the ability to declare String variables and to use them in expressions and assignment statements) is sufficiently powerful to allow us to attack some nontrivial computing tasks. As an example, Ruler (PROGRAM 1.2.1) computes a table of values of the *ruler function* that describes the relative lengths of the marks on a ruler. One noteworthy feature of this computation is that it illustrates how easy is is to craft short programs that produce huge amounts of output. If you extend this program in the obvious way to print five lines, six lines, seven lines, and so forth, you will see that each time you add just two statements to this program, you increase the size of its output by precisely one more than a factor of two.

expression	value
"Hi, " + "Bob"	"Hi, Bob"
"1" + " 2 " + "1"	"1 2 1"
"1234" + " + " + "99"	"1234 + 99"
"1234" + "99"	"123499"

Typical String expressions

Specifically, if the program prints n lines, the nth line contains $2^n - 1$ numbers. For example, if you were to add statements in this way so that the program prints 30 lines, it would attempt to print more than 1 *billion* numbers.

Program 1.2.1   *String concatenation example*

```
public class Ruler
{
   public static void main(String[] args)
   {
      String ruler1 = "1";
      String ruler2 = ruler1 + " 2 " + ruler1;
      String ruler3 = ruler2 + " 3 " + ruler2;
      String ruler4 = ruler3 + " 4 " + ruler3;
      System.out.println(ruler1);
      System.out.println(ruler2);
      System.out.println(ruler3);
      System.out.println(ruler4);
   }
}
```

This program prints the relative lengths of the subdivisions on a ruler. The nth line of output is the relative lengths of the marks on a ruler subdivided in intervals of $1/2^n$ of an inch. For example, the fourth line of output gives the relative lengths of the marks that indicate intervals of one-sixteenth of an inch on a ruler.

```
% javac Ruler.java
% java Ruler
1
1 2 1
1 2 1 3 1 2 1
1 2 1 3 1 2 1 4 1 2 1 3 1 2 1
```

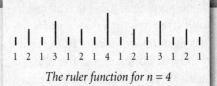

1 2 1 3 1 2 1 4 1 2 1 3 1 2 1

The ruler function for n = 4

As just discussed, our most frequent use (by far) of the concatenation operation is to put together results of computation for output with System.out.print() and System.out.println(). For example, we could simplify UseArgument (PROGRAM 1.1.2) by replacing its three statements with this single statement:

```
System.out.println("Hi, " + args[0] + ". How are you?");
```

We have considered the String type first precisely because we need it for output (and command-line input) in programs that process other types of data.

Integers   An int is an integer (natural number) between -2147483648 (-2^{31})
and 2147483647 ($2^{31}-1$). These bounds derive from the fact that integers are represented in binary with 32 binary digits: there are 2^{32} possible values. (The term
binary digit is omnipresent in computer science, and we nearly always use the abbreviation *bit*: a bit is either 0 or 1.) The range of possible int values is asymmetric
because zero is included with the positive values. See the booksite for more details
about number representation, but in the present context it suffices to know that
an int is one of the finite set of values in the range

just given. Sequences of the characters 0 through 9,
possibly with a plus or minus sign at the beginning
(that, when interpreted as decimal numbers, fall
within the defined range), are integer literal values.
We use ints frequently because they naturally arise
when implementing programs.

expression	value	comment
5 + 3	8	
5 - 3	2	
5 * 3	15	
5 / 3	1	no fractional part
5 % 3	2	remainder
1 / 0		run-time error
3 * 5 - 2	13	* has precedence
3 + 5 / 2	5	/ has precedence
3 - 5 - 2	-4	left associative
(3 - 5) - 2	-4	better style
3 - (5 - 2)	0	unambiguous

Typical int expressions

Standard arithmetic operators for addition/
subtraction (+ and -), multiplication (*), division
(/), and remainder (%) for the int data type are
built in to Java. These operators take two int operands and produce an int result, with one significant exception—division or remainder by zero is
not allowed. These operations are defined just as in
grade school (keeping in mind that all results must
be integers): given two int values a and b, the value
of a / b is the number of times b goes into a *with
the fractional part discarded*, and the value of a % b is the remainder that you get
when you divide a by b. For example, the value of 17 / 3 is 5, and the value of 17 % 3
is 2. The int results that we get from arithmetic operations are just what we expect,
except that if the result is too large to fit into int's 32-bit representation, then it
will be truncated in a well-defined manner. This situation is known as *overflow*. In

values	integers between -2^{31} and $+2^{31}-1$				
typical literals	1234 99 -99 0 1000000				
operations	add	subtract	multiply	divide	remainder
operators	+	-	*	/	%

Java's built-in int data type

Program 1.2.2   Integer multiplication and division

```java
public class IntOps
{
    public static void main(String[] args)
    {
        int a = Integer.parseInt(args[0]);
        int b = Integer.parseInt(args[1]);
        int p = a * b;
        int q = a / b;
        int r = a % b;
        System.out.println(a + " * " + b + " = " + p);
        System.out.println(a + " / " + b + " = " + q);
        System.out.println(a + " % " + b + " = " + r);
        System.out.println(a + " = " + q + " * " + b + " + " + r);
    }
}
```

Arithmetic for integers is built in to Java. Most of this code is devoted to the task of getting the values in and out; the actual arithmetic is in the simple statements in the middle of the program that assign values to p, q, and r.

```
% javac IntOps.java
% java IntOps 1234 99
1234 * 99 = 122166
1234 / 99 = 12
1234 % 99 = 46
1234 = 12 * 99 + 46
```

general, we have to take care that such a result is not misinterpreted by our code. For the moment, we will be computing with small numbers, so you do not have to worry about these boundary conditions.

PROGRAM 1.2.2 illustrates basic operations for manipulating integers, such as the use of expressions involving arithmetic operators. It also demonstrates the use of Integer.parseInt() to convert String values on the command line to int values, as well as the use of automatic type conversion to convert int values to String values for output.

Three other built-in types are different representations of integers in Java. The long, short, and byte types are the same as int except that they use 64, 16, and 8 bits respectively, so the range of allowed values is accordingly different. Programmers use long when working with huge integers, and the other types to save space. You can find a table with the maximum and minimum values for each type on the booksite, or you can figure them out for yourself from the numbers of bits.

Floating-point numbers   The double type is for representing *floating-point* numbers, for use in scientific and commercial applications. The internal representation is like scientific notation, so that we can compute with numbers in a huge range. We use floating-point numbers to represent real numbers, but they are decidedly not the same as real numbers! There are infinitely many real numbers, but we can only represent a finite number of floating-points in any digital computer representation. Floating-point numbers do approximate real numbers sufficiently well that we can use them in applications, but we often need to cope with the fact that we cannot always do exact computations.

expression	value
3.141 + .03	3.171
3.141 - .03	3.111
6.02e23 / 2.0	3.01e23
5.0 / 3.0	1.6666666666666667
10.0 % 3.141	0.577
1.0 / 0.0	Infinity
Math.sqrt(2.0)	1.4142135623730951
Math.sqrt(-1.0)	NaN

Typical double *expressions*

We can use a sequence of digits with a decimal point to type floating-point numbers. For example, 3.14159 represents a six-digit approximation to π. Alternatively, we can use a notation like scientific notation: the literal 6.022e23 represents the number 6.022×10^{23}. As with integers, you can use these conventions to write floating-point literals in your programs or to provide floating-point numbers as string parameters on the command line.

The arithmetic operators +, -, *, and / are defined for double. Beyond the built-in operators, the Java Math library defines the square root, trigonometric

values	real numbers (specified by IEEE 754 standard)			
typical literals	3.14159 6.022e23 -3.0 2.0 1.4142135623730951			
operations	add	subtract	multiply	divide
operators	+	-	*	/

Java's built-in double *data type*

Program 1.2.3   *Quadratic formula*

```
public class Quadratic
{
   public static void main(String[] args)
   {
      double b = Double.parseDouble(args[0]);
      double c = Double.parseDouble(args[1]);
      double discriminant = b*b - 4.0*c;
      double d = Math.sqrt(discriminant);
      System.out.println((-b + d) / 2.0);
      System.out.println((-b - d) / 2.0);
   }
}
```

This program prints out the roots of the polynomial $x^2 + bx + c$, using the quadratic formula. For example, the roots of $x^2 - 3x + 2$ are 1 and 2 since we can factor the equation as $(x - 1)(x - 2)$; the roots of $x^2 - x - 1$ are ϕ and $1 - \phi$, where ϕ is the golden ratio, and the roots of $x^2 + x + 1$ are not real numbers.

```
% javac Quadratic.java
% java Quadratic -3.0 2.0
2.0
1.0
```

```
% java Quadratic -1.0 -1.0
1.618033988749895
-0.6180339887498949

% java Quadratic 1.0 1.0
NaN
NaN
```

functions, logarithm/exponential functions, and other common functions for floating-point numbers. To use one of these values in an expression, we write the name of the function followed by its argument in parentheses. For example, you can use the code Math.sqrt(2.0) when you want to use the square root of 2 in an expression. We discuss in more detail the mechanism behind this arrangement in SECTION 2.1 and more details about the Math library at the end of this section.

When working with floating point numbers, one of the first things that you will encounter is the issue of *precision*: 5.0/2.0 is 2.5 but 5.0/3.0 is 1.6666666666666667. In SECTION 1.5, you will learn Java's mechanism for controlling the number of significant digits that you see in output. Until then, we will work with the Java default output format.

The result of a calculation can be one of the special values Infinity (if the number is too large to be represented) or NaN (if the result of the calculation is undefined). Though there are myriad details to consider when calculations involve these values, you can use double in a natural way and begin to write Java programs instead of using a calculator for all kinds of calculations. For example, PROGRAM 1.2.3 shows the use of double values in computing the roots of a quadratic equation using the quadratic formula. Several of the exercises at the end of this section further illustrate this point.

As with long, short, and byte for integers, there is another representation for real numbers called float. Programmers sometimes use float to save space when precision is a secondary consideration. The double type is useful for about 15 significant digits; the float type is good for only about 7 digits. We do not use float in this book.

values	true or false		
literals	true false		
operations	and	or	not
operators	&&	||	!

Java's built-in boolean *data type*

Booleans   The boolean type has just two values: true and false. These are the two possible boolean literals. Every boolean variable has one of these two values, and every boolean operation has operands and a result that takes on just one of these two values. This simplicity is deceiving—boolean values lie at the foundation of computer science.

The most important operations defined for booleans are *and* (&&), *or* (\|\|), and *not* (!), which have familiar definitions:

• a && b is true if both operands are true, and false if either is false.
• a \|\| b is false if both operands are false, and true if either is true.
• !a is true if a is false, and false if a is true.

Despite the intuitive nature of these definitions, it is worthwhile to fully specify each possibility for each operation in tables known as *truth tables*. The *not* function

a	!a		a	b	a && b	a || b
true	false		false	false	false	false
false	true		false	true	false	true
			true	false	false	true
			true	true	true	true

Truth-table definitions of boolean *operations*

a	b	a && b	!a	!b	!a || !b	!(!a || !b)
false	false	false	true	true	true	false
false	true	false	true	false	true	false
true	false	false	false	true	true	false
true	true	true	false	false	false	true

Truth-table proof that a && b *and* !(!a \|\| !b) *are identical*

has only one operand: its value for each of the two possible values of the operand is specified in the second column. The *and* and *or* functions each have two operands: there are four different possibilities for operand input values, and the values of the functions for each possibility are specified in the right two columns.

We can use these operators with parentheses to develop arbitrarily complex expressions, each of which specifies a well-defined boolean function. Often the same function appears in different guises. For example, the expressions (a && b) and !(!a \|\| !b) are equivalent.

The study of manipulating expressions of this kind is known as *Boolean logic*. This field of mathematics is fundamental to computing: it plays an essential role in the design and operation of computer hardware itself, and it is also a starting point for the theoretical foundations of computation. In the present context, we are interested in boolean expressions because we use them to control the behavior of our programs. Typically, a particular condition of interest is specified as a boolean expression and a piece of program code is written to execute one set of statements if the expression is true and a different set of statements if the expression is false. The mechanics of doing so are the topic of SECTION 1.3.

Comparisons   Some *mixed-type* operators take operands of one type and produce a result of another type. The most important operators of this kind are the comparison operators ==, !=, <, <=, >, and >=, which all are defined for each primitive numeric type and produce a boolean result. Since operations are defined only

non-negative discriminant?	(b*b - 4.0*a*c) >= 0.0
beginning of a century?	(year % 100) == 0
legal month?	(month >= 1) && (month <= 12)

Typical comparison expressions

Program 1.2.4   Leap year

```
public class LeapYear
{
   public static void main(String[] args)
   {
      int year = Integer.parseInt(args[0]);
      boolean isLeapYear;
      isLeapYear = (year % 4 == 0);
      isLeapYear = isLeapYear && (year % 100 != 0);
      isLeapYear = isLeapYear || (year % 400 == 0);
      System.out.println(isLeapYear);
   }
}
```

This program tests whether an integer corresponds to a leap year in the Gregorian calendar. A year is a leap year if it is divisible by 4 (2004), unless it is divisible by 100 in which case it is not (1900), unless it is divisible by 400 in which case it is (2000).

```
% javac LeapYear.java
% java LeapYear 2004
true
% java LeapYear 1900
false
% java LeapYear 2000
true
```

with respect to data types, each of these symbols stands for many operations, one for each data type. It is required that both operands be of the same type. The result is always boolean.

Even without going into the details of number representation, it is clear that the operations for the various types are really quite different: for example, it is one thing to compare two ints to check that (2 <= 2) is true but quite another to compare two doubles to check whether (2.0 <= 0.002e3) is true or false. Still, these operations are well-defined and useful to write code that tests for conditions such as (b*b - 4.0*a*c) >= 0.0, which is frequently needed, as you will see.

The comparison operations have lower precedence than arithmetic operators and higher precedence than boolean operators, so you do not need the parentheses in an expression like `(b*b - 4.0*a*c) >= 0.0`, and you could write an expression like `month >= 1 && month <= 12` without parentheses to test whether the value of the `int` variable `month` is between 1 and 12. (It is better style to use the parentheses, however.)

op	meaning	true	false
==	equal	2 == 2	2 == 3
!=	not equal	3 != 2	2 != 2
<	less than	2 < 13	2 < 2
<=	less than or equal	2 <= 2	3 <= 2
>	greater than	13 > 2	2 > 13
>=	greater than or equal	3 >= 2	2 >= 3

Comparisons with `int` *operands and a* `boolean` *result*

Comparison operations, together with boolean logic, provide the basis for decision-making in Java programs. PROGRAM 1.2.4 is an example of their use, and you can find other examples in the exercises at the end of this section. More importantly, in SECTION 1.3 we will see the role that boolean expressions play in more sophisticated programs.

Library methods and APIs   As we have seen, many programming tasks involve using Java library methods in addition to the built-in operations on data-type values. The number of available library methods is vast. As you learn to program, you will learn to use more and more library methods, but it is best at the beginning to restrict your attention to a relatively small set of methods. In this chapter, you have already used some of Java's methods for printing, for converting data from one type to another, and for computing mathematical functions (the Java `Math` library). In later chapters, you will learn not just how to use other methods, but how to create and use your own methods.

For convenience, we will consistently summarize the library methods that you need to know how to use in tables like this one:

```
public class System.out
```

void print(String s)	*print* s
void println(String s)	*print* s, *followed by a newline*
void println()	*print a newline*

Note: Any type of data can be used (and will be automatically converted to `String`*).*

Excerpts from Java's library for standard output

Such a table is known as an *applications programming interface (API)*. It provides the information that you need to write an *applications program* that uses the methods. Here is an API for the most commonly used methods in Java's Math library:

```
public class Math
```
---

double abs(double a)	*absolute value of a*
double max(double a, double b)	*maximum of a and b*
double min(double a, double b)	*minimum of a and b*

Note 1: abs(), max(), *and* min() *are defined also for* int, long, *and* float.

double sin(double theta)	*sine function*
double cos(double theta)	*cosine function*
double tan(double theta)	*tangent function*

Note 2: Angles are expressed in radians. Use toDegrees() *and* toRadians() *to convert.*
Note 3: Use asin(), acos(), *and* atan() *for inverse functions.*

double exp(double a)	*exponential (e^a)*
double log(double a)	*natural log ($\log_e a$, or ln a)*
double pow(double a, double b)	*raise a to the bth power (a^b)*
long round(double a)	*round to the nearest integer*
double random()	*random number in [0, 1)*
double sqrt(double a)	*square root of a*
double E	*value of e (constant)*
double PI	*value of π (constant)*

See booksite for other available functions.

Excerpts from Java's mathematics library

With the exception of random(), these methods implement mathematical functions—they use their arguments to compute a value of a specified type. Each method is described by a line in the API that specifies the information you need to know in order to use the method. The code in the tables is *not* the code that you type to use the method; it is known as the method's *signature*. The signature specifies the type of the arguments, the method name, and the type of the value that the method computes (the *return value*). When your program is executed, we say that it *calls* the system library code for the method, which *returns* the value for use in your code.

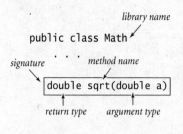

library name

```
public class Math
```

signature   *method name*

```
double sqrt(double a)
```

return type   *argument type*

. . .

Anatomy of a method signature

Note that random() does not implement a mathematical function because it does not take an argument. On the other hand, System.out.print() and System.out.println() do not implement mathematical functions because they do not return values and therefore do not have a return type. (This condition is specified in the signature by the keyword void.)

In your code, you can use a library method by typing its name followed by arguments of the specified type, enclosed in parentheses and separated by commas. You can use this code in the same way as you use variables and literals in expressions. When you do so, you can expect that method to compute a value of the appropriate type, as documented in the left column of the API. For example, you can write expressions like Math.sin(x) * Math.cos(y) and so on. Method arguments may also be expressions, as in Math.sqrt(b*b - 4.0*a*c).

library name   *method name*

```
double d = Math.sqrt(b*b - 4.0*a*c);
```

return type   *argument*

Using a library method

The Math library also defines the precise constant values PI (for π) and E (for e), so that you can use those names to refer to those constants in your programs. For example, the value of Math.sin(Math.PI/2) is 1.0 and the value of Math.log(Math.E) is 1.0 (because Math.sin() takes its argument in radians and Math.log() implements the natural logarithm function).

To be complete, we also include here the following API for Java's conversion methods, which we use for command-line arguments:

int Integer.parseInt(String s)	*convert* s *to an* int *value*
double Double.parseDouble(String s)	*convert* s *to a* double *value*
long Long.parseLong(String s)	*convert* s *to a* long *value*

Java library methods for converting strings to primitive types

You *do not* need to use methods like these to convert from int, double, and long values to String values for *output*, because Java automatically converts any value used as an argument to System.out.print() or System.out.println() to String for output.

expression	library	type	value
Integer.parseInt("123")	Integer	int	123
Math.sqrt(5.0*5.0 - 4.0*4.0)	Math	double	3.0
Math.random()	Math	double	*random in* $[0, 1)$
Math.round(3.14159)	Math	long	3

Typical expressions that use Java library methods

These APIs are typical of the online documentation that is the standard in modern programming. There is extensive online documentation of the Java APIs that is used by professional programmers, and it is available to you (if you are interested) directly from the Java website or through our booksite. You do not need to go to the online documentation to understand the code in this book or to write similar code, because we present and explain in the text all of the library methods that we use in APIs like these and summarize them in the endpapers. More important, in CHAPTERS 2 AND 3 you will learn in this book how to develop your own APIs and to implement functions for your own use.

Type conversion   One of the primary rules of modern programming is that you should always be aware of the type of data that your program is processing. Only by knowing the type can you know precisely which set of values each variable can have, which literals you can use, and which operations you can perform. Typical programming tasks involve processing multiple types of data, so we often need to convert data from one type to another. There are several ways to do so in Java.

Explicit type conversion. You can use a method that takes an argument of one type (the value to be converted) and produces a result of another type. We have already used the Integer.parseInt() and Double.parseDouble() library methods to convert String values to int and double values, respectively. Many other methods are available for conversion among other types. For example, the library method Math.round() takes a double argument and returns a long result: the nearest integer to the argument. Thus, for example, Math.round(3.14159) and Math.round(2.71828) are both of type long and have the same value (3).

Explicit cast. Java has some built-in type conversion conventions for primitive types that you can take advantage of when you are aware that you might lose information. You have to make your intention to do so explicit by using a device called a *cast*. You cast an expression from one primitive type to another by prepending the desired type name within parentheses. For example, the expression (int) 2.71828 is a cast from double to int that produces an int with value 2. The conversion methods defined for casts throw away information in a reasonable way (for a full list, see the booksite). For example, casting a floating-point number to an integer discards the fractional part by rounding towards zero. If you want a different result, such as rounding to the nearest integer, you must use the explicit conversion method Math.round(), as just discussed (but you then need to use an explicit cast to int, since that method returns a long). RandomInt (PROGRAM 1.2.5) is an example that uses a cast for a practical computation.

Automatic promotion for numbers. You can use data of any primitive numeric type where a value whose type has a larger range of values is expected, because Java automatically converts to the type with the larger range. This kind of conversion is called *promotion*. For example, we used numbers all of type double in PROGRAM 1.2.3, so there is no conversion. If we had chosen to make b and c of type int (using Integer.parseInt() to convert the command-line arguments), automatic promotion would be used to evaluate the expression b*b - 4.0*c. First, c is promoted to double to multiply by the double literal 4.0, with a double result. Then, the int value b*b is promoted to double for the subtraction, leaving a double result. Or, we might have written b*b - 4*c. In that case, the expression b*b - 4*c would be evaluated as an int and then the result promoted to double, because that is what Math.sqrt() expects. Promotion is appropriate because your intent is clear and it can be done with no loss of information. On the other hand, a conversion that might involve loss of information (for example, assigning a double to an int) leads to a compile-time error.

expression	expression type	expression value
"1234" + 99	String	"123499"
Integer.parseInt("123")	int	123
(int) 2.71828	int	2
Math.round(2.71828)	long	3
(int) Math.round(2.71828)	int	3
(int) Math.round(3.14159)	int	3
11 * 0.3	double	3.3
(int) 11 * 0.3	double	3.3
11 * (int) 0.3	int	0
(int) (11 * 0.3)	int	3

Typical type conversions

Program 1.2.5   *Casting to get a random integer*

```java
public class RandomInt
{
    public static void main(String[] args)
    {
        int N = Integer.parseInt(args[0]);
        double r = Math.random();   // uniform between 0 and 1
        int n = (int) (r * N);      // uniform between 0 and N-1
        System.out.println(n);
    }
}
```

This program uses the Java method `Math.random()` *to generate a random number r in the interval* [0, 1), *then multiplies r by the command-line argument* N *to get a random number greater than or equal to 0 and less than* N, *then uses a cast to truncate the result to be an integer n between 0 and* N-1.

```
% javac RandomInt.java

% java RandomInt 1000
548

% java RandomInt 1000
141

% java RandomInt 1000000
135032
```

Casting has higher precedence than arithmetic operations—any cast is applied to the value that immediately follows it. For example, if we write int n = (int) 11 * 0.3, the cast is no help: the literal 11 is already an integer, so the cast (int) has no effect. In this example, the compiler produces a possible loss of precision error message because there would be a loss of precision in converting the resulting value (3.3) to an int for assignment to n. The error is helpful because the intended computation for this code is likely (int) (11 * 0.3), which has the value 3, not 3.3.

BEGINNING PROGRAMMERS TEND TO FIND TYPE conversion to be an annoyance, but experienced programmers know that paying careful attention to data types is a key to success in programming. It is well worth your while to take the time to understand what type conversion is all about. After you have written just a few programs, you will understand that these rules help you to make your intentions explicit and to avoid subtle bugs in your programs.

Summary   *A data type is a set of values and a set of operations on those values.* Java has eight primitive data types: boolean, char, byte, short, int, long, float, and double. In Java code, we use operators and expressions like those in familiar mathematical expressions to invoke the operations associated with each type. The boolean type is for computing with the logical values true and false; the char type is the set of character values that we type; and the other six are numeric types, for computing with numbers. In this book, we most often use boolean, int, and double; we do not use short or float. Another data type that we use frequently, String, is not primitive, but Java has some built-in facilities for Strings that are like those for primitive types.

When programming in Java, we have to be aware that every operation is defined only in the context of its data type (so we may need type conversions) and that all types can have only a finite number of values (so we may need to live with imprecise results).

The boolean type and its operations— &&, ||, and ! —are the basis for logical decision-making in Java programs, when used in conjunction with the mixed-type comparison operators ==, !=, <, >, <=, and >=. Specifically, we use boolean expressions to control Java's conditional (if) and loop (for and while) constructs, which we will study in detail in the next section.

The numeric types and Java's libraries give us the ability to use Java as an extensive mathematical calculator. We write arithmetic expressions using the built-in operators +, -, *, /, and % along with Java methods from the Math library. Although the programs in this section are quite rudimentary by the standards of what we will be able to do after the next section, this class of programs is quite useful in its own right. You will use primitive types and basic mathematical functions extensively in Java programming, so the effort that you spend now understanding them will certainly be worthwhile.

Q. What happens if I forget to declare a variable?

A. The compiler complains, as shown below for a program IntOpsBad, which is the same as PROGRAM 1.2.2 except that the int variable p is omitted from the declaration statement.

```
% javac IntOpsBad.java
IntOpsBad.java:7: cannot resolve symbol
symbol : variable p
location: class IntOpsBad
p = a * b;
        ^
IntOpsBad.java:10: cannot resolve symbol
symbol : variable p
location: class IntOpsBad
System.out.println(a + " * " + b + " = " + p);
                                             ^
2 errors
```

The compiler says that there are two errors, but there is really just one: the declaration of p is missing. If you forget to declare a variable that you use often, you will get quite a few error messages. A good strategy is to correct the *first* error and check that correction before addressing later ones.

Q. What happens if I forget to initialize a variable?

A. The compiler checks for this condition and will give you a `variable might not have been initialized` error message if you try to use the variable in an expression.

Q. Is there a difference between = and == ?

A. Yes, they are quite different! The first is an assignment operator that changes the value of a variable, and the second is a comparison operator that produces a boolean result. Your ability to understand this answer is a sure test of whether you understood the material in this section. Think about how you might explain the difference to a friend.

Q. Why do `int` values sometime become negative when they get large?

A. If you have not experienced this phenomenon, see Exercise 1.2.10. The problem has to do with the way integers are represented in the computer. You can learn the details on the booksite. In the meantime, a safe strategy is using the `int` type when you know the values to be less than ten digits and the `long` type when you think the values might get to be ten digits or more.

Q. It seems wrong that Java should just let `int`s overflow and give bad values. Shouldn't Java automatically check for overflow?

A. Yes, this issue is a contentious one among programmers. The short answer for now is that the lack of such checking is one reason such types are called *primitive* data types. A little knowledge can go a long way in avoiding such problems. Again, it is fine to use the `int` type for small numbers, but when values run into the billions, you cannot.

Q. What is the value of `Math.abs(-2147483648)`?

A. -2147483648. This strange (but true) result is a typical example of the effects of integer overflow.

Q. It is annoying to see all those digits when printing a `float` or a `double`. Can we get `System.out.println()` to print out just two or three digits after the decimal point?

A. That sort of task involves a closer look at the method used to convert from `double` to `String`. The Java library function `System.out.printf()` is one way to do the job, and it is similar to the basic printing method in the C programming language and many modern languages, as discussed in Section 1.5. Until then, we will live with the extra digits (which is not all bad, since doing so helps us to get used to the different primitive types of numbers).

Q. How can I initialize a `double` variable to infinity?

A. Java has built-in constants available for this purpose: `Double.POSITIVE_IN-FINITY` and `Double.NEGATIVE_INFINITY`.

Q. What is the value of `Math.round(6.022e23)`?

A. You should get in the habit of typing in a tiny Java program to answer such questions yourself (and trying to understand why your program produces the result that it does).

Q. Can you compare a `double` to an `int`?

A. Not without doing a type conversion, but remember that Java usually does the requisite type conversion automatically. For example, if `x` is an `int` with the value 3, then the expression `(x < 3.1)` is true—Java converts `x` to `double` (because `3.1` is a `double` literal) before performing the comparison.

Q. Are expressions like `1/0` and `1.0/0.0` legal in Java?

A. No and yes. The first generates a run-time *exception* for division by zero (which stops your program because the value is undefined); the second is legal and has the value `Infinity`.

Q. Are there functions in Java's `Math` library for other trigonometric functions, like cosecant, secant, and cotangent?

A No, because you could use `Math.sin()`, `Math.cos()`, and `Math.tan()` to compute them. Choosing which functions to include in an API is a tradeoff between the convenience of having every function that you need and the annoyance of having to find one of the few that you need in a long list. No choice will satisfy all users, and the Java designers have many users to satisfy. Note that there are plenty of redundancies even in the APIs that we have listed. For example, you could use `Math.sin(x)/Math.cos(x)` instead of `Math.tan(x)`.

Q. Can you use `<` and `>` to compare `String` variables?

A. No. Those operators are defined only for primitive types.

Q. How about `==` and `!=`?

A. Yes, but the result may not be what you expect, because of the meanings these operators have for non-primitive types. For example, there is a distinction between

a String and its value. The expression "abc" == "ab" + x is false when x is a String with value "c" because the two operands are stored in different places in memory (even though they have the same value). This distinction is essential, as you will learn when we discuss it in more detail in SECTION 3.1.

Q. What is the result of division and remainder for negative integers?

A. The quotient a / b rounds toward 0; the remainder a % b is defined such that (a / b) * b + a % b is always equal to a. For example, -14/3 and 14/-3 are both -4, but -14 % 3 is -2 and 14 % -3 is 2.

Q. Will (a < b < c) test whether three numbers are in order?

A. No, that will not compile. You need to say (a < b && b < c).

Q. Fifteen digits for floating-point numbers certainly seems enough to me. Do I really need to worry much about precision?

A. Yes, because you are used to mathematics based on real numbers with infinite precision, whereas the computer always deals with approximations. For example, (0.1 + 0.1 == 0.2) is true but (0.1 + 0.1 + 0.1 == 0.3) is false! Pitfalls like this are not at all unusual in scientific computing. Novice programmers should avoid comparing two floating-point numbers for equality.

Q. Why do we say (a && b) and not (a & b)?

A. Java also has a & operator that we do not use in this book but which you may encounter if you pursue advanced programming courses.

Q. Why is the value of 10^6 not 1000000 but 12?

A. The ^ operator is not an exponentiation operator, which you must have been thinking. Instead, it is an operator like & that we do not use in this book. You want the literal 1e6. You could also use Math.pow(10, 6) but doing so is wasteful if you are raising 10 to a known power.

Exercises

1.2.1 Suppose that a and b are int values. What does the following sequence of statements do?

```
int t = a; b = t; a = b;
```

1.2.2 Write a program that uses Math.sin() and Math.cos() to check that the value of $\cos^2\theta + \sin^2\theta$ is approximately 1 for any θ entered as a command-line argument. Just print the value. Why are the values not always exactly 1?

1.2.3 Suppose that a and b are int values. Show that the expression

```
(!(a && b) && (a || b)) || ((a && b) || !(a || b))
```

is equivalent to true.

1.2.4 Suppose that a and b are int values. Simplify the following expression: (!(a < b) && !(a > b)).

1.2.5 The *exclusive or* operator ∧ for boolean operands is defined to be true if they are different, false if they are the same. Give a truth table for this function.

1.2.6 Why does 10/3 give 3 and not 3.333333333?

Solution. Since both 10 and 3 are integer literals, Java sees no need for type conversion and uses integer division. You should write 10.0/3.0 if you mean the numbers to be double literals. If you write 10/3.0 or 10.0/3, Java does implicit conversion to get the same result.

1.2.7 What do each of the following print?
  a. System.out.println(2 + "bc");
  b. System.out.println(2 + 3 + "bc");
  c. System.out.println((2+3) + "bc");
  d. System.out.println("bc" + (2+3));
  e. System.out.println("bc" + 2 + 3);

Explain each outcome.

1.2.8 Explain how to use PROGRAM 1.2.3 to find the square root of a number.

1.2.9 What do each of the following print?

 a. `System.out.println('b');`

 b. `System.out.println('b' + 'c');`

 c. `System.out.println((char) ('a' + 4));`

Explain each outcome.

1.2.10 Suppose that a variable a is declared as int a = 2147483647 (or equivalently, Integer.MAX_VALUE). What do each of the following print?

 a. `System.out.println(a);`

 b. `System.out.println(a+1);`

 c. `System.out.println(2-a);`

 d. `System.out.println(-2-a);`

 e. `System.out.println(2*a);`

 f. `System.out.println(4*a);`

Explain each outcome.

1.2.11 Suppose that a variable a is declared as double a = 3.14159. What do each of the following print?

 a. `System.out.println(a);`

 b. `System.out.println(a+1);`

 c. `System.out.println(8/(int) a);`

 d. `System.out.println(8/a);`

 e. `System.out.println((int) (8/a));`

Explain each outcome.

1.2.12 Describe what happens if you write sqrt instead of Math.sqrt in PROGRAM 1.2.3.

1.2.13 What is the value of (Math.sqrt(2) * Math.sqrt(2) == 2) ?

1.2.14 Write a program that takes two positive integers as command-line arguments and prints `true` if either evenly divides the other.

1.2.15 Write a program that takes three positive integers as command-line arguments and prints `true` if any one of them is greater than or equal to the sum of the other two and `false` otherwise. (*Note:* This computation tests whether the three numbers could be the lengths of the sides of some triangle.)

1.2.16 A physics student gets unexpected results when using the code

```
F = G * mass1 * mass2 / r * r;
```

to compute values according to the formula $F = Gm_1m_2 / r^2$. Explain the problem and correct the code.

1.2.17 Give the value of a after the execution of each of the following sequences:

```
int a = 1;            boolean a = true;       int a = 2;
a = a + a;            a = !a;                 a = a * a;
a = a + a;            a = !a;                 a = a * a;
a = a + a;            a = !a;                 a = a * a;
```

1.2.18 Suppose that x and y are `double` values that represent the Cartesian coordinates of a point (x, y) in the plane. Give an expression whose value is the distance of the point from the origin.

1.2.19 Write a program that takes two `int` values a and b from the command line and prints a random integer between a and b.

1.2.20 Write a program that prints the sum of two random integers between 1 and 6 (such as you might get when rolling dice).

1.2.21 Write a program that takes a `double` value t from the command line and prints the value of $\sin(2t) + \sin(3t)$.

1.2.22 Write a program that takes three `double` values x_0, v_0, and t from the command line and prints the value of $x_0 + v_0t + gt^2/2$, where g is the constant 9.78033. (*Note:* This value the displacement in meters after t seconds when an object is thrown straight up from initial position x_0 at velocity v_0 meters per second.)

1.2.23 Write a program that takes two `int` values m and d from the command line and prints `true` if day d of month m is between 3/20 and 6/20, `false` otherwise.

Creative Exercises

1.2.24 *Loan payments.* Write a program that calculates the monthly payments you would have to make over a given number of years to pay off a loan at a given interest rate compounded continuously, taking the number of years t, the principal P, and the annual interest rate r as command-line arguments. The desired value is given by the formula Pe^{rt}. Use Math.exp().

1.2.25 *Wind chill.* Given the temperature t (in Fahrenheit) and the wind speed v (in miles per hour), the National Weather Service defines the effective temperature (the wind chill) to be:

$$w = 35.74 + 0.6215\,t + (0.4275\,t - 35.75)v^{0.16}$$

Write a program that takes two double command-line arguments t and v and prints out the wind chill. Use Math.pow(a, b) to compute a^b. *Note:* The formula is not valid if t is larger than 50 in absolute value or if v is larger than 120 or less than 3 (you may assume that the values you get are in that range).

1.2.26 *Polar coordinates.* Write a program that converts from Cartesian to polar coordinates. Your program should take two real numbers x and y on the command line and print the polar coordinates r and θ. Use the Java method Math.atan2(y, x) which computes the arctangent value of y/x that is in the range from $-\pi$ to π.

Polar coordinates

1.2.27 *Gaussian random numbers.* One way to generate a random number taken from the Gaussian distribution is to use the *Box-Muller* formula

$$w = \sin(2\,\pi\,v)\,(-2\ln u)^{1/2}$$

where u and v are real numbers between 0 and 1 generated by the Math.random() method. Write a program StdGaussian that prints out a standard Gaussian random variable.

1.2.28 *Order check.* Write a program that takes three double values x, y, and z as command-line arguments and prints true if the values are strictly ascending or descending ($x < y < z$ or $x > y > z$), and false otherwise.

1.2.29 *Day of the week.* Write a program that takes a date as input and prints the day of the week that date falls on. Your program should take three command line

parameters: m (month), d (day), and y (year). For m, use 1 for January, 2 for February, and so forth. For output, print 0 for Sunday, 1 for Monday, 2 for Tuesday, and so forth. Use the following formulas, for the Gregorian calendar:

$$y_0 = y - (14 - m) / 12$$
$$x = y_0 + y_0/4 - y_0/100 + y_0/400$$
$$m_0 = m + 12 \times ((14 - m) / 12) - 2$$
$$d_0 = (d + x + (31 \times m_0)/12) \% 7$$

Example: On what day of the week was February 14, 2000?

$$y_0 = 2000 - 1 = 1999$$
$$x = 1999 + 1999/4 - 1999/100 + 1999/400 = 2483$$
$$m_0 = 2 + 12 \times 1 - 2 = 12$$
$$d_0 = (14 + 2483 + (31 \times 12) / 12) \% 7 = 2500 \% 7 = 1$$

Answer: Monday.

1.2.30 *Uniform random numbers.* Write a program that prints five uniform random values between 0 and 1, their average value, and their minimum and maximum value. Use Math.random(), Math.min(), and Math.max().

1.2.31 *Mercator projection.* The *Mercator projection* is a conformal (angle preserving) projection that maps latitude φ and longitude λ to rectangular coordinates (x, y). It is widely used—for example, in nautical charts and in the maps that you print from the web. The projection is defined by the equations $x = \lambda - \lambda_0$ and $y = 1/2 \ln((1 + \sin\varphi) / (1 - \sin\varphi))$, where λ_0 is the longitude of the point in the center of the map. Write a program that takes λ_0 and the latitude and longitude of a point from the command line and prints its projection.

1.2.32 *Color conversion.* Several different formats are used to represent color. For example, the primary format for LCD displays, digital cameras, and web pages, known as the *RGB format,* specifies the level of red (R), green (G), and blue (B) on an integer scale from 0 to 255. The primary format for publishing books and magazines, known as the *CMYK format,* specifies the level of cyan (C), magenta (M), yellow (Y), and black (K) on a real scale from 0.0 to 1.0. Write a program RGBtoCMYK that converts RGB to CMYK. Take three integers—r, g, and b—from the

command line and print the equivalent CMYK values. If the RGB values are all 0, then the CMY values are all 0 and the K value is 1; otherwise, use these formulas:

$$w = \max(r/255, g/255, b/255)$$
$$c = (w - (r/255))/w$$
$$m = (w - (g/255))/w$$
$$y = (w - (b/255))/w$$
$$k = 1 - w$$

1.2.33 *Great circle.* Write a program GreatCircle that takes four command-line arguments—x1, y1, x2, and y2—(the latitude and longitude, in degrees, of two points on the earth) and prints out the great-circle distance between them. The great-circle distance (in nautical miles) is given by the equation:

$$d = 60 \arccos(\sin(x_1) \sin(x_2) + \cos(x_1) \cos(x_2) \cos(y_1 - y_2))$$

Note that this equation uses degrees, whereas Java's trigonometric functions use radians. Use Math.toRadians() and Math.toDegrees() to convert between the two. Use your program to compute the great-circle distance between Paris (48.87° N and $-2.33°$ W) and San Francisco (37.8° N and 122.4° W).

1.2.34 *Three-sort.* Write a program that takes three int values from the command line and prints them in ascending order. Use Math.min() and Math.max().

1.2.35 *Dragon curves.* Write a program to print the instructions for drawing the dragon curves of order 0 through 5. The instructions are strings of F, L, and R characters, where F means "draw line while moving 1 unit forward," L means "turn left," and R means "turn right." A dragon curve of order N is formed when you fold a strip of paper in half N times, then unfold to right angles. The key to solving this problem is to note that a curve of order N is a curve of order $N-1$ followed by an L followed by a curve of order $N-1$ traversed in reverse order, and then to figure out a similar description for the reverse curve .

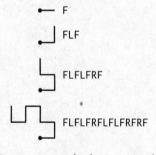

Dragon curves of order 0, 1, 2, and 3

1.3 Conditionals and Loops

IN THE PROGRAMS THAT WE HAVE examined to this point, each of the statements in the program is executed once, in the order given. Most programs are more complicated because the sequence of statements and the number of times each is executed can vary. We use the term *control flow* to refer to statement sequencing in a program. In this section, we introduce statements that allow us to change the control flow, using logic about the values of program variables. This feature is an essential component of programming.

Specifically, we consider Java statements that implement *conditionals*, where some other statements may or may not be executed depending on certain conditions, and *loops*, where some other statements may be executed multiple times, again depending on certain conditions. As you will see in numerous examples in this section, conditionals and loops truly harness the power of the computer and will equip you to write programs to accomplish a broad variety of tasks that you could not contemplate attempting without a computer.

If statements Most computations require different actions for different inputs. One way to express these differences in Java is the if statement:

```
if (<boolean expression>) { <statements> }
```

This description introduces a formal notation known as a *template* that we will use to specify the format of Java constructs. We put within angle brackets (< >) a construct that we have already defined, to indicate that we can use any instance of that construct where specified. In this case, *<boolean expression>* represents an expression that has a boolean value, such as one involving a comparison operation, and *<statements>* represents a *statement block* (a sequence of Java statements, each terminated by a semicolon). This latter construct is familiar to you: the body of main() is such a sequence. If the sequence is a single statement, the curly braces are optional. It is possible to make formal definitions of *<boolean expression>* and *<statements>*, but we refrain from going into that level of detail. The meaning

of an if statement is self-explanatory: the statement(s) in the sequence are to be
executed if and only if the expression is true.

As a simple example, suppose that you want to compute the absolute value of
an int value x. This statement does the job:

```
if (x < 0) x = -x;
```

As a second simple example, consider the following statement:

```
if (x > y)
{
    int t = x;
    x = y;
    y = t;
}
```

This code puts x and y in ascending order by exchanging them if
necessary.

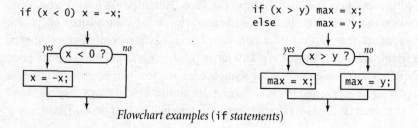

boolean expression

```
if ( x > y )
{
    int t = x;
    x = y;
    y = t;
}
```

sequence of statements

Anatomy of an if statement

You can also add an else clause to an if statement, to express the concept of
executing either one statement (or sequence of statements) or another, depending
on whether the boolean expression is true or false, as in the following template:

```
if (<boolean expression>) <statements T>
else                      <statements F>
```

As a simple example of the need for an else clause, consider the following code,
which assigns the maximum of two int values to the variable max:

```
if (x > y) max = x;
else       max = y;
```

One way to understand control flow is to visualize it with a diagram called a *flowchart*. Paths through the flowchart correspond to flow-of-control paths in the pro-

```
if (x < 0) x = -x;
```

```
yes   x < 0 ?   no

x = -x;
```

```
if (x > y) max = x;
else       max = y;
```

```
yes   x > y ?   no

max = x;      max = y;
```

Flowchart examples (if statements)

absolute value	`if (x < 0) x = -x;`
| *put x and y into sorted order* | ```
if (x > y)
{
    int t = x;
    y = x;
    x = t;
}
``` |
| *maximum of x and y* | ```
if (x > y) max = x;
else       max = y;
``` |
| *error check for division operation* | ```
if (den == 0) System.out.println("Division by zero");
else          System.out.println("Quotient = " + num/den);
``` |
| *error check for quadratic formula* | ```
double discriminant = b*b - 4.0*c;
if (discriminant < 0.0)
{
    System.out.println("No real roots");
}
else
{
    System.out.println((-b + Math.sqrt(discriminant))/2.0);
    System.out.println((-b - Math.sqrt(discriminant))/2.0);
}
``` |

Typical examples of using `if` statements

gram. In the early days of computing, when programmers used low-level languages and difficult-to-understand flows of control, flowcharts were an essential part of programming. With modern languages, we use flowcharts just to understand basic building blocks like the `if` statement.

The accompanying table contains some examples of the use of `if` and `if-else` statements. These examples are typical of simple calculations you might need in programs that you write. Conditional statements are an essential part of programming. Since the *semantics* (meaning) of statements like these is similar to their meanings as natural-language phrases, you will quickly grow used to them.

PROGRAM 1.3.1 is another example of the use of the `if-else` statement, in this case for the task of simulating a coin flip. The body of the program is a single statement, like the ones in the table above, but it is worth special attention because it introduces an interesting philosophical issue that is worth contemplating: can a computer program produce *random* values? Certainly not, but a program *can* produce numbers that have many of the properties of random numbers.

Program 1.3.1   *Flipping a fair coin*

```
public class Flip
{
    public static void main(String[] args)
    {  // Simulate a coin flip.
        if (Math.random() < 0.5) System.out.println("Heads");
        else                     System.out.println("Tails");
    }
}
```

This program uses Math.random() *to simulate a coin flip. Each time you run it, it prints either heads or tails. A sequence of flips will have many of the same properties as a sequence that you would get by flipping a fair coin, but it is not a truly random sequence.*

```
% java Flip
Heads
% java Flip
Tails
% java Flip
Tails
```

While loops   Many computations are inherently repetitive. The basic Java construct for handling such computations has the following format:

```
while (<boolean expression>) { <statements> }
```

The while statement has the same form as the if statement (the only difference being the use of the keyword while instead of if), but the meaning is quite different. It is an instruction to the computer to behave as follows: if the expression is false, do nothing; if the expression is true, execute the sequence of statements (just as with if) but then check the expression again, execute the sequence of statements again if the expression is true, and *continue* as long as the expression is true. We often refer to the statement block in a loop as the *body* of the loop. As with the if statement, the braces are optional if a while loop body has just one statement. The while statement is equivalent to a sequence of identical if statements:

```
if (<boolean expression>) { <statements> }
if (<boolean expression>) { <statements> }
if (<boolean expression>) { <statements> }
    ...
```

initialization is a separate statement

loop continuation condition

```
int v = 1;
while ( v <= N/2 )
{
    v = 2*v;
}
```

braces are optional when body is a single statement

body

Anatomy of a while *statement*

At some point, the code in one of the statements must change something (such as the value of some variable in the boolean expression) to make the boolean expression false, and then the sequence is broken.

A common programming paradigm involves maintaining an integer value that keeps track of the number of times a loop iterates. We start at some initial value, and then increment the value by 1 each time through the loop, testing whether it exceeds a predetermined maximum before deciding to continue. TenHellos (PROGRAM 1.3.2) is a simple example of this paradigm that uses a while statement. The key to the computation is the statement

```
int i = 4;
while (i <= 10)
{
    System.out.println(i + "th Hello");
    i = i + 1;
}
```

Flowchart example (while statement)

```
i = i + 1;
```

As a mathematical equation, this statement is nonsense, but as a Java assignment statement it makes perfect sense: it says to compute the value i + 1 and then assign the result to the variable i. If the value of i was 4 before the statement, it becomes 5 afterwards; if it was 5 it becomes 6; and so forth. With the initial condition in TenHellos that the value of i starts at 4, the statement block is executed five times until the sequence is broken, when the value of i becomes 11.

Using the while loop is barely worthwhile for this simple task, but you will soon be addressing tasks where you will need to specify that statements be repeated far too many times to contemplate doing it without loops. There is a profound difference between programs with while statements and programs without them, because while statements allow us to specify a potentially unlimited number of statements to be executed in a program. In particular, the while statement allows us to specify lengthy computations in short programs. This ability opens the door to writing programs for tasks that we could not contemplate addressing without a

Program 1.3.2　*Your first while loop*

```
public class TenHellos
{
   public static void main(String[] args)
   { // Print 10 Hellos.
      System.out.println("1st Hello");
      System.out.println("2nd Hello");
      System.out.println("3rd Hello");
      int i = 4;
      while (i <= 10)
      { // Print the ith Hello.
         System.out.println(i + "th Hello");
         i = i + 1;
      }
   }
}
```

This program uses a while *loop for the simple, repetitive task of printing the output shown below. After the third line, the lines to be printed differ only in the value of the index counting the line printed, so we define a variable* i *to contain that index. After initializing the value of* i *to 4, we enter into a* while *loop where we use the value of* i *in the* System.out.println() *statement and increment it each time through the loop. After printing* 10th Hello, *the value of* i *becomes 11 and the loop terminates.*

```
% java TenHellos
1st Hello
2nd Hello
3rd Hello
4th Hello
5th Hello
6th Hello
7th Hello
8th Hello
9th Hello
10th Hello
```

i	i <= 10	*output*
4	true	4th Hello
5	true	5th Hello
6	true	6th Hello
7	true	7th Hello
8	true	8th Hello
9	true	9th Hello
10	true	10th Hello
11	false	

Trace of java TenHellos

computer. But there is also a price to pay: as your programs become more sophisticated, they become more difficult to understand.

PowersOfTwo (PROGRAM 1.3.3) uses a while loop to print out a table of the powers of 2. Beyond the loop control counter i, it maintains a variable v that holds the powers of two as it computes them. The loop body contains three statements: one to print the current power of 2, one to compute the next (multiply the current one by 2), and one to increment the loop control counter.

There are many situations in computer science where it is useful to be familiar with powers of 2. You should know at least the first 10 values in this table and you should note that 2^{10} is about 1 thousand, 2^{20} is about 1 million, and 2^{30} is about 1 billion.

PowersOfTwo is the prototype for many useful computations. By varying the computations that change the accumulated value and the way that the loop control variable is incremented, we can print out tables of a variety of functions (see EXERCISE 1.3.11).

It is worthwhile to carefully examine the behavior of programs that use loops by studying a *trace* of the program. For example, a trace of the operation of PowersOfTwo should show the value of each variable before each iteration of the loop and the value of the conditional expression that controls the loop. Tracing the operation of a loop can be very tedious, but it is nearly always worthwhile to run a trace because it clearly exposes what a program is doing.

PowersOfTwo is nearly a self-tracing program, because it prints the values of its variables each time through the loop. Clearly, you can make any program produce a trace of itself by adding appropriate System. out.println() statements. Modern programming environments provide sophisticated tools for tracing, but

i	v	i <= N
0	1	true
1	2	true
2	4	true
3	8	true
4	16	true
5	32	true
6	64	true
7	128	true
8	256	true
9	512	true
10	1024	true
11	2048	true
12	4096	true
13	8192	true
14	16384	true
15	32768	true
16	65536	true
17	131072	true
18	262144	true
19	524288	true
20	1048576	true
21	2097152	true
22	4194304	true
23	8388608	true
24	16777216	true
25	33554432	true
26	67108864	true
27	134217728	true
28	268435456	true
29	536870912	true
30	1073741824	false

Trace of java PowersOfTwo 29

Program 1.3.3   *Computing powers of two*

```java
public class PowersOfTwo
{
   public static void main(String[] args)
   { // Print the first N powers of 2.
      int N = Integer.parseInt(args[0]);
      int v = 1;
      int i = 0;
      while (i <= N)
      { // Print ith power of 2.
         System.out.println(i + " " + v);
         v = 2 * v;
         i = i + 1;
      }
   }
}
```

N	loop termination value
i	loop control counter
v	current power of 2

This program takes a command-line argument N and prints a table of the powers of 2 that are less than or equal to 2^N. Each time through the loop, we increment the value of i and double the value of v. We show only the first three and the last three lines of the table; the program prints N+1 lines.

```
% java PowersOfTwo 5
0 1
1 2
2 4
3 8
4 16
5 32
```

```
% java PowersOfTwo 29
0 1
1 2
2 4
...
27 134217728
28 268435456
29 536870912
```

this tried-and-true method is simple and effective. You certainly should add print statements to the first few loops that you write, to be sure that they are doing precisely what you expect.

There is a hidden trap in PowersOfTwo, because the largest integer in Java's int data type is $2^{31} - 1$ and the program does not test for that possibility. If you invoke it with `java PowersOfTwo 31`, you may be surprised by the last line of output:

```
. . .
1073741824
-2147483648
```

The variable v becomes too large and takes on a negative value because of the way Java represents integers. The maximum value of an `int` is available for us to use as `Integer.MAX_VALUE`. A better version of PROGRAM 1.3.3 would use this value to test for overflow and print an error message if the user types too large a value, though getting such a program to work properly for all inputs is trickier than you might think. (For a similar challenge, see EXERCISE 1.3.14.)

As a more complicated example, suppose that we want to compute the largest power of two that is less than or equal to a given positive integer N. If N is 13 we want the result 8; if N is 1000, we want the result 512; if N is 64, we want the result 64; and so forth. This computation is simple to perform with a `while` loop:

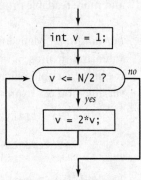

```
int v = 1;
while (v <= N/2)
    v = 2*v;
```

It takes some thought to convince yourself that this simple piece of code produces the desired result. You can do so by making these observations:

Flowchart for the statements
```
int v = 1;
while (v <= N/2)
    v = 2*v;
```

- v is always a power of 2.
- v is never greater than N.
- v increases each time through the loop, so the loop must terminate.
- After the loop terminates, 2*v is greater than N.

Reasoning of this sort is often important in understanding how `while` loops work. Even though many of the loops you will write are much simpler than this one, you should be sure to convince yourself that each loop you write is going to behave as you expect.

The logic behind such arguments is the same whether the loop iterates just a few times, as in `TenHellos`, dozens of times, as in `PowersOfTwo`, or millions of times, as in several examples that we will soon consider. That leap from a few tiny cases to a huge computation is profound. When writing loops, understanding how the values of the variables change each time through the loop (and checking that understanding by adding statements to trace their values and running for a small number of iterations) is essential. Having done so, you can confidently remove those training wheels and truly unleash the power of the computer.

For loops   As you will see, the while loop allows us to write programs for all manner of applications. Before considering more examples, we will look at an alternate Java construct that allows us even more flexibility when writing programs with loops. This alternate notation is not fundamentally different from the basic while loop, but it is widely used because it often allows us to write more compact and more readable programs than if we used only while statements.

For notation.   Many loops follow this scheme: initialize an index variable to some value and then use a while loop to test a loop continuation condition involving the index variable, where the last statement in the while loop increments the index variable. You can express such loops directly with Java's for notation:

```
for (<initialize>; <boolean expression>; <increment>)
{
    <statements>
}
```

This code is, with only a few exceptions, equivalent to

```
<initialize>;
while (<boolean expression>)
{
    <statements>
    <increment>;
}
```

Your Java compiler might even produce identical results for the two loops. In truth, *<initialize>* and *<increment>* can be any statements at all, but we nearly always use for loops to support this typical initialize-and-increment programming idiom. For example, the following two lines of code are equivalent to the corresponding lines of code in TenHellos (PROGRAM 1.3.2):

```
for (int i = 4; i <= 10; i = i + 1)
    System.out.println(i + "th Hello");
```

Typically, we work with a slightly more compact version of this code, using the shorthand notation discussed next.

Compound assignment idioms. Modifying the value of a variable is something that we do so often in programming that Java provides a variety of different shorthand notations for the purpose. For example, the following four statements all increment the value of i by 1 in Java:

```
i = i + 1;    i++;    ++i;    i += 1;
```

You can also say i-- or --i or i -= 1 or i = i-1 to decrement that value of i by 1. Most programmers use i++ or i-- in for loops, though any of the others would do. The ++ and -- constructs are normally used for integers, but the *compound assignment* constructs are useful operations for any arithmetic operator in any primitive numeric type. For example, you can say v *= 2 or v += v instead of v = 2*v. All of these idioms are for notational convenience, nothing more. This combination of shortcuts came into widespread use with the C programming language in the 1970s and have become standard. They have survived the test of time because they lead to compact, elegant, and easily understood programs. When you learn to write (and to read) programs that use them, you will be able to transfer that skill to programming in numerous modern languages, not just Java.

Scope. The scope of a variable is the part of the program where it is defined. Generally the scope of a variable is comprised of the statements that follow the declaration in the same block as the declaration. For this purpose, the code in the for loop header is considered to be in the same block as the for loop body. Therefore, the while and for formulations of loops are not quite equivalent: in a typical for loop, the incrementing variable is *not* available for use in later statements; in the corresponding while loop, it is. This distinction is often a reason to use a while instead of a for loop.

CHOOSING AMONG DIFFERENT FORMULATIONS OF THE same computation is a matter of each programmer's taste, as when a writer picks from among synonyms or chooses between using active and passive voice when composing a sentence. You will not find good hard-and-fast rules on how to compose a program any more than you will find such rules on how to compose a paragraph. Your goal should be to find a style that suits you, gets the computation done, and can be appreciated by others.

The accompanying table includes several code fragments with typical examples of loops used in Java code. Some of these relate to code that you have already seen; others are new code for straightforward computations. To cement your understanding of loops in Java, put these code snippets into a class's code that takes an integer N from the command line (like PowersOfTwo) and *compile and run them*. Then, write

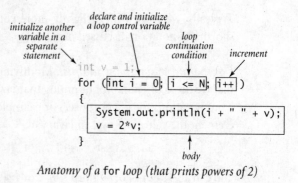

Anatomy of a for *loop (that prints powers of 2)*

some loops of your own for similar computations of your own invention, or do some of the early exercises at the end of this section. There is no substitute for the experience gained by running code that you create yourself, and it is imperative that you develop an understanding of how to write Java code that uses loops.

print largest power of two less than or equal to N	```int v = 1;while (v <= N/2) v = 2*v;System.out.println(v);```
compute a finite sum (1 + 2 + ... + N)	```int sum = 0;for (int i = 1; i <= N; i++) sum += i;System.out.println(sum);```
compute a finite product (N! = 1 × 2 × ... × N)	```int product = 1;for (int i = 1; i <= N; i++) product *= i;System.out.println(product);```
print a table of function values	```for (int i = 0; i <= N; i++) System.out.println(i + " " + 2*Math.PI*i/N);```
print the ruler function (see Program 1.2.1)	```String ruler = " ";for (int i = 1; i <= N; i++) ruler = ruler + i + ruler;System.out.println(ruler);```

Typical examples of using for *and* while *statements*

Nesting The if, while, and for statements have the same status as assignment statements or any other statements in Java. That is, we can use them whenever a statement is called for. In particular, we can use one or more of them in the <*body*> of another to make compound statements. As a first example, DivisorPattern (PROGRAM 1.3.4) has a for loop whose statements are a for loop (whose statement is an if statement) and a print statement. It prints a pattern of asterisks where the *i*th row has an asterisk in each position corresponding to divisors of *i* (the same holds true for the columns).

To emphasize the nesting, we use indentation in the program code. We refer to the i loop as the *outer* loop and the j loop as the *inner* loop. The inner loop iterates all the way through for each iteration of the outer loop. As usual, the best way to understand a new programming construct like this is to study a trace.

DivisorPattern has a complicated control structure, as you can see from its flowchart. A diagram like this illustrates the importance of using a limited number of simple control structures in programming. With nesting, you can compose loops and conditionals to build programs that are easy to understand even though they may have a complicated control structure. A great many useful computations can be accomplished with just one or two levels of nesting. For example, many programs in this book have the same general structure as DivisorPattern.

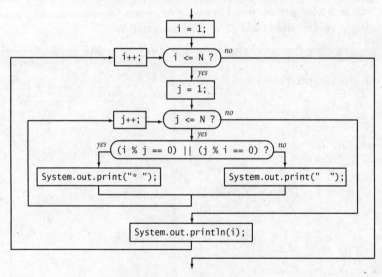

Flowchart for DivisorPattern

Program 1.3.4   Your first nested loops

```java
public class DivisorPattern
{
   public static void main(String[] args)
   { // Print a square that visualizes divisors.
      int N = Integer.parseInt(args[0]);
      for (int i = 1; i <= N; i++)
      { // Print the ith line
         for (int j = 1; j <= N; j++)
         { // Print the jth entry in the ith line.
            if ((i % j == 0) || (j % i == 0))
               System.out.print("* ");
            else
               System.out.print("  ");
         }
         System.out.println(i);
      }
   }
}
```

N	number of rows and columns
i	row index
j	column index

This program takes an integer N as the command-line argument and uses nested for loops to print an N-by-N table with an asterisk in row i and column j if either i divides j or j divides i. The loop control variables i and j control the computation.

```
% java DivisorPattern 3
* * *  1
* *    2
*   *  3

% java DivisorPattern 16
* * * * * * * * * * * * * * * *  1
* *   *   *   *   *   *   *   *  2
*   *     *     *     *     *    3
* *   *       *       *       *  4
*       *         *           *  5
* * *     *         *            6
*           *           *        7
* *   *       *               *  8
*       *         *              9
* *       *           *         10
*           *               *   11
* * * *   *           *         12
*               *               13
* *     *           *           14
*   *   *                   *   15
* *   *       *               * 16
```

i	j	i % j	j % i	output
1	1	0	0	*
1	2	1	0	*
1	3	1	0	*
				1
2	1	0	1	*
2	2	0	0	*
2	3	2	1	
				2
3	1	0	1	*
3	2	1	2	
3	3	0	0	*
				3

Trace of java DivisorPattern 3

As a second example of nesting, consider the following program fragment, which a tax preparation program might use to compute income tax rates:

```
if        (income <        0) rate = 0.0;
else if (income <   47450) rate = .22;
else if (income < 114650) rate = .25;
else if (income < 174700) rate = .28;
else if (income < 311950) rate = .33;
else                       rate = .35;
```

In this case, a number of `if` statements are nested to test from among a number of mutually exclusive possibilities. This construct is a special one that we use often. Otherwise, it is best to use braces to resolve ambiguities when nesting `if` statements. This issue and more examples are addressed in the Q&A and exercises.

Applications   The ability to program with loops immediately opens up the full world of computation. To emphasize this fact, we next consider a variety of examples. These examples all involve working with the types of data that we considered in SECTION 1.2, but rest assured that the same mechanisms serve us well for any computational application. The sample programs are carefully crafted, and by studying and appreciating them, you will be prepared to write your own programs containing loops, as requested in many of the exercises at the end of this section.

The examples that we consider here involve computing with numbers. Several of our examples are tied to problems faced by mathematicians and scientists throughout the past several centuries. While computers have existed for only 50 years or so, many of the computational methods that we use are based on a rich mathematical tradition tracing back to antiquity.

Finite sum.   The computational paradigm used by `PowersOfTwo` is one that you will use frequently. It uses two variables—one as an index that controls a loop and the other to accumulate a computational result. `Harmonic` (PROGRAM 1.3.5) uses the same paradigm to evaluate the finite sum $H_N = 1 + 1/2 + 1/3 + ... + 1/N$. These numbers, which are known as the *Harmonic numbers*, arise frequently in discrete mathematics. Harmonic numbers are the discrete analog of the logarithm. They also approximate the area under the curve $y = 1/x$. You can use PROGRAM 1.3.5 as a model for computing the values of other sums (see EXERCISE 1.3.16).

Program 1.3.5   Harmonic numbers

```
public class Harmonic
{
    public static void main(String[] args)
    {  // Compute the Nth Harmonic number.
       int N = Integer.parseInt(args[0]);
       double sum = 0.0;
       for (int i = 1; i <= N; i++)
       {  // Add the ith term to the sum
          sum += 1.0/i;
       }
       System.out.println(sum);
    }
}
```

N	number of terms in sum
i	loop index
sum	cumulated sum

This program computes the value of the Nth Harmonic number. The value is known from mathematical analysis to be about $ln(N) + 0.57721$ for large N. Note that $ln(10000) \approx 9.21034$.

```
% java Harmonic 2
1.5
% java Harmonic 10
2.9289682539682538
% java Harmonic 10000
9.787606036044348
```

Computing the square root. How are functions in Java's Math library, such as Math.sqrt(), implemented? Sqrt (PROGRAM 1.3.6) illustrates one technique. To compute the square root function, it uses an iterative computation that was known to the Babylonians over 4,000 years ago. It is also a special case of a general computational technique that was developed in the 17th century by Isaac Newton and Joseph Raphson and is widely known as *Newton's method*. Under generous conditions on a given function $f(x)$, Newton's method is an effective way to find roots (values of x for which the function is 0). Start with an initial estimate, t_0. Given the

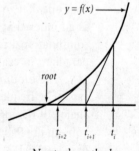

Newton's method

Program 1.3.6   Newton's method

```
public class Sqrt
{
    public static void main(String[] args)
    {
        double c = Double.parseDouble(args[0]);
        double epsilon = 1e-15;
        double t = c;
        while (Math.abs(t - c/t) > epsilon * t)
        {  // Replace t by the average of t and c/t.
            t = (c/t + t) / 2.0;
        }
        System.out.println(t);
    }
}
```

c	*argument*
epsilon	*error tolerance*
t	*estimate of c*

This program computes the square root of its command-line argument to 15 decimal places of accuracy, using Newton's method (see text).

```
% java Sqrt 2.0
1.414213562373095
% java Sqrt 2544545
1595.1630010754388
```

iteration	t	c/t
	2.0000000000000000	1.0
1	1.5000000000000000	1.3333333333333333
2	1.4166666666666665	1.4117647058823530
3	1.4142156862745097	1.4142114384748700
4	1.4142135623746899	1.4142135623715002
5	1.4142135623730950	1.4142135623730951

Trace of java Sqrt 2.0

estimate t_i, compute a new estimate by drawing a line tangent to the curve $y = f(x)$ at the point $(t_i, f(t_i))$ and set t_{i+1} to the x-coordinate of the point where that line hits the x-axis. Iterating this process, we get closer to the root.

Computing the square root of a positive number c is equivalent to finding the positive root of the function $f(x) = x^2 - c$. For this special case, Newton's method amounts to the process implemented in Sqrt (see EXERCISE 1.3.17). Start with the estimate $t = c$. If t is equal to c/t, then t is equal to the square root of c, so the computation is complete. If not, refine the estimate by replacing t with the average of t

and c/t. With Newton's method, we get the value of the square root of 2 accurate to 15 places in just 5 iterations of the loop.

Newton's method is important in scientific computing because the same iterative approach is effective for finding the roots of a broad class of functions, including many for which analytic solutions are not known (so the Java `Math` library would be no help). Nowadays, we take for granted that we can find whatever values we need of mathematical functions; before computers, scientists and engineers had to use tables or computed values by hand. Computational techniques that were developed to enable calculations by hand needed to be very efficient, so it is not surprising that many of those same techniques are effective when we use computers. Newton's method is a classic example of this phenomenon. Another useful approach for evaluating mathematical functions is to use Taylor series expansions (see EXERCISES 1.3.35–36).

Number conversion. `Binary` (PROGRAM 1.3.7) prints the binary (base 2) representation of the decimal number typed as the command-line argument. It is based on decomposing a number into a sum of powers of two. For example, the binary representation of 19 is 10011, which is the same as saying that $19 = 16 + 2 + 1$. To compute the binary representation of N, we consider the powers of 2 less than or equal to N in decreasing order to determine which belong in the binary decomposition (and therefore correspond to a 1 bit in the binary representation). The process corresponds precisely to using a balance scale to weigh an object, using weights whose values are powers of two. First, we find largest weight not heavier than the object. Then, considering the weights in decreasing order, we add each weight to test whether the object is lighter. If so, we remove the

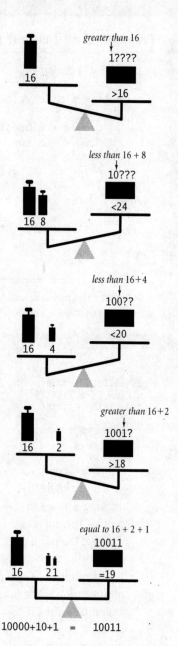

Scale analog to binary conversion

Program 1.3.7 Converting to binary

```
public class Binary
{
    public static void main(String[] args)
    { // Print binary representation of N.
        int N = Integer.parseInt(args[0]);
        int v = 1;
        while (v <= N/2)
            v = 2*v;
        // Now v is the largest power of 2 <= N.

        int n = N;
        while (v > 0)
        { // Cast out powers of 2 in decreasing order.
            if (n < v) { System.out.print(0);              }
            else       { System.out.print(1); n -= v; }
            v = v/2;
        }
        System.out.println();
    }
}
```

N	integer to convert
v	current power of 2
n	current excess

This program prints the binary representation of a positive integer given as the command-line argument, by casting out powers of 2 in decreasing order (see text).

```
% java Binary 19
10011
% java Binary 100000000
101111101011110000100000000
```

weight; if not, we leave the weight and try the next one. Each weight corresponds to a bit in the binary representation of the weight of the object: leaving a weight corresponds to a 1 bit in the binary representation of the object's weight, and removing a weight corresponds to a 0 bit in the binary representation of the object's weight.

In Binary, the variable v corresponds to the current weight being tested, and the variable n accounts for the excess (unknown) part of the object's weight (to

n	binary representation	v	v > 0	binary representation	n < v	output
19	10011	16	true	10000	false	1
3	0011	8	true	1000	true	0
3	011	4	true	100	true	0
3	01	2	true	10	false	1
1	1	1	true	1	false	1
0		0	false			

Trace of casting-out-powers-of-two loop for java Binary 19

simulate leaving a weight on the balance, we just subtract that weight from n). The value of v decreases through the powers of two. When it is larger than n, Binary prints 0; otherwise, it prints 1 and subtracts v from n. As usual, a trace (of the values of n, v, n < v, and the output bit for each loop iteration) can be very useful in helping you to understand the program. Read from top to bottom in the rightmost column of the trace, the output is 10011, the binary representation of 19.

Converting data from one representation to another is a frequent theme in writing computer programs. Thinking about conversion emphasizes the distinction between an abstraction (an integer like the number of hours in a day) and a representation of that abstraction (24 or 11000). The irony here is that the computer's representation of an integer is actually based on its binary representation.

Simulation. Our next example is different in character from the ones we have been considering, but it is representative of a common situation where we use computers to simulate what might happen in the real world so that we can make informed decisions. The specific example that we consider now is from a thoroughly studied class of problems known as *gambler's ruin*. Suppose that a gambler makes a series of fair $1 bets, starting with some given initial stake. The gambler always goes broke eventually, but when we set other limits on the game, various questions arise. For example, suppose that the gam-

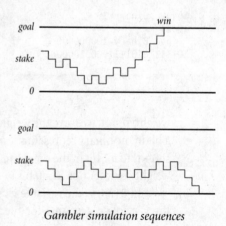

Gambler simulation sequences

Program 1.3.8   Gambler's ruin simulation

```
public class Gambler
{
    public static void main(String[] args)
    {  // Run T experiments that start with $stake
       // and terminate on $0 or $goal.
       int stake = Integer.parseInt(args[0]);
       int goal  = Integer.parseInt(args[1]);
       int T     = Integer.parseInt(args[2]);
       int bets = 0;
       int wins = 0;
       for (int t = 0; t < T; t++)
       {  // Run one experiment.
          int cash = stake;
          while (cash > 0 && cash < goal)
          {  // Simulate one bet.
             bets++;
             if (Math.random() < 0.5) cash++;
             else                     cash--;
          }  // Cash is either 0 (ruin) or $goal (win).
          if (cash == goal) wins++;
       }
       System.out.println(100*wins/T + "% wins");
       System.out.println("Avg # bets: " + bets/T);
    }
}
```

stake	initial stake
goal	walkaway goal
T	number of trials
bets	bet count
wins	win count
cash	cash on hand

The inner while *loop in this program simulates a gambler with $stake who makes a series of $1 bets, continuing until going broke or reaching $goal. The running time of this program is proportional to T times the average number of bets. For example, the third command below causes nearly 100 million random numbers to be generated.*

```
% java Gambler 10 20 1000
50% wins
Avg # bets: 100
% java Gambler 50 250 100
19% wins
Avg # bets: 11050
% java Gambler 500 2500 100
21% wins
Avg # bets: 998071
```

bler decides ahead of time to walk away after reaching a certain goal. What are the chances that the gambler will win? How many bets might be needed to win or lose the game? What is the maximum amount of money that the gambler will have during the course of the game?

Gambler (PROGRAM 1.3.8) is a simulation that can help answer these questions. It does a sequence of trials, using Math.random() to simulate the sequence of bets, continuing until the gambler is broke or the goal is reached, and keeping track of the number of wins and the number of bets. After running the experiment for the specified number of trials, it averages and prints out the results. You might wish to run this program for various values of the command-line arguments, not necessarily just to plan your next trip to the casino, but to help you think about the following questions: Is the simulation an accurate reflection of what would happen in real life? How many trials are needed to get an accurate answer? What are the computational limits on performing such a simulation? Simulations are widely used in applications in economics, science, and engineering, and questions of this sort are important in any simulation.

In the case of Gambler, we are verifying classical results from probability theory, which say the *probability of success is the ratio of the stake to the goal* and that the *expected number of bets is the product of the stake and the desired gain* (the difference between the goal and the stake). For example, if you want to go to Monte Carlo to try to turn $500 into $2,500, you have a reasonable (20%) chance of success, but you should expect to make a million $1 bets! If you try to turn $1 into $1,000, you have a .1% chance and can expect to be done (ruin, most likely) in about 999 bets.

Simulation and analysis go hand-in-hand, each validating the other. In practice, the value of simulation is that it can suggest answers to questions that might be too difficult to resolve with analysis. For example, suppose that our gambler, recognizing that there will never be enough time to make a million bets, decides ahead of time to set an upper limit on the number of bets. How much money can the gambler expect to take home in that case? You can address this question with an easy change to PROGRAM 1.3.8 (see EXERCISE 1.3.24), but addressing it with mathematical analysis is not so easy.

Factoring. A *prime* is an integer greater than one whose only positive divisors are one and itself. The prime factorization of an integer is the multiset of primes whose product is the integer. For example, 3757208 = 2*2*2*7*13*13*397. Factors (PROGRAM 1.3.9) computes the prime factorization of any given positive integer. In contrast to many of the other programs that we have seen (which we could do in a few minutes with a calculator or even a pencil and paper), this computation would not be feasible without a computer. How would you go about trying to find the factors of a number like 287994837222311? You might find the factor 17 quickly, but even with a calculator it would take you quite a while to find 1739347.

i	N	output
2	3757208	2 2 2
3	469651	
4	469651	
5	469651	
6	469651	
7	469651	7
8	67093	
9	67093	
10	67093	
11	67093	
12	67093	
13	67093	13 13
14	397	
15	397	
16	397	
17	397	
18	397	
19	397	
20	397	
		397

Trace of java Factors 3757208

Although Factors is compact and straightforward, it certainly will take some thought to for you to convince yourself that it produces the desired result for any given integer. As usual, following a trace that shows the values of the variables at the beginning of each iteration of the outer for loop is a good way to understand the computation. For the case where the initial value of N is 3757208, the inner while loop iterates three times when i is 2, to remove the three factors of 2; then zero times when i is 3, 4, 5, and 6, since none of those numbers divide 469651; and so forth. Tracing the program for a few example inputs clearly reveals its basic operation. To convince ourselves that the program will behave as expected for all inputs, we reason about what we expect each of the loops to do. The while loop clearly prints and removes from n all factors of i, but the key to understanding the program is to see that the following fact holds at the beginning of each iteration of the for loop: n has no factors between 2 and i-1. Thus, if i is not prime, it will not divide n; if i is prime, the while loop will do its job. Once we know that n has no factors less than or equal to i, we also know that it has no factors greater than n/i, so we need look no further when i is greater than n/i.

In a more naïve implementation, we might simply have used the condition (i < n) to terminate the for loop. Even given the blinding speed of modern computers, such a decision would have a dramatic effect on the size of the numbers that we could factor. EXERCISE 1.3.26 encourages you to experiment with the program to

Program 1.3.9   *Factoring integers*

```
public class Factors
{
    public static void main(String[] args)
    { // Print the prime factors of N.
      long N = Long.parseLong(args[0]);
      long n = N;
      for (long i = 2; i <= n/i; i++)
      { // Test whether i is a factor.
        while (n % i == 0)
        { // Cast out and print i factors.
          n /= i;
          System.out.print(i + " ");
        } // Any factors of n are greater than i.
      }
      if (n > 1) System.out.print(n);
      System.out.println();
    }
}
```

N	integer to factor
n	unfactored part
i	potential factor

This program prints the prime factorization of any positive integer in Java's long *data type. The code is simple, but it takes some thought to convince oneself that it is correct (see text).*

```
% java Factors 3757208
2 2 2 7 13 13 397
```

```
% java Factors 287994837222311
17 1739347 9739789
```

learn the effectiveness of this simple change. On a computer that can do billions of operations per second, we could factor numbers on the order of 10^9 in a few seconds; with the (i <= n/i) test we can factor numbers on the order of 10^{18} in a comparable amount of time. Loops give us the ability to solve difficult problems, but they also give us the ability to construct simple programs that run slowly, so we must always be cognizant of performance.

In modern applications in cryptography, there are important situations where we wish to factor truly huge numbers (with, say, hundreds or thousands of digits). Such a computation is prohibitively difficult even *with* the use of a computer.

Other conditional and loop constructs To more fully cover the Java language, we consider here four more control-flow constructs. You need not think about using these constructs for every program that you write, because you are likely to encounter them much less frequently than the if, while, and for statements. You certainly do not need to worry about using these constructs until you are comfortable using if, while, and for. You might encounter one of them in a program in a book or on the web, but many programmers do not use them at all and we do not use any of them outside this section.

Break statement. In some situations, we want to immediately exit a loop without letting it run to completion. Java provides the break statement for this purpose. For example, the following code is an effective way to test whether a given integer N>1 is prime:

```
int i;
for (i = 2; i <= N/i; i++)
    if (N % i == 0) break;
if (i > N/i) System.out.println(N + " is prime");
```

There are two different ways to leave this loop: either the break statement is executed (because i divides N, so N is not prime) or the for loop condition is not satisfied (because no i with i <= N/i was found that divides N, which implies that N is prime). Note that we have to declare i outside the for loop instead of in the initialization statement so that its scope extends beyond the loop.

Continue statement. Java also provides a way to skip to the next iteration of a loop: the continue statement. When a continue is executed within a loop body, the flow of control transfers directly to the increment statement for the next iteration of the loop.

Switch statement. The if and if-else statements allow one or two alternatives in directing the flow of control. Sometimes, a computation naturally suggests more than two mutually exclusive alternatives. We could use a sequence or a chain of if-else statements, but the Java switch statement provides a direct solution. Let us move right to a typical example. Rather than printing an int variable day in a program that works with days of the weeks (such as a solution to EXERCISE 1.2.29), it is easier to use a switch statement, as follows:

```
switch (day)
{
    case 0: System.out.println("Sun"); break;
    case 1: System.out.println("Mon"); break;
    case 2: System.out.println("Tue"); break;
    case 3: System.out.println("Wed"); break;
    case 4: System.out.println("Thu"); break;
    case 5: System.out.println("Fri"); break;
    case 6: System.out.println("Sat"); break;
}
```

When you have a program that seems to have a long and regular sequence of `if` statements, you might consider consulting the booksite and using a `switch` statement, or using an alternate approach described in SECTION 1.4.

Do-while statement. Another way to write a loop is to use the template

```
do { <statements> } while (<boolean expression>);
```

The meaning of this statement is the same as

```
while (<boolean expression>) { <statements> }
```

except that the first test of the condition is omitted. If the condition initially holds, there is no difference. For an example in which `do-while` is useful, consider the problem of generating points that are randomly distributed in the unit disk. We can use `Math.random()` to generate x and y coordinates independently to get points that are randomly distributed in the 2-by-2 square centered on the origin. Most points fall within the unit disk, so we just reject those that do not. We always want to generate at least one point, so a `do-while` loop is ideal for this computation. The following code sets x and y such that the point (x, y) is randomly distributed in the unit disk:

```
do
{   // Scale x and y to be random in (-1, 1).
    x = 2.0*Math.random() - 1.0;
    y = 2.0*Math.random() - 1.0;
} while (Math.sqrt(x*x + y*y) > 1.0);
```

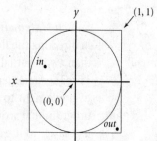

Since the area of the disk is π and the area of the square is 4, the expected number of times the loop is iterated is $4/\pi$ (about 1.27).

Infinite loops   Before you write programs that use loops, you need to think about the following issue: what if the loop-continuation condition in a `while` loop is always satisfied? With the statements that you have learned so far, one of two bad things could happen, both of which you need to learn to cope with.

First, suppose that such a loop calls `System.out.println()`. For example, if the condition in TenHellos were (i > 3) instead of (i <= 10), it would always be `true`. What happens? Nowadays, we use *print* as an abstraction to mean *display in a terminal window* and the result of attempting to display an unlimited number of lines in a terminal window is dependent on operating-system conventions. If your system is set up to have *print* mean *print characters on a piece of paper*, you might run out of paper or have to un-plug the printer. In a terminal window, you need a *stop printing* operation. Before running programs with loops on your own, you make sure that you know what to do to "pull the plug" on an infinite loop of `System.out.println()` calls and then test out the strategy by making the change to TenHellos indicated above and trying to stop it. On most systems, `<ctrl-c>` means *stop the current program*, and should do the job.

```
public class BadHellos
...
int i = 4;
while (i > 3)
{
   System.out.println
      (i + "th Hello");
   i = i + 1;
}
...

% java BadHellos
1st Hello
2nd Hello
3rd Hello
5th Hello
6th Hello
7th Hello
...
```

An infinite loop

Second, *nothing* might happen. If your program has an infinite loop that does not produce any output, it will spin through the loop and you will see no results at all. When you find yourself in such a situation, you can inspect the loops to make sure that the loop exit condition always happens, but the problem may not be easy to identify. One way to locate such a bug is to insert calls to `System.out.println()` to produce a trace. If these calls fall within an infinite loop, this strategy reduces the problem to the case discussed in the previous paragraph, but the output might give you a clue about what to do.

You might not know (or it might not matter) whether a loop is infinite or just very long. Even BadHellos eventually would terminate after printing over a billion lines because of overflow. If you invoke PROGRAM 1.3.8 with arguments such as `java Gambler 100000 200000 100`, you may not want to wait for the answer. You will learn to be aware of and to estimate the running time of your programs.

Why not have Java detect infinite loops and warn us about them? You might be surprised to know that it is not possible to do so, in general. This counterintuitive fact is one of the fundamental results of theoretical computer science.

Summary   For reference, the accompanying table lists the programs that we have considered in this section. They are representative of the kinds of tasks we can address with short programs comprised of `if`, `while`, and `for` statements processing built-in types of data. These types of computations are an appropriate way to become familiar with the basic Java flow-of-control constructs. The time that you spend now working with as many such programs as you can will certainly pay off for you in the future.

program	description
Flip	simulate a coin flip
TenHellos	your first loop
PowersOfTwo	compute and print a table of values
DivisorPattern	your first nested loop
Harmonic	compute finite sum
Sqrt	classic iterative algorithm
Binary	basic number conversion
Gambler	simulation with nested loops
Factors	`while` loop within a `for` loop

Summary of programs in this section

To learn how to use conditionals and loops, you must practice writing and debugging programs with `if`, `while`, and `for` statements. The exercises at the end of this section provide many opportunities for you to begin this process. For each exercise, you will write a Java program, then run and test it. All programmers know that it is unusual to have a program work as planned the first time it is run, so you will want to have an understanding of your program and an expectation of what it should do, step by step. At first, use explicit traces to check your understanding and expectation. As you gain experience, you will find yourself thinking in terms of what a trace might produce as you compose your loops. Ask yourself the following kinds of questions: What will be the values of the variables after the loop iterates the first time? The second time? The final time? Is there any way this program could get stuck in an infinite loop?

Loops and conditionals are a giant step in our ability to compute: `if`, `while`, and `for` statements take us from simple straight-line programs to arbitrarily complicated flow of control. In the next several chapters, we will take more giant steps that will allow us to process large amounts of input data and allow us to define and process types of data other than simple numeric types. The `if`, `while`, and `for` statements of this section will play an essential role in the programs that we consider as we take these steps.

Q&A

Q. What is the difference between = and ==?

A. We repeat this question here to remind you to be sure not to use = when you mean == in a conditional expression. The expression (x = y) assigns the value of y to x, whereas the expression (x == y) tests whether the two variables currently have the same values. In some programming languages, this difference can wreak havoc in a program and be difficult to detect, but Java's type safety usually will come to the rescue. For example, if we make the mistake of typing (t = goal) instead of (t == goal) in PROGRAM 1.3.8, the compiler finds the bug for us:

```
javac Gambler.java
Gambler.java:18: incompatible types
found  : int
required: boolean
if (t = goal) wins++;
    ^
1 error
```

Be careful about writing if (x = y) when x and y are boolean variables, since this will be treated as an assignment statement, which assigns the value of y to x and evaluates to the truth value of y. For example, instead of writing if (isPrime = false), you should write if (!isPrime).

Q. So I need to pay attention to using == instead of = when writing loops and conditionals. Is there something else in particular that I should watch out for?

A. Another common mistake is to forget the braces in a loop or conditional with a multi-statement body. For example, consider this version of the code in Gambler:

```
for (int t = 0; t < T; t++)
   for (cash = stake; cash > 0 && cash < goal; bets++)
      if (Math.random() < 0.5) cash++;
      else                     cash--;
   if (cash == goal) wins++;
```

The code appears correct, but it is dysfunctional because the second if is outside both for loops and gets executed just once. Our practice of using explicit braces for long statements is precisely to avoid such insidious bugs.

Q. Anything else?

A. The third classic pitfall is ambiguity in nested if statements:

```
if <expr1> if <expr2> <stmntA> else <stmntB>
```

In Java this is equivalent to

```
if <expr1> { if <expr2> <stmntA> else <stmntB> }
```

even if you might have been thinking

```
if <expr1> { if <expr2> <stmntA> } else <stmntB>
```

Again, using explicit braces is a good way to avoid this pitfall.

Q. Are there cases where I must use a for loop but not a while, or vice versa?

A. No. Generally, you should use a for loop when you have an initialization, an increment, and a loop continuation test (if you do not need the loop control variable outside the loop). But the equivalent while loop still might be fine.

Q. What are the rules on where we declare the loop-control variables?

A. Opinions differ. In older programming languages, it was required that all variables be declared at the beginning of a *<body>*, so many programmers are in this habit and there is a lot of code out there that follows this convention. But it makes a lot of sense to declare variables where they are first used, particularly in for loops, when it is normally the case that the variable is not needed outside the loop. However, it is not uncommon to need to test (and therefore declare) the loop-control variable outside the loop, as in the primality-testing code we considered as an example of the break statement.

Q. What is the difference between ++i and i++?

A. As statements, there is no difference. In expressions, both increment i, but ++i has the value after the increment and i++ the value before the increment. In this book, we avoid statements like x = ++i that have the side effect of changing variable values. So, it is safe to not worry much about this distinction and just use i++

in for loops and as a statement. When we do use ++i in this book, we will call attention to it and say why we are using it.

Q. So, *<initialize>* and *<increment>* can be any statements whatsoever in a for loop. How can I take advantage of that?

A. Some experts take advantage of this ability to create compact code fragments, but, as a beginner, it is best for you to use a while loop in such situations. In fact, the situation is even more complicated because *<initialize>* and *<increment>* can be *sequences* of statements, separated by commas. This notation allows for code that initializes and modifies other variables besides the loop index. In some cases, this ability leads to compact code. For example, the following two lines of code could replace the last eight lines in the body of the main() method in PowersOfTwo (PROGRAM 1.3.3):

```
for (int i = 0, v = 1; i <= n; i++, v *= 2)
    System.out.println(i + " " + v);
```

Such code is rarely necessary and better avoided, particularly by beginners.

Q Can I use a double value as in index in a for loop?

A It is legal, but generally bad practice to do so. Consider the following loop:

```
for (double x = 0.0; x <= 1.0; x += 0.1)
    System.out.println(x + " " + Math.sin(x));
```

How many times does it iterate? The number of iterations depends on an equality test between double values, which may not always give the result that you expect.

Q. Anything else tricky about loops?

A. Not all parts of a for loop need to be filled in with code. The initialization statement, the boolean expression, the increment statement, and the loop body can each be omitted. It is generally better style to use a while statement than null statements in a for loop. In the code in this book, we avoid null statements.

```
int v = 1;
while (v <= N/2)          null increment
    v *= 2;                   statement
                                 ↓
for (int v = 1; v <= N/2; )
    v *= 2;

for (int v = 1; v <= N/2; v *= 2)
    ;  ← null loop body
```

Three equivalent loops

Exercises

1.3.1 Write a program that takes three integer command-line arguments and prints `equal` if all three are equal, and `not equal` otherwise.

1.3.2 Write a more general and more robust version of `Quadratic` (PROGRAM 1.2.3) that prints the roots of the polynomial $ax^2 + bx + c$, prints an appropriate message if the discriminant is negative, and behaves appropriately (avoiding division by zero) if a is zero.

1.3.3 What (if anything) is wrong with each of the following statements?
  a. `if (a > b) then c = 0;`
  b. `if a > b { c = 0; }`
  c. `if (a > b) c = 0;`
  d. `if (a > b) c = 0 else b = 0;`

1.3.4 Write a code fragment that prints `true` if the `double` variables x and y are both strictly between 0 and 1 and `false` otherwise.

1.3.5 Improve your solution to EXERCISE 1.2.25 by adding code to check that the values of the command-line arguments fall within the ranges of validity of the formula, and also adding code to print out an error message if that is not the case.

1.3.6 Suppose that i and j are both of type `int`. What is the value of j after each of the following statements is executed?
  a. `for (i = 0, j = 0; i < 10; i++)  j += i;`
  b. `for (i = 0, j = 1; i < 10; i++)  j += j;`
  c. `for (j = 0; j < 10; j++) j += j;`
  d. `for (i = 0, j = 0; i < 10; i++) j += j++;`

1.3.7 Rewrite `TenHellos` to make a program `Hellos` that takes the number of lines to print as a command-line argument. You may assume that the argument is less than 1000. Hint: Use i % 10 and i % 100 to determine when to use st, nd, rd, or th for printing the ith Hello.

1.3.8 Write a program that, using one `for` loop and one `if` statement, prints the

integers from 1,000 to 2,000 with five integers per line. Hint: Use the % operation.

1.3.9   Write a program that takes an integer N as a command-line argument, uses Math.random() to print N uniform random values between 0 and 1, and then prints their average value (see EXERCISE 1.2.30).

1.3.10   Describe what happens when you try to print a ruler function (see the table on page 57) with a value of N that is too large, such as 100.

1.3.11   Write a program FunctionGrowth that prints a table of the values $\log N$, N, $N \log N$, N^2, N^3, and 2^N for $N = 16, 32, 64, \ldots, 2048$. Use tabs (\t characters) to line up columns.

1.3.12   What are the values of m and n after executing the following code?

```
int n = 123456789;
int m = 0;
while (n != 0)
{
    m = (10 * m) + (n % 10);
    n = n / 10;
}
```

1.3.13   What does the following program print ?

```
int f = 0, g = 1;
for (int i = 0; i <= 15; i++)
{
    System.out.println(f);
    f = f + g;
    g = f - g;
}
```

Solution.   Even an expert programmer will tell you that the only way to understand a program like this is to trace it. When you do, you will find that it prints the values 0, 1, 1, 2, 3, 5, 8, 13, 21, 34, 55, 89, 134, 233, 377, and 610. These numbers are the first sixteen of the famous *Fibonacci sequence*, which are defined by the following formulas: $F_0 = 0$, $F_1 = 1$, and $F_n = F_{n-1} + F_{n-2}$ for $n > 1$. The Fibonacci sequence arises in a surprising variety of contexts, they have been studied for centuries, and

many of their properties are well-known. For example, the ratio of successive numbers approaches the *golden ratio* φ (about 1.618) as *n* approaches infinity.

1.3.14 Write a program that takes a command-line argument N and prints all the positive powers of two less than or equal to N. Make sure that your program works properly for all values of N. (`Integer.parseInt()` will generate an error if N is too large, and your program should print nothing if N is negative.)

1.3.15 Expand your solution to EXERCISE 1.2.24 to print a table giving the total amount paid and the remaining principal after each monthly payment.

1.3.16 Unlike the harmonic numbers, the sum $1/1^2 + 1/2^2 + ... + 1/N^2$ *does* converge to a constant as N grows to infinity. (Indeed, the constant is $\pi^2/6$, so this formula can be used to estimate the value of π.) Which of the following for loops computes this sum? Assume that N is an int initialized to 1000000 and sum is a double initialized to 0.0.

a. `for (int i = 1; i <= N; i++) sum += 1 / (i*i);`

b. `for (int i = 1; i <= N; i++) sum += 1.0 / i*i;`

c. `for (int i = 1; i <= N; i++) sum += 1.0 / (i*i);`

d. `for (int i = 1; i <= N; i++) sum += 1 / (1.0*i*i);`

1.3.17 Show that PROGRAM 1.3.6 implements Newton's method for finding the square root of *c*. *Hint*: Use the fact that the slope of the tangent to a (differentiable) function $f(x)$ at $x = t$ is $f'(t)$ to find the equation of the tangent line and then use that equation to find the point where the tangent line intersects the *x*-axis to show that you can use Newton's method to find a root of any function as follows: at each iteration, replace the estimate t by $t - f(t) / f'(t)$.

1.3.18 Using Newton's method, develop a program that takes integers N and k as command-line arguments and prints the kth root of N (*Hint*: see EXERCISE 1.3.17).

1.3.19 Modify Binary to get a program Kary that takes i and k as command-line arguments and converts i to base k. Assume that i is an integer in Java's long data type and that k is an integer between 2 and 16. For bases greater than 10, use the letters A through F to represent the 11th through 16th digits, respectively.

1.3.20 Write a code fragment that puts the binary representation of a positive integer N into a String s.

Solution.   Java has a built-in method Integer.toBinaryString(N) for this job, but the point of the exercise is to see how such a method might be implemented. Working from PROGRAM 1.3.7, we get the solution

```
String s = "";
int v = 1;
while (v <= n/2) v = 2*v;
while (v > 0)
{
    if (n < v) { s += 0;           }
    else       { s += 1; n -= v; }
    v = v/2;
}
```

A simpler option is to work from right to left:

```
String s = "";
for (int n = N; n > 0; n /= 2)
    s = (n % 2) + s;
```

Both of these methods are worthy of careful study.

1.3.21 Write a version of Gambler that uses two nested while loops or two nested for loops instead of a while loop inside a for loop.

1.3.22 Write a program GamblerPlot that traces a gambler's ruin simulation by printing a line after each bet in which one asterisk corresponds to each dollar held by the gambler.

1.3.23 Modify Gambler to take an extra command-line argument that specifies the (fixed) probability that the gambler wins each bet. Use your program to try to learn how this probability affects the chance of winning and the expected number of bets. Try a value of p close to .5 (say, .48).

1.3.24 Modify Gambler to take an extra command-line argument that specifies the number of bets the gambler is willing to make, so that there are three possible

ways for the game to end: the gambler wins, loses, or runs out of time. Add to the output to give the expected amount of money the gambler will have when the game ends. *Extra credit*: Use your program to plan your next trip to Monte Carlo.

1.3.25 Modify Factors to print just one copy each of the prime divisors.

1.3.26 Run quick experiments to determine the impact of using the termination condition (i <= N/i) instead of (i < N) in Factors in PROGRAM 1.3.9. For each method, find the largest *n* such that when you type in an *n* digit number, the program is sure to finish within 10 seconds.

1.3.27 Write a program Checkerboard that takes one command-line argument N and uses a loop within a loop to print out a two-dimensional N-by-N checkerboard pattern with alternating spaces and asterisks.

1.3.28 Write a program GCD that finds the greatest common divisor (gcd) of two integers using *Euclid's algorithm*, which is an iterative computation based on the following observation: if x is greater than y, then if y divides x, the gcd of x and y is y; otherwise, the gcd of x and y is the same as the gcd of x % y and y.

1.3.29 Write a program RelativelyPrime that takes one command-line argument N and prints out an N-by-N table such that there is an * in row i and column j if the gcd of i and j is 1 (i and j are relatively prime) and a space in that position otherwise.

1.3.30 Write a program PowersOfK that takes an integer k as command-line argument and prints all the positive powers of k in the Java long data type. *Note*: The constant Long.MAX_VALUE is the value of the largest integer in long.

1.3.31 Generate a random point (x, y, z) on the surface of a sphere using Marsaglia's method: Pick a random point (a, b) in the unit disk using the method described at the end of this section. Then, set $x = 2\,a\,\sqrt{1 - a^2 - b^2}$. $y = 2\,b\,\sqrt{1 - a^2 - b^2}$. and $z = 1 - 2\,(a^2 + b^2)$.

Creative Exercises

1.3.32 *Ramanujan's taxi.* Srinivasa Ramanujan was an Indian mathematician who became famous for his intuition for numbers. When the English mathematician G. H. Hardy came to visit him one day, Hardy remarked that the number of his taxi was 1729, a rather dull number. To which Ramanujan replied, "No, Hardy! No, Hardy! It is a very interesting number. It is the smallest number expressible as the sum of two cubes in two different ways." Verify this claim by writing a program that takes a command-line argument N and prints out all integers less than or equal to N that can be expressed as the sum of two cubes in two different ways. In other words, find distinct positive integers a, b, c, and d such that $a^3 + b^3 = c^3 + d^3$. Use four nested for loops.

1.3.33 *Checksum.* The International Standard Book Number (ISBN) is a 10-digit code that uniquely specifies a book. The rightmost digit is a checksum digit that can be uniquely determined from the other 9 digits, from the condition that $d_1 + 2d_2 + 3d_3 + ... + 10d_{10}$ must be a multiple of 11 (here d_i denotes the ith digit from the right). The checksum digit d_i can be any value from 0 to 10. The ISBN convention is to use the character `'X'` to denote 10. Example: the checksum digit corresponding to 020131452 is 5 since 5 is the only value of x between 0 and 10 for which

$$10 \cdot 0 + 9 \cdot 2 + 8 \cdot 0 + 7 \cdot 1 + 6 \cdot 3 + 5 \cdot 1 + 4 \cdot 4 + 3 \cdot 5 + 2 \cdot 2 + 1 \cdot x$$

is a multiple of 11. Write a program that takes a 9-digit integer as a command-line argument, computes the checksum, and prints out the the ISBN number.

1.3.34 *Counting primes.* Write a program `PrimeCounter` that takes a command-line argument N and finds the number of primes less than or equal to N. Use it to print out the number of primes less than or equal to 10 million. *Note*: if you are not careful, your program may not finish in a reasonable amount of time!

1.3.35 *2D random walk.* A two-dimensional random walk simulates the behavior of a particle moving in a grid of points. At each step, the random walker moves north, south, east, or west with probability equal to 1/4, independent of previous moves. Write a program `RandomWalker` that takes a command-line argument N and estimates how long it will take a random walker to hit the boundary of a 2N-by-2N square centered at the starting point.

1.3.36 *Exponential function.* Assume that x is a positive variable of type double. Write a code fragment that uses the Taylor series expansion to set the value of sum to $e^x = 1 + x + x^2/2! + x^3/3! + \ldots$.

Solution. The purpose of this exercise is to get you to think about how a library function like Math.exp() might be implemented in terms of elementary operators. Try solving it, then compare your solution with the one developed here.

We start by considering the problem of computing one term. Suppose that x and term are variables of type double and n is a variable of type int. The following code fragment sets term to $x^N / N!$ using the direct method of having one loop for the numerator and another loop for the denominator, then dividing the results:

```
double num = 1.0, dem = 1.0;
for (int i = 1; i <= n; i++) num *= x;
for (int i = 1; i <= n; i++) den *= i;
double term = num/den;
```

A better approach is to use just a single for loop:

```
double term = 1.0;
for (i = 1; i <= n; i++) term *= x/i;
```

Besides being more compact and elegant, the latter solution is preferable because it avoids inaccuracies caused by computing with huge numbers. For example, the two-loop approach breaks down for values like $x = 10$ and $N = 100$ because 100! is too large to represent as a double.

To compute e^x, we nest this for loop within another for loop:

```
double term = 1.0;
double sum = 0.0;
for (int n = 1; sum != sum + term; n++)
{
    sum += term;
    term = 1.0;
    for (int i = 1; i <= n; i++) term *= x/i;
}
```

The number of times the loop iterates depends on the relative values of the next term and the accumulated sum. Once the value of the sum stops changing, we

leave the loop. (This strategy is more efficient than using the termination condition (term > 0) because it avoids a significant number of iterations that do not change the value of the sum.) This code is effective, but it is inefficient because the inner for loop recomputes all the values it computed on the previous iteration of the outer for loop. Instead, we can make use of the term that was added in on the previous loop iteration and solve the problem with a single for loop:

```
double term = 1.0;
double sum = 0.0;
for (int n = 1; sum != sum + term; n++)
{
    sum += term;
    term *= x/n;
}
```

1.3.37 *Trigonometric functions.* Write two programs, Sin and Cos, that compute the sine and cosine functions using their Taylor series expansions $\sin x = -x + x^3/3! - x^5/5! + \dots$ and $\cos x = 1 + x^2/2! - x^4/4! + \dots$.

1.3.38 *Experimental analysis.* Run experiments to determine the relative costs of Math.exp() and the methods from EXERCISE 1.3.36 for computing e^x: the direct method with nested for loops, the improvement with a single for loop, and the latter with the termination condition (term > 0). Use trial-and-error with a command-line argument to determine how many times your computer can perform each computation in 10 seconds.

1.3.39 *Pepys problem.* In 1693 Samuel Pepys asked Isaac Newton which is more likely: getting 1 at least once when rolling a fair die six times or getting 1 at least twice when rolling it 12 times. Write a program that could have provided Newton with a quick answer.

1.3.40 *Game simulation.* In the 1970s game show *Let's Make a Deal*, a contestant is presented with three doors. Behind one of them is a valuable prize. After the contestant chooses a door, the host opens one of the other two doors (never revealing the prize, of course). The contestant is then given the opportunity to switch to the other unopened door. Should the contestant do so? Intuitively, it might seem that

the contestant's initial choice door and the other unopened door are equally likely to contain the prize, so there would be no incentive to switch. Write a program Mon-teHall to test this intuition by simulation. Your program should take a command-line argument N, play the game N times using each of the two strategies (switch or do not switch), and print the chance of success for each of the two strategies.

1.3.41 *Median-of-5.* Write a program that takes five distinct integers from the command line and prints the median value (the value such that two of the others are smaller and two are larger). *Extra credit*: Solve the problem with a program that compares values fewer than seven times for any given input.

1.3.42 *Sorting three numbers.* Suppose that the variables a, b, c, and t are all of the same numeric primitive type. Prove that the following code puts a, b, and c in ascending order:

```
if (a > b) { t = a; a = b; b = t; }
if (a > c) { t = a; a = c; c = t; }
if (b > c) { t = b; b = c; c = t; }
```

1.3.43 *Chaos.* Write a program to study the following simple model for popula-tion growth, which might be applied to study fish in a pond, bacteria in a test tube, or any of a host of similar situations. We suppose that the population ranges from 0 (extinct) to 1 (maximum population that can be sustained). If the population at time t is x, then we suppose the population at time $t + 1$ to be $rx(1-x)$, where the argument r, known as the *fecundity parameter*, controls the rate of growth. Start with a small population—say, $x = 0.01$—and study the result of iterating the model, for various values of r. For which values of r does the population stabilize at $x = 1 - 1/r$? Can you say anything about the population when r is 3.5? 3.8? 5?

1.3.44 *Euler's sum-of-powers conjecture.* In 1769 Leonhard Euler formulated a generalized version of Fermat's Last Theorem, conjecturing that at least n nth pow-ers are needed to obtain a sum that is itself an nth power, for $n > 2$. Write a program to disprove Euler's conjecture (which stood until 1967), using a quintuply nested loop to find four positive integers whose 5th power sums to the 5th power of an-other positive integer. That is, find $a, b, c, d,$ and e such that $a^5 + b^5 + c^5 + d^5 = e^5$. Use the long data type.

1.4 Arrays

IN THIS SECTION, WE CONSIDER A fundamental programming construct known as the *array*. The primary purpose of an array is to facilitate storing and manipulating large quantities of data. Arrays play an essential role in many data processing tasks. They also correspond to vectors and matrices, which are widely used in science and in scientific programming. We will consider basic properties of array processing in Java, with many examples illustrating why they are useful.

An array stores a sequence of values that are all of the same type. Processing such a set of values is very common. We
might have exam scores, stock prices, nucleotides in a DNA strand, or characters in a book. Each of these examples involve a large number of values that are all of the same type.

We want not only to store values but also directly access each in-
dividual value. The method that we use to refer to individual values in an array is numbering and then *indexing* them. If we have N values, we think of them as being numbered from 0 to $N-1$. Then, we can unam-
biguously specify one of them by referring to the ith value for any value of i from 0 to $N-1$. To refer to the ith value in an array a, we use the notation a[i]. This Java construct is known as a *one-dimensional* array.

The one-dimensional array is our first example in this book of a *data structure* (a method for organizing data). We also consider in this section a more complicated data structure known as *a two-dimensional array*. Data structures play an essential role in modern programming—
CHAPTER 4 is largely devoted to the topic.

An array

Typically, when we have a large amount of data to process, we first put all of the data into one or more arrays. Then we use array indexing to refer to individual values and to process the data. We consider such applications when we discuss data input in SECTION 1.5 and in the case study that is the subject of SECTION 1.6. In this section, we expose the basic properties of arrays by considering examples where our programs first populate arrays with computed values from experimental studies and then process them.

Arrays in Java   Making an array in a Java program involves three distinct steps:
  • Declare the array name and type.
  • Create the array.
  • Initialize the array values.
To declare the array, you need to specify a name and the type of data it will contain.
To create it, you need to specify its size (the number of values). For example, the
following code makes an array of N numbers of type double, all initialized to 0.0:

```
double[] a;
a = new double[N];
for (int i = 0; i < N; i++)
    a[i] = 0.0;
```

The first statement is the array declaration. It is just like a declaration of a variable
of the corresponding primitive type except for the square brackets following the
type name, which specify that we are declaring an array. The second statement creates the array. This action is unnecessary for variables of a primitive type (so we
have not seen a similar action before), but it is needed for all other types of data in
Java (see SECTION 3.1). In the code in this book, we normally keep the array length in
an integer variable N, but any integer-valued expression will do. The for statement
initializes the N array values. We refer to each value by putting its index in brackets
after the array name. This code sets all of the array entries to the value 0.0.

   When you begin to write code that uses an array, you must be sure that your
code declares, creates, and initializes it. Omitting one of these steps is a common
programming mistake. For economy in code, we often take advantage of Java's default array initialization convention and combine all three steps into a single statement. For example, the following statement is equivalent to the code above:

```
double[] a = new double[N];
```

The code to the left of the equal sign constitutes the declaration; the code to the
right constitutes the creation. The for loop is unnecessary in this case because the
default initial value of variables of type double in a Java array is 0.0, but it would
be required if a nonzero value were desired. The default initial value is zero for all
numbers and false for type boolean. For String and other non-primitive types,
the default is the value null, which you will learn about in CHAPTER 3.

   After declaring and creating an array, you can refer to any individual value
anywhere you would use a variable name in a program by enclosing an integer in-

dex in braces after the array name. We refer to the i th item with the code a[i]. The explicit initialization code shown earlier is an example of such a use. The obvious advantage of using arrays is to avoid explicitly naming each variable individually. Using an array index is virtually the same as appending the index to the array name: for example, if we wanted to process eight variables of type double, we could declare each of them individually with the declaration

```
double a0, a1, a2, a3, a4, a5, a6, a7;
```

and then refer to them as a0, a1 and so forth instead of declaring them with double[] a = new double[8] and referring to them as a[0], a[1], and so forth. But naming dozens of individual variables in this way would be cumbersome and naming millions is untenable.

As an example of code that uses arrays, consider using arrays to represent *vectors*. We consider vectors in detail in SECTION 3.3; for the moment, think of a vector as a sequence of real numbers. The *dot product* of two vectors (of the same length) is the sum of the products of their corresponding components. The dot product of two vectors that are represented as one-dimensional arrays x[] and y[] that are each of length 3 is the expression x[0]*y[0] + x[1]*y[1] + x[2]*y[2]. If we represent the two vectors as one-dimensional arrays x[] and y[] that are each of length N and of type double, the dot product is easy to compute:

```
double sum = 0.0;
for (int i = 0; i < N; i++)
    sum += x[i]*y[i];
```

i	x[i]	y[i]	x[i]*y[i]	sum
				0
0	.30	.50	.15	.15
1	.60	.10	.06	.21
2	.10	.40	.04	.25
				.25

Trace of dot product computation

The simplicity of coding such computations makes the use of arrays the natural choice for all kinds of applications. (Note that when we use the notation x[], we are referring to the whole array, as opposed to x[i], which is a reference to the i th entry.)

The accompanying table has many examples of array-processing code, and we will consider even more examples later in the book, because arrays play a central role in processing data in many applications. Before considering more sophisticated examples, we describe a number of important characteristics of programming with arrays.

| *create an array with random values* | ```java
double[] a = new double[N];
for (int i = 0; i < N; i++)
    a[i] = Math.random();
``` |
| *print the array values, one per line* | ```java
for (int i = 0; i < N; i++)
    System.out.println(a[i]);
``` |
| *find the maximum of the array values* | ```java
double max = Double.NEGATIVE_INFINITY;
for (int i = 0; i < N; i++)
    if (a[i] > max) max = a[i];
``` |
| *compute the average of the array values* | ```java
double sum = 0.0;
for (int i = 0; i < N; i++)
    sum += a[i];
double average = sum / N;
``` |
| *copy to another array* | ```java
double[] b = new double[N];
for (int i = 0; i < N; i++)
    b[i] = a[i];
``` |
| *reverse the elements within an array* | ```java
for (int i = 0; i < N/2; i++)
{
    double temp = b[i];
    b[i] = b[N-1-i];
    b[N-i-1] = temp;
}
``` |

Typical array-processing code (for arrays of N double *values)*

Zero-based indexing. We always refer to the first element of an array as a[0], the second as a[1], and so forth. It might seem more natural to you to refer to the first element as a[1], the second value as a[2], and so forth, but starting the indexing with 0 has some advantages and has emerged as the convention used in most modern programming languages. Misunderstanding this convention often leads to *off-by one-errors* that are notoriously difficult to avoid and debug, so be careful!

Array length. Once we create an array, its size is fixed. The reason that we need to explicitly create arrays at runtime is that the Java compiler cannot know how much space to reserve for the array at compile time (as it can for primitive-type values). Our convention is to keep the size of the array in a variable N whose value can be set at runtime (usually it is the value of a command-line argument). Java's standard mechanism is to allow a program to refer to the length of an array a[] with the code a.length; we normally use N to create the array, or set the value of N to a.length. Note that the last element of an array is always a[a.length-1].

Memory representation. Arrays are fundamental data structures in that they have a direct correspondence with memory systems on virtually all computers. The elements of an array are stored consecutively in memory, so that it is easy to quickly access any array value. Indeed, we can view memory itself as a giant array. On modern computers, memory is implemented in hardware as a sequence of indexed memory locations that each can be quickly accessed with an appropriate index. When referring to computer memory, we normally refer to a location's index as its *address*. It is convenient to think of the name of the array—say, a—as storing the memory address of the first element of the array a[0]. For the purposes of illustration, suppose that the computer's memory is organized as 1,000 values, with addresses from 000 to 999. (This simplified model ignores the fact that array elements can occupy differing amounts of memory depending on their type, but you can ignore such details for the moment.) Now, suppose that an array of eight elements is stored in memory locations 523 through 530. In such a situation, Java would store the memory address (index) of the first array value somewhere else in memory, along with the array length. We refer to the address as a *pointer* and think of it as *pointing to* the referenced memory location. When we specify a[i], the compiler generates code that accesses the desired value by adding the index i to the memory address of the array a[]. For example, the Java code a[4] would generate machine code that finds the value at memory location 523 + 4 = 527. Accessing element i of an array is an efficient operation because it simply requires adding two integers and then referencing memory—just two elementary operations. Extending the model to handle different-sized array elements just involves multiplying the index by the element size before adding to the array address.

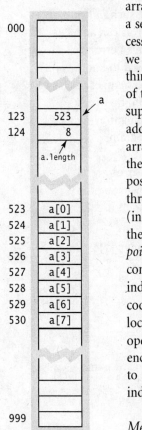

Memory representation

Memory allocation. When you use new to create an array, Java reserves space in memory for it. This process is called *memory allocation*. The same process is required for all variables that you use in a program. We call attention to it now because it is your responsibility to use new to allocate memory for an array before accessing any of its elements. If you fail to adhere to this rule, you will get a compile-time *uninitialized variable* error. Java automatically initializes all of the values in an array when it is created. You should remember that the time required to create an array is proportional to its length.

Bounds checking. As already indicated, you must be careful when programming with arrays. It is your responsibility to use legal indices when accessing an array element. If you have created an array of size N and use an index whose value is less than 0 or greater than N-1, your program will terminate with an ArrayIndex-OutOfBounds run-time exception. (In many programming languages, such *buffer overflow* conditions are not checked by the system. Such unchecked errors can and do lead to debugging nightmares, but it is also not uncommon for such an error to go unnoticed and remain in a finished program. You might be surprised to know that such a mistake can be exploited by a hacker to take control of a system, even your personal computer, to spread viruses, steal personal information, or wreak other malicious havoc.) The error messages provided by Java may seem annoying to you at first, but they are small price to pay to have a more secure program.

Setting array values at compile time. When we have a small number of literal values that we want to keep in array, we can declare and initialize it by listing the values between curly braces, separated by commas. For example, we might use the following code in a program that processes playing cards.

```
String[] suit = { "Clubs", "Diamonds", "Hearts", "Spades" };

String[] rank =
{
    "2", "3", "4", "5", "6", "7", "8", "9", "10",
    "Jack", "Queen", "King", "Ace"
};
```

After creating the two arrays, we can use them to print out a random card name, such as Queen of Clubs, as follows:

```
int i = (int) (Math.random() * rank.length);
int j = (int) (Math.random() * suit.length);
System.out.println(rank[i] + " of " + suit[j]);
```

This code uses the idiom introduced in SECTION 1.2 to generate random indices and then uses the indices to pick strings out of the arrays. Whenever the values of all array entries are known at compile time (and the size of the array is not too large) it makes sense to use this method of initializing the array—just put all the values in braces on the right hand side of an assignment in the array declaration. Doing so implies array creation, so the new keyword is not needed.

Setting array values at runtime. A more typical situation is when we wish to compute the values to be stored in an array. In this case, we can use array names with indices in the same way we use variable names on the left side of assignment statements. For example, we might use the following code to initialize an array of size 52 that represents a deck of playing cards, using the two arrays just defined:

```
String[] deck = new String[suit.length * rank.length];
for (int i = 0; i < suit.length; i++)
   for (int j = 0; j < rank.length; j++)
      deck[rank.length*i + j] = rank[i] + " of " + suit[j];
```

After this code has been executed, if you were to print out the contents of deck in order from deck[0] through deck[51] using System.out.println(), you would get the sequence

```
2 of Clubs
2 of Diamonds
2 of Hearts
2 of Spades
3 of Clubs
3 of Diamonds
...
Ace of Hearts
Ace of Spades
```

Exchange. Frequently, we wish to exchange two values in an array. Continuing our example with playing cards, the following code exchanges the cards at position i and j using the same idiom that we traced as our first example of the use of assignment statements in SECTION 1.2:

```
String t = deck[i];
deck[i] = deck[j];
deck[j] = t;
```

When we use this code, we are assured that we are perhaps changing the *order* of the values in the array but not the *set* of values in the array. When i and j are equal, the array is unchanged. When i and j are not equal, the values a[i] and a[j] are found in different places in the array. For example, if we were to use this code with i equal to 1 and j equal to 4 in the deck array of the previous example, it would leave 3 of Clubs in deck[1] and 2 of Diamonds in deck[4].

Shuffle. The following code shuffles our deck of cards:

```
int N = deck.length;
for (int i = 0; i < N; i++)
{
   int r = i + (int) (Math.random() * (N-i));
   String t = deck[i];
   deck[i] = deck[r];
   deck[r] = t;
}
```

Proceeding from left to right, we pick a random card from deck[i] through deck[N-1] (each card equally likely) and exchange it with deck[i]. This code is more sophisticated than it might seem: First, we ensure that the cards in the deck after the shuffle are the same as the cards in the deck before the shuffle by using the exchange idiom. Second, we ensure that the shuffle is random by choosing uniformly from the cards not yet chosen.

Sampling without replacement. In many situations, we want to draw a random sample from a set such that each member of the set appears at most once in the sample. Drawing numbered ping-pong balls from a basket for a lottery is an example of this kind of sample, as is dealing a hand from a deck of cards. Sample (PROGRAM 1.4.1) illustrates how to sample, using the basic operation underlying shuffling. It takes command-line arguments M and N and creates a *permutation* of size N (a rearrangement of the integers from 0 to N-1) whose first M entries com-

i	r	perm															
		0	1	2	3	4	5	6	7	8	9	10	11	12	13	14	15
		0	1	2	3	4	5	6	7	8	9	10	11	12	13	14	15
0	9	9	1	2	3	4	5	6	7	8	0	10	11	12	13	14	15
1	5	9	5	2	3	4	1	6	7	8	0	10	11	12	13	14	15
2	13	9	5	13	3	4	1	6	7	8	0	10	11	12	2	14	15
3	5	9	5	13	1	4	3	6	7	8	0	10	11	12	2	14	15
4	11	9	5	13	1	11	3	6	7	8	0	10	4	12	2	14	15
5	8	9	5	13	1	11	8	6	7	3	0	10	4	12	2	14	15
		9	5	13	1	11	8	6	7	3	0	10	4	12	2	14	15

Trace of java Sample 6 16

Program 1.4.1 Sampling without replacement

```
public class Sample
{
    public static void main(String[] args)
    {   // Print a random sample of M integers
        // from 0 ... N-1 (no duplicates).
        int M = Integer.parseInt(args[0]);
        int N = Integer.parseInt(args[1]);
        int[] perm = new int[N];

        // Initialize perm[].
        for (int j = 0; j < N; j++)
            perm[j] = j;

        // Take sample.
        for (int i = 0; i < M; i++)
        {   // Exchange perm[i] with a random element to its right.
            int r = i + (int) (Math.random() * (N-i));
            int t = perm[r];
            perm[r] = perm[i];
            perm[i] = t;
        }

        // Print sample.
        for (int i = 0; i < M; i++)
            System.out.print(perm[i] + " ");
        System.out.println();
    }
}
```

M	sample size
N	range
perm[]	permutation of 0 to N-1

This program takes two command-line arguments M and N and produces a sample of M of the integers from 0 to N-1. This process is useful, not just in state and local lotteries, but in scientific applications of all sorts. If the first argument is equal to the second, the result is a random permutation of the integers from 0 to N-1. If the first argument is greater than the second, the program will terminate with an ArrayOutOfBounds exception.

```
% java Sample 6 16
9 5 13 1 11 8

% java Sample 10 1000
656 488 298 534 811 97 813 156 424 109

% java Sample 20 20
6 12 9 8 13 19 0 2 4 5 18 1 14 16 17 3 7 11 10 15
```

prise a random sample. The accompanying trace of the contents of the perm[] array at the end of each iteration of the main loop (for a run where the values of *M* and *N* are 6 and 16, respectively) illustrates the process.

If the values of r are chosen such that each value in the given range is equally likely, then perm[0] through perm[M-1] are a random sample at the end of the process (even though some elements might move multiple times) because each element in the sample is chosen by taking each item not yet sampled, with equal probability for each choice. One important reason to explicitly compute the permutation is that we can use it to print out a random sample of *any* array by using the elements of the permutation as indices into the array. Doing so is often an attractive alternative to actually rearranging the array because it may need to be in order for some other reason (for instance, a company might wish to draw a random sample from a list of customers that is kept in alphabetical order). To see how this trick works, suppose that we wish to draw a random poker hand from our deck[] array, constructed as just described. We use the code in Sample with *N* = 52 and *M* = 5 and replace perm[i] with deck[perm[i]] in the System.out.print() statement (and change it to println()), resulting in output such as the following:

```
3 of Clubs
Jack of Hearts
6 of Spades
Ace of Clubs
10 of Diamonds
```

Sampling like this is widely used as the basis for statistical studies in polling, scientific research, and many other applications, whenever we want to draw conclusions about a large population by analyzing a small random sample.

Precomputed values. One simple application of arrays is to save values that you have computed, for later use. As an example, suppose that you are writing a program that performs calculations using small values of the harmonic numbers (see PROGRAM 1.3.5). An efficient approach is to save the values in an array, as follows:

```
double[] H = new double[N];
for (int i = 1; i < N; i++)
    H[i] = H[i-1] + 1.0/i;
```

Then you can just use the code H[i] to refer to any of the values. Precomputing values in this way is an example of a *space-time tradeoff*: by investing in space (to save the values) we save time (since we do not need to recompute them). This method is not effective if we need values for huge N, but it is very effective if we need values for small N many different times.

Simplifying repetitive code. As an example of another simple application of arrays, consider the following code fragment, which prints out the name of a month given its number (1 for January, 2 for February, and so forth):

```
if      (m ==  1) System.out.println("Jan");
else if (m ==  2) System.out.println("Feb");
else if (m ==  3) System.out.println("Mar");
else if (m ==  4) System.out.println("Apr");
else if (m ==  5) System.out.println("May");
else if (m ==  6) System.out.println("Jun");
else if (m ==  7) System.out.println("Jul");
else if (m ==  8) System.out.println("Aug");
else if (m ==  9) System.out.println("Sep");
else if (m == 10) System.out.println("Oct");
else if (m == 11) System.out.println("Nov");
else if (m == 12) System.out.println("Dec");
```

We could also use a switch statement, but a much more compact alternative is to use a String array consisting of the names of each month:

```
String[] months =
{
    "", "Jan", "Feb", "Mar", "Apr", "May", "Jun",
        "Jul", "Aug", "Sep", "Oct", "Nov", "Dec"
};
System.out.println(months[m]);
```

This technique would be especially useful if you needed to access the name of a month by its number in several different places in your program. Note that we intentionally waste one slot in the array (element 0) to make months[1] correspond to January, as required.

Assignments and equality tests. Suppose that you have created the two arrays a[] and b[]. What does it mean to assign one to the other with the code a = b; ? Similarly, what does it mean to test whether the two arrays are equal with the code (a == b)? The answers to these questions may not be what you first assume, but if you think about the array memory representation, you will see that Java's interpretation of these operations makes sense: An assignment makes the names a and b refer to the same array. The alternative would be to have an implied loop that assigns each value in b to the corresponding value in a. Similarly, an equality test checks whether the two names refer to the same array. The alternative would be to have an implied loop that tests whether each value in one array is equal to the corresponding value in the other array. In both cases, the implementation in Java is very simple: it just performs the standard operation as if the array name were a variable whose value is the memory address of the array. Note that there are many other operations that you might want to perform on arrays: for example, it would be nice in some applications to say a = a + b and have it mean "add the corresponding element in b[] to each element in a[]," but that statement is not legal in Java. Instead, we write an explicit loop to perform all the additions. We will consider in detail Java's mechanism for satisfying such higher-level programming needs in SECTION 3.2. In typical applications, we use this mechanism, so we rarely need to use Java's assignments and equality tests with arrays.

WITH THESE BASIC DEFINITIONS AND EXAMPLES out of the way, we can now consider two applications that both address interesting classical problems and illustrate the fundamental importance of arrays in efficient computation. In both cases, the idea of using data to index into an array plays a central role and enables a computation that would not otherwise be feasible.

Coupon collector   Suppose that you have a shuffled deck of cards and you turn them face up, one by one. How many cards do you need to turn up before you have seen one of each suit? How many cards do you need to turn up before seeing one of each value? These are examples of the famous *coupon collector* problem. In general, suppose that a trading card company 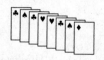 issues trading cards with N different possible cards: how many do you have to collect before you have all N possibilities, assuming that each possibility is equally likely for each card that you collect?

Coupon collection

Coupon collecting is no toy problem. For example, it is very often the case that scientists want to know whether a sequence that arises in nature has the same characteristics as a random sequence. If so, that fact might be of interest; if not, further investigation may be warranted to look for patterns that might be of importance. For example, such tests are used by scientists to decide which parts of genomes are worth studying. One effective test for whether a sequence is truly random is

Program 1.4.2 *Coupon collector simulation*

```
public class CouponCollector
{
    public static void main(String[] args)
    { // Generate random values in (0..N] until finding each one.
        int N = Integer.parseInt(args[0]);
        boolean[] found = new boolean[N];
        int cardcnt = 0, valcnt = 0;
        while (valcnt < N)
        { // Generate another value.
            int val = (int) (Math.random() * N);
            cardcnt++;
            if (!found[val])
            {
                valcnt++;
                found[val] = true;
            }
        } // N different values found.
        System.out.println(cardcnt);
    }
}
```

N	range
cardcnt	*values generated*
valcnt	*different values found*
found[]	*table of found values*

This program simulates coupon collection by taking a command-line argument N *and generating random numbers between* 0 *and* N-1 *until getting every possible value.*

```
% java CouponCollector 1000
6583
% java CouponCollector 1000
6477
% java CouponCollector 1000000
12782673
```

the *coupon collector test*: compare the number of elements that need to be examined before all values are found against the corresponding number for a uniformly random sequence. CouponCollector (PROGRAM 1.4.2) is an example program that simulates this process and illustrates the utility of arrays. It takes the value of *N* from the command line and generates a sequence of random integer values between 0 and $N-1$ using the code (int) (Math.random() * N) (see PROGRAM 1.2.5). Each value represents a card: for each card, we want to know if we have seen that value before. To maintain that knowledge, we use an array found[], which uses the card value as an index: found[i] is true if we have seen a card with value i and false if we have not. When we get a new card that is represented by the integer val, we check whether we have seen its value before simply by accessing found[val]. The computation consists of keeping count of the number of distinct values seen and the number of cards generated and printing the latter when the former gets to N.

As usual, the best way to understand a program is to consider a trace of the values of its variables for a typical run. It is easy to add code to CouponCollector that produces a trace that gives the values of the variables at the end of the while loop for a typical run. In the accompanying figure, we use F for the value false and T for the value true to make the trace easier to follow. Tracing programs that use large arrays can be a challenge: when you have an array of size N in your program, it represents N variables, so you have to list them all. Tracing programs

val	found						valcnt	cardcnt
	0	1	2	3	4	5		
	F	F	F	F	F	F	0	0
2	F	F	T	F	F	F	1	1
0	T	F	T	F	F	F	2	2
4	T	F	T	F	T	F	3	3
0	T	F	T	F	T	F	3	4
1	T	T	T	F	T	F	4	5
2	T	T	T	F	T	F	4	6
5	T	T	T	F	T	T	5	7
0	T	T	T	F	T	T	5	8
1	T	T	T	F	T	T	5	9
3	T	T	T	T	T	T	6	10

Trace for a typical run of
java CouponCollector 6

that use Math.random() also can be a challenge because you get a different trace every time you run the program. Accordingly, we check relationships among variables carefully. Here, note that valcnt always is equal to the number of true values in found[].

Without arrays, we could not contemplate simulating the coupon collector process for huge N; with arrays it is easy to do so. We will see many examples of such processes throughout the book.

Sieve of Eratosthenes   Prime numbers play an important role in mathematics and computation, including cryptography. A *prime number* is an integer greater than one whose only positive divisors are one and itself. The prime counting function $\pi(N)$ is the number of primes less than or equal to N. For example, $\pi(25) = 9$ since the first nine primes are 2, 3, 5, 7, 11, 13, 17, 19, and 23. This function plays a central role in number theory.

Program 1.4.3   Sieve of Eratosthenes

```java
public class PrimeSieve
{
    public static void main(String[] args)
    {  // Print the number of primes <= N.
        int N = Integer.parseInt(args[0]);
        boolean[] isPrime = new boolean[N+1];
        for (int i = 2; i < N; i++)
            isPrime[i] = true;

        for (int i = 2; i <= N/i; i++)
        {  if (isPrime[i])
            {  // Mark multiples of i as nonprime.
                for (int j = i; j <= N/i; j++)
                    isPrime[i * j] = false;
            }
        }

        // Count the primes.
        int primes = 0;
        for (int i = 2; i <= N; i++)
            if (isPrime[i]) primes++;
        System.out.println(primes);
    }
}
```

N	argument
isPrime[i]	is i *prime?*
primes	*prime counter*

This program takes a command-line argument N *and computes the number of primes less than or equal to* N. *To do so, it computes an array of boolean values with* isPrime[i] *set to* true *if* i *is prime, and to* false *otherwise. First, it sets to* true *all array elements in order to indicate that no numbers are initially known to be nonprime. Then it sets to* false *array elements corresponding to indices that are known to be nonprime (multiples of known primes). If* a[i] *is still* true *after all multiples of smaller primes have been set to* false, *then we know* i *to be prime. The termination test in the second* for *loop is* i <= N/i *instead of the naive* i <= N *because any number with no factor less than* N/i *has no factor greater than* N/i, *so we do not have to look for such factors. This improvement makes it possible to run the program for large* N.

```
% java PrimeSieve 25
9
% java PrimeSieve 100
25
% java PrimeSieve 1000000000
50847534
```

i	isPrime																							
	2	3	4	5	6	7	8	9	10	11	12	13	14	15	16	17	18	19	20	21	22	23	24	25
	T	T	T	T	T	T	T	T	T	T	T	T	T	T	T	T	T	T	T	T	T	T	T	T
2			F		F		F		F		F		F		F		F		F		F		F	
3								F			F			F			F			F			F	
5																								F
	T	T	F	T	F	T	F	F	F	T	F	T	F	F	F	T	F	T	F	F	F	T	F	F

Trace of java PrimeSieve 25

One approach to counting primes is to use a program like Factors (PROGRAM 1.3.9). Specifically, we could modify the code in Factors to set a boolean value to be true if a given number is prime and false otherwise (instead of printing out factors), then enclose that code in a loop that increments a counter for each prime number. This approach is effective for small N, but becomes too slow as N grows.

PrimeSieve (PROGRAM 1.4.3) takes a command-line integer N and computes the prime count using a technique known as the *Sieve of Eratosthenes*. The program uses a boolean array isPrime[] to record which integers are prime. The goal is to set isPrime[i] to true if i is prime, and to false otherwise. The sieve works as follows: Initially, set all array elements to true, indicating that no factors of any integer have yet been found. Then, repeat the following steps as long as i <= N/i:

• Find the next smallest i for which no factors have been found.
• Leave isPrime[i] as true since i has no smaller factors.
• Set the isPrime[] entries for all multiples of i to be false.

When the nested for loop ends, we have set the isPrime[] entries for all nonprimes to be false and have left the isPrime[] entries for all primes as true. With one more pass through the array, we can count the number of primes less than or equal to N. As usual, it is easy to add code to print a trace. For programs such as Prime-Sieve, you have to be a bit careful—it contains a nested for-if-for, so you have to pay attention to the braces in order to put the print code in the correct place. Note that we stop when i > N/i, just as we did for Factors.

With PrimeSieve, we can compute $\pi(N)$ for large N, limited primarily by the maximum array size allowed by Java. This is another example of a space-time tradeoff. Programs like PrimeSieve play an important role in helping mathematicians to develop the theory of numbers, which has many important applications.

Two-dimensional arrays In many applications, a convenient way to store information is to use a table of numbers organized in a rectangular table and refer to *rows* and *columns* in the table. For example, a teacher might need to maintain a table with a row corresponding to each student and a column corresponding to each assignment, a scientist might need to maintain a table of experimental data with rows corresponding to experiments and columns corresponding to various outcomes, or a programmer might want to prepare an image for display by setting a table of pixels to various grayscale values or colors.

a[1][2]

99	85	98
98	57	78
92	77	76
94	32	11
99	34	22
90	46	54
76	59	88
92	66	89
97	71	24
89	29	38

row 1 → (second row); column 2 (third column)

Anatomy of a two-dimensional array

The mathematical abstraction corresponding to such tables is a *matrix*; the corresponding Java construct is a *two-dimensional array*. You are likely to have already encountered many applications of matrices and two-dimensional arrays, and you will certainly encounter many others in science, in engineering, and in computing applications, as we will demonstrate with examples throughout this book. As with vectors and one-dimensional arrays, many of the most important applications involve processing large amounts of data, and we defer considering those applications until we consider input and output, in SECTION 1.5.

Extending Java array constructs to handle two-dimensional arrays is straightforward. To refer to the element in row i and column j of a two-dimensional array a[][], we use the notation a[i][j]; to declare a two-dimensional array, we add another pair of brackets; and to create the array, we specify the number of rows followed by the number of columns after the type name (both within brackets), as follows:

```
double[][] a = new double[M][N];
```

We refer to such an array as an *M*-by-*N* array. By convention, the first dimension is the number of rows and the second is the number of columns. As with one-dimensional arrays, Java initializes all entries in arrays of numbers to zero and in arrays of boolean values to `false`.

Initialization. Default initialization of two-dimensional arrays is useful because it masks more code than for one-dimensional arrays. The following code is equivalent to the single-line create-and-initialize idiom that we just considered:

```
double[][] a;
a = new double[M][N];
for (int i = 0; i < M; i++)
{  // Initialize the ith row.
   for (int j = 0; j < N; j++)
      a[i][j] = 0.0;
}
```

This code is superfluous when initializing to zero, but the nested for loops are needed to initialize to some other value(s). As you will see, this code is a model for the code that we use to access or modify each element of a two-dimensional array.

Output. We use nested for loops for many array-processing operations. For example, to print an *M*-by-*N* array in the familiar tabular format, we would use the following code

```
for (int i = 0; i < M; i++)
{  // Print the ith row.
   for (int j = 0; j < N; j++)
      System.out.print(a[i][j] + " ");
   System.out.println();
}
```

regardless of the array elements' type. If desired, we could add code to embellish the output with row and column numbers (see Exercise 1.4.6), but Java programmers typically tabulate arrays with row numbers running top to bottom from 0 and column number running left to right from 0. Generally, we also do so and do not bother to use labels.

Memory representation. Java represents a two-dimensional array as an array of arrays. A matrix with *M* rows and *N* columns is actually an array of length *M*, each entry of which is an array of length *N*. In a two-dimensional Java array a[][], we can use the code a[i] to refer to the ith row (which is a one-dimensional array), but we have no corresponding way to refer to a column.

a[][]

a[0][0]	a[0][1]	a[0][2]
a[1][0]	a[1][1]	a[1][2]
a[2][0]	a[2][1]	a[2][2]
a[3][0]	a[3][1]	a[3][2]
a[4][0]	a[4][1]	a[4][2]
a[5][0]	a[5][1]	a[5][2]
a[6][0]	a[6][1]	a[6][2]
a[7][0]	a[7][1]	a[7][2]
a[8][0]	a[8][1]	a[8][2]
a[9][0]	a[9][1]	a[9][2]

a[5] →

A 10-by-3 array

Setting values at compile time. The Java method for initializing an array of values at compile time follows immediately from the representation. A two-dimensional array is an array of rows, each row initialized as a one-dimensional array. To initialize a two-dimensional array, we enclose in braces a list of terms to initialize the rows, separated by commas. Each term in the list is itself a list: the values for the array elements in the row, enclosed in braces and separated by commas.

Spreadsheets. One familiar use of arrays is a *spreadsheet* for maintaining a table of numbers. For example, a teacher with M students and N test grades for each student might maintain an $(M+1)$-by-$(N+1)$ array, reserving the last column for each student's average grade and the last row for the average test grades. Even though we typically do such computations within specialized applications, it is worthwhile to study the underlying code as an introduction to array processing. To compute the average grade for each student (average values for each row), sum the entries for each row and divide by N. The row-by-row order in which this code processes the matrix

```
int[][] a =
{
    { 99, 85, 98,  0 },
    { 98, 57, 78,  0 },
    { 92, 77, 76,  0 },
    { 94, 32, 11,  0 },
    { 99, 34, 22,  0 },
    { 90, 46, 54,  0 },
    { 76, 59, 88,  0 },
    { 92, 66, 89,  0 },
    { 97, 71, 24,  0 },
    { 89, 29, 38,  0 },
    {  0,  0,  0,  0 }
};
```

Compile-time initialization of a two-dimensional array

Compute row averages

```
for (int i = 0; i < M; i++)
{  // Compute average for row i
    double sum = 0.0;
    for (int j = 0; j < N; j++)
        sum += a[i][j];
    a[i][N] = (int) Math.round(sum/N);
}
```

Compute column averages

```
for (int j = 0; j < N; j++)
{  // Compute average for column j
    double sum = 0.0;
    for (int i = 0; i < M; i++)
        sum += a[i][j];
    a[M][j] = (int) Math.round(sum/M);
}
```

Typical spreadsheet calculations

entries is known as *row-major* order. Similarly, to compute the average test grade (average values for each column), sum the entries for each column and divide by M. The column-by-column order in which this code processes the matrix entries is known as *column-major* order.

a[][]   a[1][2]
```
.70 .20 .10
.30 .60 .10
.50 .10 .40
```

b[][]   b[1][2]
```
.80 .30 .50
.10 .40 .10
.10 .30 .40
```

c[][]   c[1][2]
```
1.5 .50 .60
.40 1.0 .20
.60 .40 .80
```

Matrix addition

Matrix operations. Typical applications in science and engineering involve representing matrices as two-dimensional arrays and then implementing various mathematical operations with matrix operands. Again, even though such processing is often done within specialized applications, it is worthwhile for you to understand the underlying computation. For example, we can *add* two N-by-N matrices as follows:

```
double[][] c = new double[N][N];
for (int i = 0; i < N; i++)
    for (int j = 0; j < N; j++)
        c[i][j] = a[i][j] + b[i][j];
```

Similarly, we can *multiply* two matrices. You may have learned matrix multiplication, but if you do not recall or are not familiar with it, the Java code below for square matrices is essentially the same as the mathematical definition. Each entry c[i][j] in the product of a[] and b[] is computed by taking the dot product of row i of a[] with column j of b[].

```
double[][] c = new double[N][N];
for (int i = 0; i < N; i++)
{
    for (int j = 0; j < N; j++)
    {
        // Compute dot product of row i and column j.
        for (int k = 0; k < N; k++)
            c[i][j] += a[i][k]*b[k][j];
    }
}
```

The definition extends to matrices that are not necessarily square (see EXERCISE 1.4.17).

a[][]
```
.70 .20 .10
.30 .60 .10   ← row 1
.50 .10 .40
```

b[][]   *column 2*
```
.80 .30 .50
.10 .40 .10
.10 .30 .40
```

```
c[1][2] =  .3 *.5
        +  .6 *.1
        +  .1 *.4
        ≐ .25
```

c[][]
```
.59 .32 .41
.31 .36 .25   ← ≐ .25
.45 .31 .42
```

Matrix multiplication

Special cases of matrix multiplication. Two special cases of matrix multiplication are important. These special cases occur when one of the dimensions of one of the matrices is 1, so it may be viewed as a vector. We have *matrix-vector multiplication*, where we multiply an M-by-N matrix by a *column vector* (an N-by-1 matrix) to get an M-by-1 column vector result (each entry in the result is the dot product of the corresponding row in the matrix with the operand vector). The second case is *vector-matrix multiplication*, where we multiply a *row vector* (a 1-by-M matrix) by an M-by-N matrix to get a 1-by-N row vector result (each entry in the result is the dot product of the operand vector with the corresponding column in the matrix). These operations provide a succinct way to express numerous matrix calculations. For example, the row-average computation for such a spreadsheet with M rows and N columns is equivalent to a matrix-vector multiplication where the column vector has M entries all equal to $1/M$. Similarly, the column-average computation in such a spreadsheet is equivalent to a vector-matrix multiplication where the row vector has N entries all equal to $1/N$. We return to vector-matrix multiplication in the context of an important application at the end of this chapter.

Ragged arrays. There is actually no requirement that all rows in a two-dimensional array have the same length—an array with rows of nonuniform length is known as a *ragged array* (see EXERCISE 1.4.32 for an example application). The possibility of ragged arrays creates the need for more care in crafting array-processing code. For example, this code prints the contents of a ragged array:

Matrix-vector multiplication `a[][]*x[] = b[]`

```
for (int i = 0; i < M; i++)
{  // Dot product of row i and x[].
   for (int j = 0; j < N; j++)
      b[i] += a[i][j]*x[j];
}
```

Vector-matrix multiplication `y[]*a[][] = c[]`

```
for (int j = 0; j < N; j++)
{  // Dot product of y[] and column j.
   for (int i = 0; i < M; i++)
      c[j] += y[i]*a[i][j];
}
```

Matrix-vector and vector-matrix multiplication

```
for (int i = 0; i < a.length; i++)
{
   for (int j = 0; j < a[i].length; j++)
      System.out.print(a[i][j] + " ");
   System.out.println();
}
```

This code tests your understanding of Java arrays, so you should take the time to study it. In this book, we normally use square or rectangular arrays, whose dimension is given by a variable M or N. Code that uses a[i].length in this way is a clear signal to you that an array is ragged.

Multidimensional arrays. The same notation extends to allow us to write code using arrays that have any number of dimensions. For instance, we can declare and initialize a three-dimensional array with the code

```
double[][][] a = new double[N][N][N];
```

and then refer to an entry with code like a[i][j][k], and so forth.

TWO-DIMENSIONAL ARRAYS PROVIDE A NATURAL REPRESENTATION for matrices, which are omnipresent in science, mathematics, and engineering. They also provide a natural way to organize large amounts of data, a key factor in spreadsheets and many other computing applications. Through Cartesian coordinates, two- and three-dimensional arrays also provide the basis for a models of the physical world. We consider their use in all three arenas throughout this book.

Example: self-avoiding random walks   Suppose that you leave your dog in the middle of a large city whose streets form a familiar grid pattern. We assume that there are N north-south streets and N east-west streets all regularly spaced and fully intersecting in a pattern known as a *lattice.* Trying to escape the city, the dog makes a random choice of which way to go at each intersection, but knows by scent to avoid visiting any place previously visited. But it is possible for the dog to get stuck in a dead end where there is no choice but to revisit some intersection. What is the chance that this will happen? This amusing problem is a simple example of a famous model known as the *self-avoiding random walk,* which has important scientific applications in the study of polymers and in statistical mechanics, among many others. For example, you can see

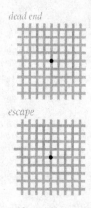

dead end

escape

Self-avoiding walks

that this process models a chain of material growing a bit at a time, until no growth is possible. To better understand such processes, scientists seek to understand the properties of self-avoiding walks.

The dog's escape probability is certainly dependent on the size of the city. In a tiny 5-by-5 city, it is easy to convince yourself that the dog is certain to escape. But what are the chances of escape when the city is large? We are also interested in other parameters. For example, how long is the dog's path, on the average? How often does the dog come within one block of a previous position other than the one just left, on the average? How often does the dog come within one block of escaping? These sorts of properties are important in the various applications just mentioned.

SelfAvoidingWalk (PROGRAM 1.4.4) is a simulation of this situation that uses a two-dimensional boolean array, where each entry represents an intersection. The value true indicates that the dog has visited the intersection; false indicates that the dog has not visited the intersection. The path starts in the center and takes random steps to places not yet visited until getting stuck or escaping at a boundary. For simplicity, the code is written so that if a random choice is made to go to a spot that has already been visited, it takes no action, trusting that some subsequent random choice will find a new place (which is assured because the code explicitly tests for a dead end and leaves the loop in that case).

Note that the code depends on Java initializing all of the array entries to false for each experiment. It also exhibits an important programming technique where we code the loop exit test in the while statement as a *guard* against an illegal statement in the body of the loop. In this case, the while loop continuation test serves as a guard against an out-of-bounds array access within the loop. This corresponds to checking whether the dog has escaped. Within the loop, a successful dead-end test results in a break out of the loop.

As you can see from the sample runs, the unfortunate truth is that your dog is nearly certain to get trapped in a dead end in a large city. If you are interested in learning more about self-avoiding walks, you can find several suggestions in the exercises. For example, the dog is virtually certain to escape in the three-dimensional version of the problem. While this is an intuitive result that is confirmed by our tests, the development of a mathematical model that explains the behavior of self-avoiding walks is a famous open problem: despite extensive research, no one knows a succinct mathematical expression for the escape probability, the average length of the path, or any other important parameter.

Program 1.4.4   *Self-avoiding random walks*

```
public class SelfAvoidingWalk
{
    public static void main(String[] args)
    { // Do T random self-avoiding walks
      //    in an N-by-N lattice
      int N = Integer.parseInt(args[0]);
      int T = Integer.parseInt(args[1]);
      int deadEnds = 0;
      for (int t = 0; t < T; t++)
      {
          boolean[][] a = new boolean[N][N];
          int x = N/2, y = N/2;
          while (x > 0 && x < N-1 && y > 0 && y < N-1)
          { // Check for dead end and make a random move.
              a[x][y] = true;
              if (a[x-1][y] && a[x+1][y] && a[x][y-1] && a[x][y+1])
              { deadEnds++; break;  }
              double r = Math.random();
              if      (r < 0.25) { if (!a[x+1][y]) x++; }
              else if (r < 0.50) { if (!a[x-1][y]) x--; }
              else if (r < 0.75) { if (!a[x][y+1]) y++; }
              else if (r < 1.00) { if (!a[x][y-1]) y--; }
          }
      }
      System.out.println(100*deadEnds/T + "% dead ends");
    }
}
```

N	lattice size
T	number of trials
deadEnds	trials resulting in a dead end
a[][]	intersections visited
x, y	current position
r	random number in (0, 1)

This program takes command-line arguments N and T and computes T self-avoiding walks in an N-by-N lattice. For each walk, it creates a boolean array, starts the walk in the center, and continues until either a dead end or a boundary is reached. The result of the computation is the percentage of dead ends. As usual, increasing the number of experiments increases the precision of the results.

```
% java SelfAvoidingWalk 5 100
0% dead ends
% java SelfAvoidingWalk 20 100
36% dead ends
% java SelfAvoidingWalk 40 100
80% dead ends
% java SelfAvoidingWalk 80 100
98% dead ends
% java SelfAvoidingWalk 160 100
100% dead ends
```

```
% java SelfAvoidingWalk 5 1000
0% dead ends
% java SelfAvoidingWalk 20 1000
32% dead ends
% java SelfAvoidingWalk 40 1000
70% dead ends
% java SelfAvoidingWalk 80 1000
95% dead ends
% java SelfAvoidingWalk 160 1000
100% dead ends
```

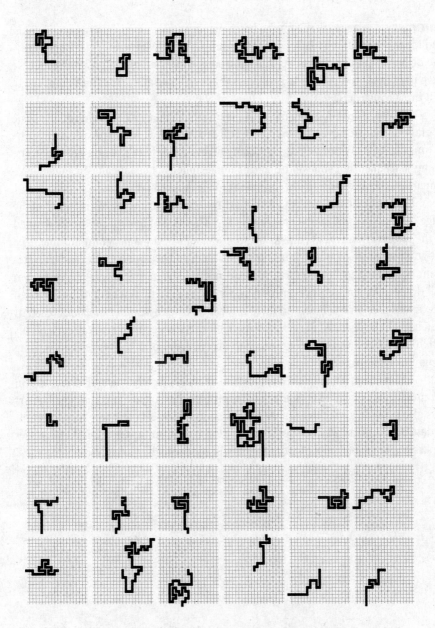

Self-avoiding random walks in a 21-by-21 grid

Summary   Arrays are the fourth basic element (after assignments, conditionals, and loops) found in virtually every programming language, completing our coverage of basic Java constructs. As you have seen with the sample programs that we have presented, you can write programs that can solve all sorts of problems using just these constructs.

Arrays are prominent in many of the programs that we consider, and the basic operations that we have discussed here will serve you well in addressing many programming tasks. When you are not using arrays explicitly (and you are sure to be doing so frequently), you will be using them implicitly, because all computers have a memory that is conceptually equivalent to an indexed array.

The fundamental ingredient that arrays add to our programs is a potentially huge increase in the size of a program's *state*. The state of a program can be defined as the information you need to know to understand what a program is doing. In a program without arrays, if you know the values of the variables and which statement is the next to be executed, you can normally determine what the program will do next. When we trace a program, we are essentially tracking its state. When a program uses arrays, however, there can be too huge a number of values (each of which might be changed in each statement) for us to effectively track them all. This difference makes writing programs with arrays more of a challenge than writing programs without them.

Arrays directly represent vectors and matrices, so they are of direct use in computations associated with many basic problems in science and engineering. Arrays also provide a succinct notation for manipulating a potentially huge amount of data in a uniform way, so they play a critical role in any application that involves processing large amounts of data, as you will see throughout this book.

Q. Some Java programmers use int a[] instead of int[] a to declare arrays. What's the difference?

A. In Java, both are legal and equivalent. The former is how arrays are declared in C. The latter is the preferred style in Java since the type of the variable int[] more clearly indicates that it is an *array* of integers.

Q. Why do array indices start at 0 instead of 1?

A. This convention originated with machine-language programming, where the address of an array element would be computed by adding the index to the address of the beginning of an array. Starting indices at 1 would entail either a waste of space at the beginning of the array or a waste of time to subtract the 1.

Q. What happens if I use a negative number to index an array?

A. The same thing as when you use an index that is too big. Whenever a program attempts to index an array with an index that is not between zero and the array length minus one, Java will issue an ArrayIndexOutOfBoundsException and terminate the program.

Q. What happens when I compare two arrays with (a == b)?

A. The expression evaluates to true only if a[] and b[] refer to the same array, not if they have the same sequence of elements. Unfortunately, this is rarely what you want.

Q. If a[] is an array, why does System.out.println(a) print out a hexadecimal integer, like @f62373 , instead of the elements of the array?

A. Good question. It is printing out the memory address of the array, which, unfortunately, is rarely what you want.

Q. What other pitfalls should I watch out for when using arrays?

A. It is very important to remember that Java *always* initializes arrays when you create them, so that *creating an array takes time proportional to the size of the array.*

Exercises

1.4.1 Write a program that declares and initializes an array a[] of size 1000 and accesses a[1000]. Does your program compile? What happens when you run it?

1.4.2 Describe and explain what happens when you try to compile a program with the following statement:

```
int N = 1000;
int[] a = new int[N*N*N*N];
```

1.4.3 Given two vectors of length N that are represented with one-dimensional arrays, write a code fragment that computes the *Euclidean distance* between them (the square root of the sums of the squares of the differences between corresponding entries).

1.4.4 Write a code fragment that reverses the order of a one-dimensional array a[] of String values. Do not create another array to hold the result. *Hint*: Use the code in the text for exchanging two elements.

1.4.5 What is wrong with the following code fragment?

```
int[] a;
for (int i = 0; i < 10; i++)
    a[i] = i * i;
```

Solution. It does not allocate memory for a[] with new. This code results in a `variable a might not have been initialized` compile-time error.

1.4.6 Write a code fragment that prints the contents of a two-dimensional boolean array, using * to represent true and a space to represent false. Include row and column numbers.

1.4.7 What does the following code fragment print?

```
int[] a = new int[10];
for (int i = 0; i < 10; i++)
    a[i] = 9 - i;
for (int i = 0; i < 10; i++)
    a[i] = a[a[i]];
for (int i = 0; i < 10; i++)
    System.out.println(a[i]);
```

1.4.8 What values does the following code put in the array a[]?

```
int N = 10;
int[] a = new int[N];
a[0] = 1;
a[1] = 1;
for (int i = 2; i < N; i++)
    a[i] = a[i-1] + a[i-2];
```

1.4.9 What does the following code fragment print?

```
int[] a = { 1, 2, 3 };
int[] b = { 1, 2, 3 };
System.out.println(a == b);
```

1.4.10 Write a program Deal that takes an command-line argument N and prints N poker hands (five cards each) from a shuffled deck, separated by blank lines.

1.4.11 Write code fragments to create a two-dimensional array b[][] that is a copy of an existing two-dimensional array a[][], under each of the following assumptions:

a. a[][] is square

b. a[][] is rectangular

c. a[][] may be ragged

Your solution to *b* should work for *a*, and your solution to *c* should work for both *b* and *a*, but your code should get progressively more complicated.

1.4.12 Write a code fragment to print the *transposition* (rows and columns changed) of a square two-dimensional array. For the example spreadsheet array in the text, you code would print the following:

```
99  98  92  94  99  90  76  92  97  89
85  57  77  32  34  46  59  66  71  29
98  78  76  11  22  54  88  89  24  38
```

1.4.13 Write a code fragment to transpose a square two-dimensional array *in place* without creating a second array.

1.4.14 Write a program that takes an integer *N* from the command line and creates an *N*-by-*N* boolean array a[][] such that a[i][j] is true if i and j are relatively prime (have no common factors), and false otherwise. Use your solution to EXERCISE 1.4.6 to print the array. *Hint*: Use sieving.

1.4.15 Write a program that computes the product of two square matrices of boolean values, using the *or* operation instead of + and the *and* operation instead of *.

1.4.16 Modify the spreadsheet code fragment in the text to compute a *weighted* average of the rows, where the weights of each test score are in a one-dimensional array weights[]. For example, to assign the last of the three tests in our example to be twice the weight of the others, you would use

```
double[] weights = { .25, .25, .50 };
```

Note that the weights should sum to 1.

1.4.17 Write a code fragment to multiply two rectangular matrices that are not necessarily square. *Note*: For the dot product to be well-defined, the number of columns in the first matrix must be equal to the number of rows in the second matrix. Print an error message if the dimensions do not satisfy this condition.

1.4.18 Modify SelfAvoidingWalk (PROGRAM 1.4.4) to calculate and print the average length of the paths as well as the dead-end probability. Keep separate the average lengths of escape paths and dead-end paths.

1.4.19 Modify SelfAvoidingWalk to calculate and print the average area of the smallest axis-oriented rectangle that encloses the path. Keep separate statistics for escape paths and dead-end paths.

Creative Exercises

1.4.20 *Dice simulation.* The following code computes the exact probability distribution for the sum of two dice:

```
double[] dist = new double[13];
for (int i = 1; i <= 6; i++)
   for (int j = 1; j <= 6; j++)
      dist[i+j] += 1.0;

for (int k = 1; k <= 12; k++)
   dist[k] /= 36.0;
```

The value `dist[k]` is the probability that the dice sum to k. Run experiments to validate this calculation simulating N dice throws, keeping track of the frequencies of occurrence of each value when you compute the sum of two random integers between 1 and 6. How large does N have to be before your empirical results match the exact results to three decimal places?

1.4.21 *Longest plateau.* Given an array of integers, find the length and location of the longest contiguous sequence of equal values where the values of the elements just before and just after this sequence are smaller.

1.4.22 *Empirical shuffle check.* Run computational experiments to check that our shuffling code works as advertised. Write a program `ShuffleTest` that takes command-line arguments M and N, does N shuffles of an array of size M that is initialized with `a[i]` = `i` before each shuffle, and prints an M-by-M table such that row i gives the number of times i wound up in position j for all j. All entries in the array should be close to N/M.

1.4.23 *Bad shuffling.* Suppose that you choose a random integer between 0 and N-1 in our shuffling code instead of one between i and N-1. Show that the resulting order is *not* equally likely to be one of the $N!$ possibilities. Run the test of the previous exercise for this version.

1.4.24 *Music shuffling.* You set your music player to shuffle mode. It plays each of the N songs before repeating any. Write a program to estimate the likelihood that you will not hear any sequential pair of songs (that is, song 3 does not follow song 2, song 10 does not follow song 9, and so on).

1.4.24 *Minima in permutations.* Write a program that takes an integer N from the command line, generates a random permutation, prints the permutation, and prints the number of left-to-right minima in the permutation (the number of times an element is the smallest seen so far). Then write a program that takes integers M and N from the command line, generates M random permutations of size N, and prints the average number of left-to-right minima in the permutations generated. *Extra credit*: Formulate a hypothesis about the number of left-to-right minima in a permutation of size N, as a function of N.

1.4.25 *Inverse permutation.* Write a program that reads in a permutation of the integers 0 to N-1 from N command-line arguments and prints the inverse permutation. (If the permutation is in an array a[], its inverse is the array b[] such that a[b[i]] = b[a[i]] = i.) Be sure to check that the input is a valid permutation.

1.4.26 *Hadamard matrix.* The N-by-N Hadamard matrix H(N) is a boolean matrix with the remarkable property that any two rows differ in exactly N/2 entries. (This property makes it useful for designing error-correcting codes.) H(1) is a 1-by-1 matrix with the single entry true, and for N>1, H(2N) is obtained by aligning four copies of H(N) in a large square, and then inverting all of the entries in the lower right N-by-N copy, as shown in the following examples (with T representing true and F representing false, as usual).

H(1)	H(2)	H(4)
T	T T	T T T T
	T F	T F T F
		T T F F
		T F F T

Write a program that takes one command-line argument N and prints H(N). Assume that N is a power of 2.

1.4.27 *Rumors.* Alice is throwing a party with N other guests, including Bob. Bob starts a rumor about Alice by telling it to one of the other guests. A person hearing this rumor for the first time will immediately tell it to one other guest, chosen at random from all the people at the party except Alice and the person from whom

they heard it. If a person (including Bob) hears the rumor for a second time, he or she will not propagate it further. Write a program to estimate the probability that everyone at the party (except Alice) will hear the rumor before it stops propagating. Also calculate an estimate of the expected number of people to hear the rumor.

1.4.28 *Find a duplicate.* Given an array of N elements with each element between 1 and N, write an algorithm to determine whether there are any duplicates. You do not need to preserve the contents of the given array, but do not use an extra array.

1.4.29 *Counting primes.* Compare PrimeSieve with the method that we used to demonstrate the break statement, at the end of SECTION 1.3. This is a classic example of a time-space tradeoff: PrimeSieve is fast, but requires a boolean array of size *N*; the other approach uses only two integer variables, but is substantially slower. Estimate the magnitude of this difference by finding the value of *N* for which this second approach can complete the computation in about the same time as java PrimeSeive 1000000.

1.4.30 *Minesweeper.* Write a program that takes 3 command-line arguments *M*, *N*, and *p* and produces an *M*-by-*N* boolean array where each entry is occupied with probability *p*. In the minesweeper game, occupied cells represent bombs and empty cells represent safe cells. Print out the array using an asterisk for bombs and a period for safe cells. Then, replace each safe square with the number of neighboring bombs (above, below, left, right, or diagonal) and print out the solution.

```
* * . . .        * * 1 0 0
. . . . .        3 3 2 0 0
. * . . .        1 * 1 0 0
```

Try to write your code so that you have as few special cases as possible to deal with, by using an (*M*+2)-by-(*N*+2) boolean array.

1.4.31 *Self-avoiding walk length.* Suppose that there is no limit on the size of the grid. Run experiments to estimate the average walk length.

1.4.32 *Three-dimensional self-avoiding walks.* Run experiments to verify that the dead-end probability is 0 for a three-dimensional self-avoiding walk and to compute the average walk length for various values of *N*.

1.4.33 *Random walkers.* Suppose that N random walkers, starting in the center of an N-by-N grid, move one step at a time, choosing to go left, right, up, or down with equal probability at each step. Write a program to help formulate and test a hypothesis about the number of steps taken before all cells are touched.

1.4.34 *Bridge hands.* In the game of bridge, four players are dealt hands of 13 cards each. An important statistic is the distribution of the number of cards in each suit in a hand. Which is the most likely, 5-3-3-2, 4-4-3-2, or 4-3-3-3?

1.4.35 *Birthday problem.* Suppose that people enter an empty room until a pair of people share a birthday. On average, how many people will have to enter before there is a match? Run experiments to estimate the value of this quantity. Assume birthdays to be uniform random integers between 0 and 364.

1.4.36 *Coupon collector.* Run experiments to validate the classical mathematical result that the expected number of coupons needed to collect N values is about NH_N. For example, if you are observing the cards carefully at the blackjack table (and the dealer has enough decks randomly shuffled together), you will wait until about 235 cards are dealt, on average, before seeing every card value.

1.4.37 *Binomial coefficients.* Write a program that builds and prints a two-dimensional ragged array a such that a[N][k] contains the probability that you get exactly k heads when you toss a coin N times. Take a command-line argument to specify the maximum value of N. These numbers are known as the *binomial distribution*: if you multiply each entry in row *i* by 2^N, you get the *binomial coefficients* (the coefficients of x^k in $(x+1)^N$) arranged in *Pascal's triangle*. To compute them, start with a[N][0] = 0 for all N and a[1][1] = 1, then compute values in successive rows, left to right, with a[N][k] = (a[N-1][k] + a[N-1][k-1])/2.

Pascal's triangle				binomial distribution				
1				1				
1 1				1/2	1/2			
1 2 1				1/4	1/2	1/4		
1 3 3 1				1/8	3/8	3/8	1/8	
1 4 6 4 1				1/16	1/4	3/8	1/4	1/16

1.5   Input and Output

IN THIS SECTION WE EXTEND THE set of simple abstractions (command-line input and standard output) that we have been using as the interface between our Java programs and the outside world to include *standard input, standard drawing,* and *standard audio*. Standard input makes it convenient for us to write programs that process arbitrary amounts of input and to interact with our programs; standard drawing makes it possible for us to work with graphical representations of images, freeing us from having to encode everything as text; and standard audio adds

1.5.1	Generating a random sequence
1.5.2	Interactive user input
1.5.3	Averaging a stream of numbers
1.5.4	A simple filter
1.5.5	Input-to-drawing filter
1.5.6	Bouncing ball
1.5.7	Digital signal processing

Programs in this section

sound. These extensions are easy to use, and you will find that they bring you to yet another new world of programming.

The abbreviation *I/O* is universally understood to mean *input/output*, a collective term that refers to the mechanisms by which programs communicate with the outside world. Your computer's operating system controls the physical devices that are connected to your computer. To implement the standard I/O abstractions, we use libraries of methods that interface to the operating system.

You have already been accepting argument values from the command line and printing strings in a terminal window; the purpose of this section is to provide you with a much richer set of tools for processing and presenting data. Like the System.out.print() and System.out.println() methods that you have been using, these methods do not implement mathematical functions—their purpose is to cause some side effect, either on an input device or an output device. Our prime concern is using such devices to get information into and out of our programs.

An essential feature of standard I/O mechanisms is that there is no limit on the amount of input or output data, from the point of view of the program. Your programs can consume input or produce output indefinitely.

One use of standard I/O mechanisms is to connect your programs to *files* on your computer's disk. It is easy to connect standard input, standard output, standard drawing, and standard audio to files. Such connections make it easy to have your Java programs save or load results to files for archival purposes or for later reference by other programs or other applications.

Bird's-eye view   The conventional model that we have been using for Java programming has served us since SECTION 1.1. To build context, we begin by briefly reviewing the model.

A Java program takes input values from the command line and prints a string of characters as output. By default, both *command-line input* and *standard output* are associated with the application that takes commands (the one in which you have been typing the java and javac commands). We use the generic term *terminal window* to refer to this application. This model has proven to be a convenient and direct way for us to interact with our programs and data.

Command-line input. This mechanism, which we have been using to provide input values to our programs, is a standard part of Java programming. All classes have a main() method that takes a String array args[] as its argument. That array is the sequence of command-line arguments that we type, provided to Java by the operating system. By convention, both Java and the operating system process the arguments as strings, so if we intend for an argument to be a number, we use a method such as Integer.parseInt() or Double.parseDouble() to convert it from String to the appropriate type.

Standard output. To print output values in our programs, we have been using the system methods System.out.println() and System.out.print(). Java puts the results of a program's sequence of calls on these methods into the form of an abstract stream of characters known as *standard output*. By default, the operating system connects standard output to the terminal window. All of the output in our programs so far has been appearing in the terminal window.

For reference, and as a starting point, RandomSeq (PROGRAM 1.5.1) is a program that uses this model. It takes a command-line argument N and produces an output sequence of N random numbers between 0 and 1.

NOW WE ARE GOING TO COMPLEMENT command-line input and standard output with three additional mechanisms that address their limitations and provide us with a far more useful programming model. These mechanisms give us a new bird's-eye view of a Java program in which the program converts a standard input stream and a sequence of command-line arguments into a standard output stream, a standard drawing, and a standard audio stream.

Program 1.5.1   Generating a random sequence

```java
public class RandomSeq
{
    public static void main(String[] args)
    { // Print a random sequence of N real values in [0, 1)
        int N = Integer.parseInt(args[0]);
        for (int i = 0; i < N; i++)
            System.out.println(Math.random());
    }
}
```

This program illustrates the conventional model that we have been using so far for Java programming. It takes a command-line argument N and prints N random numbers between 0 and 1. From the program's point of view, there is no limit on the length of the output sequence.

```
% java RandomSeq 1000000
0.2498362534343327
0.5578468691774513
0.5702167639727175
0.32191774192688727
0.6865902823177537
...
```

Standard input. Our class StdIn is a library that implements a standard input abstraction to complement the standard output abstraction. Just as you can print a value to standard output at any time during the execution of your program, you can read a value from a standard input stream at any time.

Standard drawing. Our class StdDraw allows you to create drawings with your programs. It uses a simple graphics model that allows you to create drawings consisting of points and lines in a window on your computer. StdDraw also includes facilities for text, color, and animation.

Standard audio. Our class StdAudio allows you to create sound with your programs. It uses a standard format to convert arrays of numbers into sound.

To use both command-line input and standard output, you have been using built-in Java facilities. Java also has built-in facilities that support abstractions like standard input, standard draw, and standard audio, but they are somewhat more complicated to use, so we have developed a simpler interface to them in our StdIn, StdDraw, and StdAudio libraries. To logically complete our programming model, we also include a StdOut library. To use these libraries, download StdIn.java, StdOut. java, StdDraw.java, and StdAudio.java and place them in the same directory as your program (or use one of the other mechanisms for sharing libraries described on the booksite).

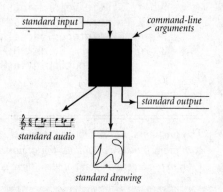

A bird's-eye view of a Java program (revisited)

The standard input and standard output abstractions date back to the development of the UNIX operating system in the 1970s and are found in some form on all modern systems. Although they are primitive by comparison to various mechanisms developed since, modern programmers still depend on them as a reliable way to connect data to programs. We have developed for this book standard draw and standard audio in the same spirit as these earlier abstractions to provide you with an easy way to produce visual and aural output.

Standard output   Java's System.out.print() and System.out.println() methods implement the basic standard output abstraction that we need. Nevertheless, to treat standard input and standard output in a uniform manner (and to provide a few technical improvements), starting in this section and continuing through the rest of the book, we use similar methods that are defined in our StdOut library. StdOut.print() and StdOut.println() are nearly the same as the Java methods that you have been using (see the booksite for a discussion of the differences, which need not concern you now). The StdOut.printf() method is a main topic of this section and will be of interest to you now because it gives you more control over the appearance of the output. It was a feature of the C language of the early 1970s that still survives in modern languages because it is so useful.

Since the first time that we printed double values, we have been distracted by excessive precision in the printed output. For example, when we use System.out. print(Math.PI) we get the output 3.141592653589793, even though we might

```
public class StdOut
```
---
void print(String s)	*print* s
void println(String s)	*print* s, *followed by newline*
void println()	*print a new line*
void printf(String f, ...)	*formatted print*

API for our library of static methods for standard output

prefer to see 3.14 or 3.14159. The print() and println() methods present each number to 15 decimal places even when we would be happy with just a few digits of precision. The printf() method is more flexible: it allows us to specify the number of digits and the precision when converting data type values to strings for output. With printf(), we can write StdOut.printf("%7.5f", Math.PI) to get 3.14159, and we can replace System.out.print(t) with

```
StdOut.printf("The square root of %.1f is %.6f", c, t);
```

in Newton (PROGRAM 1.3.6) to get output like

```
The square root of 2.0 is 1.414214
```

Next, we describe the meaning and operation of these statements, along with extensions to handle the other built-in types of data.

Formatted printing basics. In its simplest form, printf() takes two arguments. The first argument is a *format string* that describes how to convert the second argument into a string for output. The simplest type of format string begins with % and ends with a one-letter *conversion code*. The conversion codes that we use most frequently are d (for decimal values from Java's integer types), f (for floating-point values), and s (for String values). Between the % and the conversion code is an integer that specifies the *field width* of the converted value (the number of characters in the converted output string). By default, blanks are added on the left to make the length of the converted output equal to the field width; if we want the blanks on the right, we can insert a minus sign before the field width. (If the

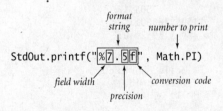

Anatomy of a formatted print statement

converted output string is larger than the field width, the field width is ignored.) Following the width, we have the option of including a period followed by the number of digits to put after the decimal point (the precision) for a `double` value or the number of characters to take from the beginning of the string for a `String` value. The most important thing to remember about using `printf()` is that *the conversion code in the format and the type of the corresponding argument must match.* That is, Java must be able to convert from the type of the argument to the type required by the conversion code. Every type of data can be converted to `String`, but if you write `StdOut.printf("%12d", Math.PI)` or `StdOut.printf("%4.2f", 512)`, you will get an `IllegalFormatConversionException` run-time error.

Format string. The first argument of `printf()` is a `String` that may contain characters other than a format string. Any part of the argument that is not part of a format string passes through to the output, with the format string replaced by the argument value (converted to a string as specified). For example, the statement

```
StdOut.printf("PI is approximately %.2f\n", Math.PI);
```

prints the line

```
PI is approximately 3.14
```

Note that we need to explicitly include the newline character \n in the argument in order to print a new line with `printf()`.

type	code	typical literal	sample format strings	converted string values for output
int	d	512	"%14d" "%-14d"	" 512" "512 "
double	f e	1595.1680010754388	"%14.2f" "%.7f" "%14.4e"	" 1595.17" "1595.1680011" " 1.5952e+03"
String	s	"Hello, World"	"%14s" "%-14s" "%-14.5s"	" Hello, World" "Hello, World " "Hello "

Format conventions for `printf()` *(see the booksite for many other options)*

Multiple arguments. The printf() function can take more than two arguments. In this case, the format string will have a format specifier for each additional argument, perhaps separated by other characters to pass through to the output. For example, if you were making payments on a loan, you might use code whose inner loop contains the statements

```
String formats = "%3s  $%6.2f   $%7.2f   $%5.2f\n";
StdOut.printf(formats, month[i], pay, balance, interest);
```

to print the second and subsequent lines in a table like this (see EXERCISE 1.5.14):

```
     payment    balance  interest
Jan  $299.00  $9742.67   $41.67
Feb  $299.00  $9484.26   $40.59
Mar  $299.00  $9224.78   $39.52
...
```

Formatted printing is convenient because this sort of code is much more compact than the string-concatenation code that we have been using.

Standard input   Our StdIn library takes data from a *standard input stream* that may be empty or may contain a sequence of values separated by whitespace (spaces, tabs, newline characters, and the like). Each value is a String or a value from one of Java's primitive types. One of the key features of the standard input stream is that your program *consumes* values when it reads them. Once your program has read a value, it cannot back up and read it again. This assumption is restrictive, but it reflects physical characteristics of some input devices and simplifies implementing the abstraction. The library consists of the nine methods: isEmpty(), readInt(), readDouble(), readLong(), readBoolean(), readChar(), readString(), read-Line(), and readAll(). Within the input stream model, these methods are largely self-documenting (the names describe their effect), but their precise operation is worthy of careful consideration, so we will consider several examples in detail.

Typing input. When you use the java command to invoke a Java program from the command line, you actually are doing three things: issuing a command to start executing your program, specifying the values of the command line arguments, and beginning to define the standard input stream. The string of characters that you type in the terminal window after the command line *is* the standard input stream. When you type characters, you are interacting with your program. The

```
public class StdIn
```

boolean	isEmpty()	true *if no more values,* false *otherwise*
int	readInt()	*read a value of type* int
double	readDouble()	*read a value of type* double
long	readLong()	*read a value of type long*
boolean	readBoolean()	*read a value of type* boolean
char	readChar()	*read a value of type* char
String	readString()	*read a value of type* String
String	readLine()	*read the rest of the line*
String	readAll()	*read the rest of the text*

API for our library of static methods for standard input

program *waits* for you to create the standard input stream. For example, consider the following program, which takes a command-line argument *N*, then reads *N* numbers from standard input and adds them:

```
public class AddInts
{
    public static void main(String[] args)
    {
        int N = Integer.parseInt(args[0]);
        int sum = 0;
        for (int i = 0; i < N; i++)
        {
            int value = StdIn.readInt();
            sum += value;
        }
        StdOut.println("Sum is " + sum);
    }
}
```

When you type java AddInts 4, after the program takes the command-line argument, it calls the method StdIn.readInt() and waits for you to type an integer. Suppose that you want 144 to be the first value. As you type 1, then 4, and then 4, nothing happens, because StdIn does not know that you are done typing the integer. But when you then type <return> to signify the end of your integer, StdIn. readInt() immediately returns the value 144, which your program adds to sum and then calls StdIn.readInt() again. Again, nothing happens until you type the second value: if you type 2, then 3, then 3, and then <return> to end the number, StdIn.readInt() returns the value 233, which your program again adds to sum. After you have typed four numbers in this way, AddInts expects no more input and prints out the sum, as desired.

Input format. If you type abc or 12.2 or true when StdIn.readInt() is expecting an int, it will respond with a NumberFormatException. The format for each type is the same as you have been using for literal values within Java programs. For convenience, StdIn treats strings of consecutive whitespace characters as identical to one space and allows you to delimit your numbers with such strings. It does not matter how many spaces you put between numbers, or whether you enter numbers on one line or separate them with tab characters or spread them out over several lines, (except that your

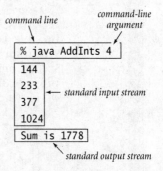

Anatomy of a command

terminal application processes standard input one line at a time, so it will wait until you type <return> before sending all of the numbers on that line to standard input). You can mix values of different types in an input stream, but whenever the program expects a value of a particular type, the input stream must have a value of that type.

Interactive user input. TwentyQuestions (PROGRAM 1.5.2) is a simple example of a program that interacts with its user. The program generates a random integer and then gives clues to a user trying to guess the number. (As a side note: by using *binary search*, you can always get to the answer in at most twenty questions. See SECTION 4.2.) The fundamental difference between this program and others that we have written is that the user has the ability to change the control flow *while* the program is executing. This capability was very important in early applications of computing, but we rarely write such programs nowadays because modern applications typically take such input through the graphical user interface, as discussed in CHAPTER 3. Even a simple program like TwentyQuestions illustrates that writing programs that support user interaction is potentially very difficult because you have to plan for all possible user inputs.

Program 1.5.2   Interactive user input

```
public class TwentyQuestions
{
    public static void main(String[] args)
    { // Generate a number and answer questions
      // while the user tries to guess the value.
      int N = 1 + (int) (Math.random() * 1000000);
      StdOut.print("I'm thinking of a number ");
      StdOut.println("between 1 and 1,000,000");
      int m = 0;
      while (m != N)
      { // Solicit one guess and provide one answer
         StdOut.print("What's your guess? ");
         m = StdIn.readInt();
         if (m == N) StdOut.println("You win!");
         if (m < N)  StdOut.println("Too low ");
         if (m > N)  StdOut.println("Too high");
      }
    }
}
```

N	hidden value
m	user's guess

This program plays a simple guessing game. You type numbers, each of which is an implicit question ("Is this the number?") and the program tells you whether your guess is too high or too low. You can always get it to print You win! *with less than twenty questions. To use this program, you need to first download* StdIn.java *and* StdOut.java *into the same directory as this code (which is in a file named* TwentyQuestions.java*).*

```
% java TwentyQuestions
I'm thinking of a number between 1 and 1,000,000
What's your guess? 500000
Too high
What's your guess? 250000
Too low
What's your guess? 375000
Too high
What's your guess? 312500
Too high
What's your guess? 300500
Too low
...
```

Program 1.5.3   *Averaging a stream of numbers*

```
public class Average
{
   public static void main(String[] args)
   { // Average the numbers on the input stream.
      double sum = 0.0;
      int cnt = 0;
      while (!StdIn.isEmpty())
      { // Read a number and cumulate the sum.
         double value = StdIn.readDouble();
         sum += value;
         cnt++;
      }
      double average = sum / cnt;
      StdOut.println("Average is " + average);
   }
}
```

cnt	count of numbers read
sum	cumulated sum

This program reads in a sequence of real numbers from standard input and prints their average on standard output (provided that the sum does not overflow). From its point of view, there is no limit on the size of the input stream. The commands on the right below use redirection and piping (discussed in the next subsection) to provide 100,000 numbers to average.

```
% java Average
10.0 5.0 6.0
3.0
7.0 32.0
<ctrl-d>
Average is 10.5
```

```
% java RandomSeq 100000 > data.txt
% java Average < data.txt
Average is 0.5010473676174824

% java RandomSeq 100000 | java Average
Average is 0.5000499417963857
```

Processing an arbitrary-size input stream. Typically, input streams are finite: your program marches through the input stream, consuming values until the stream is empty. But there is no restriction of the size of the input stream, and some programs simply process all the input presented to them. Average (PROGRAM 1.5.3) is an example that reads in a sequence of real numbers from standard input and prints their average. It illustrates a key property of using an input stream: the length of the stream is not known to the program. We type all the numbers that we have, and then the program averages them. Before reading each number, the program uses the method StdIn.isEmpty() to check whether there are any more numbers in the input stream. How do we signal that we have no more data to type? By convention, we type a special sequence of characters known as the *end-of-file* sequence. Unfortunately, the terminal applications that we typically encounter on modern operating systems use different conventions for this critically important sequence. In this book, we use <ctrl-d> (many systems require <ctrl-d> to be on a line by itself); the other widely used convention is <ctrl-z> on a line by itself. Average is a simple program, but it represents a profound new capability in programming: with standard input, we can write programs that process an unlimited amount of data. As you will see, writing such programs is an effective approach for numerous data-processing applications.

STANDARD INPUT IS A SUBSTANTIAL STEP up from the command-line input model that we have been using, for two reasons, as illustrated by TwentyQuestions and Average. First, we can interact with our program—with command-line arguments, we can only provide data to the program *before* it begins execution. Second, we can read in large amounts of data—with command-line arguments, we can only enter values that fit on the command line. Indeed, as illustrated by Average, the amount of data can be potentially unlimited, and many programs are made simpler by that assumption. A third *raison d'être* for standard input is that your operating system makes it possible to change the source of standard input, so that you do not have to type all the input. Next, we consider the mechanisms that enable this possibility.

Redirection and piping   For many applications, typing input data as a standard input stream from the terminal window is untenable because our program's processing power is then limited by the amount of data that we can type (and our typing speed). Similarly, we often want to save the information printed on the standard output stream for later use. To address such limitations, we next focus on the idea that standard input is an *abstraction*—the program just expects its input and has no dependence on the source of the input stream. Standard output is a similar abstraction. The power of these abstractions derives from our ability (through the operating system) to specify various other sources for standard input and standard output, such as a file, the network, or another program. All modern operating systems implement these mechanisms.

Redirecting standard output to a file. By adding a simple directive to the command that invokes a program, we can *redirect* its standard output to a file, either for permanent storage or for input to another program at a later time. For example,

```
% java RandomSeq 1000 > data.txt
```

specifies that the standard output stream is not to be printed in the terminal window, but instead is to be written to a text file named data.txt. Each call to System.out.print() or System.out.println() appends text at the end of that file. In this example, the end result is a file that contains 1,000 random values. No output appears in the terminal window: it goes directly into the file named after the > symbol. Thus, we can save away information for later retrieval. Note that we do not have to change RandomSeq (PROGRAM 1.5.1) in any way for this mechanism to work—it is using the standard output abstraction and is unaffected by our use of a different implementation of that abstraction. You can use this mechanism to save output from any program that you write. Once we have expended a significant amount of effort to obtain a result, we often want to save the result for later reference. In a modern system, you can save some information by using cut-and-paste or some similar mechanism that is provided by the operating system, but cut-and-paste is inconvenient for large amounts of data. By contrast, redirection is specifically designed to make it easy to handle large amounts of data.

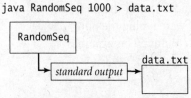

java RandomSeq 1000 > data.txt

Redirecting standard output to a file

Redirecting from a file to standard input. Similarly, we can redirect standard input so that StdIn reads data from a file instead of the terminal application:

```
% java Average < data.txt
```

This command reads a sequence of numbers from the file data.txt and computes their average value. Specifically, the < symbol is a directive that tells the operating system to implement the standard input stream by reading from the text file data.txt instead of waiting for the user to type something into the terminal window. When the program calls StdIn.readDouble(), the operating system reads the value from the file. The file data.txt could

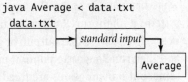

java Average < data.txt

Redirecting from a file to standard input

have been created by any application, not just a Java program—virtually every application on your computer can create text files. This facility to redirect from a file to standard input enables us to create *data-driven code* where we can change the data processed by a program without having to change the program at all. Instead, we keep data in files and write programs that read from standard input.

Connecting two programs. The most flexible way to implement the standard input and standard output abstractions is to specify that they are implemented by our own programs! This mechanism is called *piping*. For example, the command

```
% java RandomSeq 1000 | java Average
```

specifies that the standard output for RandomSeq and the standard input stream for Average are the *same* stream. The effect is as if RandomSeq were typing the numbers it generates into the terminal window while Average is running. This example also has the same effect as the following sequence of commands:

```
% java RandomSeq 1000 > data.txt
% java Average < data.txt
```

In this case, the file data.txt is not created. This difference is profound, because it removes another limitation on the size of the input and output streams that we can process. For example, we could replace 1000 in our example with 1000000000, even though we might not have the space to save a billion numbers on our computer (we do need the *time* to process them, however). When RandomSeq calls System.out.println(), a string is added to the end of the stream; when Average calls StdIn.readInt(), a string is removed from the beginning of the stream. The timing of precisely what happens is up to the operating

```
java RandomSeq 1000 | java Average
```

Piping the output of one program to the input of another

system: it might run RandomSeq until it produces some output, and then run Average to consume that output, or it might run Average until it needs some output, and then run RandomSeq until it produces the needed output. The end result is the same, but our programs are freed from worrying about such details because they work solely with the standard input and standard output abstractions.

Program 1.5.4   A simple filter

```java
public class RangeFilter
{
    public static void main(String[] args)
    { // Filter out numbers not between lo and hi.
        int lo = Integer.parseInt(args[0]);
        int hi = Integer.parseInt(args[1]);
        while (!StdIn.isEmpty())
        { // Process one number.
            int t = StdIn.readInt();
            if (t >= lo && t <= hi) StdOut.print(t + " ");
        }
        StdOut.println();
    }
}
```

lo	lower bound of range
hi	upper bound of range
t	current number

This filter copies to the output stream the numbers from the input stream that fall inside the range given by the command-line parameters. There is no limit on the length of the streams.

```
% java RangeFilter 100 400
358 1330 55 165 689 1014 3066 387 575 843 203 48 292 877 65 998
<ctrl-d>
358 165 387 203 292
```

Filters. Piping, a core feature of the original UNIX system of the early 1970s, still survives in modern systems because it is a simple abstraction for communicating among disparate programs. Testimony to the power of this abstraction is that many UNIX programs are still being used today to process files that are thousands or millions of times larger than imagined by the programs' authors. We can communicate with other Java programs via calls on methods, but standard input and standard output allow us to communicate with programs that were written at another time and, perhaps, in another language. With standard input and standard output, we are agreeing on a simple interface to the outside world. For many common tasks, it is convenient to think of each program as a *filter* that converts a standard input stream to a standard output stream in some way, with piping as the command mechanism to connect programs together. For example, RangeFilter (PROGRAM 1.5.4) takes two command-line arguments and prints on standard output those numbers from standard input that fall within the specified range. You might imagine standard input to be measurement data from some instrument, with the filter being used to throw away data outside the range of interest for the experiment at hand. Several standard filters that were designed for UNIX still survive (sometimes with different names) as commands in modern operating systems. For example, the sort filter puts the lines on standard input in sorted order:

```
% java RandomSeq 6 | sort
0.035813305516568916
0.14306638757584322
0.348292877655532103
0.5761644592016527
0.7234592733392126
0.9795908813988247
```

We discuss sorting in SECTION 4.2. A second useful filter is grep, which prints the lines from standard input that match a given pattern. For example, if you type

```
% grep lo < RangeFilter.java
```

you get the result

```
// Filter out numbers not between lo and hi.
int lo = Integer.parseInt(args[0]);
    if (t >= lo && t <= hi) StdOut.print(t + " ");
```

Programmers often use tools such as grep to get a quick reminder of variable names or language usage details. A third useful filter is more, which reads data from standard input and displays it in your terminal window one screenful at a time. For example, if you type

```
% java RandomSeq 1000 | more
```

you will see as many numbers as fit in your terminal window, but more will wait for you to hit the space bar before displaying each succeeding screenful. The term *filter* is perhaps misleading: it was meant to describe programs like RangeFilter that write some subsequence of standard input to standard output, but it is now often used to describe any program that reads from standard input and writes to standard output.

Multiple streams. For many common tasks, we want to write programs that take input from multiple sources and/or produce output intended for multiple destinations. In SECTION 3.1 we discuss our Out and In libraries, which generalize StdOut and StdIn to allow for multiple input and output streams. These libraries include provisions not just for redirecting these streams to and from files, but also from arbitrary web pages.

PROCESSING LARGE AMOUNTS OF INFORMATION PLAYS an essential role in many applications of computing. A scientist may need to analyze data collected from a series of experiments, a stock trader may wish to analyze information about recent financial transactions, or a student may wish to maintain collections of music and movies. In these and countless other applications, data-driven programs are the norm. Standard output, standard input, redirection, and piping provides us with the capability to address such applications with our Java programs. We can collect data into files on our computer through the web or any of the standard devices and use redirection and piping to connect data to our programs. Many (if not most) of the programming examples that we consider throughout this book have this ability.

Standard drawing Up to this point, our input/output abstractions have focused exclusively on text strings. Now we introduce an abstraction for producing drawings as output. This library is easy to use and allows us to take advantage of a visual medium to cope with far more information than is possible with just text.

As with standard input, our standard drawing abstraction is implemented in a library that you need to download from the booksite, StdDraw.java. Standard drawing is very simple: we imagine an abstract drawing device capable of drawing lines and points on a two-dimensional canvas. The device is capable of responding to the commands that our programs issue in the form of calls to methods in Std-Draw such as the following:

public class StdDraw (*basic drawing commands*)
_____

```
    void line(double x0, double y0, double x1, double y1)
    void point(double x, double y)
```

Like the methods for standard input and standard output, these methods are nearly self-documenting: StdDraw.line() draws a straight line segment connecting the

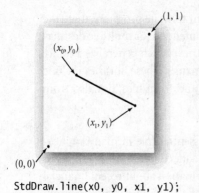

StdDraw.line(x0, y0, x1, y1);

point (x_0, y_0) with the point (x_1, y_1) whose coordinates are given as arguments. StdDraw.point() draws a spot centered on the point (x, y) whose coordinates are given as arguments. The default scale is the unit square (all coordinates between 0 and 1). The standard implementation displays the canvas in a window on your computer's screen, with black lines and points on a white background. The window includes a menu option to save your drawing to a file, in a format suitable for publishing on paper or on the web.

Your first drawing. The HelloWorld equivalent for graphics programming with StdDraw is to draw a triangle with a point inside. To form the triangle, we draw three lines: one from the point $(0, 0)$ at the lower left corner to the point $(1, 0)$, one from that point to the third point at $(1/2, \sqrt{3}/2)$, and one from that point back to $(0, 0)$. As a final flourish, we draw a spot in the middle of the triangle. Once you have successfully downloaded StdDraw.java and then compiled and run Triangle, you are off and running to write your own programs that draw figures comprised of lines and points. This ability literally adds a new dimension to the output that you can produce.

```
public class Triangle
{
    public static void main(String[] args)
    {
        double t = Math.sqrt(3.0)/2.0;
        StdDraw.line(0.0, 0.0, 1.0, 0.0);
        StdDraw.line(1.0, 0.0, 0.5,    t);
        StdDraw.line(0.5,    t, 0.0, 0.0);
        StdDraw.point(0.5, t/3.0);
    }
}
```

When you use a computer to create drawings, you get immediate feedback (the drawing) so that you can refine and improve your program quickly. With a computer program, you can create drawings that you could not contemplate making by hand. In particular, instead of viewing our data as just numbers, we can use pictures, which are far more expressive. We will consider other graphics examples after we discuss a few other drawing commands.

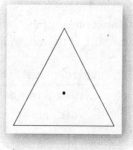

Your first drawing

Control commands. The default coordinate system for standard drawing is the unit square, but we often want to draw plots at different scales. For example, a typical situation is to use coordinates in some range for the *x*-coordinate, or the *y*-coordinate, or both. Also, we often want to draw lines of different thickness and points of different size than the standard. To accommodate these needs, StdDraw has the following methods:

---

public class StdDraw (*basic control commands*)

void setXscale(double x0, double x1)	*reset x range to (x_0, x_1)*
void setYscale(double y0, double y1)	*reset y range to (y_0, y_1)*
void setPenRadius(double r)	*set pen radius to r*

Note: Methods with the same names but no arguments reset to default values.

For example, when we issue the command StdDraw.setXscale(0, N), we are telling the drawing device that we will be using *x*-coordinates between 0 and N. Note that the two-call sequence

```
StdDraw.setXscale(x0, x1);
StdDraw.setYscale(y0, y1);
```

sets the drawing coordinates to be within a *bounding box* whose lower left corner is at (x_0, y_0) and whose upper right corner is at (x_1, y_1). If you use integer coordinates, Java casts them to double, as expected. Scaling is the simplest of the transformations commonly used in graphics. In the applications that we consider in this chapter, we use it in a straightforward way to match our drawings to our data.

The pen is circular, so that lines have rounded ends, and when you set the pen radius to *r* and draw a point, you get a circle of radius *r*. The default pen radius is .005 and is not affected by coordinate scaling. This default is about 1/200 the width of the default window, so that if you draw 50 points equally spaced along a horizontal or vertical line, you will

```
int N = 50;
StdDraw.setXscale(0, N);
StdDraw.setYscale(0, N);
for (int i = 0; i <= N; i++)
    StdDraw.line(0, N-i, i, 0);
```

(N, N)

$(0, 0)$

Scaling to integer coordinates

Program 1.5.5 *Input-to-drawing filter*

```java
public class PlotFilter
{
   public static void main(String[] args)
   { // Plot points in standard input.

      // Scale as per first four values.
      double x0 = StdIn.readDouble();
      double y0 = StdIn.readDouble();
      double x1 = StdIn.readDouble();
      double y1 = StdIn.readDouble();
      StdDraw.setXscale(x0, x1);
      StdDraw.setYscale(y0, y1);

      // Read and plot the rest of the points.
      while (!StdIn.isEmpty())
      { // Read and plot a point.
         double x = StdIn.readDouble();
         double y = StdIn.readDouble();
         StdDraw.point(x, y);
      }
   }
}
```

x0	*left bound*
y0	*bottom bound*
x1	*right bound*
y1	*top bound*
x, y	*current point*

Some data is inherently visual. The file USA.txt *on the booksite has the coordinates of the US cities with populations over 500 (by convention, the first four numbers are the minimum and maximum x and y values).*

```
% java PlotFilter < USA.txt
```

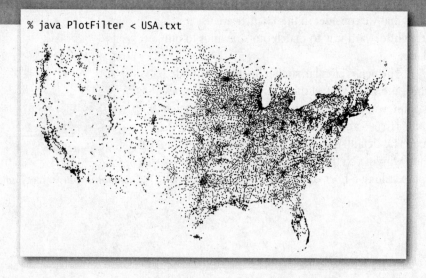

be able to see individual circles, but if you draw 100 such points, the result will look like a line. When you issue the command StdDraw.setPenRadius(.01), you are saying that you want the thickness of the lines and the size of the points to be two times the .005 standard.

Filtering data to a standard drawing. One of the simplest applications of standard draw is to plot data, by filtering it from standard input to the drawing. Plot-Filter (PROGRAM 1.5.5) is such a filter: it reads a sequence of points defined by (*x*, *y*) coordinates and draws a spot at each point. It adopts the convention that the first four numbers on standard input specify the bounding box, so that it can scale the plot without having to make an extra pass through all the points to determine the scale (this kind of convention is typical with such data files). The graphical representation of points plotted in this way is far more expressive (and far more compact) than the numbers themselves or anything that we could create with the standard output representation that our programs have been limited to until now. The plotted image that is produced by PROGRAM 1.5.5 makes it far easier for us to infer properties of the cities (such as, for example, clustering of population centers) than does a list of the coordinates. Whenever we are processing data that represents the physical world, a visual image is likely to be one of the most meaningful ways that we can use to display output. PlotFilter illustrates just how easily you can create such an image.

Plotting a function graph. Another important use of StdDraw is to plot experimental data or the values of a mathematical function. For example, suppose that we want to plot values of the function $y = \sin(4x) + \sin(20x)$ in the interval $(0, \pi)$. Accomplishing this task is a prototypical example of *sampling*: there are an infinite number of points in the interval, so we have to make do with evaluating the function at a finite number of points within the interval. We sample the function by choosing a set of *x*-values, then computing *y*-values by evaluating the function at each *x*-value. Plotting the function by connecting successive points with lines produces what is known as a *piecewise linear approximation*. The simplest way to proceed is to regularly space the *x* values: we decide ahead of time on a sample size, then space the *x*-coordinates by the interval size divided by the sample size. To make sure that the values we plot fall in the visible canvas, we scale the *x*-axis corresponding to the sample size and the *y*-axis corresponding to the maximum and minimum values of the function within the interval. The smoothness of the curve depends on properties of the function and the size of the sample. If the sample size is too small, the rendition of the function may not be at all accurate (it might not be very smooth, and it might miss major fluctuations); if the sample is too large, producing the plot may be time-consuming, since some functions are time-consuming to compute. (In SECTION 2.4, we will look at a method for plotting a smooth curve without using an excessive number of points.) You can use this same technique to plot the function graph of any function you choose: decide on an *x*-interval where you want to plot the function, compute function values evenly spaced through that interval and store them in an array, determine and set the *y*-scale, and draw the line segments.

```
double[] a = new double[N+1];
for (int i = 0; i <= N; i++)
   a[i] = Math.sin(4*Math.PI*i/N)
          + Math.sin(20*Math.PI*i/N);
StdDraw.setXscale(0, N);
StdDraw.setYscale(-2.0, 2.0);
for (int i = 1; i <= N; i++)
   StdDraw.line(i-1, a[i-1], i, a[i]);
```

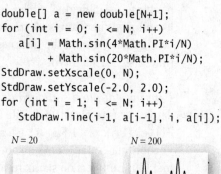

$N = 20$ $N = 200$

Plotting a function graph

Outline and filled shapes. StdDraw also includes methods to draw circles, rectangles, and arbitrary polygons. Each shape defines an outline. When the method name is just the shape name, that outline is traced by the drawing pen. When the name begins with filled, the named shape is instead filled solid, not traced. As usual, we summarize the available methods in an API:

---

public class StdDraw (*shapes*)

   void circle(double x, double y, double r)

   void filledCircle(double x, double y, double r)

   void square(double x, double y, double r)

   void filledSquare(double x, double y, double r)

   void polygon(double[] x, double[] y)

   void filledPolygon(double[] x, double[] y)

The arguments for circle() and filledCircle() define a circle of radius *r* centered at (x, y); the arguments for square() and filledSquare() define a square of side length $2r$ centered on (x, y); and the arguments for polygon() and filled-Polygon() define a sequence of points that we connect by lines, including one from the last point to the first point. If you want to define shapes other than squares or circles, use one of these methods. For example,

```
double[] xd = { x-r, x, x+r, x };
double[] yd = { y, y+r, y, y-r };
StdDraw.polygon(xd, yd);
```

plots a diamond (a rotated $2r$-by-$2r$ square) centered on the point (x, y).

Text and color. Occasionally, you may wish to annotate or highlight various elements in your drawings. StdDraw has a method for drawing text, another for setting parameters associated with text, and another for changing the color of the ink in the pen. We make scant use of these features in this book, but they can be very useful, particularly for drawings on your computer screen. You will find many examples of their use on the booksite.

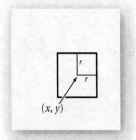

StdDraw.circle(x, y, r);

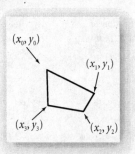

StdDraw.square(x, y, r);

public class StdDraw *(text and color commands)*

```
void text(double x, double y, String s)
void setFont(Font f)
void setPenColor(Color c)
```

In this code, Font and Color are non-primitive types that you will learn about in SECTION 3.1. Until then, we leave the details to StdDraw. The available pen colors are BLACK, BLUE, CYAN, DARK_GRAY, GRAY, GREEN, LIGHT_GRAY, MAGENTA, ORANGE, PINK, RED, WHITE, and YELLOW, defined as constants within StdDraw. For example, the call StdDraw.setPenColor(StdDraw.GRAY) changes to gray ink. The default ink color is BLACK. The default font in StdDraw suffices for most of the drawings that you need (and you can find information on using other fonts on

```
double[] x = {x0, x1, x2, x3};
double[] y = {y0, y1, y2, y3};
StdDraw.polygon(x, y);
```

the booksite). For example, you might wish to use these methods to annotate function plots to highlight relevant values, and you might find it useful to develop similar methods to annotate other parts of your drawings.

Shapes, color, and text are basic tools that you can use to produce a dizzying variety of images, but you should use them sparingly. Use of such artifacts usually presents a design challenge, and our Std-Draw commands are crude by the standards of modern graphics libraries, so that you are likely to need an extensive number of calls to them to produce the beautiful images that you may imagine. On the other hand, using color or labels to help focus on important information in drawings is often worthwhile, as is using color to represent data values.

Animation. The StdDraw library supplies additional methods that provide limitless opportunities for creating interesting effects.

```
StdDraw.square(.2, .8, .1);
StdDraw.filledSquare(.8, .8, .2);
StdDraw.circle(.8, .2, .2);
double[] xd = { .1, .2, .3, .2 };
double[] yd = { .2, .3, .2, .1 };
StdDraw.filledPolygon(xd, yd);
StdDraw.text(.2, .5, "black text");
StdDraw.setPenColor(StdDraw.WHITE);
StdDraw.text(.8, .8, "white text");
```

Shape and text examples

public class StdDraw (advanced control commands)

void setCanvasSize(int w, int h)	*create canvas in screen window of width from* w *and height* h *(in pixels)*
void clear()	*clear the canvas to white (default)*
void clear(Color c)	*clear the canvas; color it* c
void show(int dt)	*draw, then pause* dt *milliseconds*
void show()	*draw, turn off pause mode*

The default canvas size is 512-by-512 pixels; if you want to change it, call set-CanvasSize() before any drawing commands. The clear() and show() methods support dynamic changes in the images on the computer screen. Such effects can provide compelling visualizations. We give an example next that also works for the printed page. There are more examples in the booksite that are likely to capture your imagination.

Bouncing ball. The `HelloWorld` of animation is to produce a black ball that appears to move around on the canvas. Suppose that the ball is at position (r_x, r_y) and we want to create the impression of moving it to a new position nearby, such as, for example, $(r_x + .01, r_y + .02)$. We do so in two steps:

- Erase the drawing.
- Draw a black ball at the new position.

To create the illusion of movement, we iterate these steps for a whole sequence of positions (one that will form a straight line, in this case). But these two steps do not suffice, because the computer is so quick at drawing that the image of the ball will rapidly flicker between black and white instead of creating an animated image. Accordingly, `StdDraw` has a `show()` method that allows us to control when the results of drawing actions are actually shown on the display. You can think of it as collecting all of the lines, points, shapes, and text that we tell it to draw, and then immediately drawing them all when we issue the `show()` command. To control the apparent speed, `show()` takes an argument `dt` that tells `StdDraw` to wait `dt` milliseconds after doing the drawing. By default, `StdDraw` issues a `show()` after each `line()`, `point()`, or other drawing command; we turn that option off when we call `StdDraw.show(t)` and turn it back on when we call `StdDraw.show()` with no arguments. With these commands, we can create the illusion of motion with the following steps:

- Erase the drawing (but do not show the result).
- Draw a black ball at the new position.
- Show the result of both commands, and wait for a brief time.

`BouncingBall` (PROGRAM 1.5.6) implements these steps to create the illusion of a ball moving in the 2-by-2 box centered on the origin. The current position of the ball is (r_x, r_y), and we compute the new position at each step by adding v_x to r_x and v_y to r_y. Since (v_x, v_y) is the fixed distance that the ball moves in each time unit, it represents the *velocity*. To keep the ball in the drawing, we simulate the effect of the ball bouncing off the walls according to the laws of elastic collision. This effect is easy to implement: when the ball hits a vertical wall, we just change the velocity in the x-direction from v_x to $-v_x$, and when the ball hits a horizontal wall, we change the velocity in the y-direction from v_y to $-v_y$. Of course, you have to download the code from the booksite and run it on your computer to see motion. To make the image clearer on the printed page, we modified `BouncingBall` to use a gray background that also shows the track of the ball as it moves (see EXERCISE 1.5.34).

Program 1.5.6   *Bouncing ball*

```
public class BouncingBall
{
    public static void main(String[] args)
    { // Simulate the movement of a bouncing ball.
        StdDraw.setXscale(-1.0, 1.0);
        StdDraw.setYscale(-1.0, 1.0);
        double rx = .480, ry = .860;
        double vx = .015, vy = .023;
        double radius = .05;
        int dt = 20;
        while(true)
        { // Update ball position and draw it there.
            if (Math.abs(rx + vx) + radius > 1.0) vx = -vx;
            if (Math.abs(ry + vy) + radius > 1.0) vy = -vy;
            rx = rx + vx;
            ry = ry + vy;
            StdDraw.clear();
            StdDraw.filledCircle(rx, ry, radius);
            StdDraw.show(dt);
        }
    }
}
```

rx, ry	*position*
vx, vy	*velocity*
dt	*wait time*
radius	*ball radius*

This program simulates the movement of a bouncing ball in the unit box. The ball bounces off the boundary according to the laws of elastic collision. The 20-millisecond wait for StdDraw. show() *keeps the black image of the ball persistent on the screen, even though most of the ball's pixels alternate between black and white. If you modify this code to take the wait time* dt *as a command-line argument, you can control the speed of the ball. The images below, which show the track of the ball, are produced by a modified version of this code (see Exercise 1.5.34).*

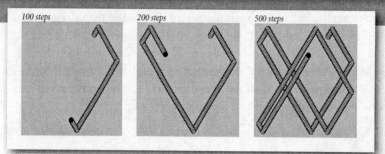

100 steps   200 steps   500 steps

STANDARD DRAWING COMPLETES OUR PROGRAMMING MODEL by adding a "picture is worth a thousand words" component. It is a natural abstraction that you can use to better open up your programs to the outside world. With it, you can easily produce the function plots and visual representations of data that are commonly used in science and engineering. We will put it to such uses frequently throughout this book. Any time that you spend now working with the sample programs on the last few pages will be well worth the investment. You can find many useful examples on the booksite and in the exercises, and you are certain to find some outlet for your creativity by using StdDraw to meet various challenges. Can you draw an *N*-pointed star? Can you make our bouncing ball actually bounce (add gravity)? You may be surprised at how easily you can accomplish these and other tasks.

```
public class StdDraw
```

`void line(double x0, double y0, double x1, double y1)`	
`void point(double x, double y)`	
`void text(double x, double y, String s)`	
`void circle(double x, double y, double r)`	
`void filledCircle(double x, double y, double r)`	
`void square(double x, double y, double r)`	
`void filledSquare(double x, double y, double r)`	
`void polygon(double[] x, double[] y)`	
`void filledPolygon(double[] x, double[] y)`	
`void setXscale(double x0, double x1)`	*reset x range to (x_0, x_1)*
`void setYscale(double y0, double y1)`	*reset y range to (y_0, y_1)*
`void setPenRadius(double r)`	*set pen radius to* r
`void setPenColor(Color c)`	*set pen color to* c
`void setFont(Font f)`	*set text font to* f
`void setCanvasSize(int w, int h)`	*set canvas to* w-by-h *window*
`void clear(Color c)`	*clear the canvas; color it* c
`void show(int dt)`	*show all; pause* dt *milliseconds*
`void save(String filename)`	*save to a* .jpg *or* w.png *file*

Note: Methods with the same names but no arguments reset to default values.

API for our library of static methods for standard drawing

Standard audio   As a final example of a basic abstraction for output, we consider StdAudio, a library that you can use to play, manipulate, and synthesize sound files. You probably have used your computer to process music. Now you can write programs to do so. At the same time, you will learn some concepts behind a venerable and important area of computer science and scientific computing: *digital signal processing*. We will only scratch the surface of this fascinating subject, but you may be surprised at the simplicity of the underlying concepts.

Concert A. Sound is the perception of the vibration of molecules, in particular, the vibration of our eardrums. Therefore, oscillation is the key to understanding sound. Perhaps the simplest place to start is to consider the musical note A above middle C, which is known as *concert A*. This note is nothing more than a sine wave, scaled to oscillate at a frequency of 440 times per second. The function $\sin(t)$ repeats itself once every 2π units on the x-axis, so if we measure t in seconds and plot the function $\sin(2\pi t \times 440)$, we get a curve that oscillates 440 times per second. When you play an A by plucking a guitar string, pushing air through a trumpet, or causing a small cone to vibrate in a speaker, this sine wave is the prominent part of the sound that you hear and recognize as concert A. We measure frequency in *hertz* (cycles per second). When you double or halve the frequency, you move up or down one octave on the scale. For example, 880 hertz is one octave above concert A and 110 hertz is two octaves below concert A. For reference, the frequency range of human hearing is about 20 to 20,000 hertz. The amplitude (y-value) of a sound corresponds to the volume. We plot our curves between -1 and $+1$ and assume that any devices that record and play sound will scale as appropriate, with further scaling controlled by you when you turn the volume knob.

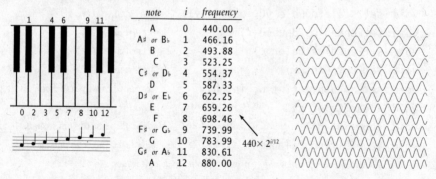

note	i	frequency
A	0	440.00
A♯ *or* B♭	1	466.16
B	2	493.88
C	3	523.25
C♯ *or* D♭	4	554.37
D	5	587.33
D♯ *or* E♭	6	622.25
E	7	659.26
F	8	698.46
F♯ *or* G♭	9	739.99
G	10	783.99
G♯ *or* A♭	11	830.61
A	12	880.00

$440 \times 2^{i/12}$

Notes, numbers, and waves

Other notes. A simple mathematical formula characterizes the other notes on the chromatic scale. There are twelve notes on the chromatic scale, divided equally on a logarithmic (base 2) scale. We get the *i*th note above a given note by multiplying its frequency by the (i/12)th power of 2. In other words, the frequency of each note in the chromatic scale is precisely the frequency of the previous note in the scale multiplied by the twelfth root of two (about 1.06). This information suffices to create music! For example, to play the tune *Frère Jacques,* we just need to play each of the notes *A B C# A* by producing sine waves of the appropriate frequency for about half a second and then repeat the pattern. The primary method in the StdAudio library, StdAudio.play(), allows you to do just that.

Sampling. For digital sound, we represent a curve by sampling it at regular intervals, in precisely the same manner as when we plot function graphs. We sample sufficiently often that we have an accurate representation of the curve—a widely used sampling rate for digital sound is 44,100 samples per second. For concert *A*, that rate corresponds to plotting each cycle of the sine wave by sampling it at about 100 points. Since we sample at regular intervals, we only need to compute the *y*-coordinates of the sample points. It is that simple: *we represent sound as an array of numbers* (double values that are between −1 and +1). Our standard sound library method StdAudio.play() takes an array as its argument and plays the sound represented by that array on your computer. For example, suppose that you want to play concert *A* for 10 seconds. At 44,100 samples per second, you need an array of 441,001 double values. To fill in the array, use a for loop that samples the function $\sin(2\pi t \times 440)$ at $t = 0/44100$,

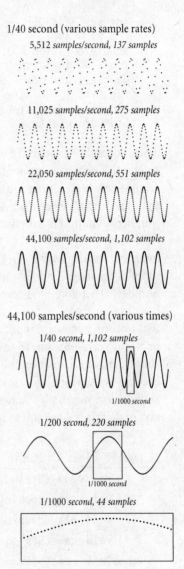

1/40 second (various sample rates)

5,512 *samples/second, 137 samples*

11,025 *samples/second, 275 samples*

22,050 *samples/second, 551 samples*

44,100 *samples/second, 1,102 samples*

44,100 samples/second (various times)

1/40 *second, 1,102 samples*

1/1000 *second*

1/200 *second, 220 samples*

1/1000 *second*

1/1000 *second, 44 samples*

Sampling a sine wave

1/44100, 2/44100, 3/44100, . . . 441000/44100. Once we fill the array with these values, we are ready for StdAudio.play(), as in the following code:

```
int sps = 44100;              // samples per second
int hz = 440;                 // concert A
double duration = 10.0;       // ten seconds
int N = (int) (sps * duration);  // total number of samples
double[] a = new double[N+1];
for (int i = 0; i <= N; i++)
   a[i] = Math.sin(2*Math.PI * i * hz / sps);
StdAudio.play(a);
```

This code is the HelloWorld of digital audio. Once you use it to get your computer to play this note, you can write code to play other notes and make music! The difference between creating sound and plotting an oscillating curve is nothing more than the output device. Indeed, it is instructive and entertaining to send the same numbers to both standard draw and standard audio (see EXERCISE 1.5.27).

Saving to a file. Music can take up a lot of space on your computer. At 44,100 samples per second, a four-minute song corresponds to $4 \times 60 \times 44100 = 10,584,000$ numbers. Therefore, it is common to represent the numbers corresponding to a song in a binary format that uses less space than the string-of-digits representation that we use for standard input and output. Many such formats have been developed in recent years—StdAudio uses the .wav format. You can find some information about the .wav format on the booksite, but you do not need to know the details, because StdAudio takes care of the conversions for you. Our standard library for audio allows you to play .wav files, to write programs to create and manipulate arrays of double values, and to read and write them as .wav files.

```
public class StdAudio
```

void play(String file)	*play the given .wav file*
void play(double[] a)	*play the given sound wave*
void play(double x)	*play sample for 1/44100 second*
void save(String file, double[] a)	*save to a .wav file*
double[] read(String file)	*read from a .wav file*

API for our library of static methods for standard audio

Program 1.5.7   Digital signal processing

```
public class PlayThatTune
{
    public static void main(String[] args)
    { // Read a tune from StdIn and play it.
        int sps = 44100;
        while (!StdIn.isEmpty())
        { // Read and play one note.
            int pitch = StdIn.readInt();
            double duration = StdIn.readDouble();
            double hz = 440 * Math.pow(2, pitch / 12.0);
            int N = (int) (sps * duration);
            double[] a = new double[N+1];
            for (int i = 0; i <= N; i++)
                a[i] = Math.sin(2*Math.PI * i * hz / sps);
            StdAudio.play(a);
        }
    }
}
```

pitch	distance from A
duration	note play time
hz	frequency
N	number of samples
a[]	sampled sine wave

This is a data-driven program that plays pure tones from the notes on the chromatic scale, specified on standard input as a pitch (distance from concert A) and a duration (in seconds). The test client reads the notes from standard input, creates an array by sampling a sine wave of the specified frequency and duration at 44100 samples per second, and then plays each note by calling StdAudio.play().

```
% more elise.txt
7 .25
6 .25
7 .25
6 .25
7 .25
2 .25
5 .25
3 .25
0 .50
```

```
% java PlayThatTune < elise.txt
```

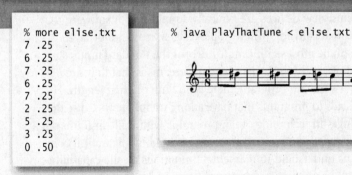

PlayThatTune (PROGRAM 1.5.7) is an example that shows how easily we can create music with StdAudio. It takes notes from standard input, indexed on the chromatic scale from concert *A*, and plays them on standard audio. You can imagine all sorts of extensions on this basic scheme, some of which are addressed in the exercises. We include StdAudio in our basic arsenal of programming tools because sound processing is one important application of scientific computing that is certainly familiar to you. Not only has the commercial application of digital signal processing had a phenomenal impact on modern society, but the science and engineering behind it combines physics and computer science in interesting ways. We will study more components of digital signal processing in some detail later in the book. (For example, you will learn in SECTION 2.1 how to create sounds that are more musical than the pure sounds produced by PlayThatTune.)

I/O IS A PARTICULARLY CONVINCING EXAMPLE of the power of abstraction because standard input, standard output, standard draw, and standard audio can be tied to different physical devices at different times without making any changes to programs. Although devices may differ dramatically, we can write programs that can do I/O without depending on the properties of specific devices. From this point forward, we will use methods from StdOut, StdIn, StdDraw, and/or StdAudio in nearly every program in this book, and you will use them in nearly all of your programs, so make sure to download copies of these libraries. For economy, we collectively refer to these libraries as Std*. One important advantage of using such libraries is that you can switch to new devices that are faster, cheaper, or hold more data without changing your program at all. In such a situation, the details of the connection are a matter to be resolved between your operating system and the Std* implementations. On modern systems, new devices are typically supplied with software that resolves such details automatically for both the operating system and for Java.

Conceptually, one of the most significant features of the standard input, standard output, standard draw, and standard audio data streams is that they are *infinite*: from the point of view of your program, there is no limit on their length. This point of view not only leads to programs that have a long useful life (because they are less sensitive to changes in technology than programs with built-in limits). It also is related to the *Turing machine*, an abstract device used by theoretical computer scientists to help us understand fundamental limitations on the capabilities of real computers. One of the essential properties of the model is the idea of a finite discrete device that works with an unlimited amount of input and output.

Q&A

Q. Why are we not using the standard Java libraries for input, graphics, and sound?

A. We *are* using them, but we prefer to work with simpler abstract models. The Java libraries behind StdIn, StdDraw, and StdAudio are built for production programming, and the libraries and their APIs are a bit unwieldy. To get an idea of what they are like, look at the code in StdIn.java, StdDraw.java, and StdAudio.java.

Q. So, let me get this straight. If I use the format %2.4f for a double value, I get two digits before the decimal point and four digits after, right?

A. No, that specifies just four digits after the decimal point. The first value is the width of the whole field. You want to use the format %7.2f to specify seven characters in total, four before the decimal point, the decimal point itself, and two digits after the decimal point.

Q. What other conversion codes are there for printf()?

A. For integer values, there is o for octal and x for hexadecimal. There are also numerous formats for dates and times. See the booksite for more information.

Q. Can my program re-read data from standard input?

A. No. You only get one shot at it, in the same way that you cannot undo a println() command.

Q. What happens if my program attempts to read data from standard input after it is exhausted?

A. You will get an error. StdIn.isEmpty() allows you to avoid such an error by checking whether there is more input available.

Q. What does the error message Exception in thread "main" java.lang.NoClassDefFoundError: StdIn mean?

A. You probably forgot to put StdIn.java in your working directory.

Q. I have a different working directory for each project that I am working on, so I have copies of StdOut.java, StdIn.java, StdDraw.java, and StdAudio.java in each of them. Is there some better way?

A. Yes. You can put them all in one directory and use the "classpath" mechanism to tell Java where to find them. This mechanism is operating-system dependent—you can find instructions on how to use it on the booksite.

Q. My terminal window hangs at the end of a program using StdAudio. How can I avoid having to use <ctrl-c> to get a command prompt?

A. Add a call to System.exit(0) as the last line in main(). Don't ask why.

Q. So I use negative integers to go below concert *A* when making input files for PlayThatTune?

A. Right. Actually, our choice to put concert *A* at 0 is arbitrary. A popular standard, known as the *MIDI Tuning Standard*, starts numbering at the *C* five octaves below concert *A*. By that convention, concert *A* is 69 and you do not need to use negative numbers.

Exercises

1.5.1 Write a program that reads in integers (as many as the user enters) from standard input and prints out the maximum and minimum values.

1.5.2 Modify your program from the previous exercise to insist that the integers must be positive (by prompting the user to enter positive integers whenever the value entered is not positive).

1.5.3 Write a program that takes an integer N from the command line, reads N double values from standard input, and prints their mean (average value) and standard deviation (square root of the sum of the squares of their differences from the average, divided by $N-1$).

1.5.4 Extend your program from the previous exercise to create a filter that prints all the values that are further than 1.5 standard deviations from the mean. Use an array.

1.5.5 Write a program that reads in a sequence of integers and prints out both the integer that appears in a longest consecutive run and the length of the run. For example, if the input is 1 2 2 1 5 1 1 7 7 7 7 1 1, then your program should print Longest run: 4 consecutive 7s.

1.5.6 Write a filter that reads in a sequence of integers and prints out the integers, removing repeated values that appear consecutively. For example, if the input i 1 2 2 1 5 1 1 7 7 7 7 1 1 1 1 1 1 1 1, your program should print out 1 2 1 5 1 7 1.

1.5.7 Write a program that takes a command-line argument N, reads in N-1 distinct integers between 1 and N, and determines the missing value.

1.5.8 Write a program that reads in positive real numbers from standard input and prints out their geometric and harmonic means. The *geometric mean* of N positive numbers $x_1, x_2, ..., x_N$ is $(x_1 \times x_2 \times ... \times x_N)^{1/N}$. The *harmonic mean* is $(1/x_1 + 1/x_2 + ... + 1/x_N) / (1/N)$. *Hint*: For the geometric mean, consider taking logs to avoid overflow.

1.5.9 Suppose that the file input.txt contains the two strings F and .F. What

does the following command do (see EXERCISE 1.2.35)?

```
java Dragon < input.txt | java Dragon | java Dragon

public class Dragon
{
   public static void main(String[] args)
   {
      String dragon = StdIn.readString();
      String nogard = StdIn.readString();
      StdOut.print(dragon + "L" + nogard);
      StdOut.print(" ");
      StdOut.print(dragon + "R" + nogard);
      StdOut.println();
   }
}
```

1.5.10 Write a filter TenPerLine that takes a sequence of integers between 0 and 99 and prints 10 integers per line, with columns aligned. Then write a program RandomIntSeq that takes two command-line arguments M and N and outputs N random integers between 0 and M-1. Test your programs with the command java RandomIntSeq 200 100 | java TenPerLine.

1.5.11 Write a program that reads in text from standard input and prints out the number of words in the text. For the purpose of this exercise, a word is a sequence of non-whitespace characters that is surrounded by whitespace.

1.5.12 Write a program that reads in lines from standard input with each line containing a name and two integers and then uses printf() to print a table with a column of the names, the integers, and the result of dividing the first by the second, accurate to three decimal places. You could use a program like this to tabulate batting averages for baseball players or grades for students.

1.5.13 Which of the following *require* saving all the values from standard input (in an array, say), and which could be implemented as a filter using only a fixed number of variables? For each, the input comes from standard input and consists of N real numbers between 0 and 1.

- Print the maximum and minimum numbers.
- Print the kth smallest value.
- Print the sum of the squares of the numbers.
- Print the average of the N numbers.
- Print the percentage of numbers greater than the average.
- Print the N numbers in increasing order.
- Print the N numbers in random order.

1.5.14 Write a program that prints a table of the monthly payments, remaining principal, and interest paid for a loan, taking three numbers as command-line arguments: the number of years, the principal, and the interest rate (see EXERCISE 1.2.24).

1.5.15 Write a program that takes three command-line arguments x, y, and z, reads from standard input a sequence of point coordinates (x_i, y_i, z_i), and prints the coordinates of the point closest to (x, y, z). Recall that the square of the distance between (x, y, z) and (x_i, y_i, z_i) is $(x - x_i)^2 + (y - y_i)^2 + (z - z_i)^2$. For efficiency, do not use Math.sqrt() or Math.pow().

1.5.16 Given the positions and masses of a sequence of objects, write a program to compute their center-of-mass, or *centroid*. The centroid is the average position of the N objects, weighted by mass. If the positions and masses are given by (x_i, y_i, m_i), then the centroid (x, y, m) is given by:

$$m = m_1 + m_2 + \dots + m_N$$
$$x = (m_1 x_1 + \dots + m_n x_N) / m$$
$$y = (m_1 y_1 + \dots + m_n y_N) / m$$

1.5.17 Write a program that reads in a sequence of real numbers between -1 and $+1$ and prints out their average magnitude, average power, and the number of zero crossings. The *average magnitude* is the average of the absolute values of the data values. The *average power* is the average of the squares of the data values. The number of *zero crossings* is the number of times a data value transitions from a strictly negative number to a strictly positive number, or vice versa. These three statistics are widely used to analyze digital signals.

1.5.18 Write a program that takes a command-line argument N and plots an N-by-N checkerboard with red and black squares. Color the lower left square red.

1.5.19 Write a program that takes as command-line arguments an integer N and a double value p (between 0 and 1), plots N equally spaced points of size on the circumference of a circle, and then, with probability p for each pair of points, draws a gray line connecting them.

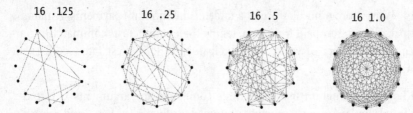

1.5.20 Write code to draw hearts, spades, clubs, and diamonds. To draw a heart, draw a diamond, then attach two semicircles to the upper left and upper right sides.

1.5.21 Write a program that takes a command-line argument N and plots a rose with N petals (if N is odd) or $2N$ petals (if N is even), by plotting the polar coordinates (r, θ) of the function $r = \sin(N\theta)$ for θ ranging from 0 to 2π radians.

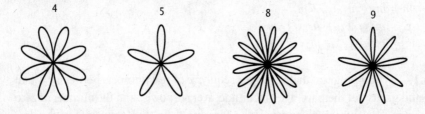

1.5.22 Write a program that takes a string s from the command line and displays it in banner style on the screen, moving from left to right and wrapping back to the beginning of the string as the end is reached. Add a second command-line argument to control the speed.

1.5.23 Modify PlayThatTune to take additional command-line arguments that control the volume (multiply each sample value by the volume) and the tempo (multiply each note's duration by the tempo).

1.5.24 Write a program that takes the name of a .wav file and a playback rate r as command-line arguments and plays the file at the given rate. First, use StdAudio. read() to read the file into an array a[]. If $r = 1$, just play a[]; otherwise create a new array b[] of approximate size r times a.length. If $r < 1$, populate b[] by *sampling* from the original; if $r > 1$, populate b[] by *interpolating* from the original. Then play b[].

1.5.25 Write programs that uses StdDraw to create each of the following designs.

1.5.26 Write a program Circles that draws filled circles of random size at random positions in the unit square, producing images like those below. Your program should take four command-line arguments: the number of circles, the probability that each circle is black, the minimum radius, and the maximum radius.

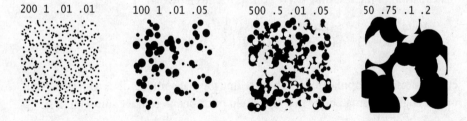

200 1 .01 .01   100 1 .01 .05   500 .5 .01 .05   50 .75 .1 .2

Creative Exercises

1.5.27 *Visualizing audio.* Modify PlayThatTune to send the values played to standard drawing, so that you can watch the sound waves as they are played. You will have to experiment with plotting multiple curves in the drawing canvas to synchronize the sound and the picture.

1.5.28 *Statistical polling.* When collecting statistical data for certain political polls, it is very important to obtain an unbiased sample of registered voters. Assume that you have a file with N registered voters, one per line. Write a filter that prints out a random sample of size M (see PROGRAM 1.4.1).

1.5.29 *Terrain analysis.* Suppose that a terrain is represented by a two-dimensional grid of elevation values (in meters). A *peak* is a grid point whose four neighboring cells (left, right, up, and down) have strictly lower elevation values. Write a program Peaks that reads a terrain from standard input and then computes and prints the number of peaks in the terrain.

1.5.30 *Histogram.* Suppose that the standard input stream is a sequence of double values. Write a program that takes an integer N and two double values l and r from the command line and uses StdDraw to plot a histogram of the count of the numbers in the standard input stream that fall in each of the N intervals defined by dividing (l, r) into N equal-sized intervals.

1.5.31 *Spirographs.* Write a program that takes three parameters R, r, and a from the command line and draws the resulting *spirograph*. A spirograph (technically, an epicycloid) is a curve formed by rolling a circle of radius r around a larger fixed circle of radius R. If the pen offset from the center of the rolling circle is $(r+a)$, then the equation of the resulting curve at time t is given by

$$x(t) = (R + r) \cos(t) - (r + a) \cos((R + r)t/r)$$
$$y(t) = (R + r) \sin(t) - (r + a) \sin((R + r)t/r)$$

Such curves were popularized by a best-selling toy that contains discs with gear teeth on the edges and small holes that you could put a pen in to trace spirographs.

1.5.32 *Clock.* Write a program that displays an animation of the second, minute, and hour hands of an analog clock. Use the method StdDraw.show(1000) to update the display roughly once per second.

1.5.33 *Oscilloscope.* Write a program to simulate the output of an oscilloscope and produce Lissajous patterns. These patterns are named after the French physicist, Jules A. Lissajous, who studied the patterns that arise when two mutually perpendicular periodic disturbances occur simultaneously. Assume that the inputs are sinusoidal, so that the following parametric equations describe the curve:

$$x(t) = A_x \sin (w_x t + \theta_x)$$
$$y(t) = A_y \sin (w_y t + \theta_y)$$

Take the six parameters A_x, w_x, θ_x, A_y, w_y, and θ_y from the command line.

1.5.34 *Bouncing ball with tracks.* Modify BouncingBall to produce images like the ones shown in the text, which show the track of the ball on a gray background.

1.5.35 *Bouncing ball with gravity.* Modify BouncingBall to incorporate gravity in the vertical direction. Add calls to StdAudio.play() to add one sound effect when the ball hits a wall and a different one when it hits the floor.

1.5.36 *Random tunes.* Write a program that uses StdAudio to play random tunes. Experiment with keeping in key, assigning high probabilities to whole steps, repetition, and other rules to produce reasonable melodies.

1.5.37 *Tile patterns.* Using your solution to EXERCISE 1.5.25, write a program TilePattern that takes a command-line argument N and draws an N-by-N pattern, using the tile of your choice. Add a second command-line argument that adds a checkerboard option. Add a third command-line argument for color selection. Using the patterns on the facing page as a starting point, design a tile floor. Be creative! *Note*: These are all designs from antiquity that you can find in many ancient (and modern) buildings.

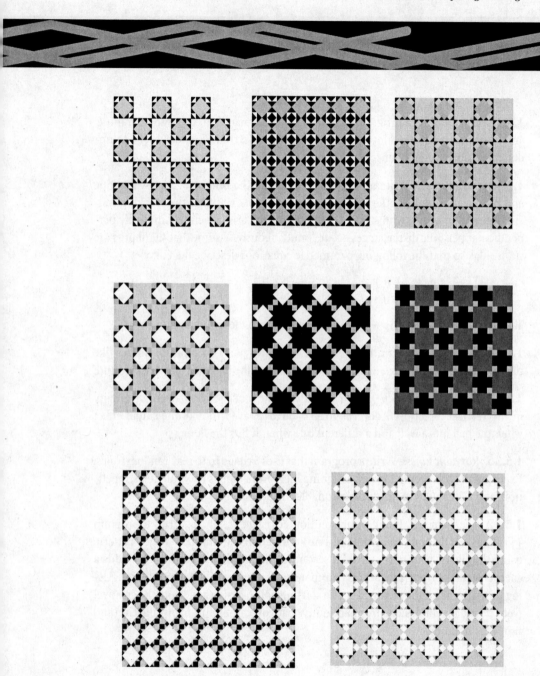

1.6   Case Study: Random Web Surfer

COMMUNICATING ACROSS THE WEB HAS BECOME an integral part of everyday life. This communication is enabled in part by scientific studies of the structure of the web, a subject of active research since its inception. We next consider a simple model of the web that has proven to be a particularly successful approach to understanding some of its properties. Variants of this model are widely used and have been a key factor in the explosive growth of search applications on the web.

The model is known as the *random surfer* model, and is simple to describe. We consider the web to be a fixed set of *pages*, with each page containing a fixed set of *hyperlinks* (for brevity, we use the term *links*), and each link a reference to some other page. We study what happens to a person (the random surfer) who randomly moves from page to page, either by typing a page name into the address bar or by clicking a link on the current page.

The underlying mathematical model behind the web model is known as the *graph*, which we will consider in detail at the end of the book (in SECTION 4.5). We defer discussion of details about processing graphs until then. Instead, we concentrate on calculations associated with a natural and well-studied probabilistic model that accurately describes the behavior of the random surfer.

The first step in studying the random surfer model is to formulate it more precisely. The crux of the matter is to specify what it means to randomly move from page to page. The following intuitive *90-10 rule* captures both methods of moving to a new page: *Assume that 90 per cent of the time the random surfer clicks a random link on the current page (each link chosen with equal probability) and that 10 percent of the time the random surfer goes directly to a random page (all pages on the web chosen with equal probability).*

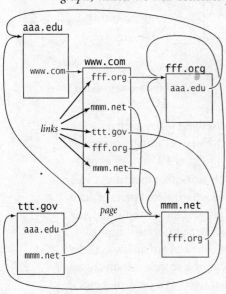

Pages and links

You can immediately see that this model has flaws, because you know from your own experience that the behavior of a real web surfer is not quite so simple:

- No one chooses links or pages with equal probability.
- There is no real potential to surf directly to each page on the web.
- The 90-10 (or any fixed) breakdown is just a guess.
- It does not take the back button or bookmarks into account.
- We can only afford to work with a small sample of the web.

Despite these flaws, the model is sufficiently rich that computer scientists have learned a great deal about properties of the web by studying it. To appreciate the model, consider the small example on the previous page. Which page do you think the random surfer is most likely to visit?

Each person using the web behaves a bit like the random surfer, so understanding the fate of the random surfer is of intense interest to people building web infrastructure and web applications. The model is a tool for understanding the experience of each of the hundreds of millions of web users. In this section, you will use the basic programming tools from this chapter to study the model and its implications.

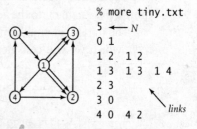

Input format　We want to be able to study the behavior of the random surfer on various web models, not just one example. Consequently, we want to write *data-driven code*, where we keep data in files and write programs that read the data from standard input. The first step in this approach is to define an *input format* that we can use to structure the information in the input files. We are free to define any convenient input format.

Random surfer input format

Later in the book, you will learn how to read web pages in Java programs (SECTION 3.1) and to convert from names to numbers (SECTION 4.4) as well as other techniques for efficient graph processing. For now, we assume that there are *N* web pages, numbered from 0 to N-1, and we represent links with ordered pairs of such numbers, the first specifying the page containing the link and the second specifying the page to which it refers. Given these conventions, a straightforward input format for the random surfer problem is an input stream consisting of an integer (the value of *N*) followed by a sequence of pairs of integers (the representations of all the links). StdIn treats all sequences of whitespace characters as a single delimiter, so we are free to either put one link per line or arrange them several to a line.

Transition matrix   We use a two-dimensional matrix, that we refer to as the *transition matrix*, to completely specify the behavior of the random surfer. With N web pages, we define an N-by-N matrix such that the entry in row i and column j is the probability that the random surfer moves to page j when on page i. Our first task is to write code that can create such a matrix for any given input. By the 90-10 rule, this computation is not difficult. We do so in three steps:

- Read N, and then create arrays counts[][] and outDegree[].
- Read the links and accumulate counts so that counts[i][j] counts the links from i to j and outDegree[i] counts the links from i to anywhere.
- Use the 90-10 rule to compute the probabilities.

The first two steps are elementary, and the third is not much more difficult: multiply counts[i][j] by .90/degree[i] if there is a link from i to j (take a random link with probability .9), and then add .10/N to each entry (go to a random page with probability .1). Transition (PROGRAM 1.6.1) performs this calculation: It is a filter that converts the list-of-links representation of a web model into a transition-matrix representation.

The transition matrix is significant because each row represents a *discrete probability distribution*—the entries fully specify the behavior of the random surfer's next move, giving the probability of surfing to each page. Note in particular that the entries sum to 1 (the surfer always goes somewhere).

The output of Transition defines another file format, one for matrices of double values: the numbers of rows and columns followed by the values for matrix entries. Now, we can write programs that read and process transition matrices.

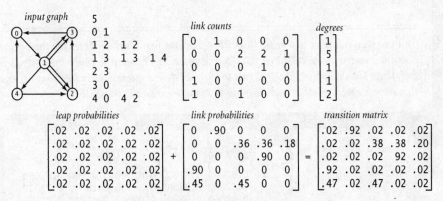

Transition matrix computation

Program 1.6.1 *Computing the transition matrix*

```
public class Transition
{
   public static void main(String[] args)
   { // Print random-surfer probabilites.
      int N = StdIn.readInt();
      int[][] counts = new int[N][N];
      int[] outDegree = new int[N];
      while (!StdIn.isEmpty())
      { // Accumulate link counts.
         int i = StdIn.readInt();
         int j = StdIn.readInt();
         outDegree[i]++;
         counts[i][j]++;
      }

      StdOut.println(N + " " + N);
      for (int i = 0; i < N; i++)
      { // Print probability distribution for row i.
         for (int j = 0; j < N; j++)
         { // Print probability for column j.
            double p = .90*counts[i][j]/outDegree[i] + .10/N;
            StdOut.printf("%8.5f", p);
         }
         StdOut.println();
      }
   }
}
```

N	number of pages
counts[i][j]	count of links from page i to page j
outDegree[i]	count of links from page i to anywhere
p	transition probability

This program is a filter that reads links from standard input and produces the corresponding transition matrix on standard output. First, it processes the input to count the outlinks from each page. Then it applies the 90-10 rule to compute the transition matrix (see text). It assumes that there are no pages that have no outlinks in the input (see Exercise 1.6.3).

```
% more tiny.txt
5
0 1
1 2   1 2
1 3   1 3   1 4
2 3
3 0
4 0   4 2
```

```
% java Transition < tiny.txt
5 5
 0.02000 0.92000 0.02000 0.02000 0.02000
 0.02000 0.02000 0.38000 0.38000 0.20000
 0.02000 0.02000 0.02000 0.92000 0.02000
 0.92000 0.02000 0.02000 0.02000 0.02000
 0.47000 0.02000 0.47000 0.02000 0.02000
```

Simulation   Given the transition matrix, simulating the behavior of the random surfer involves surprisingly little code, as you can see in RandomSurfer (PROGRAM 1.6.2). This program reads a transition matrix and surfs according to the rules, starting at page 0 and taking the number of moves as a command-line argument. It counts the number of times that the surfer visits each page. Dividing that count by the number of moves yields an estimate of the probability that a random surfer winds up on the page. This probability is known as the page's *rank*. In other words, RandomSurfer computes an estimate of all page ranks.

One random move. The key to the computation is the random move, which is specified by the transition matrix. We maintain a variable page whose value is the current location of the surfer. Row page of the matrix gives, for each j, the probability that the surfer next goes to j. In other words, when the surfer is at page, our task is to generate a random integer between 0 and N-1 according to the distribution given by row page in the transition matrix (the one-dimensional array p[page]). How can we accomplish this task? We can use Math.random() to generate a random number r between 0 and 1, but how does that help us get to a random page? One way to answer this question is to think of the probabilities in row page as defining a set of N intervals in (0, 1) with each probability corresponding to an interval length. Then our random variable r falls into one of the intervals, with probability precisely specified by the interval length. This reasoning leads to the following code:

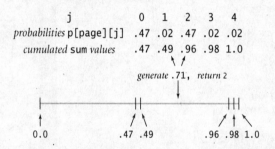

Generating a random integer from a discrete distribution

```
double sum = 0.0;
for (int j = 0; j < N; j++)
{  // Find interval containing r.
   sum += p[page][j];
   if (r < sum) { page = j; break; }
}
```

The variable sum tracks the endpoints of the intervals defined in row p[page], and the for loop finds the interval containing the random value r. For example, suppose that the surfer is at page 4 in our example. The transition probabilities are .47,

---

Program 1.6.2   *Simulating a random surfer*

```java
public class RandomSurfer
{
    public static void main(String[] args)
    { // Simulate random-surfer leaps and links.
        int T = Integer.parseInt(args[0]);
        int N = StdIn.readInt();
        StdIn.readInt();

        // Read transition matrix.
        double[][] p = new double[N][N];
        for (int i = 0; i < N; i++)
            for (int j = 0; j < N; j++)
                p[i][j] = StdIn.readDouble();

        int page = 0; // Start at page 0.
        int[] freq = new int[N];
        for (int t = 0; t < T; t++)
        {   // Make one random move.
            double r = Math.random();
            double sum = 0.0;
            for (int j = 0; j < N; j++)
            {  // Find interval containing r.
                sum += p[page][j];
                if (r < sum) { page = j; break; }
            }
            freq[page]++;
        }

        for (int i = 0; i < N; i++)      // Print page ranks.
            StdOut.printf("%8.5f", (double) freq[i] / T);
        StdOut.println();
    }
}
```

T	*number of moves*
N	*number of pages*
page	*current page*
p[i][j]	*probability that the surfer moves from page i to page j*
freq[i]	*number of times the surfer hits page i*

This program uses a transition matrix to simulate the behavior of a random surfer. It takes the number of moves as a command-line argument, reads the transition matrix, performs the indicated number of moves as prescribed by the matrix, and prints the relative frequency of hitting each page. The key to the computation is the random move to the next page (see text).

```
% java Transition < tiny.txt | java RandomSurfer 100
 0.24000 0.23000 0.16000 0.25000 0.12000
% java Transition < tiny.txt | java RandomSurfer 10000
 0.27280 0.26530 0.14820 0.24830 0.06540
% java Transition < tiny.txt | java RandomSurfer 1000000
0.27324 0.26568 0.14581 0.24737 0.06790
```

.02, .47, .02, and .02, and sum takes on the values 0.0, 0.47, 0.49, 0.96, 0.98, and 1.0. These values indicate that the probabilities define the five intervals (0, .47), (.47, .49), (.49, .96), (.96, .98), and (.98, 1), one for each page. Now, suppose that Math.random() returns the value .71. We increment j from 0 to 1 to 2 and stop there, which indicates that .71 is in the interval (.49, .96), so we send the surfer to the third page (page 2). Then, we perform the same computation for p[2], and the random surfer is off and surfing. For large *N*, we can use *binary search* to substantially speed up this computation (see EXERCISE 4.2.36). Typically, we are interested in speeding up the search in this situation because we are likely to need a huge number of random moves, as you will see.

Markov chains. The random process that describes the surfer's behavior is known as a *Markov chain*, named after the Russian mathematician Andrey Markov, who developed the concept in the early 20th century. Markov chains are widely applicable, well-studied, and have many remarkable and useful properties. For example, you may have wondered why RandomSurfer starts the random surfer at page 0 whereas you might have expected a random choice. A basic limit theorem for Markov chains says that the surfer could start *anywhere*, because the probability that a random surfer eventually winds up on any particular page is the same for all starting pages! No matter where the surfer starts, the process eventually stabilizes to a point where further surfing provides no further information. This phenomenon is known as *mixing*. Though this phenomenon is perhaps counterintuitive at first, it explains coherent behavior in a situation that might seem chaotic. In the present context, it captures the idea that the web looks pretty much the same to everyone after surfing for a sufficiently long time. However, not all Markov chains have this mixing property. For example, if we eliminate the random leap from our model, certain configurations of web pages can present problems for the surfer. Indeed, there exist on the web sets of pages known as *spider traps,* which are designed to attract incoming links but have no outgoing links. Without the random leap, the surfer could get stuck in a spider trap. The primary purpose of the 90-10 rule is to guarantee mixing and eliminate such anomalies.

Page ranks. The RandomSurfer simulation is straightforward: it loops for the indicated number of moves, randomly surfing through the graph. Because of the mixing phenomenon, increasing the number of iterations gives increasingly accurate estimates of the probability that the surfer lands on each page (the page ranks). How do the results compare with your intuition when you first thought about the question? You might have guessed that page 4 was the lowest-ranked page, but did you think that pages 0 and 1 would rank higher than page 3? If we want to know which page is the highest rank, we need more precision and more accuracy. RandomSurfer needs 10^n moves to get answers precise to n decimal places and many more moves for those answers to stabilize to an accurate value. For our example, it takes tens of thousands of iterations to get answers accurate to two decimal places and millions of iterations to get answers accurate to three places (see Exercise 1.6.5). The end result is that page 0 beats page 1 by 27.3% to 26.6%. That such a tiny difference would appear in such a small problem is quite surprising: if you guessed that page 0 is the most likely spot for the surfer to end up, you were lucky! Accurate page rank estimates for the web are valuable in practice for many reasons. First, using them to put in order the pages that match the search criteria for web searches proved to be vastly more in line with people's expectations than previous methods. Next, this measure of confidence and reliability led to the investment of huge amounts of money in web advertising based on page ranks. Even in our tiny example, page ranks might be used to convince advertisers to pay up to four times as much to place an ad on page 0 as on page 4. Computing page ranks is mathematically sound, an interesting computer science problem, and big business, all rolled into one.

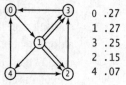

```
0 .27
1 .27
3 .25
2 .15
4 .07
```

Visualizing the histogram. With StdDraw, it is also easy to create a visual representation that can give you a feeling for how the random surfer visit frequencies converge to the page ranks. Simply add

Page ranks with histogram

```
StdDraw.clear();
StdDraw.setXscale(-1, N);
StdDraw.setYscale(0, t);
StdDraw.setPenRadius(.5/N);
for (int i = 0; i < N; i++)
    StdDraw.line(i, 0, i, freq[i]);
StdDraw.show(20);
```

to the random move loop, run RandomSurfer for large values of T, and you will see a drawing of the frequency histogram that eventually stabilizes to the page ranks. After you have used this tool once, you are likely to find yourself using it *every* time you want to study a new model (perhaps with some minor adjustments to handle larger models).

Studying other models. RandomSurfer and Transition are excellent examples of data-driven programs. You can easily create a data model just by creating a file like tiny.txt that starts with an integer N and then specifies pairs of integers between 0 and N-1 that represent links connecting pages. You are encouraged to run it for various data models as suggested in the exercises, or to make up some models of your own to study. If you have ever wondered how web page ranking works, this calculation is your chance to develop better intuition about what causes one page to be ranked more highly than another. What kind of page is likely to be rated highly? One that has many links to other pages, or one that has just a few links to other pages? The exercises in this section present many opportunities to study the behavior of the random surfer. Since RandomSurfer uses standard input, you can write simple programs that generate large input models, pipe their output to RandomSurfer, and therefore study the random surfer on large models. Such flexibility is an important reason to use standard input and standard output.

DIRECTLY SIMULATING THE BEHAVIOR OF A random surfer to understand the structure of the web is appealing, but it has limitations. Think about the following question: Could you use it to compute page ranks for a web model with millions (or billions!) of web pages and links? The quick answer to this question is *no*, because you cannot even afford to store the transition matrix for such a large number of pages. A matrix for millions of pages would have *trillions* of entries. Do you have that much space on your computer? Could you use RandomSurfer to find page ranks for a smaller model with, say, thousands of pages? To answer this question, you might run multiple simulations, record the results for a large number of trials, and then interpret those experimental results. We do use this approach for many scientific problems (the gambler's ruin problem is one example; SECTION 2.4 is devoted to another), but it can be very time-consuming, as a huge number of trials may be necessary to get the desired accuracy. Even for our tiny example, we saw that it takes millions of iterations to get the page ranks accurate to three or four decimal places. For larger models, the required number of iterations to obtain accurate estimates becomes truly huge.

Mixing a Markov chain   It is important to remember that the page ranks are a property of the web model, not any particular approach for computing it. That is, RandomSurfer is just *one* way to compute page ranks. Fortunately, a simple computational model based on a well-studied area of mathematics provides a far more efficient approach than simulation to the problem of computing page ranks. That model makes use of the basic arithmetic operations on two-dimensional matrices that we considered in SECTION 1.4.

Squaring a Markov chain. What is the probability that the random surfer will move from page i to page·j in *two* moves? The first move goes to an intermediate page k, so we calculate the probability of moving from i to k and then from k to j for all possible k and add up the results. For our example, the probability of moving from 1 to 2 in two moves is the probability of moving from 1 to 0 to 2 (.02×.02), plus the probability of moving from 1 to 1 to 2 (.02×.38), plus the probability of moving from 1 to 2 to 2 (.38×.02), plus the probability of moving from 1 to 3 to 2 (.38×.02), plus the probability of moving from 1 to 4 to 2 (.20×.47), which adds up to a grand total of .1172. The same process works for each pair of pages. *This calculation is one that we have seen before*, in the definition of matrix multiplication: the entry in row i and column j in the result is the dot product of row i and column j in the original. In other words, the result of multiplying p[][] by itself is a matrix where the entry in row i and column j is the probability that the random surfer moves from page i to page j in two moves. Studying the entries of the two-move transition matrix for our example is well worth your time and will help you better understand the movement of the random surfer. For instance, the largest entry in the square is the one in row 2 and column 0, reflecting the fact that a surfer starting on page 2 has only one link out, to page 3, where there is also only one link out, to page 0. Therefore, by far the most likely outcome for a surfer start-

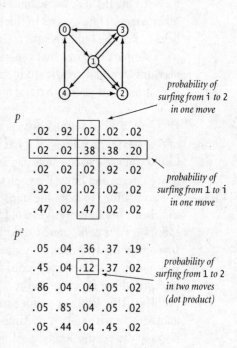

probability of
surfing from i to 2
in one move

probability of
surfing from 1 to i
in one move

probability of
surfing from 1 to 2
in two moves
(dot product)

Squaring a Markov chain

ing on page 2 is to end up in page 0 after two moves. All of the other two-move routes involve more choices and are less probable. It is important to note that this is an exact computation (up to the limitations of Java's floating-point precision), in contrast to RandomSurfer, which produces an estimate and needs more iterations to get a more accurate estimate.

The power method. We might then calculate the probabilities for three moves by multiplying by p[][] again, and for four moves by multiplying by p[][] yet again, and so forth. However, matrix-matrix multiplication is expensive, and we are actually interested in a *vector*-matrix calculation. For our example, we start with the vector

```
[1.0 0.0 0.0 0.0 0.0 ]
```

which specifies that the random surfer starts on page 0. Multiplying this vector by the transition matrix gives the vector

```
[.02 .92 .02 .02 .02 ]
```

which is the probabilities that the surfer winds up on each of the pages after one step. Now, multiplying *this* vector by the transition matrix gives the vector

```
[.05 .04 .36 .37 .19 ]
```

which contains the probabilities that the surfer winds up on each of the pages after *two* steps. For example, the probability of moving from 0 to 2 in two moves is the probability of moving from 0 to 0 to 2 (.02×.02), plus the probability of moving from 0 to 1 to 2 (.92×.38), plus the probability of moving from 0 to 2 to 2 (.02×.02), plus the probability of moving from 0 to 3 to 2 (.02×.02), plus the probability of moving from 0 to 4 to 2 (.02×.47), which adds up to a grand total of .36 . From these initial calculations, the pattern is clear: *The vector giving the probabilities that the random surfer is at each page after t steps is precisely the product of the corresponding vector for t − 1 steps and the transition matrix.* By the basic limit theorem for Markov chains, this process converges to the same vector no matter where we start; in other words, after a sufficient number of moves, the probability that the surfer ends up on any given page is independent of the starting point. Markov (PROGRAM 1.6.3) is an implementation that you can use to check convergence for our example. For instance, it gets the same results (the page ranks accurate to two decimal places) as RandomSurfer, but with just 20 matrix-vector multiplications

rank[]   p[][]   newRank[]

first move

$$[\ 1.0\ 0.0\ 0.0\ 0.0\ 0.0\ ]\ *\ \begin{bmatrix} .02 & .92 & .02 & .02 & .02 \\ .02 & .02 & .38 & .38 & .20 \\ .02 & .02 & .02 & .92 & .02 \\ .92 & .02 & .02 & .02 & .02 \\ .47 & .02 & .47 & .02 & .02 \end{bmatrix} = [\ .02\ .92\ .02\ .02\ .02\ ]$$

probabilities of surfing
from 0 to i in one move

second move

probabilities of surfing
from i to 2 in one move

probabilities of surfing
from 0 to i in one move

probability of surfing from 0 to 2
in two moves (dot product)

$$[\ .02\ .92\ .02\ .02\ .02\ ]\ *\ \begin{bmatrix} .02 & .92 & .02 & .02 & .02 \\ .02 & .02 & .38 & .38 & .20 \\ .02 & .02 & .02 & .92 & .02 \\ .92 & .02 & .02 & .02 & .02 \\ .47 & .02 & .47 & .02 & .02 \end{bmatrix} = [\ .05\ .04\ .36\ .37\ .19\ ]$$

probabilities of surfing
from 0 to i in two moves

third move

probabilities of surfing
from 0 to i in two moves

$$[\ .05\ .04\ .36\ .37\ .19\ ]\ *\ \begin{bmatrix} .02 & .92 & .02 & .02 & .02 \\ .02 & .02 & .38 & .38 & .20 \\ .02 & .02 & .02 & .92 & .02 \\ .92 & .02 & .02 & .02 & .02 \\ .47 & .02 & .47 & .02 & .02 \end{bmatrix} = [\ .44\ .06\ .12\ .36\ .03\ ]$$

probabilities of surfing
from 0 to i in three moves

.
.
.

20th move

probabilities of surfing
from 0 to i in 19 moves

$$[\ .27\ .26\ .15\ .25\ .07\ ]\ *\ \begin{bmatrix} .02 & .92 & .02 & .02 & .02 \\ .02 & .02 & .38 & .38 & .20 \\ .02 & .02 & .02 & .92 & .02 \\ .92 & .02 & .02 & .02 & .02 \\ .47 & .02 & .47 & .02 & .02 \end{bmatrix} = [\ .27\ .26\ .15\ .25\ .07\ ]$$

probabilities of surfing
from 0 to i in 20 moves
(steady state)

The power method for computing page ranks (limit values of transition probabilities)

Program 1.6.3 Mixing a Markov chain

```
public class Markov
{  // Compute page ranks after T moves.
   public static void main(String[] args)
   {
      int T = Integer.parseInt(args[0]);
      int N = StdIn.readInt();
      StdIn.readInt();

      // Read p[][] from StdIn.
      double[][] p = new double[N][N];
      for (int i = 0; i < N; i++)
         for (int j = 0; j < N; j++)
            p[i][j] = StdIn.readDouble();

      // Use the power method to compute page ranks.
      double[] rank = new double[N];
      rank[0] = 1.0;
      for (int t = 0; t < T; t++)
      {  // Compute effect of next move on page ranks.
         double[] newRank = new double[N];
         for (int j = 0; j < N; j++)
         {  //  New rank of page j is dot product
            //  of old ranks and column j of p[][].
            for (int k = 0; k < N; k++)
               newRank[j] += rank[k]*p[k][j];
         }

         for (int j = 0; j < N; j++)
            rank[j] = newRank[j];
      }

      for (int i = 0; i < N; i++)    // Print page ranks.
         StdOut.printf("%8.5f", rank[i]);
      StdOut.println();
   }
}
```

T	number of iterations
N	number of pages
p[][]	transition matrix
rank[]	page ranks
newRank[]	new page ranks

This program reads a transition matrix from standard input and computes the probabilities that a random surfer lands on each page (page ranks) after the number of steps specified as command-line argument.

```
% java Transition < tiny.txt | java Markov 20
 0.27245 0.26515 0.14669 0.24764 0.06806

% java Transition < tiny.txt | java Markov 40
 0.27303 0.26573 0.14618 0.24723 0.06783
```

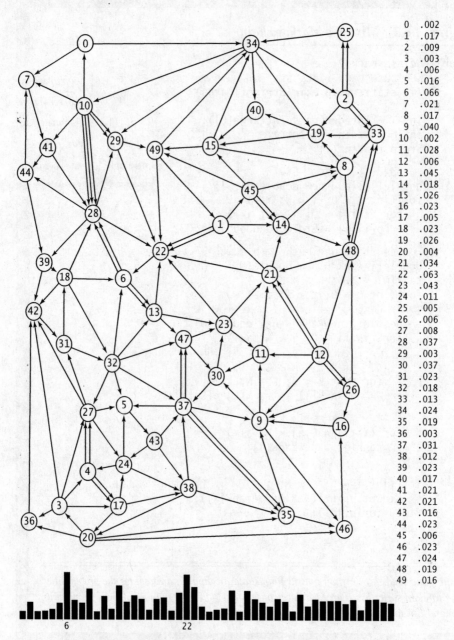

0	.002
1	.017
2	.009
3	.003
4	.006
5	.016
6	.066
7	.021
8	.017
9	.040
10	.002
11	.028
12	.006
13	.045
14	.018
15	.026
16	.023
17	.005
18	.023
19	.026
20	.004
21	.034
22	.063
23	.043
24	.011
25	.005
26	.006
27	.008
28	.037
29	.003
30	.037
31	.023
32	.018
33	.013
34	.024
35	.019
36	.003
37	.031
38	.012
39	.023
40	.017
41	.021
42	.021
43	.016
44	.023
45	.006
46	.023
47	.024
48	.019
49	.016

Page ranks with histogram for a larger example

instead of the tens of thousands of iterations needed by RandomSurfer. Another 20 multiplications gives the results accurate to three decimal places, as compared with millions of iterations for RandomSurfer, and just a few more give the results to full precision (see EXERCISE 1.6.6).

MARKOV CHAINS ARE WELL-STUDIED, BUT THEIR impact on the web was not truly felt until 1998, when two graduate students, Sergey Brin and Lawrence Page, had the audacity to build a Markov chain and compute the probabilities that a random surfer hits each page for *the whole web*. Their work revolutionized web search and is the basis for the page ranking method used by GOOGLE, the highly successful web search company that they founded. Specifically, the company periodically recomputes the random surfer's probability for each page. Then, when you do a search, it lists the pages related to your search keywords in order of these ranks. Such page ranks now predominate because they somehow correspond to the expectations of typical web users, reliably providing them with *relevant* web pages for typical searches. The computation that is involved is enormously time-consuming, due to the huge number of pages on the web, but the result has turned out to be enormously profitable and well worth the expense. The method used in Markov is far more efficient than simulating the behavior of a random surfer, but it is still too slow to actually compute the probabilities for a huge matrix corresponding to all the pages on the web. That computation is enabled by better data structures for graphs (see CHAPTER 4).

Lessons   Developing a full understanding of the random surfer model is beyond the scope of this book. Instead, our purpose is to show you an application that involves writing a bit more code than the short programs that we have been using to teach specific concepts. What specific lessons can we learn from this case study?

We already have a full computational model.   Primitive types of data and strings, conditionals and loops, arrays, and standard input/output enable you to address interesting problems of all sorts. Indeed, it is a basic precept of theoretical computer science that this model suffices to specify any computation that can be performed on any reasonable computing device. In the next two chapters, we discuss two critical ways in which the model has been extended to drastically reduce the amount of time and effort required to develop large and complex programs.

Data-driven code is prevalent. The concept of using standard input and output streams and saving data in files is a powerful one. We write filters to convert from one kind of input to another, generators that can produce huge input files for study, and programs that can handle a wide variety of different models. We can save data for archiving or later use. We can also process data derived from some other source and then save it in a file, whether it is from a scientific instrument or a distant website. The concept of data-driven code is an easy and flexible way to support this suite of activities.

Accuracy can be elusive. It is a mistake to assume that a program produces accurate answers simply because it can print numbers to many decimal places of precision. Often, the most difficult challenge that we face is ensuring that we have accurate answers.

Uniform random numbers are only a start. When we speak informally about random behavior, we often are thinking of something more complicated than the "every value equally likely" model that Math.random() gives us. Many of the problems that we consider involve working with random numbers from other distributions, such as RandomSurfer.

Efficiency matters. It is also a mistake to assume that your computer is so fast that it can do *any* computation. Some problems require much more computational effort than others. CHAPTER 4 is devoted to a thorough discussion of evaluating the performance of the programs that you write. We defer detailed consideration of such issues until then, but remember that you always need to have some general idea of the performance requirements of your programs.

PERHAPS THE MOST IMPORTANT LESSON TO learn from writing programs for complicated problems like the example in this section is that *debugging is difficult.* The polished programs in the book mask that lesson, but you can rest assured that each one is the product of a long bout of testing, fixing bugs, and running the programs on numerous inputs. Generally we avoid describing bugs and the process of fixing them in the text because that makes for a boring account and overly focuses attention on bad code, but you can find some examples and descriptions in the exercises and on the booksite.

Exercises

1.6.1 Modify Transition to take the leap probability from the command line and use your modified version to examine the effect on page ranks of switching to an 80-20 rule or a 95-5 rule.

1.6.2 Modify Transition to ignore the effect of multiple links. That is, if there are multiple links from one page to another, count them as one link. Create a small example that shows how this modification can change the order of page ranks.

1.6.3 Modify Transition to handle pages with no outgoing links, by filling rows corresponding to such pages with the value $1/N$.

1.6.4 The code fragment in RandomSurfer that generates the random move fails if the probabilities in the row p[page] do not add up to 1. Explain what happens in that case, and suggest a way to fix the problem.

1.6.5 Determine, to within a factor of 10, the number of iterations required by RandomSurfer to compute page ranks to four decimal places and to five decimal places for tiny.txt.

1.6.6. Determine the number of iterations required by Markov to compute page ranks to three decimal places, to four decimal places, and to ten decimal places for tiny.txt.

1.6.7 Download the file medium.txt from the booksite (which reflects the 50-page example depicted in this section) and add to it links *from* page 23 *to* every other page. Observe the effect on the page ranks, and discuss the result.

1.6.8 Add to medium.txt (see the previous exercise) links *to* page 23 *from* every other page, observe the effect on the page ranks, and discuss the result.

1.6.9 Suppose that your page is page 23 in medium.txt. Is there a link that you could add from your page to some other page that would *raise* the rank of *your* page?

1.6.10 Suppose that your page is page 23 in medium.txt. Is there a link that you could add from your page to some other page that would *lower* the rank of *that* page?

1.6.11 Use `Transition` and `RandomSurfer` to determine the transition probabilities for the eight-page example shown below.

1.6.12 Use `Transition` and `Markov` to determine the transition probabilities for the eight-page example shown below.

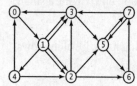

Eight-page example

Creative Exercises

1.6.13 *Matrix squaring.* Write a program like Markov that computes page ranks by repeatedly squaring the matrix, thus computing the sequence p, p^2, p^4, p^8, p^{16}, and so forth. Verify that all of the rows in the matrix converge to the same values.

1.6.14 *Random web.* Write a generator for Transition that takes as input a page count N and a link count M and prints to standard output N followed by M random pairs of integers from 0 to N-1. (See SECTION 4.5 for a discussion of more realistic web models.)

1.6.15 *Hubs and authorities.* Add to your generator from the previous exercise a fixed number of *hubs*, which have links pointing to them from 10% of the pages, chosen at random, and *authorities*, which have links pointing from them to 10% of the pages. Compute page ranks. Which rank higher, hubs or authorities?

1.6.16 *Page ranks.* Design an array of pages and links where the highest-ranking page has fewer links pointing to it than some other page.

1.6.17 *Hitting time.* The hitting time for a page is the expected number of moves between times the random surfer visits the page. Run experiments to estimate page hitting times for tiny.txt, compare with page ranks, formulate a hypothesis about the relationship, and test your hypothesis on medium.txt.

1.6.18 *Cover time.* Write a program that estimates the time required for the random surfer to visit every page at least once, starting from a random page.

1.6.19 *Graphical simulation.* Create a graphical simulation where the size of the dot representing each page is proportional to its rank. To make your program data-driven, design a file format that includes coordinates specifying where each page should be drawn. Test your program on medium.txt.

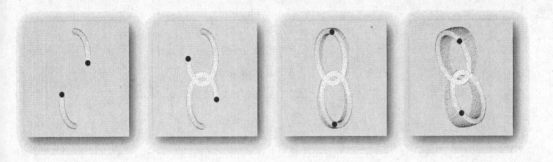

Chapter Two

Functions and Modules

THIS CHAPTER IS CENTERED ON A construct that has as profound an impact on control flow as do conditionals and loops: the *function*, which allows us to transfer control back and forth between different pieces of code. Functions (which are known as *static methods* in Java) are important because they allow us to clearly separate tasks within a program and because they provide a general mechanism that enables us to reuse code.

We group functions together in *modules*, which we can compile independently. We use modules to break a computational task into subtasks of a reasonable size. You will learn in this chapter how to build modules of your own and to use them, in a style of programming known as *modular programming*.

Some modules are developed with the primary intent of providing code that can be reused later by many other programs. We refer to such modules as *libraries*. In particular, we consider in this chapter libraries for generating random numbers, analyzing data, and input/output for arrays. Libraries vastly extend the set of operations that we use in our programs.

We pay special attention to functions that transfer control to themselves. This process is known as *recursion*. At first, recursion may seem counterintuitive, but it allows us to develop simple programs that can address complex tasks that would otherwise be much more difficult to handle.

Whenever you can clearly separate tasks within programs, you should do so. We repeat this mantra throughout this chapter, and end the chapter with an example showing how a complex programming task can be handled by breaking it into smaller subtasks, then independently developing modules that interact with one another to address the subtasks.

2.1   Static Methods

THE JAVA CONSTRUCT FOR IMPLEMENTING FUNCTIONS is known as the *static method*. The modifier `static` distinguishes this kind of method from the kind discussed later in CHAPTER 3—we will apply it consistently for now and discuss the difference then. You have actually been using static methods since the beginning of this book, from printing with `System.out.print-ln()` to mathematical functions such as `Math.abs()` and `Math.sqrt()` to all of the methods in `StdIn`, `StdOut`, `StdDraw`, and `StdAudio`. Indeed, every Java program that you have written has a static method named `main()`. In this section, you will learn how to define and use static methods.

In mathematics, a *function* maps a value of a specified type (the *domain*) to another value of another specified type (the *range*). For example, the function $f(x) = x^2$ maps 2 to 4, 3 to 9, 4 to 16, and so forth. At first, we work with static methods that implement mathematical functions, because they are so familiar. Many standard functions are implemented in Java's `Math` library, but scientists and engineers work with a broad variety of mathematical functions, which cannot all be included in the library. At the beginning of this section, you will learn how to implement and use such functions on your own.

Later, you will learn that we can do more with static methods than implement mathematical functions: static methods can have strings and other types as their range or domain, and they can have side effects such as producing output. We also consider in this section how to use static methods to organize programs and thus to simplify complicated programming tasks.

Static methods support a key concept that will pervade your approach to programming from this point forward: *Whenever you can clearly separate tasks within programs, you should do so.* We will be overemphasizing this point throughout this section and reinforcing it throughout this book. When you write an essay, you break it up into paragraphs; when you write a program, you will break it up into methods. Separating a larger task into smaller ones is much more important in programming than in writing, because it greatly facilitates *debugging*, *maintenance*, and *reuse*, which are all critical in developing good software.

Using and defining static methods

As you know from using Java's Math library, the use of static methods is easy to understand. For example, when you write Math.abs(a-b) in a program, the effect is as if you were to replace that code by the value that is computed by Java's Math.abs() method when presented with the value a-b. This usage is so intuitive that we have hardly needed to comment on it. If you think about what the system has to do to create this effect, you will see that it involves changing a program's *control flow*. The implications of being able to change the control flow in this way is as profound as doing so for conditionals and loops.

You can define static methods other than main() in a .java file, as illustrated in Newton (PROGRAM 2.1.1). This implementation is better than our original implementation of Newton's algorithm (PROGRAM 1.3.6) because it clearly separates the two primary tasks performed by the program: calculating the square root and interacting with the user. *Whenever you can clearly separate tasks within programs, you should do so.* The code here differs from PROGRAM 1.3.6 in two additional respects. First, sqrt() returns Double.NaN when its argument is negative; second, main() tests sqrt() not just for one value, but for all the values given on the command line. A static method must return a well-defined value for each possible argument, and taking multiple command-line arguments facilitates testing that Newton operates as expected for various input values.

While Newton appeals to our familiarity with mathematical functions, we will examine it in detail so that you can think carefully about what a static method is and how it operates.

Control flow. Newton comprises two static methods: sqrt() and main(). Even though sqrt() appears first in the code, the first statement executed when the program is executed is, as always, the first statement in main(). The next few statements operate as usual, except that the code sqrt(a[i]), which is known as a *function call* on the static method sqrt(), causes a *transfer of control* (to the first line of code in sqrt()), each time that it is encountered. Moreover, the value of c within

```
public class Newton
{
    public static double sqrt(double c)
    {
        if (c < 0) return Double.NaN;
        double err = 1e-15;
        double t = c;
        while (Math.abs(t - c/t) > err * t)
            t = (c/t + t) / 2.0;
        return t;
    }

    public static void main(String[] args)
    {
        int N = args.length;
        double[] a = new double[N];
        for (int i = 0; i < N; i++)
            a[i] = Double.parseDouble(args[i]);
        for (int i = 0; i < N; i++)
        {
            double x = sqrt(a[i]);

            StdOut.println(x);
        }
    }
}
```

Flow of control for a call on a static method

Program 2.1.1   Newton's method (revisited)

```java
public class Newton
{
    public static double sqrt(double c)
    {  // Compute the square root of c.
        if (c < 0) return Double.NaN;
        double err = 1e-15;
        double t = c;
        while (Math.abs(t - c/t) > err * t)
            t = (c/t + t) / 2.0;
        return t;
    }

    public static void main(String[] args)
    {  // Print square roots of arguments.
        int N = args.length;
        double[] a = new double[N];
        for (int i = 0; i < N; i++)
            a[i] = Double.parseDouble(args[i]);
        for (int i = 0; i < N; i++)
        {  // Print square root of ith argument.
            double x = sqrt(a[i]);
            StdOut.println(x);
        }
    }
}
```

err	*desired precision*
t	*current estimate*

N	*argument count*
a[]	*argument values*

This program defines two static methods, one named sqrt() *that computes the square root of its argument using Newton's algorithm (see Program 1.3.6) and one named* main(), *which tests* sqrt() *on command-line argument values. The constant values* NaN *and* Infinity *stand for "not a number" and infinity, respectively.*

```
% java Newton 1.0 2.0 3.0 1000000.1
1.0
1.414213562373095
1.7320508075688772
1000.000499999875

% java Newton NaN Infinity 0 -0 -2
NaN
Infinity
0.0
-0.0
NaN
```

sqrt() is initialized to the value of a[i] within main() at the time of the call. Then the statements in sqrt() are executed in sequence, as usual, until reaching a return statement, which transfers control back to the statement in main() containing the call on sqrt(). Moreover, the effect of the call is the same as if sqrt(a[0]) were a variable whose value is the value of t in sqrt() when the return t statement is executed. The end result exactly matches our intuition: the first value assigned to x and printed is precisely the value computed by code in sqrt() (with the value of c initialized to a[0]). Next, the same process transfers control to sqrt again (with the value of c initialized to a[1]), and so forth.

Function call trace. One simple approach to following the control flow through function calls is to imagine that each function prints its name and argument when it is called and its return value just before returning, with indentation added on calls and subtracted on returns. The result is a special case of the process of tracing a program by printing the values of its variables, which we have been using since SECTION 1.2. However, the added indentation exposes the flow of the control, and helps us check that each function has the effect that we expect. Adding calls on StdOut.printf() to trace

```
main({1, 2})
   sqrt(1)
      Math.abs(0)
      return 0.0
   return 1.0
   sqrt(2)
      Math.abs(1.0)
      return 1.0
      Math.abs(1.416666666666667)
      return 1.416666666666667
      ...
   return 1.414213562373095
return
```

Function call trace for java Newton 1 2

a program's control flow in this way is a fine way to begin to understand what it is doing (see EXERCISE 2.1.7). If the return values match our expectations, we need not trace the function code in detail, saving us a substantial amount of work.

Anatomy of a static method. The square root function maps a nonnegative real number to a nonnegative real number; the sqrt() static method in Newton maps a double to a double. The first line of a static method, known as its *signature*, describes this information. The type of the domain is indicated in parentheses after the function name, along with a name called an *argument variable* that we will use to refer to the argument. The type of the range is indicated before the function name—we can put code that calls this function anywhere we could put an expression of that type. We will discuss the meaning of the public keyword in the next section and the meaning of the static keyword in CHAPTER 3. (Technically, the signature in Java does not include these keyword modifiers or the return type, but we

leave that distinction for experts.)
Following the signature is the
body of the method, enclosed
in braces. For sqrt() this code
is the same as we discussed in
SECTION 1.3, except that the last
statement is a return statement,
which causes a transfer of control
back to the point where the static
method was called. For any given
initial value of the argument variable, the method must compute
a return value. The variables that

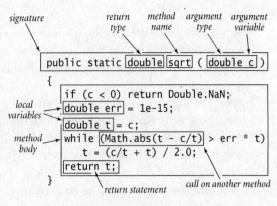

Anatomy of a static method

are declared and used in the body of the method are known as *local variables*. There
are two local variables in sqrt(): err and t. These variables are local to the code in
the body of the method and cannot be used outside of the method.

Properties of static methods   For the rest of this chapter, your programming
will be centered on creating and using static methods, so it is worthwhile to consider in more detail their basic properties.

Terminology. As we have been doing throughout, it is useful to draw a distinction
between abstract concepts and Java mechanisms to implement them (the Java if
statement implements the conditional, the while statement implements the loop,
and so forth). There are several concepts rolled up in the idea of a function, and
Java constructs corresponding to each, as summarized in the following table:

concept	Java construct	description
function	static method	mapping
domain	argument type	set of values where function is defined
range	return type	set of values a function can return
formula	method body	function definition

When we use a symbolic name in a formula that defines a mathematical function
(such as $f(x) = 1 + x + x^2$), the symbol is a placeholder for some value in the domain

that will be substituted into the formula when computing the function value. In Java, the symbol that we use is the name of an argument variable. It represents the particular value of interest where the function is to be evaluated.

Scope. The *scope* of a variable name is the set of statements that can refer to that name. The general rule in Java is that the scope of the variables in a block of statements is limited to the statements in that block. In particular, the scope of a variable in a static method is limited to that method's body. Therefore, you cannot refer to a variable in one static method that is declared in another. If the method includes smaller blocks—for example, the body of an if or a for statement—the scope of any variables declared in one of those blocks is limited to just the statements within the block. Indeed, it is common practice to use the same variable names in independent blocks of code. When we do so, we are declaring different independent variables. For example, we have been following this practice when we use an index i in two different for loops in the same program. A guiding principle when designing software is that each variable should be defined so that its scope is as small as possible. One of the important reasons that we use static methods is that they ease debugging by limiting variable scope.

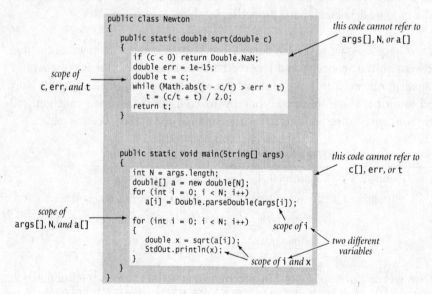

Scope of local and argument variables

Argument variables. You can use argument variables anywhere in the code in the body of the function in the same way you use local variables. The only difference between an argument variable and a local variable is that the argument variable is initialized with the argument value provided by the calling code. This approach is known as *pass by value.* The method works with the *value* of its arguments, not the arguments themselves. One consequence of this approach is that changing the value of an argument variable within a static method has no effect on the calling code. An alternative known as *pass by reference,* where the method actually works with the calling code's variable, is favored in some programming environments (and actually is akin to the way Java works for nonprimitive arguments, as we will see). For clarity, we do not change argument variables in the code in this book: our static methods take the values of argument variables and produce a result.

Multiple methods. You can define as many static methods as you want in a `.java` file. Each has a body that consists of a sequence of statements enclosed in braces. These methods are independent, except that they may refer to each other through calls. They can appear in any order in the file.

Calling other static methods. As evidenced by `main()` calling `sqrt()` and `sqrt()` calling `Math.abs()` in `Newton`, any static method defined in a `.java` file can call any other static method in the same file or any static method in a Java library such as `Math`. Also, as we see in the next section, a static method can call a static method in any `.java` file in the same directory. In SECTION 2.3, we consider the ramifications of the idea that a static method can even call *itself.*

Multiple arguments. Like a mathematical function, a Java static method can take on more than one argument, and therefore can have more than one argument variable. For example, the following method computes the length of the hypotenuse of a right triangle with sides of length a and b:

```
public static double hypotenuse(double a, double b)
{   return Math.sqrt(a*a + b*b);   }
```

Although the argument variables are of the same type in this case, in general they can be of different types. The type and the name of each argument variable is declared in the function signature, separated by commas.

| *absolute value of an* int *value* | ```java
public static int abs(int x)
{
   if (x < 0) return -x;
   else        return  x;
}
``` |
| *absolute value of a* double *value* | ```java
public static double abs(double x)
{
   if (x < 0.0) return -x;
   else          return  x;
}
``` |
| *primality test* | ```java
public static boolean isPrime(int N)
{
   if (N < 2) return false;
   for (int i = 2; i <= N/i; i++)
      if (N % i == 0) return false;
   return true;
}
``` |
| *hypotenuse of a right triangle* | ```java
public static double hypotenuse(double a, double b)
{   return Math.sqrt(a*a + b*b);   }
``` |
| *Harmonic number* | ```java
public static double H(int N)
{
   double sum = 0.0;
   for (int i = 1; i <= N; i++)
      sum += 1.0 / i;
   return sum;
}
``` |
| *uniform random integer in* $[0, N)$ | ```java
public static int uniform(int N)
{   return (int) (Math.random() * N);   }
``` |
| *draw a triangle* | ```java
public static void drawTriangle(double x0, double y0,
                                double x1, double y1,
                                double x2, double y2 )
{
   StdDraw.line(x0, y0, x1, y1);
   StdDraw.line(x1, y1, x2, y2);
   StdDraw.line(x2, y2, x0, y0);
}
``` |

Typical code for implementing functions
```

Overloading. Static methods whose signatures differ are different static methods. For example, we often want to define the same operation for values of different numeric types, as in the following static methods for computing absolute values:

```
public static int abs(int x)
{
   if (x < 0) return -x;
   else       return  x;
}

public static double abs(double x)
{
   if (x < 0.0) return -x;
   else          return  x;
}
```

These are two different methods, but sufficiently similar so as to justify using the same name (abs). Using one name for two static methods whose signatures differ is known as *overloading*, and is common in Java programming. For example, the Java Math library uses this approach to provide implementations of Math.abs(), Math.min(), and Math.max() for all primitive numeric types. Another common use of overloading is to define two different versions of a function, one that takes an argument and another that uses a default value of that argument.

Single return value. Like a mathematical function, a Java static method can provide only one return value, of the type declared in the method signature. This policy is not as restrictive as it might seem. First, you will see in CHAPTER 3 that many types of data in Java can contain more information than a value of a single primitive type. Second, you will see later in this section that we can use arrays as arguments and return values for static methods.

Multiple return statements. Control goes back to the calling program as soon as the first return statement in a static method is reached. You can put return statements wherever you need them, as in sqrt(). Even though there may be multiple return statements, any static method returns a single value each time it is invoked: the value following the first return statement encountered. Some programmers insist on having only one return per function, but we are not so strict in this book.

Side effects. A static method may use the keyword void as its return type, to indicate that it has no return value. An explicit return is not necessary in a void static method: control returns to the caller after the last statement. In this book, we use void static methods for two primary purposes:

  • For I/O, using StdIn, StdOut, StdDraw, and StdAudio
  • To manipulate the contents of arrays

You have been using void static methods for output since main() in HelloWorld, and we will discuss their use with arrays later in this section. A void static method is said to produce *side effects* (consume input, produce output, or otherwise change the state of the system). For example, the main() static method in our programs has a void return type because its purpose is to produce output. It is possible in Java to write methods that have other side effects, but we will avoid doing so until CHAPTER 3, where we do so in a specific manner supported by Java. Technically, void static methods do not implement mathematical functions (and neither does Math.random() or the methods in StdIn, which take no arguments but do produce return values).

Implementing mathematical functions   Why not just use the static methods that are defined within Java, such as Math.sqrt()? The answer to this question is that we *do* use such implementations when they are present. Unfortunately, there are an unlimited number of mathematical functions that we may wish to use and only a small set of basic functions in the library. When you encounter a function that is not in the library, you need to implement a corresponding static method.

   As an example, we consider the kind of code required for a familiar and important application that is of interest to many high school and college students in the United States. In a recent year, over 1 million students took a standard college entrance examination. Scores range from 400 (lowest) to 1600 (highest) on the multiple-choice parts of the test. These scores play a role in making important decisions: for example, student athletes are required to have a score of at least 820, and the minimum eligibility requirement for certain academic scholarships is 1500. What percentage of test takers are ineligible for athletics? What percentage are eligible for the scholarships?

   Two functions from statistics enable us to compute accurate answers to these questions. The *Gaussian (normal) distribution function* is characterized by the familiar bell-shaped curve and defined by the formula $\phi(x) = e^{-x^2/2} / \sqrt{2\pi}$. The *cumulative Gaussian distribution function* $\Phi(z)$ is defined to be the area under the curve defined by $\phi(x)$ above the x-axis and to the left of the vertical line $x = z$. These functions play an important role in science, engineering, and finance because they arise as accurate models throughout the natural world and because they are essential in understanding experimental error.

In particular, these functions are known to accurately describe the distribution of test scores in our example, as a function of the mean (average value of the scores) and the standard deviation (square root of the sum of the squares of the differences between each score and the mean), which are published each year. Given the mean μ and the standard deviation σ of the test scores, the percentage of students with scores less than a given value z is closely approximated by the function $\Phi((z-\mu)/\sigma)$. Static methods to calculate ϕ and Φ are not available in Java's Math library, so we need to develop our own implementations.

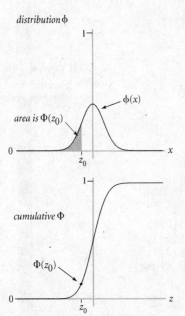

Gaussian probability functions

Closed form. In the simplest situation, we have a closed-form mathematical formula defining our function in terms of functions that are implemented in the library. This situation is the case for ϕ—the Java Math library includes methods to compute the exponential and the square root functions (and a constant value for π), so a static method phi() corresponding to the mathematical definition is easy to implement (see PROGRAM 2.1.2).

No closed form. Otherwise, we may need a more complicated algorithm to compute function values. This situation is the case for Φ—no closed-form expression exists for this function. Such algorithms sometimes follow immediately from Taylor series approximations, but developing reliably accurate implementations of mathematical functions is an art that needs to be addressed carefully, taking advantage of the knowledge built up in mathematics over the past several centuries. Many different approaches have been studied for evaluating Φ. For example, a Taylor series approximation to the ratio of Φ and ϕ turns out to be an effective basis for evaluating the function:

$$\Phi(z) = 1/2 + \phi(z)\,(z + z^3/3 + z^5/(3\cdot5) + z^7/(3\cdot5\cdot7) + \dots\,).$$

Program 2.1.2   *Gaussian functions*

```java
public class Gaussian
{ // Implement Gaussian (normal) distribution functions.
   public static double phi(double x)
   {
      return Math.exp(-x*x/2) / Math.sqrt(2*Math.PI);
   }

   public static double Phi(double z)
   {
      if (z < -8.0) return 0.0;
      if (z >  8.0) return 1.0;
      double sum = 0.0, term = z;
      for (int i = 3; sum != sum + term; i += 2)
      {
         sum  = sum + term;
         term = term * z * z / i;
      }
      return 0.5 + phi(z) * sum;
   }

   public static void main(String[] args)
   {
      double z     = Double.parseDouble(args[0]);
      double mu    = Double.parseDouble(args[1]);
      double sigma = Double.parseDouble(args[2]);
      StdOut.printf("%.3f\n", Phi((z - mu) / sigma));
   }
}
```

| sum | *cumulated sum* |
| term | *current term* |

This code implements the Gaussian (normal) density (phi) and cumulative distribution (Phi) functions, which are not implemented in Java's Math library. The phi() implementation follows directly from its definition, and the Phi() implementation uses a Taylor series and also calls phi() (see accompanying text at left and Exercise 1.3.36).

```
% java Gaussian 820 1019 209
0.171

% java Gaussian 1500 1019 209
0.989

% java Gaussian 1500 1025 231
0.980
```

This formula readily translates to the Java code for the static method Phi() in PRO-GRAM 2.1.2. For small (respectively large) z, the value is extremely close to 0 (respectively 1), so the code directly returns 0 (respectively 1); otherwise, it uses the Taylor series to add terms until the sum converges.

Running Gaussian with the appropriate arguments on the command line tells us that about 17% of the test takers were ineligible for athletics and that only about 1% qualified for the scholarship. In a year when the mean was 1025 and the standard deviation 231, about 2% qualified for the scholarship.

COMPUTING WITH MATHEMATICAL FUNCTIONS OF ALL sorts has always played a central role in science and engineering. In a great many applications, the functions that you need are expressed in terms of the functions in Java's Math library as we have just seen with phi(), or in terms of Taylor series approximations that are easy to compute, as we have just seen with Phi(). Indeed, support for such computations has played a central role throughout the evolution of computing systems and programming languages. You will find many examples on the booksite and throughout this book.

Using static methods to organize code   Beyond evaluating mathematical functions, the process of calculating a result value on the basis of an input value is important as a general technique for organizing control flow in *any* computation. Doing so is a simple example of an extremely important principle that is a prime guiding force for any good programmer: *Whenever you can clearly separate tasks within programs, you should do so.*

Functions are natural and universal for expressing computational tasks. Indeed, the "bird's-eye view" of a Java program that we began with in SECTION 1.1 was equivalent to a function: we began by thinking of a Java program as a function that transforms command-line arguments into an output string. This view expresses itself at many different levels of computation. In particular, it is generally the case that a long program is more naturally expressed in terms of functions instead of as a sequence of Java assignment, conditional, and loop statements. With the ability to define functions, we can better organize our programs by defining functions within them when appropriate.

For example, Coupon (PROGRAM 2.1.3) is a version of CouponCollector (PRO-GRAM 1.4.2) that better separates the individual components of the computation. If you study PROGRAM 1.4.2, you will identify three separate tasks:

Program 2.1.3   Coupon collector (revisited)

```java
public class Coupon
{
   public static int uniform(int N)
   {  // Generate a random integer between 0 and N-1.
      return (int) (Math.random() * N);
   }

   public static int collect(int N)
   {  // Collect coupons until getting one of each value.
      boolean[] found = new boolean[N];
      int cardcnt = 0, valcnt = 0;
      while (valcnt < N)
      {
         int val = uniform(N);
         cardcnt++;
         if (!found[val]) valcnt++;
         found[val] = true;
      }
      return cardcnt;
   }

   public static void main(String[] args)
   {  // Print the number of coupons collected
      // to get N different coupons.
      int N = Integer.parseInt(args[0]);
      int count = collect(N);
      StdOut.println(count);
   }
}
```

found[]	*cumulated sum*
cardcnt	*number collected*
valcnt	*number that differ*
val	*current value*

This version of Program 1.4.2 illustrates the style of encapsulating computations in static methods. This code has the same effect as CouponCollector, *but better separates the code into its three constituent pieces: generating a random integer between 0 and N-1, running a collection experiment, and managing the I/O.*

```
% java Coupon 1000
6522

% java Coupon 1000
6481

% java Coupon 1000000
12783771
```

- Given *N*, compute a random coupon value.
- Given *N*, do the coupon collection experiment.
- Get *N* from the command line, then compute and print the result.

Coupon rearranges the code in CouponCollect to reflect the reality that these three functions underlie the computation.

With this organization, we could change uniform() (for example, we might want to draw the random numbers from a different distribution) or main() (for example, we might want to take multiple inputs or run multiple experiments) without worrying about the effect of any changes on collect().

Using static methods isolates the implementation of each component of the collection experiment from others, or *encapsulates* them. Typically, programs have many independent components, which magnifies the benefits of separating them into different static methods. We will discuss these benefits in further detail after we have seen several other examples, but you certainly can appreciate that it is better to express a computation in a program by breaking it up into functions, just as it is better to express an idea in an essay by breaking it up into paragraphs. *Whenever you can clearly separate tasks within programs, you should do so.*

Implementing static methods for arrays   A static method can take an array as an argument or as a return value. This capability is a special case of Java's object orientation, which is the subject of CHAPTER 3. We consider it in the present context because the basic mechanisms are easy to understand and to use, leading us to compact solutions to a number of problems that naturally arise when we use arrays to help us process large amounts of data.

Arrays as arguments. When a static method takes an array as an argument, it implements a function that operates on an arbitrary number of values of the same type. For example, the following static method computes the mean (average) value of an array of double values.

```
public static double mean(double[] a)
{
    double sum = 0.0;
    for (int i = 0; i < a.length; i++)
        sum = sum + a[i];
    return sum / a.length;
}
```

We have been using arrays as arguments from the beginning. The code

```java
public static void main(String[] args)
```

defines `main()` as a static method that takes an array of strings as an argument and returns nothing. By convention, the Java system collects the strings that you type after the program name in the `java` command into an array `args[]` and calls `main()` with that array as argument. (Most programmers use the name `args` for the argument variable, even though any name at all would do.) Within `main()`, we can manipulate that array just like any other array. The `main()` method in Newton (PROGRAM 2.1.1) is an example of such code.

Side effects with arrays. It is often the case that the purpose of a static method that takes an array as argument is to produce a side effect (change values of array elements). A prototypical example of such a method is one that exchanges the values at two given indices in a given array. We can adapt the code that we examined at the beginning of SECTION 1.4:

```java
public static void exch(String[] a, int i, int j)
{
   String t = a[i];
   a[i] = a[j];
   a[j] = t;
}
```

This implementation stems naturally from the Java array representation. The argument variable in `exch()` is a reference to the array, not to all of the array's values: when you pass an array as argument to a static method, you are giving it the opportunity to operate on that array (not a copy of it). A second prototypical example of a static method that takes an array argument and produces side effects is one that randomly shuffles the values in the array, using this version of the algorithm that we examined in SECTION 1.4 (and the `exch()` and `uniform()` methods just defined):

```java
public static void shuffle(String[] a)
{
   int N = a.length;
   for (int i = 0; i < N; i++)
      exch(a, i, i + uniform(N-i));
}
```

| *find the maximum of the array values* | ```java
public static double max(double[] a)
{
   double max = Double.NEGATIVE_INFINITY;
   for (int i = 0; i < a.length; i++)
      if (a[i] > max) max = a[i];
   return max;
}
``` |
| *dot product* | ```java
public static double dot(double[] a, double[] b)
{
   double sum = 0.0;
   for (int i = 0; i < a.length; i++)
      sum += a[i] * b[i];
   return sum;
}
``` |
| *exchange two elements in an array* | ```java
public static void exch(String[] a, int i, int j)
{
   String t = a[i];
   a[i] = a[j];
   a[j] = t;
}
``` |
| *print a 1D array (and its length)* | ```java
public static void print(double[] a)
{
   StdOut.println(a.length);
   for (int i = 0; i < a.length; i++)
      StdOut.println(a[i]);
}
``` |
| *read a 2D array of double values (with dimensions) in row-major order* | ```java
public static double[][] readDouble2D()
{
   int M = StdIn.readInt();
   int N = StdIn.readInt();
   double[][] a = new double[M][N];
   for (int i = 0; i < M; i++)
      for (int j = 0; j < N; j++)
         a[i][j] = StdIn.readDouble();
   return a;
}
``` |

Typical code for implementing functions with arrays
```

Similarly, we will consider in SECTION 4.2 methods that *sort* an array (rearrange its values so that they are in order). All of these examples highlight the basic fact that the mechanism for passing arrays in Java is a *call-by-reference* mechanism with respect to the contents of the array. Unlike primitive-type arguments, the changes that a method makes in the contents of an array *are* reflected in the client program. A method that takes an array as argument cannot change the array itself—the reference is the same memory location assigned when the array was created, and the length is the value set when the array was created—but it can change the contents of the array to any values whatsoever.

Arrays as return values. A method that sorts, shuffles, or otherwise modifies an array taken as argument does not have to return a reference to that array, because it is changing the contents of a client array, not a copy. But there are many situations where it is useful for a static method to provide an array as a return value. Chief among these are static methods that create arrays for the purpose of returning multiple values of the same type to a client. For example, the following static method produces an array of the kind used by StdAudio (see PROGRAM 1.5.7) that contains values sampled from a sine wave of a given frequency (in hertz) and duration (in seconds), sampled at the standard 44,100 samples per second.

```
public static double[] tone(double hz, double t)
{
    int sps = 44100;
    int N = (int) (sps * t);
    double[] a = new double[N+1];
    for (int i = 0; i <= N; i++)
        a[i] = Math.sin(2 * Math.PI * i * hz / sps);
    return a;
}
```

In this code, the size of the array returned depends on the duration: if the given duration is t, the size of the array is about 44100*t. With static methods like this one, we can write code that treats a sound wave as a single entity (an array containing sampled values), as we will see next in PROGRAM 2.1.4.

Example: superposition of sound waves   As discussed in SECTION 1.5, the simple audio model that we studied there needs to be embellished in order to create sound that resembles the sound produced by a musical instrument. Many different embellishments are possible; with static methods we can systematically apply them to produce sound waves that are far more complicated than the simple sine waves that we produced in SECTION 1.5. As an illustration of the effective use of static methods to solve an interesting computational problem, we consider a program that has essentially the same functionality as PlayThatTune (PROGRAM 1.5.7), but adds harmonic tones one octave above and one octave below each note in order to produce a more realistic sound.

Chords and harmonics.   Notes like concert *A* have a pure sound that is not very musical, because the sounds that you are accustomed to hearing have many other components. The sound from the guitar string echoes off the wooden part of the instrument, the walls of the room that you are in, and so forth. You may think of such effects as modifying the basic sine wave. For example, most musical instruments produce harmonics (the same note in different octaves and not as loud), or you might play chords (multiple notes at the same time). To combine multiple sounds, we use *superposition*: simply add their waves together and rescale to make sure that all values stay between -1 and $+1$. As it turns out, when

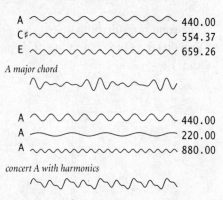

Superposing waves to make composite sounds

we superpose sine waves of different frequencies in this way, we can get arbitrarily complicated waves. Indeed, one of the triumphs of 19th century mathematics was the development of the idea that any smooth periodic function can be expressed as a sum of sine and cosine waves, known as a *Fourier series*. This mathematical idea corresponds to the notion that we can create a large range of sounds with musical instruments or our vocal chords and that all sound consists of a composition of various oscillating curves. Any sound corresponds to a curve and any curve corresponds to a sound, and we can create arbitrarily complex curves with superposition.

Superposition. Since we represent sound waves by arrays of numbers that represent their values at the same sample points, superposition is simple to implement: we add together their sample values at each sample point to produce the combined result and then rescale. For greater control, we specify a relative weight for each of the two waves to be added, with the property that the weights are positive and sum to 1. For example, if we want the first sound to have three times the effect of the second, we would assign the first a weight of .75 and the second a weight of .25. Now, if one wave is in an array a[] with relative weight awt and the other is in an array b[] with relative weight bwt, we compute their weighted sum with the following code:

```
double[] c = new double[a.length];
for (int i = 0; i < a.length; i++)
    c[i] = a[i]*awt + b[i]*bwt;
```

The conditions that the weights are positive and sum to 1 ensure that this operation preserves our convention of keeping the values of all of our waves between -1 and $+1$.

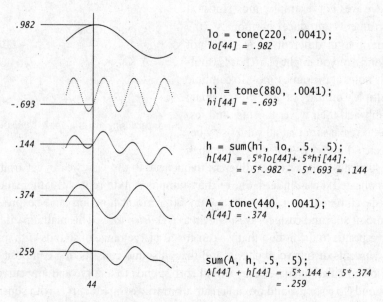

```
lo = tone(220, .0041);
lo[44] = .982

hi = tone(880, .0041);
hi[44] = -.693

h = sum(hi, lo, .5, .5);
h[44] = .5*lo[44]+.5*hi[44];
     = .5*.982 - .5*.693 = .144

A = tone(440, .0041);
A[44] = .374

sum(A, h, .5, .5);
A[44] + h[44] = .5*.144 + .5*.374
             = .259
```

Adding harmonics to concert A (180 samples at 44,100 samples/sec)

PROGRAM 2.1.4 IS AN IMPLEMENTATION THAT applies these concepts to produce a more realistic sound than that produced by PROGRAM 1.5.7. In order to do so, it makes use of functions to divide the computation into four parts:

- Given a frequency and duration, create a pure tone.
- Given two sound waves and relative weight, superpose them.
- Given a pitch and duration, create a note with harmonics.
- Read and play a sequence of pitch/duration pairs from standard input.

These tasks are each amenable to implementation as functions, which depend on one another. Each function is well-defined and straightforward to implement. All of them (and StdAudio) represent sound as a series of discrete values kept in an array, corresponding to sampling a sound wave at 44,100 samples per second.

Up to this point, the use of functions has been somewhat of a notational convenience. For example, the control flow in PROGRAMS 2.1.1–2.1.3 is simple—each function is called in just one place in the code. By contrast, PROGRAM 2.1.4 is a convincing example of the effectiveness of defining functions to organize a computation because

```
public class PlayThatTune
{
    public static double[] sum(double[] a, double[] b,
                               double awt, double bwt)
    {
        double[] c = new double[a.length];
        for (int i = 0; i < a.length; i++)
            c[i] = a[i]*awt + b[i]*bwt;
        return c;
    }

    public static double[] tone(double hz, double t)
    {
        int sps = 44100;
        int N = (int) (sps * t);
        double[] a = new double[N+1];
        for (int i = 0; i <= N; i++)
            a[i] = Math.sin(2 * Math.PI * i * hz / sps);
        return a;
    }

    public static double[] note(int pitch, double t)
    {
        double hz = 440.0 * Math.pow(2, pitch / 12.0);
        double[] a  = tone(hz, t);
        double[] hi = tone(2*hz, t);
        double[] lo = tone(hz/2, t);
        double[] h  = sum(hi, lo, .5, .5);
        return sum(a, h, .5, .5);
    }

    public static void main(String[] args)
    {
        while (!StdIn.isEmpty())
        {
            int pitch = StdIn.readInt();
            double duration = StdIn.readDouble();
            double[] a = note(pitch, duration);
            StdAudio.play(a);
        }
    }
}
```

Flow of control among several static methods

the functions are each called multiple times. For example, the function note() calls the function tone() three times and the function sum() twice. Without static methods, we would need multiple copies of the code in tone() and sum(); with

Program 2.1.4 *Play that Tune (revisited)*

```
public class PlayThatTune
{
   public static double[] sum(double[] a, double[] b,
                              double awt, double bwt)
   {  // Superpose a and b, weighted.
      double[] c = new double[a.length];
      for (int i = 0; i < a.length; i++)
         c[i] = a[i]*awt + b[i]*bwt;
      return c;.
   }

   public static double[] tone(double hz, double t)
      // see text

   public static double[] note(int pitch, double t)
   {  // Play note of given pitch, with harmonics.
      double hz = 440.0 * Math.pow(2, pitch / 12.0);
      double[] a  = tone(hz, t);
      double[] hi = tone(2*hz, t);
      double[] lo = tone(hz/2, t);
      double[] h  = sum(hi, lo, .5, .5);
      return sum(a, h, .5, .5);
   }

   public static void main(String[] args)
   {  // Read and play a tune, with harmonics.
      while (!StdIn.isEmpty())
      {  // Read and play a note, with harmonics.
         int pitch = StdIn.readInt();
         double duration = StdIn.readDouble();
         double[] a = note(pitch, duration);
         StdAudio.play(a);
      }
   }
}
```

hz	frequency
a[]	pure tone
hi[]	upper harmonic
lo[]	lower harmonic
h[]	tone with harmonics

This code embellishes the sounds produced by Program 1.5.7 by using static methods to create harmonics, which results in a more realistic sound than the pure tone.

```
% more elise.txt
7 .25
6 .25
7 .25
6 .25
7 .25
...
```

```
% java PlayThatTune < elise.txt
```

static methods, we can deal directly with concepts close to the application. As with loops, methods have a simple but profound effect: we have one sequence of statements (those in the method definition) executed multiple times during the execution of our program—once for each time the method is called in the control flow in main().

STATIC METHODS ARE IMPORTANT BECAUSE THEY give us the ability to *extend* the Java language within a program. Having implemented and debugged static methods such as sqrt(), phi(), Phi(), mean(), abs(), exch(), shuffle(), isPrime(), H(), uniform(), sum(), note(), and tone(), we can use them almost as if they were built into Java. The flexibility to do so opens up a whole new world of programming. Before, you were safe in thinking about a Java program as a sequence of statements. Now you need to think of a Java program as a *set of static methods* that can call one another. The statement-to-statement control flow to which you have been accustomed is still present within static methods, but programs have a higher-level control flow defined by static method calls and returns. This ability enables you to think in terms of operations called for by the application, not just the simple arithmetic operations on primitive types that are built in to Java.

Whenever you can clearly separate tasks within programs, you should do so. The examples in this section (and the programs throughout the rest of the book) clearly illustrate the benefits of adhering to this maxim. With static methods, we can

- Divide a long sequence of statements into independent parts.
- Reuse code without having to copy it.
- Work with higher-level concepts (such as sound waves).

This produces code that is easier to understand, maintain, and debug than a long program composed solely of Java assignment, conditional, and loop statements. In the next section, we discuss the idea of using static methods defined in *other* programs, which again takes us to another level of programming.

Q. Why do I need to use the return type void? Why not just omit the return type?

A. Java requires it; we have to include it. Second-guessing a decision made by a programming-language designer is the first step on the road to becoming one.

Q. Can I return from a void function by using return? If so, what return value should I use?

A. Yes. Use the statement return; with no return value.

Q. What happens if I leave out the keyword static?

A. As usual, the best way to answer a question like this is to try it yourself and see what happens. Here is the result of omitting static for sqrt() in Newton:

```
Newton.java:13: non-static method sqrt(double)
cannot be referenced from a static context
        double x = sqrt(i);
                   ^
1 error
```

Non-static methods are different from static methods. You will learn about the former in CHAPTER 3.

Q. What happens if I write code after a return statement?

A. Once a return statement is reached, control immediately returns to the caller, so any code after a return statement is useless. The Java compiler identifies this situation as an error, reporting unreachable code.

Q. What happens if I do not include a return statement?

A. No problem, if the return type is void. In this case, control will return to the caller after the last statement. When the return type is not void, the compiler will report a missing return statement error if there is *any* path through the code that does not end in a return.

Q. This issue with side effects and arrays passed as arguments in confusing. Is it really all that important?

A. Yes. Properly controlling side effects is one of a programmer's most important tasks in large systems. Taking the time to be sure that you understand the difference between passing a value (when arguments are of a primitive type) and passing a reference (when arguments are arrays) will certainly be worthwhile. The very same mechanism is used for all other types of data, as you will learn in CHAPTER 3.

Q. So why not just eliminate the possibility of side effects by making all arguments pass-by-value, including arrays?

A. Think of a huge array with, say, millions of elements. Does it make sense to copy all of those values for a static method that is just going to exchange two of them? For this reason, most programming languages support passing an array to a function without creating a copy of the array elements—MATLAB is a notable exception.

Exercises

2.1.1 Write a static method max3() that takes three int values as arguments and returns the value of the largest one. Add an overloaded function that does the same thing with three double values.

2.1.2 Write a static method odd() that takes three boolean inputs and returns true if an odd number of inputs are true, and false otherwise.

2.1.3 Write a static method majority() that takes three boolean arguments and returns true if at least two of the arguments have the value true, and false otherwise. Do not use an if statement.

2.1.4 Write a static method eq() that takes two arrays of integers as arguments and returns true if they contain the same number of elements and all corresponding pairs of elements are equal.

2.1.5 Write a static method areTriangular() that takes three double values as arguments and returns true if they could be the sides of a triangle (none of them is greater than or equal to the sum of the other two). See EXERCISE 1.2.15.

2.1.6 Write a static method sigmoid() that takes a double argument x and returns the double value obtained from the formula $1/(1-e^{-x})$.

2.1.7 If the argument of sqrt() in Newton (PROGRAM 2.1.1) has the value Infinity, then Newton.sqrt() returns the value Infinity, as desired. Explain why.

2.1.8 Add a method abs() to Newton (PROGRAM 2.1.1), change sqrt() to use abs() instead of Math.abs(), and add print statements to produce a function call trace, as described in the text. *Hint*: You need to add an argument to each function to give the level of indentation.

2.1.9 Give the function call trace for java Newton 4.0 9.0.

2.1.10 Write a static method lg() that takes a double value N as argument and returns the base 2 logarithm of N. You may use Java's Math library.

2.1.11 Write a static method lg() that takes an int value N as argument and returns the largest int not larger than the base-2 logarithm of N. Do *not* use Math.

2.1.12 Write a static method `signum()` that takes an `int` value N as argument and returns -1 if N is less than 0, 0 if N is equal to 0, and +1 if N is greater than 0.

2.1.13 Consider the static method `duplicate()` below.

```
public static String duplicate(String s)
{
    String t = s + s;
    return t;
}
```

What does the following code fragment do?

```
String s = "Hello";
s = duplicate(s);
String t = "Bye";
t = duplicate(duplicate(duplicate(t)));
StdOut.println(s + t);
```

2.1.14 Consider the static method `cube()` below.

```
public static void cube(int i)
{
    i = i * i * i;
}
```

How many times is the following for loop iterated?

```
for (int i = 0; i < 1000; i++)
    cube(i);
```

Answer: Just 1,000 times. A call to `cube()` has no effect on client code. It changes the value of its local argument variable `i`, but that change has no effect on the `i` in the for loop, which is a different variable. If you replace the call to `cube(i)` with the statement `i = i * i * i;` (maybe that was what you were thinking), then the loop is iterated five times, with `i` taking on the values 0, 1, 2, 9, and 730 at the beginning of the five iterations.

2.1.15 The following *checksum* formula is widely used by banks and credit card

companies to validate legal account numbers:

$$d_0 + f(d_1) + d_2 + f(d_3) + d_4 + f(d_5) + \ldots = 0 \pmod{10}$$

The d_i are the decimal digits of the account number and $f(d)$ is the sum of the decimal digits of $2d$ (for example, $f(7) = 5$ because $2\times7 = 14$ and $1+ 4 = 5$). For example 17327 is valid because $1+5+3+4+7=20$, which is a multiple of 10. Implement the function f and write a program to take a 10-digit integer as a command-line argument and print a valid 11-digit number with the given integer as its first 10 digits and the checksum as the last digit.

2.1.16 Given two stars with angles of declination and right ascension (d_1, a_1) and (d_2, a_2), the angle they subtend is given by the formula

$$2 \arcsin((\sin^2(d/2) + \cos(d_1)\cos(d_2)\sin^2(a/2))^{1/2}),$$

where a_1 and a_2 are angles between -180 and 180 degrees, d_1 and d_2 are angles between -90 and 90 degrees, $a = a_2 - a_1$, and $d = d_2 - d_1$. Write a program to take the declination and right ascension of two stars as command-line arguments and print the angle they subtend. *Hint*: Be careful about converting from degrees to radians.

2.1.17 Write a readBoolean2D() method that reads a two-dimensional boolean matrix (with dimensions) into an array.

Solution: The body of the method is virtually the same as for the corresponding method given in the table in the text for 2D arrays of double values:

```
public static boolean[][] readBoolean2D()
{
    int M = StdIn.readInt();
    int N = StdIn.readInt();
    boolean[][] a = new boolean[M][N];
    for (int i = 0; i < M; i++)
        for (int j = 0; j < N; j++)
            a[i][j] = StdIn.readBoolean();
    return a;
}
```

Note that StdIn accepts 0 and 1 as boolean values in the input stream.

2.1.18 Write a method that takes an array of double values as argument and re-

scales the array so that each element is between 0 and 1 (by subtracting the minimum value from each element and then dividing each element by the difference between the minimum and maximum values). Use the max() method defined in the table in the text, and write and use a matching min() method.

2.1.19 Write a method histogram() that takes an array a[] of int values and an integer M as argument and returns an array of length M whose ith entry is the number of times the integer i appeared in the argument array. If the values in a[] are all between 0 and M-1, the sum of the values in the returned array should be equal to a.length.

2.1.20 Assemble code fragments in this section and in SECTION 1.4 to develop a program that takes N from the command line and prints N five-card hands, separated by blank lines, drawn from a randomly shuffled card deck, one card per line using card names like Ace of Clubs.

2.1.21 Write a method multiply() that takes two square matrices of the same dimension as arguments and produces their product (another square matrix of that same dimension). *Extra credit*: Make your program work whenever the number of rows in the first matrix is equal to the number of columns in the second matrix.

2.1.22 Write a method any() that takes an array of boolean values as argument and returns true if any of the entries in the array is true, and false otherwise. Write a method all() that takes an array of boolean values as argument and returns true if all of the entries in the array are true, and false otherwise.

2.1.23 Develop a version of getCoupon() that better models the situation when one of the coupons is rare: choose one value at random, return that value with probability $N/1000$, and return all other values with equal probability. *Extra credit*: How does this change affect the average value of the coupon collector function?

2.1.24 Modify PlayThatTune to add harmonics two octaves away from each note, with half the weight of the one-octave harmonics.

Creative Exercises

2.1.25 *Birthday problem.* Develop a class with appropriate static methods for studying the birthday problem (see EXERCISE 1.4.35).

2.1.26 *Euler's totient function.* Euler's totient function is an important function in number theory: $\varphi(n)$ is defined as the number of positive integers less than or equal to n that are relatively prime with n (no factors in common with n other than 1). Write a class with a function that takes an integer argument n and returns $\varphi(n)$, and a main() that takes an integer from the command line, calls the function, and prints the result.

2.1.27 *Harmonic numbers.* Write a program Harmonic that contains three static methods H(), Hsmall(), and Hlarge() for computing the Harmonic numbers. The Hsmall() method should just compute the sum (as in PROGRAM 1.3.5), the Hlarge() method should use the approximation $H_N = \log_e(N) + \gamma + 1/(2N) - 1/(12N^2) + 1/(120N^4)$ (the number $\gamma = .577215664901532...$ is known as *Euler's constant*), and the H() method should call Hsmall() for $N < 100$ and Hlarge() otherwise.

2.1.28 *Gaussian random values.* Experiment with the following method for generating random variables from the Gaussian distribution, which is based on generating a random point in the unit circle and using a form of the Box-Muller formula (see EXERCISE 1.2.27 and the discussion of do-while at the end of SECTION 1.3).

```
public static double gaussian()
{
    double r, x, y;
    do
    {
        x = uniform(-1.0, 1.0);
        y = uniform(-1.0, 1.0);
        r = x*x + y*y;
    } while (r >= 1 || r == 0);
    return x * Math.sqrt(-2 * Math.log(r) / r);
}
```

Take a command-line argument N and generate N random numbers, using an array a[20] to count the numbers generated that fall between i*.05 and (i+1)*.05 for

i from 0 to 19. Then use StdDraw to plot the values and to compare your result with the normal bell curve.

2.1.29 *Binary search.* A general method that we study in detail in SECTION 4.2 is effective for computing the inverse of a cumulative probability density function like Phi(). Such functions are continuous and nondecreasing from $(0,0)$ to $(1,1)$. To find the value x_0 for which $f(x_0) = y_0$, check the value of $f(.5)$. If it is greater than y_0, then x_0 must be between 0 and .5; otherwise, it must be between .5 and 1. Either way, we halve the length of the interval known to contain x_0. Iterating, we can compute x_0 to within a given tolerance. Add a method PhiInverse() to Gaussian that uses binary search to compute the inverse. Change main() to take a number p between 0 and 100 as a third command-line argument and print the minimum score that a student would need to be in the top p percent of students taking the SAT in a year when the mean and standard deviation were the first two command-line arguments.

2.1.30 *Black-Scholes option valuation.* The Black-Scholes formula supplies the theoretical value of a European call option on a stock that pays no dividends, given the current stock price s, the exercise price x, the continuously compounded risk-free interest rate r, the standard deviation σ of the stock's return (volatility), and the time (in years) to maturity t. The value is given by the formula $s\,\Phi(a) - xe^{-rt}\Phi(b)$, where $\Phi(z)$ is the Gaussian cumulative distribution function, $a = (\ln(s/x) + (r + \sigma^2/2)\,t)/(\sigma\sqrt{t})$, and $b = a - \sigma\sqrt{t}$. Write a program that takes $s, x, r, \texttt{sigma}$, and t from the command line and prints the Black-Scholes value.

2.1.31 *Implied volatility.* Typically the volatility is the unknown value in the Black-Scholes formula. Write a program that reads s, x, r, t, and the current price of the European call option from the command line and uses binary search (see EXERCISE 2.1.29) to compute σ.

2.1.32 *Horner's method.* Write a class Horner with a method double eval (double x, double[] p) that evaluates the polynomial $p(x)$ whose coefficients are the entries in p[]:

$$p_0 + p_1 x^1 + p_2 x^2 + \ldots + p_{N-2} x^{N-2} + p_{N-1} x^{N-1}$$

Use *Horner's method*, an efficient way to perform the computations that is suggested by the following parenthesization:

$$p_0 + x\,(p_1 + x\,(p_2 + \ldots + x\,(p_{N-2} + xp_{N-1})) \ldots)$$

Write a test client with a static method exp() that uses Horner.eval() to compute an approximation to e^x, using the first N terms of the Taylor series expansion $e^x = 1 + x + x^2/2! + x^3/3! + \ldots$. Take an argument x from the command-line, and compare your result against that computed by Math.exp(x).

2.1.33 *Benford's law.* The American astronomer Simon Newcomb observed a quirk in a book that compiled logarithm tables: the beginning pages were much grubbier than the ending pages. He suspected that scientists performed more computations with numbers starting with 1 than with 8 or 9, and postulated the first digit law, which says that under general circumstances, the leading digit is much more likely to be 1 (roughly 30%) than the digit 9 (less than 4%). This phenomenon is known as *Benford's law* and is now often used as a statistical test. For example, IRS forensic accountants rely on it to discover tax fraud. Write a program that reads in a sequence of integers from standard input and tabulates the number of times each of the digits 1–9 is the leading digit, breaking the computation into a set of appropriate static methods. Use your program to test the law on some tables of information from your computer or from the web. Then, write a program to foil the IRS by generating random amounts from \$1.00 to \$1,000.00 with the same distribution that you observed.

2.1.34 *Binomial distribution.* Write a function

```
public static double binomial(int N, int k, double p)
```

to compute the probability of obtaining exactly k heads in N biased coin flips (heads with probability p) using the formula

$$f(N, k, p) = p^k(1-p)^{N-k}\,N!\,/\,(k!(N-k)!).$$

Hint: To stave off overflow, compute $x = \ln f(N, k, p)$ and then return e^x. In main(), take N and p from the command line and check that the sum over all values of k between 0 and N is (approximately) 1. Also, compare every value computed with the normal approximation

$$f(N, k, p) \approx \phi(Np, Np(1-p))$$

(see EXERCISE 2.2.1).

2.1.35 *Coupon collecting from a binomial distribution.* Develop a version of get-Coupon() that uses binomial() from the previous exercise to return coupon values according to the binomial distribution with $p = 1/2$. *Hint*: Generate a uniformly distributed random number x between 0 and 1, then return the smallest value of k for which the sum of $f(N, j, p)$ for all $j < k$ exceeds x. *Extra credit*: Develop a hypothesis for describing the behavior of the coupon collector function under this assumption.

2.1.36 *Chords.* Develop a version of PlayThatTune that can handle songs with chords (including harmonics). Develop an input format that allows you to specify different durations for each chord and different amplitude weights for each note within a chord. Create test files that exercise your program with various chords and harmonics, and create a version of *Für Elise* that uses them.

0 |I|₁₁
1 ₁₁₁II
2 ₁₁I₁I
3 ₁₁II₁
4 ₁I₁₁I
5 ₁I₁I₁
6 ₁III₁₁
7 I₁₁₁I
8 I₁₁I₁
9 I₁I₁₁

2.1.37 *Postal bar codes.* The barcode used by the U.S. Postal System to route mail is defined as follows: Each decimal digit in the zip code is encoded using a sequence of three half-height and two full-height bars. The barcode starts and ends with a full-height bar (the guard rail) and includes a checksum digit (after the five-digit zip code or ZIP+4), computed by summing up the original digits modulo 10. Implement the following functions

• Draw a half-height or full-height bar on StdDraw.
• Given a digit, draw its sequence of bars.
• Compute the checksum digit.

and a test client that reads in a five- (or nine-) digit zip code as the command-line argument and draws the corresponding postal bar code.

2.1.38 *Calendar.* Write a program Calendar that takes two command-line arguments M and Y and prints out the monthly calendar for the Mth month of year Y, as in this example:

```
% java Calendar 2 2009
February 2009
 S  M Tu  W Th  F  S
 1  2  3  4  5  6  7
 8  9 10 11 12 13 14
15 16 17 18 19 20 21
22 23 24 25 26 27 28
```

Hint: See LeapYear (PROGRAM 1.2.4) and EXERCISE 1.2.29.

2.1.39 *Fourier spikes.* Write a program that takes a command-line argument N and plots the function

$$(\cos(t) + \cos(2t) + \cos(3t) + \ldots + \cos(Nt)) / N$$

for 500 equally spaced samples of t from -10 to 10 (in radians). Run your program for $N = 5$ and $N = 500$. *Note*: You will observe that the sum converges to a spike (0 everywhere except a single value). This property is the basis for a proof that *any* smooth function can be expressed as a sum of sinusoids.

2.2 Libraries and Clients

EACH PROGRAM THAT YOU HAVE WRITTEN consists of Java code that resides in a single .java file. For large programs, keeping all the code in a single file in this way is restrictive and unnecessary. Fortunately, it is very easy in Java to refer to a method in one file that is defined in another. This ability has two important consequences on our style of programming.

First, it enables *code reuse*. One program can make use of code that is already written and debugged, not by copying the code, but just by referring to it. This ability to define code that can be reused is an essential part of modern programming. It amounts to extending Java—you can define and use your own operations on data.

Second, it enables *modular programming*. You can not only divide a program up into static methods, as just described in SECTION 2.1, but also keep them in different files, grouped together according to the needs of the application. Modular programming is important because it allows us to *independently* develop, compile, and debug parts of big programs one piece at a time, leaving each finished piece in its own file for later use without having to worry about its details again. We develop libraries of static methods for use by any other program, keeping each library in its own file and using its methods in any other program. Java's Math library and our Std* libraries for input/output are examples that you have already used. More important, you will soon see that it is very easy to define libraries of your own. The ability to define libraries and then to use them in multiple programs is a critical ingredient in our ability to build programs to address complex tasks.

Having just moved in SECTION 2.1 from thinking of a Java program as a sequence of statements to thinking of a Java program as a class comprising a set of methods (one of which is main()), you will be ready after this section to think of a Java program as a set of *classes*, each of which is an independent module consisting of a set of methods. Since each method can call a method in another class, all of your code can interact as a network of methods that call one another, grouped together in classes. With this capability, you can start to think about managing complexity when programming by breaking up programming tasks into classes that can be implemented and tested independently.

Using static methods in other programs   To refer to a static method in one class that is defined in another, we use the same mechanism that we have been using to invoke methods such as StdOut.printf() and StdAudio.play():

• Keep both classes in the same directory in your computer.

• To call a method, prepend its class name and a period separator.

For example, consider Gaussian (PROGRAM 2.1.2). The definition of one of its methods requires the square root function. For purposes of illustration, suppose that we wish to use the sqrt() implementation from Newton (PROGRAM 2.1.1). All that we need to do is to keep Gaussian.java in the same directory as Newton.java and prepend the class name when calling sqrt(). If we want to use the standard

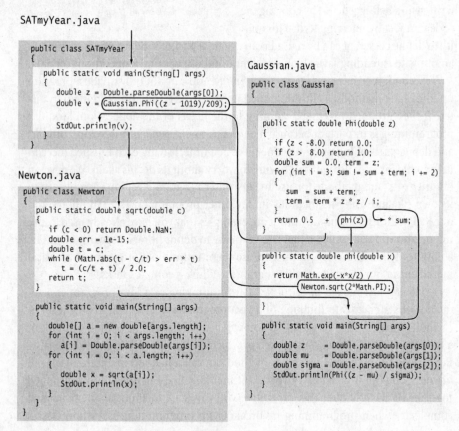

A modular program

Java implementation, we call Math.sqrt(); if we want to use our own implementation, we call Newton.sqrt(). Moreover, any other class in that directory can make use of the methods defined in Gaussian, by calling Gaussian.phi() or Gaussian.Phi(). For example, we might wish to have a simple client SATmyYear.java that takes a value z from the command line and prints $\Phi((z-1019)/209)$, so that we do not need to type in the mean and standard deviation each time we want to know the percentage scoring less than a given value for a certain year. The files Gaussian.java, Newton.java, and SATmyYear.java implement Java classes that interact with one another: SATmyYear calls a method in Gaussian, which calls a method that calls a method in Newton.

The potential effect of programming by defining multiple files, each an independent class with multiple methods, is another profound change in our programming style. Generally, we refer to this approach as *modular programming*. We independently develop and debug methods for an application and then utilize them at any later time. In this section, we will consider numerous illustrative examples to help you get used to the idea. However, there are several details about the process that we need to discuss before considering more examples.

The public *keyword.* We have been identifying every method as public since HelloWorld. This modifier identifies the method as available for use by any other program with access to the file. You can also identify methods as private (and there are a few other categories), but you have no reason to do so at this point. We will discuss various options in SECTION 3.3.

Each module is a class. We use the term *module* to refer to all the code that we keep in a single file. In Java, by convention, each module is a Java class that is kept in a file with the same name of the class but has a .java extension. In this chapter, each class is merely a set of static methods (one of which is main()). You will learn much more about the general structure of the Java class in CHAPTER 3.

The .class *file.* When you compile the program (by typing javac followed by the class name), the Java compiler makes a file with the class name followed by a .class extension that has the code of your program in a language more suited to your computer. If you have a .class file, you can use the module's methods in another program even without having the source code in the corresponding .java file (but you are on your own if you discover a bug!).

Compile when necessary. When you compile a program, the Java compiler will compile everything that needs to be compiled in order to run that program. If you call Newton.sqrt() in Gaussian, then, when you type javac Gaussian.java, the compiler will also check whether you modified Newton.java since the last time it was compiled (by checking the time it was last changed against the time Newton.class was created). If so, it will also compile Newton! If you think about this policy, you will agree that it is actually quite helpful. If you find a bug in Newton (and fix it), you want all the classes that call Newton.sqrt() to use the new version.

Multiple main methods. Another subtle point is to note that more than one class might have a main() method. In our example, SATmyYear, Newton and Gaussian each have main() methods. If you recall the rule for executing a program, you will see that there is no confusion: when you type java followed by a class name, Java transfers control to the machine code corresponding to the main() static method defined in that class. Typically, we put a main() static method in every class, to test and debug its methods. When we want to run SATmyYear, we type java SATmy-Year; when we want to debug Newton or Gaussian, we type java Newton or java Gaussian (with appropriate command-line arguments).

IF YOU THINK OF EACH PROGRAM that you write as something that you might want to make use of later, you will soon find yourself with all sorts of useful tools. Modular programming allows us to view every solution to a computational problem that we may develop as adding value to our computational environment.

For example, suppose that you need to evaluate Φ for some future application. Why not just cut and paste the code that implements Phi() from Gaussian? That would work, but would leave you with two copies of the code, making it more difficult to maintain. If you later want to fix or improve it, you would need to do so in both copies. Instead, you can just call Gaussian.Phi(). Our implementations and uses of them are soon going to proliferate, so having just one copy of each is a worthy goal.

From this point forward, you should write *every* program by identifying a reasonable way to divide the computation into separate parts of a manageable size and implementing each part as if someone will want to use it later. Most frequently, that someone will be you, and you will have yourself to thank for saving the effort of rewriting and re-debugging code.

Libraries We refer to a module whose methods are primarily intended for use by many other programs as a *library*. One of the most important characteristics of programming in Java is that many, many methods have been predefined for you, in literally thousands of Java libraries that are available for your use. We reveal information about those that might be of interest to you throughout the book, but we will postpone a detailed discussion of the scope of Java libraries until the end of the book, because many of them are designed for use by experienced programmers. Instead, we focus in this chapter on the even more important idea that we can build *user-defined libraries*, which are nothing more than classes that each contain a set of related methods for use by other programs. No Java library can contain all the methods that we might need for a given computation, so this ability is a crucial step in addressing complex programming applications.

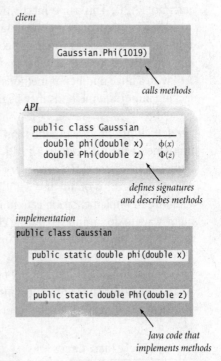

Library abstraction

Clients. We use the term *client* to refer to the program that calls a given method. When a class contains a method that is a client of a method in another class, we say that the first class is a client of the second class. In our example, Gaussian is a client of Newton. A given class might have multiple clients. For example, all of the programs that you have written that call Math.sqrt() or Math.random() are Math clients. When you implement a new static method or a new class, you need to have a very clear of idea of what it is going to do for its clients.

APIs. Programmers normally think in terms of a *contract* between the client and the implementation that is a clear specification of what the method is to do. When you are writing both clients and implementations, you are making contracts with yourself, which by itself is helpful because it provides extra help in debugging. More important, this approach enables code reuse. You have been able to write programs that are clients of Std* and Math and other built-in Java classes because of an informal contract (an English-language description of what they are supposed to do) along with a precise specification of the signatures of the methods that are available for use. Collectively, this information is known as an *applications programming interface* (API). This same mechanism is effective for user-defined libraries. The API allows any client to use the library without having to examine the code in the implementation, just as you have been doing for Math and Std*. The guiding principle in API design is to *provide to clients the methods they need and no others.* An API with a huge number of methods may be a burden to implement; an API that is lacking important methods may be unnecessarily inconvenient for clients.

Implementations. We use the term *implementation* to describe the Java code that implements the methods in an API, kept by convention in a file with the library name and a .java extension. Every Java program is an implementation of some API, and no API is of any use without some implementation. Our goal when developing an implementation is to honor the terms of the contract. Often, there are many ways to do so, and separating client code from implementation code gives us the freedom to substitute new and improved implementations.

FOR EXAMPLE, CONSIDER THE GAUSSIAN DISTRIBUTION functions. These do not appear in Java's Math library but are important in applications, so it is worthwhile for us to put them in a library for use by future client programs and to articulate this API:

```
public class Gaussian
```

double phi(double x)	$\phi(x)$
double phi(double x, double m, double s)	$\phi(x, \mu, \sigma)$
double Phi(double z)	$\Phi(z)$
double Phi(double z, double m, double s)	$\Phi(z, \mu, \sigma)$

API for our library of static methods for ϕ and Φ

Implementing these four static methods is straightforward from the code in Gaussian (PROGRAM 2.1.2)—see EXERCISE 2.2.1. Adding the three-argument versions of phi() and Phi() to the Gaussian library saves us from having to worry about those cases later on.

How much information should an API contain? This is a gray area and a hotly debated issue among programmers and computer-science educators. We might try to put as much information as possible in the API, but (as with any contract!) there are limits to the amount of information that we can productively include. In this book, we stick to a principle that parallels our guiding design principle: *provide to client programmers the information they need and no more.* Doing so gives us vastly more flexibility than the alternative of providing detailed information about implementations. Indeed, any extra information amounts to implicitly extending the contract, which is undesirable. Many programmers fall into the bad habit of checking implementation code to try to understand what it does. Doing so might lead to client code that depends on behavior not specified in the API, which would not work with a new implementation. Implementations change more often than you might think. For example, each new release of Java contains many new implementations of library functions.

Often, the implementation comes first. You might have a working module that you later decide might be useful for some task, and you can just start using its methods in other programs. In such a situation, it is wise to carefully articulate the API at some point. The methods may not have been designed for reuse, so it is worthwhile to use an API to do such a design (as we did for `Gaussian`).

The remainder of this section is devoted to several examples of libraries and clients. Our purpose in considering these libraries is twofold. First, they provide a richer programming environment for your use as you develop increasingly sophisticated client programs of your own. Second, they serve as examples for you to study as you begin to develop libraries for your own use.

Random numbers We have written several programs that use `Math.random()`, but our code often uses particular idioms that convert the random `double` values between 0 and 1 that `Math.random()` provides to the type of random numbers that we want to use (random `boolean` values or random `int` values in a specified range, for example). To effectively reuse our code that implements these idioms, we will, from now on, use the `StdRandom` library in PROGRAM 2.2.1. `StdRandom` uses overloading to generate random numbers from various distributions. You can use any of them in the same way that you use our standard I/O libraries (download `StdRandom.java` and keep it in a directory with your client programs, or use your operating system's classpath mechanism). As usual, we summarize the methods in our `StdRandom` library with an API:

```
public class StdRandom
```
---
int	uniform(int N)	*integer between* 0 *and* N-1
double	uniform(double lo, double hi)	*real between* lo *and* hi
boolean	bernoulli(double p)	true *with probability* p
double	gaussian()	*normal, mean* 0, *standard deviation* 1
double	gaussian(double m, double s)	*normal, mean* m, *standard deviation* s
int	discrete(double[] a)	i *with probability* a[i]
void	shuffle(double[] a)	*randomly shuffle the array* a[]

API for our library of static methods for random numbers

These methods are sufficiently familiar that the short descriptions in the API suffice to specify what they do. By collecting all of these methods that use Math.random() to generate random numbers of various types in one file (StdRandom.java), we concentrate our attention on generating random numbers to this one file (and reuse the code in that file) instead of spreading them through every program that uses these methods. Moreover, each program that uses one of these methods is more clear than code that calls Math.random() directly, because its purpose for using Math.random() is clearly articulated by the choice of method from StdRandom.

API design. We make certain assumptions about the values passed to each method in StdRandom. For example, we assume that clients will call uniform(N) only for positive integers N, bernoulli(p) only for p between 0 and 1, and discrete() only for an array whose entries are between 0 and 1 and sum to 1. All of these assumptions are part of the contract between the client and the implementation. We strive to design libraries such that the contract is clear and unambiguous and to avoid getting bogged down with details. As with many tasks in programming, a good API design is often the result of several iterations of trying and living with various possibilities. We always take special care in designing APIs, because when we change an API we might have to change all clients and all implementations. Our goal is to articulate what clients are to expect *separate from the code* in the API. This practice frees us to change the code, and perhaps to use an implementation that achieves the desired effect more efficiently or with more accuracy.

Program 2.2.1   *Random number library*

```java
public class StdRandom
{
    public static int uniform(int N)
    {  return (int) (Math.random() * N);  }

    public static double uniform(double lo, double hi)
    {  return lo + Math.random() * (hi - lo);  }

    public static boolean bernoulli(double p)
    {  return Math.random() < p;  }

    public static double gaussian()
    {  /* See Exercise 2.1.28. */  }

    public static double gaussian(double m, double s)
    {  return m + s * gaussian();  }

    public static int discrete(double[] a)
    {  // See Program 1.6.2.
        double r = uniform(0.0, 1.0);
        double sum = 0.0;
        for (int i = 0; i < a.length; i++)
        {
            sum += a[i];
            if (sum > r) return i;
        }
        return a.length - 1;
    }

    public static void shuffle(double[] a)
    {  /* See Exercise 2.2.4. */  }

    public static void main(String[] args)
    {  /* See text. */  }
}
```

This is a library of methods to compute various types of random numbers: random non-negative integer less than a given value, uniformly distributed in a given range, random bit (Bernoulli), Gaussian, Gaussian with given mean and standard deviation, and distributed according to a given discrete distribution.

```
% java StdRandom 5
90 26.36076 false 8.79269 0
13 18.02210 false 9.03992 1
58 56.41176 true  8.80501 0
29 16.68454 false 8.90827 0
85 86.24712 true  8.95228 0
```

Unit testing. Even though we implement StdRandom without reference to any particular client, it is good programming practice to include a *test client* main() that, although not used when a client class uses the library, is helpful for use when debugging and testing the methods in the library. *Whenever you create a library, you should include a* main() *method for unit testing and debugging.* Proper unit testing can be a significant programming challenge in itself (for example, the best way of testing whether the methods in StdRandom produce numbers that have the same characteristics as truly random numbers is still debated by experts). At a minimum, you should always include a main() method that
  • Exercises all the code
  • Provides some assurance that the code is working
  • Takes an argument from the command line to allow more testing
Then, you should refine that main() method to do more exhaustive testing as you use the library more extensively. For example, we might start with the following code for StdRandom (leaving the testing of shuffle() for an exercise):

```java
public static void main(String[] args)
{
    int N = Integer.parseInt(args[0]);
    double[] t = { .5, .3, .1, .1 };
    for (int i = 0; i < N; i++)
    {
        StdOut.printf(" %2d " , uniform(100));
        StdOut.printf("%8.5f ", uniform(10.0, 99.0));
        StdOut.printf("%5b " , bernoulli(.5));
        StdOut.printf("%7.5f ", gaussian(9.0, .2));
        StdOut.printf("%2d " , discrete(t));
        StdOut.println();
    }
}
```

When we include this code in StdRandom.java and invoke this method as illustrated in PROGRAM 2.2.1, the output carries no surprises: the numbers in the first column might be equally likely to be any value from 0 to 99; the integers in the second column might be uniformly spread between 10.0 and 99.0; about half of the values in the third column are true; the numbers in the fourth column seem to average about 9.0, and seem unlikely to be too far from 9.0; and the last column seems to be not far from 50% 0s, 30% 1s, 10% 2s, and 10% 3s. If something seems amiss in one of the columns, we can type java StdRandom 10 or 100 to see many more results. In this particular case, we can (and should) do far more extensive testing in a separate client to check that the numbers have many of the same properties as truly random numbers drawn from the cited distributions (see EXERCISE 2.2.3). One effective approach is to write test clients that use StdDraw, as data visualization can be a quick indication that a program is behaving as intended. For example, a plot of a large number of points whose *x* and *y* coordinates are both drawn from various distributions often produces a pattern that gives direct insight into the important properties of the distribution. More important, a bug in the random number generation code is likely to show up immediately in such a plot.

```
public class RandomPoints
{
   public static void main(String[] args)
   {
      int N = Integer.parseInt(args[0]);
      for (int i = 0; i < N; i++)
      {
         double x = StdRandom.gaussian(.5, .2);
         double y = StdRandom.gaussian(.5, .2);
         StdDraw.point(x, y);
      }
   }
}
```

A StdRandom *test client*

Stress testing. An extensively used library such as StdRandom should also be subject to *stress testing*, where we make sure that it does not crash when the client does not follow the contract or makes some assumption that is not explicitly covered. You can be sure that Java libraries have been subject to such testing, which requires carefully examining each line of code and questioning whether some condition might cause a problem. What should discrete() do if array entries do not sum to exactly 1? What if the argument is an array of size 0? What should the two-argument uniform() do if one or both of its arguments is NaN? Infinity? Any question that you can think of is fair game. Such cases are sometimes referred to as *corner cases*. You are certain to encounter a teacher or a supervisor who is a stickler about corner cases. With experience, most programmers learn to address them early, to avoid an unpleasant bout of debugging later. Again, a reasonable approach is to implement a stress test as a separate client.

Input and output for arrays   We have seen and will see many examples where we wish to keep data in arrays for processing. Accordingly, it is useful to build a library of static methods that complements StdIn and StdOut by providing static methods for reading arrays of primitive types from standard input and printing them to standard output, as expressed in this API:

public class StdArrayIO

double[]	readDouble1D()	*read a one-dimensional array of* double *values*
double[][]	readDouble2D()	*read a two-dimensional array of* double *values*
void	print(double[] a)	*print a one-dimensional array of* double *values*
void	print(double[][] a)	*print a two-dimensional array of* double *values*

Notes:

    1. 1D *format is an integer N followed by N values.*

    2. 2D *format is two integers M and N followed by M×N values in row-major order.*

    3. Methods for int *and* boolean *are also included.*

API for our library of static methods for array input and output

The first two notes at the bottom of the table reflect the idea that we need to settle on a *file format*. For simplicity and harmony, we adopt the convention that all values appearing in standard input include the dimension(s) and appear in the order indicated. The read*() methods expect this format, the print() methods produce output in this format, and we can easily create files in this format for data from some other source. The third note at the bottom of the table indicates that StdArrayIO actually contains twelve methods—four each for int, double, and boolean. The print() methods are overloaded (they all have the same name print() but different types of arguments), but the read*() methods need different names, formed by adding the type name (capitalized, as in StdIn) followed by 1D or 2D.

Implementing these methods is straightforward from the array-processing code that we have considered in Section 1.4 and in Section 2.1, as shown in StdArrayIO (Program 2.2.2). Packaging up all of these static methods into one file—StdArrayIO.java—allows us to easily reuse the code and saves us from having to worry about the details of reading and printing arrays when writing client programs later on.

Program 2.2.2   *Array I/O library*

```
public class StdArrayIO
{
    public static double[] readDouble1D()
    {  /* See Exercise 2.2.6 */  }

    public static double[][] readDouble2D()
    {
        int M = StdIn.readInt();
        int N = StdIn.readInt();
        double[][] a = new double[M][N];
        for (int i = 0; i < M; i++)
            for (int j = 0; j < N; j++)
                a[i][j] = StdIn.readDouble();
        return a;
    }

    public static void print(double[] a)
    {  /* See Exercise 2.2.6 */  }

    public static void print(double[][] a)
    {
        int M = a.length;
        int N = a[0].length;
        System.out.println(M + " " + N);
        for (int i = 0; i < M; i++)
        {
            for (int j = 0; j < N; j++)
                StdOut.print(a[i][j] + " ");
            StdOut.println();
        }
        StdOut.println();
    }

    // Methods for other types are similar (see booksite).

    public static void main(String[] args)
    {  print(readDouble2D());  }

}
```

```
% more tiny.txt
4 3
  .000   .270   .000
  .246   .224  -.036
  .222   .176   .0893
 -.032   .739   .270

% java StdArrayIO < tiny.txt
4 3
  0.00000   0.27000   0.00000
  0.24600   0.22400  -0.03600
  0.22200   0.17600   0.08930
 -0.03200   0.73900   0.27000
```

This library of static methods facilitates reading one-dimensional and two-dimensional arrays from standard input and printing them to standard output. The file format includes the dimensions (see accompanying text). Numbers in the output in the example are truncated.

Iterated function systems   Scientists have discovered that complex visual images can arise unexpectedly from simple computational processes. With StdRandom, StdDraw, and StdArrayIO, we can easily study the behavior of such systems.

Sierpinksi triangle. As a first example, consider the following simple process: Start by plotting a point at one of the vertices of a given equilateral triangle. Then pick one of the three vertices at random and plot a new point halfway between the point just plotted and that vertex. Continue performing this same operation. Each time, we are picking a random vertex from the triangle to establish the line whose midpoint will be the next point plotted. Since we are making a random choice, the set of points should have some of the characteristics of random points, and that does seem to be the case after the first few iterations:

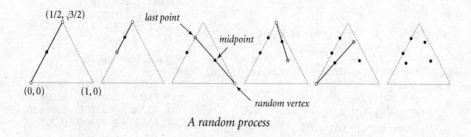

A random process

But we can study the process for a large number of iterations by writing a program to plot T points according to the rules:

```
double[] cx = { 0.000, 1.000, 0.500 };
double[] cy = { 0.000, 0.000, 0.866 };
double x = 0.0, y = 0.0;
for (int t = 0; t < T; t++)
{
    int r = StdRandom.uniform(3);
    x = (x + cx[r]) / 2.0;
    y = (y + cy[r]) / 2.0;
    StdDraw.point(x, y);
}
```

We keep the x and y coordinates of the triangle vertices in the arrays cx[] and cy[], respectively. We use StdRandom.uniform() to choose a random index r into these arrays—the coordinates of the chosen vertex are (cx[r], cy[r]). The *x*-coordinate of the midpoint of the line from (*x*, *y*) to that vertex is given by the expression (x + cx[r])/2.0, and a similar calculation gives the *y* coordinate. Adding a call to StdDraw.point() and putting this code in a loop completes the implementation. Remarkably, despite the randomness, the same figure always emerges after a large number of iterations! This figure is known as the *Sierpinski triangle* (see EXERCISE 2.3.27). Understanding why such a regular figure should arise from such a random process is a fascinating question.

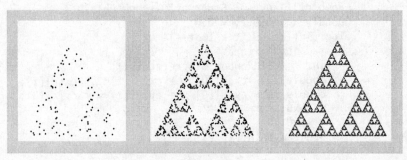

A random process?

Barnsley fern. To add to the mystery, we can produce pictures of remarkable diversity by playing the same game with different rules. One striking example is known as the *Barnsley fern*. To generate it, we use the same process, but this time driven by the following table of formulas. At each step, we choose the formulas to use to update *x* and *y* with the indicated probability (2% of the time we use the first pair of formulas, 15% of the time we use the second pair of formulas, and so forth).

probability	x-update	y-update
2%	$x = .500$	$y = .270y$
15%	$x = -.139x + .263y + .570$	$y = .246x + .224y - .036$
13%	$x = .170x - .215y + .408$	$y = .222x + .176y + .0893$
70%	$x = .781x + .034y + .1075$	$y = -.032x + .739y + .270$

We could write code just like the code we just wrote for the Sierpinski triangle to iterate these rules, but matrix processing provides a uniform way to generalize that

Program 2.2.3   *Iterated function systems*

```
public class IFS
{
   public static void main(String args[])
   {  // Plot T iterations of IFS on StdIn.
      int T = Integer.parseInt(args[0]);
      double[] dist   = StdArrayIO.readDouble1D();
      double[][] cx   = StdArrayIO.readDouble2D();
      double[][] cy   = StdArrayIO.readDouble2D();
      double x = 0.0, y = 0.0;
      for (int t = 0; t < T; t++)
      {  // Plot 1 iteration.
         int r = StdRandom.discrete(dist);
         double x0 = cx[r][0]*x + cx[r][1]*y + cx[r][2];
         double y0 = cy[r][0]*x + cy[r][1]*y + cy[r][2];
         x = x0;
         y = y0;
         StdDraw.point(x, y);
      }
   }
}
```

T	iterations
dist[]	probabilities
cx[][]	x coefficients
cy[][]	y coefficients
x, y	current point

This data-driven client of StdArrayIO, StdRandom, *and* StdDraw *iterates the function system defined by a 1-by-M vector (probabilities) and two M-by-3 matrices (coefficients for updating x and y, respectively) on standard input, plotting the result as a set of points on standard draw. Curiously, this code does not need to know the value of M, as it uses separate methods to create and process the matrices.*

```
% more sierpinski.txt

3
  .33 .33 .34
3 3
  .50 .00 .00
  .50 .00 .50
  .50 .00 .25
3 3
  .00 .50 .00
  .00 .50 .00
  .00 .50 .433
```

```
% java IFS 10000 < sierpinski.txt
```

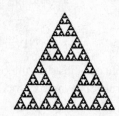

```
% more barnsley.txt
4
   .01 .85 .07 .07
4 3
   .00   .00   .500
   .85   .04   .075
   .20 -.26   .400
  -.15   .28   .575
4 3
   .00   .16   .000
  -.04   .85   .180
   .23   .22   .045
   .26   .24 -.086
```

```
% more tree.txt
6
   .1 .1 .2 .2 .2 .2
6 3
   .00   .00   .550
  -.05   .00   .525
   .46 -.15   .270
   .47 -.15   .265
   .43   .26   .290
   .42   .26   .290
6 3
   .00   .60   .000
  -.50   .00   .750
   .39   .38   .105
   .17   .42   .465
  -.25   .45   .625
  -.35   .31   .525
```

```
% more coral.txt
3
   .40 .15 .45
3 3
   .3077 -.5315   .8863
   .3077 -.0769   .2166
   .0000   .5455   .0106
3 3
  -.4615 -.2937 1.0962
   .1538 -.4476   .3384
   .6923 -.1958   .3808
```

% java IFS 20000 < barnsley.txt

% java IFS 20000 < tree.txt

% java IFS 20000 < coral.txt

Examples of iterated function systems

code to handle any set of rules. We have M different transformations, chosen from a 1-by-M vector with StdRandom.discrete(). For each transformation, we have an equation for updating x and an equation for updating y, so we use two M-by-3 matrices for the equation coefficients, one for x and one for y. IFS (PROGRAM 2.2.3) implements this data-driven version of the computation. This program enables limitless exploration: it performs the iteration for any input containing a vector that defines the probability distribution and the two matrices that define the coefficients, one for updating x and the other for updating y. For the coefficients just given, again, even though we choose a random equation at each step, the same figure emerges every time that we do this computation: an image that looks remarkably similar to a fern that you might see in the woods, not something generated by a random process on a computer.

Generating a Barnsley fern

That the same short program that takes a few numbers from standard input and plots points on standard draw can (given different data) produce both the Sierpinski triangle and the Barnsley fern (and many, many other images) is truly remarkable. Because of its simplicity and the appeal of the results, this sort of calculation is useful in making synthetic images that have a realistic appearance in computer-generated movies and games. Perhaps more significantly, the ability to produce such realistic diagrams so easily suggests intriguing scientific questions: What does computation tell us about nature? What does nature tell us about computation?

Standard statistics Next, we consider a library for a set of mathematical calculations and basic visualization tools that arise in all sorts of applications in science and engineering and are not all implemented in standard Java libraries. These calculations relate to the task of understanding the statistical properties of a set of numbers. Such a library is useful, for example, when we perform a series of scientific experiments that yield measurements of a quantity. One of the most important challenges facing modern scientists is proper analysis of such data, and computation is playing an increasingly important role in such analysis. These basic data analysis methods that we will consider are summarized in the following API:

```
public class StdStats
```
---

double	max(double[] a)	*largest value*
double	min(double[] a)	*smallest value*
double	mean(double[] a)	*average*
double	var(double[] a)	*sample variance*
double	stddev(double[] a)	*sample standard deviation*
double	median(double[] a)	*median*
void	plotPoints(double[] a)	*plot points at* (i, a[i])
void	plotLines(double[] a)	*plot lines connecting points at* (i, a[i])
void	plotBars(double[] a)	*plot bars to points at* (i, a[i])

Note: overloaded implementations are included for all numeric types

API for our library of static methods for data analysis

Basic statistics. Suppose that we have N measurements $x_0, x_1, .., x_{N-1}$. The average value of those measurements, otherwise known as the *mean*, is given by the formula $\mu = (x_0 + x_1 + \ldots + x_{N-1}) / N$ and is an estimate of the value of the quantity. The minimum and maximum values are also of interest, as is the median (the value which is smaller than and larger than half the values). Also of interest is the *sample variance*, which is given by the formula

$$\sigma^2 = ((x_0 - \mu)^2 + (x_1 - \mu)^2 + \ldots + (x_{N-1} - \mu)^2)) / (N-1)$$

Program 2.2.4   Data analysis library

```java
public class StdStats
{
    public static double max(double[] a)
    {  // Compute maximum value in a[].
        double max = Double.NEGATIVE_INFINITY;
        for (int i = 0; i < a.length; i++)
            if (a[i] > max) max = a[i];
        return max;
    }

    public static double mean(double[] a)
    {  // Compute the average of the values in a[].
        double sum = 0.0;
        for (int i = 0; i < a.length; i++)
            sum = sum + a[i];
        return sum / a.length;
    }

    public static double var(double[] a)
    {  // Compute the sample variance of the values in a[].
        double avg = mean(a);
        double sum = 0.0;
        for (int i = 0; i < a.length; i++)
            sum += (a[i] - avg) * (a[i] - avg);
        return sum / (a.length - 1);
    }

    public static double stddev(double[] a)
    {  return Math.sqrt(var(a));  }

    // See Program 2.2.5 for plotting methods.

    public static void main(String[] args)
    {  /* See text. */  }

}
```

This code implements methods to compute the maximum, mean, variance, and standard deviation of numbers in a client array. The method for computing the minimum is omitted, and plotting methods are in Program 2.2.5 (see Section 4.2 for a discussion of the median).

```
% more tiny.txt
5
3.0 1.0 2.0 5.0 4.0
```

```
% java StdStatistics < tiny.txt
     min    1.000
    mean    3.000
     max    5.000
 std dev    1.581
```

and the *sample standard deviation,* the square root of the sample variance. Std-Stats (PROGRAM 2.2.3) shows implementations of static methods for computing these basic statistics (the median is more difficult to compute than the others—we will consider the implementation of median() in SECTION 4.2). The main() test client for StdStats reads numbers from standard input into an array and calls each of the methods to print out the minimum, mean, maximum, and standard deviation, as follows:

```
public static void main(String[] args)
{
    double[] a = StdArrayIO.readDouble1D();
    StdOut.printf("     min %7.3f\n", min(a));
    StdOut.printf("    mean %7.3f\n", mean(a));
    StdOut.printf("     max %7.3f\n", max(a));
    StdOut.printf(" std dev %7.3f\n", stddev(a));
}
```

As with StdRandom, a more extensive test of the calculations is called for (see EXERCISE 2.2.3). Typically, as we debug or test new methods in the library, we adjust the unit testing code accordingly, testing the methods one at a time. A mature and widely used library like StdStats also deserves a stress-testing client for extensively testing everything after any change. If you are interested in seeing what such a client might look like, you can find one for StdStats on the booksite. Most experienced programmers will advise you that any time spent doing unit testing and stress testing will more than pay for itself later.

Plotting. One important use of StdDraw is to help us visualize data rather than relying on tables of numbers. In a typical situation, we perform experiments, save the experimental data in an array, and then compare the results against a model, perhaps a mathematical function that describes the data. To expedite this process for the typical case where values of one variable are equally spaced, our StdStats library contains static methods that you can use for plotting data in an array. PROGRAM 2.2.5 is an implementation of the plotPoints(), plotLine(), and plotBars() methods for StdStats. These methods display the values in the argument array at regularly spaced intervals in the drawing window, either connected together by line segments (lines), filled circles at each value (points), or bars from the *x*-axis to the value (bars). They all plot the points with *x* coordinate i and *y* coordinate a[i] using filled circles, lines through the points, and bars, respectively.

Program 2.2.5 *Plotting data values in an array*

```
public static void plotPoints(double[] a)
{  // Plot points at (i, a[i]).
   int N = a.length;
   StdDraw.setXscale(0, N-1);
   StdDraw.setPenRadius(1/(3.0*N));
   for (int i = 0; i < N; i++)
      StdDraw.point(i, a[i]);
}

public static void plotLines(double[] a)
{  // Plot lines through points at (i, a[i]).
   int N = a.length;
   StdDraw.setXscale(0, N-1);
   StdDraw.setPenRadius();
   for (int i = 1; i < N; i++)
      StdDraw.line(i-1, a[i-1], i, a[i]);
}

public static void plotBars(double[] a)
{  // Plot bars from (0, a[i]) to (i, a[i]).
   int N = a.length;
   StdDraw.setXscale(0, N-1);
   StdDraw.setPenRadius(0.5 / N);
   for (int i = 0; i < N; i++)
      StdDraw.line(i, 0, i, a[i]);
}
```

This code implements three methods in StdStats (Program 2.2.4) for plotting data. They plot the points (i, a[i]) with filled circles, connecting line segments, and bars, respectively.

```
int N = 20;
double[] a = new double[N];
for (int i = 0; i < N; i++)
   a[i] = 1.0/(i+1);
```

plotPoints(a);   plotLines(a);   plotBars(a);

(0.0, 1.0)

(9.0, 0.1)

They all rescale *x* to fill the drawing window (so that the points are evenly spaced along the *x*-coordinate) and leave to the client scaling the *y*-coordinates.

These methods are not intended to be a general-purpose plotting package, you can certainly think of all sorts of things that you might want to add: different types of spots, labeled axes, color, and many other artifacts are commonly found in modern systems that can plot data. Some situations might call for more complicated methods than these.

Our intent with StdStats is to introduce you to data analysis while showing you how easy it is to define a library to take care of useful tasks. Indeed, this library has already proven useful—we use these plotting methods to produce the figures in this book that depict function graphs, sound waves, and experimental results. Next, we consider several examples of their use.

Plotting function graphs. You can use the StdStats.plot*() methods to draw a plot of the function graph for any function at all: choose an *x*-interval where you want to plot the function, compute function values evenly spaced through that interval and store them in an array, determine and set the *y* scale, and then call StdStats. plotLines() or another plot*() method. For example, to plot a sine function, rescale the *y*-axis to cover values between −1 and +1. Scaling the *x*-axis is automatically handled by the StdStats methods. If

```
int N = 50;
double[] a = new double[N+1];
for (int i = 0; i <= N; i++)
    a[i] = Gaussian.phi(-4.0 + 8.0*i/N);
StdStats.plotPoints(a);
StdStats.plotLines(a);
```

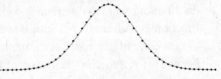

Plotting a function graph

you do not know the range, you can handle the situation by calling:

```
StdDraw.setYscale(StdStats.min(a), StdStats.max(a));
```

The smoothness of the curve is determined by properties of the function and by the number of points plotted. As we discussed when first considering StdDraw, you have to be careful to sample enough points to catch fluctuations in the function. We will consider another approach to plotting functions based on sampling values that are not equally spaced in SECTION 2.4.

Plotting sound waves. Both the StdAudio library and the StdStats plot methods work with arrays that contain sampled values at regular intervals. The diagrams of sound waves in SECTION 1.5 and at the beginning of this section were each produced by first scaling the *y*-axis with StdDraw.setYscale(-1, 1), then plotting the points with StdStats.plotPoints(). As you have seen, such plots give direct insight into processing audio. You can also produce interesting effects by plotting sound waves as you play them with StdAudio, although this task is a bit challenging because of the huge amount of data involved (see EXERCISE 1.5.23).

```
StdDraw.setYscale(-1.0, 1.0);
double[] hi;
hi = PlayThatTune.tone(880, .01);
StdStats.plotPoints(hi);
```

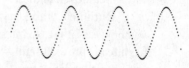

Plotting a sound wave

Plotting experimental results You can put multiple plots on the same drawing. One typical reason to do so is to compare experimental results with a theoretical model. For example, Bernoulli (PROGRAM 2.2.6) counts the number of heads found when a fair coin is flipped *N* times and compares the result with the predicted normal (Gaussian) distribution function. A famous result from probability theory is that the distribution of this quantity is the binomial distribution, which is extremely well-approximated by the normal distribution function ϕ with mean *N/2* and standard deviation $\sqrt{N}/2$. The more often we run the experiment, the more accurate the approximation. The drawing produced by Bernoulli is a succinct summary of the results of the experiment and a convincing validation of the theory. This example is prototypical of a scientific approach to applications programming that we use often throughout this book and that you should use whenever you run an experiment. If a theoretical model that can explain your results is available, a visual plot comparing the experiment to the theory can validate both.

THESE FEW EXAMPLES ARE INTENDED TO indicate to you what is possible with a well-designed library of static methods for data analysis. Several extensions and other ideas are explored in the exercises. You will find StdStats to be useful for basic plots, and you are encouraged to experiment with these implementations and to modify them or to add methods to make your own library that can draw plots of your own design. As you continue to address an ever-widening circle of programming tasks, you will naturally be drawn to the idea of developing tools like these for your own use.

Program 2.2.6 Bernoulli trials

```java
public class Bernoulli
{
    public static int binomial(int N)
    {   // Simulate flipping a coin N times.
        int heads = 0;
        for (int i = 0; i < N; i++)
            if (StdRandom.bernoulli(0.5)) heads++;
        return heads;
    }
    public static void main(String[] args)
    {   // Perform experiments, plot results and model.
        int N = Integer.parseInt(args[0]);
        int T = Integer.parseInt(args[1]);

        int[] freq = new int[N+1];
        for (int t = 0; t < T; t++)
            freq[binomial(N)]++;

        double[] norm = new double[N+1];
        for (int i = 0; i <= N; i++)
            norm[i] = (double) freq[i] / T;
        StdStats.plotBars(norm);

        double stddev = Math.sqrt(N)/2.0;
        double[] phi = new double[N+1];
        for (int i = 0; i <= N; i++)
            phi[i] = Gaussian.phi(i, N/2.0, stddev);
        StdStats.plotLines(phi);

    }
}
```

N	*number of flips per trial*
T	*number of trials*
freq[]	*experimental results*
norm[]	*normalized results*
phi[]	*Gaussian model*

This StdStats, StdRandom, *and* Gaussian *client provides convincing visual evidence that the number of heads observed when a fair coin is flipped N times obeys a Gaussian distribution. It uses the overloaded* Gaussian.phi() *that takes as arguments the mean and standard deviation (see Exercise 2.2.1).*

% java Bernoulli 20 100000

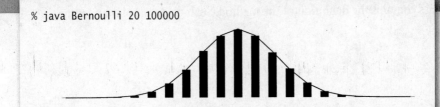

Modular programming   The library implementations that we have developed illustrate a programming style known as *modular programming*. Instead of writing a new program that is self-contained in its own file to address a new problem, we break up each task into smaller, more manageable subtasks, then implement and independently debug code that addresses each subtask. Good libraries facilitate modular programming by allowing us to define and to provide solutions of important subtasks for future clients. *Whenever you can clearly separate tasks within a program, you should do so.* Java supports such separation by allowing us to independently debug and later use classes in separate files. Traditionally, programmers use the term *module* to refer to code that can be compiled and run independently; in Java each *class* is a module.

IFS (PROGRAM 2.2.3) exemplifies modular programming because it is a relatively sophisticated computation that is implemented with several relatively small modules, developed independently. It uses StdRandom and StdArrayIO), as well as the methods from Integer and StdDraw that we are accustomed to using. If we were to put all of the code required for IFS in a single file, we would have a large amount of code on our hands to maintain and debug; with modular programming, we can study iterated function systems with some confidence that the arrays are read properly and that the

API	description
Gaussian	Gaussian distribution functions
StdRandom	random numbers
StdArrayIO	input and output for arrays
IFS	client for iterated function systems
StdStats	functions for data analysis
Bernoulli	client for Bernoulli trials experiments

Summary of classes in this section

random number generator will produce properly distributed values, because we already implemented and tested the code for these tasks in separate modules.

Similarly, Bernoulli (PROGRAM 2.2.5) also exemplifies modular programming. It is a client of Gaussian, Integer, Math, StdRandom, and StdStats. Again, we can have some confidence that the methods in these modules produce the expected results because they are system libraries or libraries that we have tested, debugged, and used before.

To describe the relationships among modules in a modular program, we often draw a *dependency graph*, where we connect two class names with an arrow labeled with the name of a method if the first class contains a call on the method and the second class contains the definition of the method. Such diagrams play an impor-

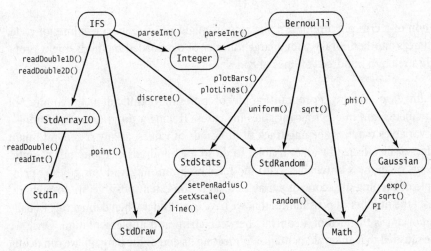

Dependency graph for the modules in this section

tant role because understanding the relationships among modules is necessary for proper development and maintenance.

We emphasize modular programming throughout this book because it has many important advantages that have come to be accepted as essential in modern programming, including the following:

- We can have programs of a reasonable size, even in large systems.
- Debugging is restricted to small pieces of code.
- We can reuse code without having to reimplement it.
- Maintaining (and improving) code is much simpler.

The importance of these advantages is difficult to overstate, so we will expand upon each of them.

Programs of a reasonable size. No large task is so complex that it cannot be divided into smaller subtasks. If you find yourself with a program that stretches to more than a few pages of code, you must ask yourself the following questions: Are there subtasks that could be implemented separately? Do some of these subtasks logically group together in a separate library? Could other clients use this code in the future? At the other end of the range, if you find yourself with a huge number of tiny modules, you must ask yourself questions such as: Is there some group of subtasks that logically belong in the same module? Is each module likely to be used by multiple clients? There is no hard-and-fast rule on module size: one implementation of a critically important abstraction might properly be a few lines of code, whereas another library with a large number of overloaded methods might properly stretch to hundreds of lines of code.

Debugging. Tracing a program rapidly becomes more difficult as the number of statements and interacting variables increases. Tracing a program with hundreds of variables requires keeping track of hundreds of values, as any statement might affect or be affected by any variable. To do so for hundreds or thousands of statements or more is untenable. With modular programming and our guiding principle of keeping the scope of variables local to the extent possible, we severely restrict the number of possibilities that we have to consider when debugging. Equally important is the idea of a contract between client and implementation. Once we are satisfied that an implementation is meeting its end of the bargain, we can debug all its clients under that assumption.

Code reuse. Once we have implemented libraries such as StdStats and StdRandom, we do not have to worry about writing code to compute averages or standard deviations or to generate random numbers again—we can simply reuse the code that we have written. Moreover, we do not need to make copies of the code: any module can just refer to any public method in any other module.

Maintenance. Like a good piece of writing, a good program can always be improved, and modular programming facilitates the process of continually improving your Java programs because improving a module improves all of its clients. For example, it is normally the case that there are several different approaches to solving a particular problem. With modular programming, you can implement more than one and try them independently. More importantly, suppose that while developing a new client, you find a bug in some module. With modular programming, fixing that bug amounts to fixing bugs in all of the module's clients.

IF YOU ENCOUNTER AN OLD PROGRAM (or a new program written by an old programmer!), you are likely to find one huge module—a long sequence of statements, stretching to several pages or more, where any statement can refer to any variable in the program. Variables whose scope extends to a whole program are known as *global variables*. We avoid global variables in modular programs, but their use is common in lower-level and older programming languages. Huge modules that use global variables are extremely difficult to understand, maintain, and debug. Old programs of this kind are found in critical parts of our computational infrastructure (for example, some nuclear power plants and some banks) precisely because the programmers charged with maintaining them cannot even understand them well enough to rewrite them in a modern language! With support for modular programming, modern languages like Java help us avoid such situations by separately developing libraries of methods in independent classes.

The ability to share static methods among different files fundamentally extends our programming model in two different ways. First, it allows us to reuse code without having to maintain multiple copies of it. Second, by allowing us to organize a program into files of manageable size that can be independently debugged and compiled, it strongly supports our basic message: *Whenever you can clearly separate tasks within a program, you should do so*. We use the term *library* to capture the idea of developing methods for later reuse and *modular programming* to capture the idea of independently developing pieces connected by well-defined interfaces instead of a big, monolithic piece of code.

In this section, we have supplemented the Std* libraries of SECTION 1.5 with several other libraries that you can use: Gaussian, StdArrayIO, StdRandom, and StdStats. Furthermore, we have illustrated their use with several client programs. These tools are centered on basic mathematical concepts that arise in any scientific project or engineering task. Our intent is not just to provide tools, but also to illustrate to you that it is easy for you to create your own tools. The first question that most modern programmers ask when addressing a complex task is "What tools do I need?" When the needed tools are not conveniently available, the second question is "How difficult would it be to implement them?" To be a good programmer, you need to have the confidence to build a software tool when you need it and the wisdom to know when it might be better to seek a solution in a library.

After libraries and modular programming, you have one more step to learn a complete modern programming model: *object-oriented programming*, the topic of CHAPTER 3. With object-oriented programming, you can build libraries of functions that use side effects (in a tightly controlled manner) to vastly extend the Java programming model. Before moving to object-oriented programming, we consider in this chapter the profound ramifications of the idea that any method can call itself (in SECTION 2.3) and a more extensive case study (in SECTION 2.4) of modular programming than the small clients in this section.

Q. I tried to use StdRandom, but got the error message Exception in thread "main" java.lang.NoClassDefFoundError: StdRandom. What's wrong?

A. You need to download StdRandom.java into the directory containing your client, or use your operating system's classpath mechanism, as described on the booksite.

Q. Is there a keyword that identifies a class as a library?

A. No, any set of public methods will do. There is a bit of a conceptual leap in this viewpoint because it is one thing to sit down to create a .java file that you will compile and run, quite another thing to create a .java file that you will rely on much later in the future, and still another thing to create a .java file for *someone else* to use in the future. You need to develop some libraries for your own use before engaging in this sort of activity, which is the province of experienced systems programmers.

Q. How do I develop a new version of a library that I have been using for a while?

A. With care. Any change to the API might break any client program, so it is best to work in a separate directory. But then you are working with a copy of the code. If you are changing a library that has a lot of clients, you can appreciate the problems faced by companies putting out new versions of their software. If you just want to add a few methods to a library, go ahead: that is usually not too dangerous, though you should realize that you might find yourself in a situation where you have to support that library for years!

Q. How do I know that an implementation behaves properly? Why not automatically check that it satisfies the API?

A. We use informal specifications because writing a detailed specification is not much different than writing a program. Moreover, a fundamental tenet of theoretical computer science says that doing so does not even solve the basic problem, because generally there is no way to check that two different programs perform the same computation.

Exercises

2.2.1 Add to Gaussian (PROGRAM 2.1.2) the method implementation phi(x, mu, sigma) specified in the API that computes the Gaussian distribution with a given mean μ and standard deviation σ, based on the formula $\phi(x,\mu,\sigma) = \phi((x-\mu)/\sigma)/\sigma$. Also include the implementation of the associated cumulative distribution function Phi(z, mu, sigma), based on the formula $\Phi(z, \mu, \sigma) = \Phi((z-\mu)/\sigma)$.

2.2.2 Write a static method library that implements the *hyperbolic* trigonometric functions based on the definitions $\sinh(x) = (e^x - e^{-x})/2$ and $\cosh(x) = (e^x + e^{-x})/2$, with $\tanh(x)$, $\coth(x)$, $\text{sech}(x)$, and $\text{csch}(x)$ defined in a manner analogous to standard trigonometric functions.

2.2.3 Write a test client for both StdStats and StdRandom that checks that the methods in both libraries operate as expected. Take a command-line argument N, generate N random numbers using each of the methods in StdRandom, and print out their statistics. *Extra credit*: Defend the results that you get by comparing them to those that are to be expected from analysis.

2.2.4 Add to StdRandom a method shuffle() that takes an array of double values as argument and rearranges them in random order. Implement a test client that checks that each permutation of the array is produced about the same number of times.

2.2.5 Develop a client that does stress testing for StdRandom. Pay particular attention to discrete(). For example, do the probabilities sum to 1?

2.2.6 Develop a full implementation of StdArrayIO (implement all 12 methods indicated in the API).

2.2.7 Write a method that takes double values ymin and ymax (with ymin strictly less than ymax), and a double array a[] as arguments and uses the StdStats library to linearly scale the values in a[] so that they are all between ymin and ymax.

2.2.8 Write a Gaussian and StdStats client that explores the effects of changing the mean and standard deviation on the Gaussian distribution curve. Create one plot with curves having a fixed mean and various standard deviations and another with curves having a fixed standard deviation and various means.

2.2.9 Add to StdRandom a static method maxwellBoltzmann() that returns a random value drawn from a *Maxwell-Boltzmann* distribution with parameter σ. To produce such a value, return the square root of the sum of the squares of three Gaussian random variables with mean 0 and standard deviation σ. The speeds of molecules in an ideal gas have a Maxwell-Boltzmann distribution.

2.2.10 Modify Bernoulli (PROGRAM 2.2.6) to animate the bar graph, replotting it after each experiment, so that you can watch it converge to the normal distribution. Then add a command-line argument and an overloaded binomial() implementation to allow you to specify the probability *p* that a biased coin comes up heads, and run experiments to get a feeling for the distribution corresponding to a biased coin. Be sure to try values of *p* that are close to 0 and close to 1.

2.2.11 Write a library Matrix that implements the following API:

```
public class Matrix
```
---

double	dot(double[] a, double[] b)	*vector dot product*
double[][]	multiply(double[][] a, double[][] b)	*matrix-matrix product*
double[][]	transpose(double[][] a)	*transpose*
double[]	multiply(double[][] a, double[] x)	*matrix-vector product*
double[]	multiply(double[] x, double[][] a)	*vector-matrix product*

(See SECTION 1.4.) As a test client, use the following code, which performs the same calculation as Markov (PROGRAM 1.6.3).

```java
public static void main(String[] args)
{
    int T = Integer.parseInt(args[0]);
    double[][] p = StdArrayIO.readDouble2D();
    double[] rank = new double[p.length];
    rank[0] = 1.0;
    for (int t = 0; t < T; t++)
        rank = Matrix.multiply(rank, p);
    StdArrayIO.print(rank);
}
```

Mathematicians and scientists use mature libraries or special-purpose matrix-processing languages for such tasks (see the CONTEXT section at the end of this book for some details). See the booksite for information on using such libraries.

2.2.12 Write a `Matrix` client that implements the version of `Markov` described in SECTION 1.6 but is based on squaring the matrix, instead of iterating the vector-matrix multiplication.

2.2.13 Rewrite `RandomSurfer` (PROGRAM 1.6.2) using the `StdArrayIO` and `StdRandom` libraries.

Partial solution.

```
...
double[][] p = StdArrayIO.readDouble2D();
int page = 0; // Start at page 0.
int[] freq = new int[N];
for (int t = 0; t < T; t++)
{
    page = StdRandom.discrete(p[page]);
    freq[page]++;
}
...
```

2.2.14 Add a method `exp()` to `StdRandom` that takes an argument λ and returns a random number from the *exponential distribution* with rate λ. *Hint*: If x is a random number uniformly distributed between 0 and 1, then $-\ln x / \lambda$ is a random number from the exponential distribution with rate λ.

2.2.15 *Sicherman dice.* Suppose that you have two six-sided dice, one with faces labeled 1, 3, 4, 5, 6, and 8 and the other with faces labeled 1, 2, 2, 3, 3, and 4. Compare the probabilities of occurrence of each of the values of the sum of the dice with those for a standard pair of dice. Use StdRandom and StdStats.

2.2.16 *Craps.* The following are the rules for a *pass bet* in the game of *craps*. Roll two six-sided dice, and let x be their sum.
  • If x is 7 or 11, you win.
  • If x is 2, 3, or 12, you lose.
Otherwise, repeatedly roll the two dice until their sum is either x or 7.
  • If their sum is x, you win.
  • If their sum is 7, you lose.
Write a modular program to estimate the probability of winning a pass bet. Modify your program to handle loaded dice, where the probability of a die landing on 1 is taken from the command line, the probability of landing on 6 is 1/6 minus that probability, and 2–5 are assumed equally likely. *Hint*: Use StdRandom.discrete().

2.2.17 *Dynamic histogram.* Suppose that the standard input stream is a sequence of double values. Write a program that takes an integer N and two double values l and r from the command line and uses StdStats to plot a histogram of the count of the numbers in the standard input stream that fall in each of the N intervals defined by dividing (l, r) into N equal-sized intervals. Use your program to add code to your solution to Exercise 2.2.3 to plot a histogram of the distribution of the numbers produced by each method, taking N from the command line.

2.2.18 *Tukey plot.* A Tukey plot is a data visualization that generalizes a histogram, and is appropriate for use when each integer in a given range is associated with a set of y values. For each integer in the range, we compute the mean, standard deviation, 10th percentile, and 90th percentile of all the associated y values; draw a vertical line with x-coordinate i running from the 10th percentile y value to the 90th percentile y value; and then draw a thin rectangle centered on the line that runs from one standard deviation below the mean to one standard deviation above the mean. Suppose that the standard input stream is a sequence of pairs of numbers

where the first number in each pair is an `int` and the second a `double` value. Write a `StdStats` and `StdDraw` client that takes an integer N from the command line and, assuming that all the `int` values on the input stream are between 0 and `N-1`, uses `StdDraw` to make a Tukey plot of the data.

2.2.19 *IFS.* Experiment with various inputs to `IFS` to create patterns of your own design like the Sierpinski triangle, the Barnsley fern, or the other examples in the table in the text. You might begin by experimenting with minor modifications to the given inputs.

2.2.20 *IFS matrix implementation.* Write a version of `IFS` that uses `Matrix.multiply()` (see EXERCISE 2.2.11) instead of the equations that compute the new values of x0 and y0.

2.2.21 *Stress test.* Develop a client that does stress testing for `StdStats`. Work with a classmate, with one person writing code and the other testing it.

2.2.22 *Gambler's ruin.* Develop a `StdRandom` client to study the gambler's ruin problem (see PROGRAM 1.3.8 and EXERCISES 1.3.21–24. *Note*: Defining a static method for the experiment is more difficult than for `Bernoulli` because you cannot return two values.

2.2.23 *Library for properties of integers.* Develop a library based on the functions that we have considered in this book for computing properties of integers. Include functions for determining whether a given integer is prime; whether two integers are relatively prime; computing all the factors of a given integer; the greatest common divisor and least common multiple of two integers; Euler's totient function (EXERCISE 2.1.26); and any other functions that you think might be useful. Include overloaded implementations for `long` values. Create an API, a client that performs stress testing, and clients that solve several of the exercises earlier in this book.

2.2.24 *Voting machines.* Develop a `StdRandom` client (with appropriate static methods of its own) to study the following problem: Suppose that in a population of 100 million voters, 51% vote for candidate A and 49% vote for candidate B. However, the voting machines are prone to make mistakes, and 5% of the time

they produce the wrong answer. Assuming the errors are made independently and at random, is a 5% error rate enough to invalidate the results of a close election? What error rate can be tolerated?

2.2.25 *Poker analysis.* Write a StdRandom and StdStats client (with appropriate static methods of its own) to estimate the probabilities of getting one pair, two pair, three of a kind, a full house, and a flush in a five-card poker hand via simulation. Divide your program into appropriate static methods and defend your design decisions. *Extra credit*: Add straight and straight flush to the list of possibilities.

2.2.26 *Music library.* Develop a library based on the functions in PlayThatTune (PROGRAM 2.1.4) that you can use to write client programs to create and manipulate songs.

2.2.27 *Animated plots.* Write a program that takes a command-line argument M and produces a bar graph of the M most recent double values on standard input. Use the same animation technique that we used for BouncingBall (PROGRAM 1.5.6): erase, redraw, show, and wait briefly. Each time your program reads a new number, it should redraw the whole graph. Since most of the picture does not change as it is redrawn slightly to the left, your program will produce the effect of a fixed-size window dynamically sliding over the input values. Use your program to plot a huge time-variant data file, such as stock prices.

2.2.28 *Array plot library.* Develop your own plot methods that improve upon those in StdStats. Be creative! Try to make a plotting library that you think will be useful for some application in the future.

2.3 Recursion

THE IDEA OF CALLING ONE FUNCTION from another immediately suggests the possibility of a function calling *itself*. The function-call mechanism in Java and most modern programming languages supports this possibility, which is known as *recursion*. In this section, we will study examples of elegant and efficient recursive solutions to a variety of problems. Once you get used to the idea, you will see that recursion is a powerful general-purpose programming technique with many attractive properties. It is a fundamental tool that we use

often in this book. Recursive programs are often more compact and easier to understand than their nonrecursive counterparts. Few programmers become sufficiently comfortable with recursion to use it in everyday code, but solving a problem with an elegantly crafted recursive program is a satisfying experience that is certainly accessible to every programmer (even you!).

A recursive model of the natural world

Recursion is much more than a programming technique. In many settings, it is a useful way to describe the natural world. For example, the recursive tree (to the left) resembles a real tree, and has a natural recursive description. Many, many phenomena are well-explained by recursive models. In particular, recursion plays a central role in computer science. It provides a simple computational model that embraces everything that can be computed with any computer; it helps us to organize and to analyze programs; and it is the key to numerous critically important computational applications, ranging from combinatorial search to tree data structures that support information processing to the Fast Fourier Transform for signal processing.

One important reason to embrace recursion is that it provides a straightforward way to build simple mathematical models that we can use to prove important facts about our programs. The proof technique that we use to do so is known as *mathematical induction*. Generally, we avoid going into the details of mathematical proofs in this book, but you will see in this section that it is worthwhile to make the effort to convince yourself that recursive programs have the intended effect.

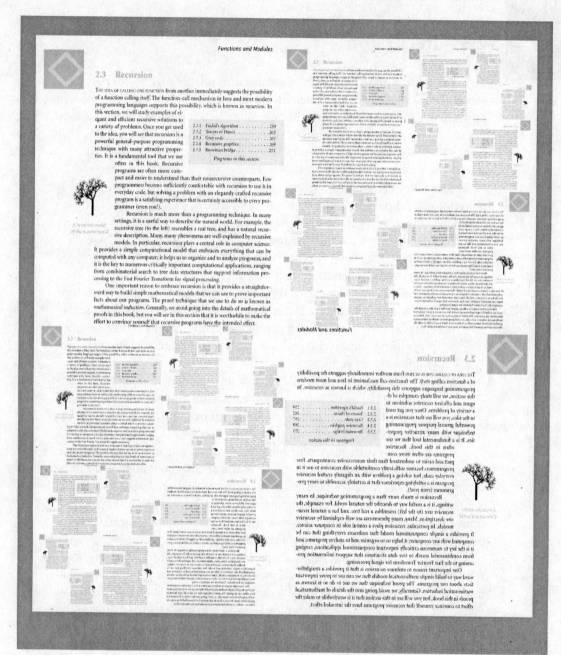

A recursive image

Your first recursive program   The HelloWorld for recursion (the first recursive program that most programmers implement) is the *factorial* function, defined for positive integers N by the equation

$$N! = N \times (N-1) \times (N-2) \times \ldots \times 2 \times 1$$

In other words, $N!$ is the product of the positive integers less than or equal to N. Now, $N!$ is easy to compute with a for loop, but an even easier method is to use the following recursive function:

```
public static long factorial(int N)
{
    if (N == 1) return 1;
    return N * factorial(N-1);
}
```

This static method calls itself. The implementation clearly produces the desired effect. You can persuade yourself that it does so by noting that factorial() returns $1 = 1!$ when N is 1 and that if it properly computes the value

$$(N-1)! = (N-1) \times (N-2) \times \ldots \times 2 \times 1$$

then it properly computes the value

$$N! = N \times (N-1)!$$

$$= N \times (N-1) \times (N-2) \times \ldots \times 2 \times 1$$

To compute factorial(5), the recursive method multiplies 5 by factorial(4); to compute factorial(4), it multiplies 4 by factorial(3); and so forth. This process is repeated until factorial(1), which directly returns the value 1. We can trace this computation in precisely the same way that we trace any sequence of function calls. Since we treat all of the calls as being independent copies of the code, the fact that they are recursive is immaterial.

```
factorial(5)
  factorial(4)
    factorial(3)
      factorial(2)
        factorial(1)
          return 1
        return 2*1 = 2
      return 3*2 = 6
    return 4*6 = 24
  return 5*24 = 120
```

Function call trace for factorial

Our factorial() implementation exhibits the two main components that are required for every recursive function. The *base case* returns a value without making any subsequent recursive calls. It does this for one or more special input values for which the function can be evaluated without recursion. For `factorial()`, the base case is $N = 1$. The *reduction step* is the central part of a recursive function. It relates the function at one (or more) inputs to the function evaluated at one (or more) other inputs. For `factorial()`, the reduction step is `N * factorial(N-1)`. All recursive functions must have these two components. Furthermore, the sequence of parameter values must converge to the base case. For `factorial()`, the value of N decreases by one for each call, so the sequence of argument values converges to the base case $N = 1$.

Tiny programs such as `factorial()` are perhaps slightly more clear if we put the reduction step in an `else` clause. However, adopting this convention for every recursive program would unnecessarily complicate larger programs because it would involve putting most of the code (for the reduction step) within braces after the `else`. Instead, we adopt the convention of always putting the base case as the first statement, ending with a `return`, and then devoting the rest of the code to the reduction step.

The `factorial()` implementation itself is not particularly useful in practice because *N!* grows so quickly that the multiplication will overflow and produce incorrect answers for $N > 20$. But the same technique is effective for computing all sorts of functions. For example, the recursive function

1	1
2	2
3	6
4	24
5	120
6	720
7	5040
8	40320
9	362880
10	3628800
11	39916800
12	479001600
13	6227020800
14	87178291200
15	1307674368000
16	20922789888000
17	355687428096000
18	6402373705728000
19	121645100408832000
20	2432902008176640000

Values of N! in `long`

```
public static double H(int N)
{
    if (N == 1) return 1.0;
    return H(N-1) + 1.0/N;
}
```

is an effective method for computing the Harmonic numbers (see PROGRAM 1.3.5) when *N* is small, based on the following equations:

$$H_N = 1 + 1/2 + \ldots + 1/N$$

$$= \left(1 + 1/2 + \ldots + 1/(N-1)\right) + 1/N = H_{N-1} + 1/N$$

Indeed, this same approach is effective for computing, with only a few lines of code, the value of *any* discrete sum for which you have a compact formula. Recursive programs like these are just loops in disguise, but recursion can help us better understand this sort of computation.

Mathematical induction   Recursive programming is directly related to *mathematical induction*, a technique for proving facts about discrete functions.

Proving that a statement involving an integer N is true for infinitely many values of N by mathematical induction involves the following two steps:
- The *base case*: prove the statement true for some specific value or values of N (usually 1).
- The *induction step* (the central part of the proof): assume the statement to be true for all positive integers less than N, then use that fact to prove it true for N.

Such a proof suffices to show that the statement is true for *all* N: we can start at the base case, and use our proof to establish that the statement is true for each larger value of N, one by one.

Everyone's first induction proof is to demonstrate that the sum of the positive integers less than or equal to N is given by the formula $N(N+1)/2$. That is, we wish to prove that the following equation is valid for all $N \geq 1$:

$$1 + 2 + 3 \ldots + (N-1) + N = N(N+1)/2$$

The equation is certainly true for $N = 1$ (base case). If we assume it to be true for all integers less than N, then, in particular, it is true for $N-1$, so

$$1 + 2 + 3 \ldots + (N-1) = (N-1)N/2$$

and we can add N to both sides of this equation and simplify to get the desired equation (induction step).

Every time we write a recursive program, we need mathematical induction to be convinced that the program has the desired effect. The correspondence between induction and recursion is self-evident. The difference in nomenclature indicates a difference in outlook: in a recursive program, our outlook is to get a computation done by reducing to a smaller problem, so we use the term *reduction step*; in an induction proof, our outlook is to establish the truth of the statement for larger problems, so we use the term *induction step*.

When we write recursive programs we usually do not write down a full formal proof that they produce the desired result, but we are always dependent upon the existence of such a proof. We do often appeal to an informal induction proof to convince ourselves that a recursive program operates as expected. For example, we just discussed an informal proof to become convinced that `factorial()` computes the product of the positive integers less than or equal to N.

Program 2.3.1 Euclid's algorithm

```java
public class Euclid
{
    public static int gcd(int p, int q)
    {
        if (q == 0) return p;
        return gcd(q, p % q);
    }
    public static void main(String[] args)
    {
        int p = Integer.parseInt(args[0]);
        int q = Integer.parseInt(args[1]);
        int d = gcd(p, q);
        StdOut.println(d);
    }
}
```

p, q	arguments
d	greatest common divisor

This program prints out the greatest common divisor of its two command-line arguments, using a recursive implementation of Euclid's algorithm.

```
% java Euclid 1440 408
24
% java Euclid 314159 271828
1
```

Euclid's algorithm The *greatest common divisor* (gcd) of two positive integers is the largest integer that divides evenly into both of them. For example, the greatest common divisor of 102 and 68 is 34 since both 102 and 68 are multiples of 34, but no integer larger than 34 divides evenly into 102 and 68. You may recall learning about the greatest common divisor when you learned to reduce fractions. For example, we can simplify 68/102 to 2/3 by dividing both numerator and denominator by 34, their gcd. Finding the gcd of huge numbers is an important problem that arises in many commercial applications, including the famous RSA cryptosystem.

We can efficiently compute the gcd using the following property, which holds for positive integers p and q:

> *If p>q, the gcd of p and q is the same as the gcd of p and p % q.*

To convince yourself of this fact, first note that the gcd of p and q is the same as the gcd of q and $p-q$, because a number divides both p and q if and only if it divides both q and $p-q$. By the same argument, q and $p-2q$, q and $p-3q$, and so forth have the same gcd, and one way to compute p % q is to subtract q from p until getting a number less than q.

```
gcd(1440, 408)
  gcd(408, 216)
    gcd(216, 24)
      gcd(192, 24)
        gcd(24, 0)
          return 24
        return 24
      return 24
    return 24
  return 24
return 24
```
Function call trace for gcd

The static method gcd() in Euclid (PROGRAM 2.3.1) is a compact recursive function whose reduction step is based on this property. The base case is when q is 0, with gcd(p, 0) = p. To see that the reduction step converges to the base case, observe that the second input strictly decreases in each recursive call since p % q < q. If $p < q$, the first recursive call switches the arguments. In fact, the second input decreases by at least a factor of two for every second recursive call, so the sequence of inputs quickly converges to the base case (see EXERCISE 2.3.11). This recursive solution to the problem of computing the greatest common divisor is known as *Euclid's algorithm* and is one of the oldest known algorithms—it is over 2,000 years old.

Towers of Hanoi No discussion of recursion would be complete without the ancient *towers of Hanoi* problem. In this problem, we have three poles and n discs that fit onto the poles. The discs differ in size and are initially stacked on one of the poles, in order from largest (disc n) at the bottom to smallest (disc 1) at the top. The task is to move all n discs to another pole, while obeying the following rules:

• Move only one disc at a time.
• Never place a larger disc on a smaller one.

One legend says that the world will end when a certain group of monks accomplishes this task in a temple with 64 golden discs on three diamond needles. But how can the monks accomplish the task at all, playing by the rules?

To solve the problem, our goal is to issue a sequence of instructions for moving the discs. We assume that the poles are arranged in a row, and that each instruction to move a disc specifies its number and whether to move it left or right. If a disc is on the left pole, an instruction to move left means to wrap to the right pole; if a disc is on the right pole, an instruction to move right means to wrap to the left pole. When the discs are all on one pole, there are two possible moves (move the smallest disc left or right); otherwise, there are three possible moves (move the smallest disc left or right, or make the one legal move involving the other two poles).

Choosing among these possibilities on each move to achieve the goal is a challenge that requires a plan. Recursion provides just the plan that we need, based on the following idea: first we move the top $n-1$ discs to an empty pole, then we move the largest disc to the other empty pole (where it does not inter-fere with the smaller ones), and then we complete the job by moving the $n-1$ discs onto the largest disc.

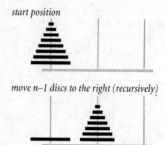

start position

TowersOfHanoi (PROGRAM 2.3.2) is a direct imple-mentation of this strategy. It reads in a command-line argu-ment n and prints out the solution to the Towers of Hanoi problem on n discs. The recursive static method moves() prints the sequence of moves to move the stack of discs to the left (if the argument left is true) or to the right (if left is false). It does so exactly according to the plan just described.

move n–1 discs to the right (recursively)

move largest disc left (wrap to rightmost)

Function call trees To better understand the behav-ior of modular programs that have multiple recursive calls (such as TowersOfHanoi), we use a visual representation known as a *function call tree*. Specifically, we represent each method call as a *tree node*, depicted as a circle labeled with the values of the arguments for that call. Below each tree node, we draw the tree nodes corresponding to each call in that use of the method (in order from left to right) and lines connecting to them. This diagram contains all the information we need to under-stand the behavior of the program. It contains a tree node for each method call.

move n–1 discs to the right (recursively)

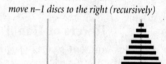

Recursive plan for towers of Hanoi

We can use function call trees to understand the behavior of any modular program, but they are particularly useful in exposing the behavior of recursive programs.

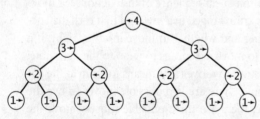

Function call tree for moves(4, true) *in* TowersOfHanoi

For example, the tree corresponding to a call to move() in TowersOfHanoi is easy to con-struct. Start by drawing a tree node labeled with the values of the command-line arguments. The first argument is the number of discs in the pile to be moved (and the label of the disc to actu-

Program 2.3.2   Towers of Hanoi

```java
public class TowersOfHanoi
{
   public static void moves(int n, boolean left)
   {
      if (n == 0) return;
      moves(n-1, !left);
      if (left) StdOut.println(n + " left");
      else      StdOut.println(n + " right");
      moves(n-1, !left);
   }
   public static void main(String[] args)
   {  // Read n, print moves to move n discs left.
      int n = Integer.parseInt(args[0]);
      moves(n, true);
   }
}
```

n	number of discs
left	direction to move pile

The recursive method moves() *prints the moves needed to move n discs to the left (if* left *is* true*) or to the right (if* left *is* false*).*

```
% java TowersOfHanoi 1
1 left

% java TowersOfHanoi 2
1 right
2 left
1 right

% java TowersOfHanoi 3
1 left
2 right
1 left
3 left
1 left
2 right
1 left
```

```
% java TowersOfHanoi 4
1 right
2 left
1 right
3 right
1 right
2 left
1 right
4 left
1 right
2 left
1 right
3 right
1 right
2 left
1 right
```

ally be moved); the second is the direction to move the pile. For clarity, we depict the direction (a `boolean` value) as an arrow that points left or right, since that is our interpretation of the value—the direction to move the piece. Then draw two tree nodes below with the number of discs decremented by 1 and the direction switched, and continue doing so until only nodes with labels corresponding to a first argument value 1 have no nodes below them. These nodes correspond to calls on `moves()` that do not lead to further recursive calls.

Take a moment to study the function call tree depicted earlier in this section and to compare it with the corresponding function call trace depicted at right. When you do so, you will see that the recursion tree is just a compact representation of the trace. In particular, reading the node labels from left to right gives the moves needed to solve the problem.

Moreover, when you study the tree, you probably notice several patterns, including the following two:

• Alternate moves involve the smallest disc.

• That disc always moves in the same direction.

These observations are relevant because they give a solution to the problem that does not require recursion (or even a computer): every other move involves the smallest disc (including the first and last), and each intervening move is the only legal move at the time not involving the smallest disc. We can *prove* that this method produces the same outcome as the recursive program, using induction. Having started centuries ago without the benefit of a computer, perhaps our monks are using this method.

Trees are relevant and important in understanding recursion because the tree is the quintessential recursive object. As an abstract mathematical model, trees play an essential role in many applications, and in CHAPTER 4, we will consider the use of trees as a computational model to structure data for efficient processing.

```
moves(4, true)
  moves(3, false)
    moves(2, true)
      moves(1, false)
        1 right

      2 left

    moves(1, true)
      1 right

  3 right
  moves(2, true)
    moves(1, false)
      1 right

    2 left

  moves(1, false)
    1 right
```

3 discs moved right

```
  4 left

moves(3, false)
  moves(2, true)
    moves(1, false)
      1 right

    2 left

  moves(1, false)
    1 right

  3 right
  moves(2, true)
    moves(1, false)
      1 right

    2 left

  moves(1, false)
    1 right
```

disc 4 moved left

3 discs moved right

Function call trace for `moves(4, true)`

Exponential time   One advantage of using recursion is that often we can develop mathematical models that allow us to prove important facts about the behavior of recursive programs. For the towers of Hanoi, we can estimate the amount of time until the end of the world (assuming that the legend is true). This exercise is important not just because it tells us that the end of the world is quite far off (even if the legend is true), but also because it provides insight that can help us avoid writing programs that will not finish until then.

For the towers of Hanoi, the mathematical model is simple: if we define the function $T(n)$ to be the number of move directives issued by `TowersOf-Hanoi` to move n discs from one peg to another, then the recursive code immediately implies that $T(n)$ must satisfy the following equation:

$T(n) = 2\ T(n-1) + 1$ for $n > 1$, with $T(1) = 1$

Such an equation is known in discrete mathematics as a *recurrence relation*. Recurrence relations naturally arise in the study of recursive programs. We can often use them to derive a closed-form expression for the quantity of interest. For $T(n)$, you may have already guessed from the initial values $T(1) = 1$, $T(2) = 3$, $T(3), = 7$, and $T(4) = 15$ that $T(n) = 2^n - 1$. The recurrence relation provides a way to *prove* this to be true, by mathematical induction:

• *Base case*: $T(1) = 2^n - 1 = 1$

• *Induction step*: if $T(n-1)= 2^{n-1} - 1$, $T(n) = 2\ (2^{n-1} - 1) + 1 = 2^n - 1$

Therefore, by induction, $T(n) = 2^n - 1$ for all $n > 0$. The minimum possible number of moves also satisfies the same recurrence (see EXERCISE 2.3.9).

Knowing the value of $T(n)$, we can estimate the amount of time required to perform all the moves. If the monks move discs at the rate of one per second, it would take more than one week for them to finish a 20-disc problem, more than 31 years to finish a 30-disc problem, and more than 348 *centuries* for them to finish a 40-disc problem (assuming that they do not make a mistake). The 64-disc problem would take more than 1.4 *million* centuries. The end of the world is likely to be even further off than that because those monks presumably never have had the benefit of using PROGRAM 2.3.2, and might not be able to move the discs so rapidly or to figure out so quickly which disc to move next.

Even computers are no match for exponential growth. A computer that can do a billion operations per second will still take centuries to do 2^{64} operations, and no computer will ever do 2^{1000} operations, say. The lesson is profound: with recur-

$(30, 2^{30})$

$(20, 2^{20})$

Exponential growth

sion, you can easily write simple short programs that take exponential time, but they simply will not run to completion when you try to run them for large n. Novices are often skeptical of this basic fact, so it is worth your while to pause now to think about it. To convince yourself that it is true, take the print statements out of `TowersOfHanoi` and run it for increasing values of n starting at 20. You can easily verify that each time you increase the value of n by 1, the running time doubles, and you will quickly lose patience waiting for it to finish. If you wait for an hour for some value of n, you will wait more than a day for $n+5$, more than a month for $n+10$, and more than a century for $n+20$ (no one has *that* much patience). Your computer is just not fast enough to run every short Java program that you write, no matter how simple the program might seem! *Beware of programs that might require exponential time.*

We are often interested in predicting the running time of our programs. In Section 4.1, we will discuss the use of the same process that we just used to help estimate the running time of other programs.

Gray codes

The towers of Hanoi problem is no toy. It is intimately related to basic algorithms for manipulating numbers and discrete objects. As an example, we consider *Gray codes*, a mathematical abstraction with numerous applications.

The playwright Samuel Beckett, perhaps best known for *Waiting for Godot*, wrote a play called *Quad* that had the following property: starting with an empty stage, characters enter and exit one at a time so that each subset of characters on the stage appears exactly once. How did Beckett generate the stage directions for this play?

One way to represent a subset of n discrete objects is to use a string of n bits. For Beckett's problem, we use a 4-bit string, with bits numbered from right to left and a bit value of 1 indicating the character onstage. For example, the string 0 1 0 1 corresponds to the scene with characters 3 and 1 onstage. This representation gives a quick proof of a basic fact: *the number different subsets of n objects is exactly 2^n*. *Quad* has four characters, so there are $2^4 = 16$ different scenes. Our task is to generate the stage directions.

An n-bit *Gray code* is a list of the 2^n different n-bit binary numbers such that each entry in the list differs in precisely one bit from its predecessor. Gray codes directly apply to Beckett's problem because changing the value of a bit from 0 to 1 corresponds to

code	subset	move
0 0 0 0	*empty*	
0 0 0 1	1	enter 1
0 0 1 1	2 1	enter 2
0 0 1 0	2	exit 1
0 1 1 0	3 2	enter 3
0 1 1 1	3 2 1	enter 1
0 1 0 1	3 1	exit 2
0 1 0 0	3	exit 1
1 1 0 0	4 3	enter 4
1 1 0 1	4 3 1	enter 1
1 1 1 1	4 3 2 1	enter 2
1 1 1 0	4 3 2	exit 1
1 0 1 0	4 2	exit 3
1 0 1 1	4 2 1	enter 1
1 0 0 1	4 1	exit 2
1 0 0 0	4	exit 1

Gray code representations

a character entering the subset onstage; changing a bit from 1 to 0 corresponds to a character exiting the subset.

How do we generate a Gray code? A recursive plan that is very similar to the one that we used for the towers of Hanoi problem is effective. The n-bit *binary-reflected Gray code* is defined recursively as follows:

- The $(n-1)$ bit code, with 0 prepended to each word, followed by
- The $(n-1)$ bit code *in reverse order*, with 1 prepended to each word

The 0-bit code is defined to be null, so the 1-bit code is 0 followed by 1. From this recursive definition, we can verify by induction that the n-bit binary reflected Gray code has the required property: adjacent codewords differ in one bit position. It is true by the inductive hypothesis, except possibly for the last codeword in the first half and the first codeword in the second half: this pair differs only in their first bit.

The recursive definition leads, after some careful thought, to the implementation in Beckett (PROGRAM 2.3.3) for printing out Beckett's stage directions. This program is remarkably similar to TowersOfHanoi. Indeed, except for nomenclature, the only difference is in the values of the second arguments in the recursive calls!

As with the directions in TowersOfHanoi, the enter and exit directions are redundant in Beckett, since exit is issued only when an actor is onstage, and enter is issued only when an actor is not onstage. Indeed, both Beckett and TowersOfHanoi directly involve the ruler function that we considered in one of our first programs (PROGRAM 1.2.1). Without the redundant instructions, they both implement a simple recursive function that could allow Ruler to print out the values of the ruler function for any value given as a command-line argument.

Gray codes have many applications, ranging from analog-to-digital converters to experimental design. They have been used in pulse code communication, the minimization of logic circuits, and hypercube architectures, and were even proposed to organize books on library shelves.

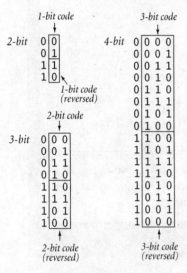

2-, 3-, and 4-bit Gray codes

Program 2.3.3   Gray code

```java
public class Beckett
{
   public static void moves(int n, boolean enter)
   {
      if (n == 0) return;
      moves(n-1, true);
      if (enter) StdOut.println("enter " + n);
      else       StdOut.println("exit  " + n);
      moves(n-1, false);
   }

   public static void main(String[] args)
   {
      int n = Integer.parseInt(args[0]);
      moves(n, true);
   }
}
```

n	number of characters
enter	stage direction

This recursive program gives Beckett's stage instructions (the bit positions that change in a binary-reflected Gray code). The bit position that changes is precisely described by the ruler function, and (of course) each character alternately enters and exits.

```
% java Beckett 1
enter 1

% java Beckett 2
enter 1
enter 2
exit  1

% java Beckett 3
enter 1
enter 2
exit  1
enter 3
enter 1
exit  2
exit  1
```

```
% java Beckett 4
enter 1
enter 2
exit  1
enter 3
enter 1
exit  2
exit  1
enter 4
enter 1
enter 2
exit  1
enter 3
enter 1
exit  2
exit  1
```

Recursive graphics   Simple recursive drawing schemes can lead to pictures that are remarkably intricate. Recursive drawings not only relate to numerous applications, but they also provide an appealing platform for developing a better understanding of properties of recursive programs, because we can watch the process of a recursive figure taking shape.

    As a first simple example, consider `Htree` (PROGRAM 2.3.4), which, given a command-line argument n, draws an *H-tree of order n*, defined as follows: The base case is to draw nothing for $n = 0$. The reduction step is to draw, within the unit square

    • three lines in the shape of the letter H

    • four H-trees of order $n-1$, one connected to each tip of the H

with the additional provisos that the H-trees of order $n-1$ are halved in size and centered in the four quadrants of the square.

order 1

order 2

order 3

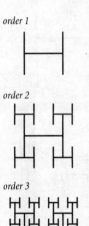

H-trees

    Drawings like these have many practical applications. For example, consider a cable company that needs to run cable to all of the homes distributed throughout its region. A reasonable strategy is to use an H-tree to get the signal to a suitable number of centers distributed throughout the region, then run cables connecting each home to the nearest center. The same problem is faced by computer designers who want to distribute power or signal throughout an integrated circuit chip.

    Though every drawing is in a fixed-size window, H-trees certainly exhibit exponential growth. An H-tree of order n connects 4^n centers, so you would be trying to plot more than a million lines with $n = 10$, more than a billion with $n = 15$, and the program will certainly not finish the drawing with $n = 30$.

    If you take a moment to run `Htree` on your computer for a drawing that takes a minute or so to complete, you will, just by watching the drawing progress, have the opportunity to gain substantial insight into the nature of recursive programs, because you can see the order in which the H figures appear and how they form into H-trees. An even more instructive exercise, which derives from the fact that the same drawing results no matter in what order the recursive `draw()` calls and the `StdDraw.line()` calls appear, is to observe the effect of rearranging the order of these calls on the order in which the lines appear in the emerging drawing (see EXERCISE 2.3.14).

Program 2.3.4   Recursive graphics

```java
public class Htree
{
    public static void draw(int n, double sz, double x, double y)
    {  // Draw an H-tree centered at x, y
       // of depth n and size sz.
       if (n == 0) return;
       double x0 = x - sz/2, x1 = x + sz/2;
       double y0 = y - sz/2, y1 = y + sz/2;
       StdDraw.line(x0,  y, x1,  y);
       StdDraw.line(x0, y0, x0, y1);
       StdDraw.line(x1, y0, x1, y1);
       draw(n-1, sz/2, x0, y0);
       draw(n-1, sz/2, x0, y1);
       draw(n-1, sz/2, x1, y0);
       draw(n-1, sz/2, x1, y1);
    }

    public static void main(String[] args)
    {
       int n = Integer.parseInt(args[0]);
       draw(n, .5, .5, .5);
    }
}
```

n	depth
sz	line length
x, y	center

This recursive program draws three lines in the shape of the letter H that connect the center (x, y) of the square with the centers of the four quadrants, then calls itself for each of the quadrants, using an integer argument to control the depth of the recursion.

% java Htree 3

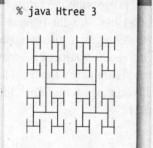

% java Htree 4

% java Htree 5

Brownian bridge   An H-tree is a simple example of a *fractal*: a geometric shape that can be divided into parts, each of which is (approximately) a reduced-size copy of the original. Fractals are easy to produce with recursive programs, although scientists, mathematicians, and programmers study them from many different points of view. We have already encountered fractals several times in this book—for example, IFS (PROGRAM 2.2.3).

The study of fractals plays an important and lasting role in artistic expression, economic analysis and scientific discovery. Artists and scientists use them to build compact models of complex shapes that arise in nature and resist description using conventional geometry, such as clouds, plants, mountains, riverbeds, human skin, and many others. Economists also use fractals to model function graphs of economic indicators.

Fractional Brownian motion is a mathematical model for creating realistic fractal models for many naturally rugged shapes. It is used in computational finance and in the study of many natural phenomena, including ocean flows and nerve membranes. Computing the exact fractals specified by the model can be a difficult challenge, but it is not difficult to compute approximations with recursive programs. We consider one simple example here; you can find much more information about the model on the booksite.

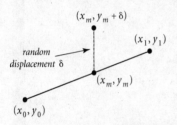

Brownian bridge calculation

Brownian (PROGRAM 2.3.5) produces a function graph that approximates a simple example of fractional Brownian motion known as a *Brownian bridge* and closely related functions. You can think of this graph as a random walk that connects two points, from (x_0, y_0) to (x_1, y_1), controlled by a few parameters. The implementation is based on the *midpoint displacement method*, which is a recursive plan for drawing the plot within the interval $[x_0, x_1]$. The base case (when the size of the interval is smaller than a given tolerance) is to draw a straight line connecting the two endpoints. The reduction case is to divide the interval into two halves, proceeding as follows:

• Compute the midpoint (x_m, y_m) of the interval.
• Add to the y-coordinate y_m of the midpoint a random value δ, chosen from the Gaussian distribution with mean 0 and a given variance.
• Recur on the subintervals, dividing the variance by a given scaling factor s.

The shape of the curve is controlled by two parameters: the *volatility* (initial value of the variance) controls the distance the graph strays from the straight line con-

Program 2.3.5   Brownian bridge

```java
public class Brownian
{
    public static void curve(double x0, double y0,
                             double x1, double y1,
                             double var, double s)
    {
        if (x1 - x0 < .01)
        {
            StdDraw.line(x0, y0, x1, y1);
            return;
        }
        double xm = (x0 + x1) / 2;
        double ym = (y0 + y1) / 2;
        double delta = StdRandom.gaussian(0, Math.sqrt(var));
        curve(x0, y0, xm, ym+delta, var/s, s);
        curve(xm, ym+delta, x1, y1, var/s, s);
    }
    public static void main(String[] args)
    {
        double H = Double.parseDouble(args[0]);
        double s = Math.pow(2, 2*H);
        curve(0, .5, 1.0, .5, .01, s);
    }
}
```

x0, y0	*left endpoint*
x1, y1	*right endpoint*
xm, ym	*middle*
delta	*displacement*
var	*variance*
H	*Hurst exponent*

By adding a small, random Gaussian to a recursive program that would otherwise plot a straight line, we get fractal curves. The command-line argument H, *known as the Hurst exponent, controls the smoothness of the curves.*

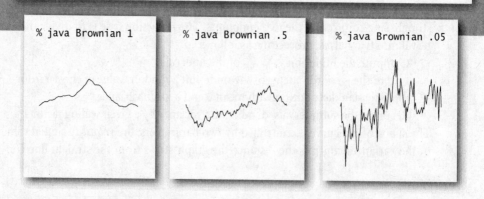

```
% java Brownian 1        % java Brownian .5        % java Brownian .05
```

necting the points, and *the Hurst exponent* controls the smoothness of the curve. We denote the Hurst exponent by H and divide the variance by 2^{2H} at each recursive level. When H is 1/2 (divide by 2 at each level) the curve is a Brownian bridge: a continuous version of the gambler's ruin problem (see PROGRAM 1.3.8). When $0 < H < 1/2$, the displacements tend to decrease, resulting in a smoother curve; and when $2 > H > 1/2$, the displacements tend to increase, resulting in a rougher curve. The value $2 - H$ is known as the *fractal dimension* of the curve.

The volatility and initial endpoints of the interval have to do with scale and positioning. The `main()` test client in `Brownian` allows you to experiment with the smoothness parameter. With values larger than 1/2, you get plots that look something like the horizon in a mountainous landscape; with values smaller than 1/2, you get plots similar to those you might see for the value of a stock index.

Extending the midpoint displacement method to two dimensions produces fractals known as *plasma clouds*. To draw a rectangular plasma cloud, we use a recursive plan where the base case is to draw a rectangle of a given color and the reduction step is to draw a plasma cloud in each quadrant with colors that are perturbed from the average with a random Gaussian. Using the same volatility and smoothness controls as in `Brownian`, we can produce synthetic clouds that are remarkably realistic. We can use the same code to produce synthetic terrain, by interpreting the color value as the altitude. Variants of this scheme are widely used in the entertainment industry to generate background scenery for movies and computer games.

A plasma cloud

Pitfalls of recursion By now, you are perhaps persuaded that recursion can help you to write compact and elegant programs. As you begin to craft your own recursive programs, you need to be aware of several common pitfalls that can arise. We have already discussed one of them in some detail (the running time of your program might grow exponentially). Once identified, these problems are generally not difficult to overcome, but you will learn to be very careful to avoid them when writing recursive programs.

Missing base case. Consider the following recursive function, which is supposed to compute Harmonic numbers, but is missing a base case:

```java
public static double H(int N)
{
    return H(N-1) + 1.0/N;
}
```

If you run a client that calls this function, it will repeatedly call itself and never return, so your program will never terminate. You probably already have encountered infinite loops, where you invoke your program and nothing happens (or perhaps you get an unending sequence of lines of output). With infinite recursion, however, the result is different because the system keeps track of each recursive call (using a mechanism that we will discuss in SECTION 4.3, based on a data structure known as a *stack*) and eventually runs out of memory trying to do so. Eventually, Java reports a StackOverflowError. When you write a recursive program, you should always try to convince yourself that it has the desired effect by an informal argument based on mathematical induction. Doing so might uncover a missing base case.

No guarantee of convergence. Another common problem is to include within a recursive function a recursive call to solve a subproblem that is not smaller than the original problem. For example, the following method will go into an infinite recursive loop for any value of its argument N except 1:

```java
public static double H(int N)
{
    if (N == 1) return 1.0;
    return H(N) + 1.0/N;
}
```

Bugs like this one are easy to spot, but subtle versions of the same problem can be harder to identify. You may find several examples in the exercises at the end of this section.

Excessive memory requirements. If a function calls itself recursively an excessive number of times before returning, the memory required by Java to keep track of the recursive calls may be prohibitive, resulting in a `StackOverflowError`. To get an idea of how much memory is involved, run a small set of experiments using our recursive program for computing the Harmonic numbers for increasing values of N:

```
public static double H(int N)
{
    if (N == 1) return 1.0;
    return H(N-1) + 1.0/N;
}
```

The point at which you get `StackOverflowError` will give you some idea of how much memory Java uses to implement recursion. By contrast, you can run PRO-GRAM 1.3.5 to compute H_N for huge N using only a tiny bit of space.

Excessive recomputation. The temptation to write a simple recursive program to solve a problem must always be tempered by the understanding that a simple program might take exponential time (unnecessarily) due to excessive recomputation. This effect is possible even in the simplest recursive programs, and you certainly need to learn to avoid it. For example, the *Fibonacci sequence*

    0 1 1 2 3 5 8 13 21 34 55 89 144 233 377 ...

is defined by the recurrence $F_n = F_{n-1} + F_{n-2}$ for $n \geq 2$ with $F_0 = 0$ and $F_1 = 1$. The Fibonacci sequence has many interesting properties and arise in numerous applications. A novice programmer might implement this recursive function to compute numbers in the Fibonacci sequence:

```
public static long F(int n)
{
    if (n == 0) return 0;
    if (n == 1) return 1;
    return F(n-1) + F(n-2);
}
```

However, this program is spectacularly inefficient! Novice programmers often refuse to believe this fact, and run code like this expecting that the computer is certainly fast enough to crank out an answer. Go ahead; see if your computer is fast enough to use this program to compute F_{50}. To see why it is futile to do so, consider what the function does to compute $F(8) = 21$.

It first computes $F(7) = 13$ and $F(6) = 8$. To compute $F(7)$, it recursively computes $F(6) = 8$ *again* and $F(5) = 5$. Things rapidly get worse because both times it computes $F(6)$, it ignores the fact that it already computed $F(5)$, and so forth. In fact, you can prove by induction that the number of times this program computes F(1) when computing F(n) is precisely F_n (see EXERCISE 2.3.12). The mistake of recomputation is compounded exponentially. As an example, to compute F(200), the number of times this method needs to compute F(1) is $F_{200} > 10^{43}$! No imaginable computer will ever be able to do this many calculations. *Beware of programs that might require exponential time.* Many calculations that arise and find natural expression as recursive programs fall into this category. Do not fall into the trap of implementing and trying to run them.

The following is one caveat: a systematic technique known as *memoization* allows us to avoid this pitfall while still taking advantage of the compact recursive description of a computation. In memoization, we maintain an array that keeps track of the values we have computed so that we can return those values and make recursive calls only for new values. This technique is a form of *dynamic programming*, a well-studied technique for organizing computations that you will learn if you take courses in algorithms or operations research.

```
F(7)
  F(6)
    F(5)
      F(4)
        F(3)
          F(2)
            F(1)
              return 1
            F(0)
              return 0
            return 1
          F(1)
            return 1
          return 2
        F(2)
          F(1)
            return 1
          F(0)
            return 0
          return 1
        return 3
      F(3)
        F(2)
          F(1)
            return 1
          F(0)
            return 0
          return 1
        F(1)
          return 1
        return 2
      return 5
    F(4)
      F(3)
        F(2)
         .
         .
         .
```

Wrong way to compute Fibonacci numbers

Perspective   Programmers who do not use recursion are missing two opportunities. First recursion leads to compact solutions to complex problems. Second, recursive solutions embody an argument that the program operates as anticipated. In the early days of computing, the overhead associated with recursive programs was prohibitive in some systems, and many people avoided recursion. In modern systems like Java, recursion is often the method of choice.

If you are intrigued by the mystery of how the Java system manages to implement the illusion of independently operating copies of the same piece of code, be assured that we will consider this issue in CHAPTER 4. You may be surprised at the simplicity of the solution. It is so easy to implement that programmers were using recursion well before the advent of high-level programming languages like Java. Indeed, you might be surprised to learn that you could write programs equivalent to the ones considered in this chapter with just the basic loops, conditionals, and arrays programming model discussed in CHAPTER 1.

Recursion has reinforced for us the idea of proving that a program operates as intended. The natural connection between recursion and mathematical induction is essential. For everyday programming, our interest in correctness is to save time and energy tracking down bugs. In modern applications, security and privacy concerns make correctness an *essential* part of programming. If the programmer cannot be convinced that an application works as intended, how can a user who wants to keep personal data private and secure be so convinced?

Recursive functions truly illustrate the power of a carefully articulated abstraction. While the concept of a function having the ability to call itself seems absurd to many people at first, the many examples that we have considered are certainly evidence that mastering recursion is essential to understanding and exploiting computation and in understanding the role of computational models in studying natural phenomena.

Recursion is the last piece in a programming model that served to build much of the computational infrastructure that was developed as computers emerged to take a central role in daily life in the latter part of the 20th century. Programs built from libraries of functions consisting of statements that operate on primitive types of data, conditionals, loops, and function calls (including recursive ones) can solve important applications of all sorts. In the next section, we emphasize this point and review these concepts in the context of a large application. In CHAPTER 3 and in CHAPTER 4, we will examine extensions to these basic ideas that embrace a more expansive style of programming that now dominates the computing landscape.

Q. Are there situations when iteration is the only option available to address a problem?

A. No, any loop can be replaced by a recursive function, though the recursive version might require excessive memory.

Q. Are there situations when recursion is the only option available to address a problem?

A. No, any recursive function can be replaced by an iterative counterpart. In SECTION 4.3, we will see how compilers produce code for function calls by using a data structure called a *stack*.

Q. Which should I prefer, recursion or iteration?

A. Whichever leads to the simpler, more easily understood, or more efficient code.

Q. I get the concern about excessive space and excessive recomputation in recursive code. Anything else to be concerned about?

A. Be extremely wary of creating arrays in recursive code. The amount of space used can pile up very quickly, as can the amount of time required for memory management.

Exercises

2.3.1 What happens if you call `factorial()` with a negative value of n? With a large value, say, 35?

2.3.2 Write a recursive function that computes the value of ln $(N!)$

2.3.3 Give the sequence of integers printed by a call to `ex233(6)`:

```
public static int ex233(int n)
{
    if (n <= 0) return;
    StdOut.println(n);
    ex233(n-2);
    ex233(n-3);
    StdOut.println(n);
}
```

2.3.4 Give the value of `ex234(6)`:

```
public static String ex234(int n)
{
    if (n <= 0) return "";
    return ex234(n-3) + n + ex234(n-2) + n;
}
```

2.3.5 Criticize the following recursive function:

```
public static String ex235(int n)
{
    String s = ex235(n-3) + n + ex235(n-2) + n;
    if (n <= 0) return "";
    return s;
}
```

Answer: The base case will never be reached. A call to `ex235(3)` will result in calls to `ex235(0)`, `ex235(-3)`, `ex235(-6)`, and so forth until a `StackOverflowError`.

2.3.6 Given four positive integers a, b, c, and d, explain what value is computed by `gcd(gcd(a, b), gcd(c, d))`.

2.3.7   Explain in terms of integers and divisors the effect of the following Euclid-like function.

```
public static boolean gcdlike(int p, int q)
{
    if (q == 0) return (p == 1);
    return gcdlike(q, p % q);
}
```

2.3.8   Consider the following recursive function.

```
public static int mystery(int a, int b)
{
    if (b == 0)       return 0;
    if (b % 2 == 0) return mystery(a+a, b/2);
    return mystery(a+a, b/2) + a;
}
```

What are the values of mystery(2, 25) and mystery(3, 11)? Given positive integers a and b, describe what value mystery(a, b) computes. Answer the same question, but replace + with *.

2.3.9   Write a recursive program Ruler to plot the subdivisions of a ruler using StdDraw as in PROGRAM 1.2.1.

2.3.10   Solve the following recurrence relations, all with $T(1) = 1$. Assume N is a power of two.
- $T(N) = T(N/2) + 1$.
- $T(N) = 2T(N/2) + 1$.
- $T(N) = 2T(N/2) + N$.
- $T(N) = 4T(N/2) + 3$.

2.3.11   Prove by induction that the minimum possible number of moves needed to solve the towers of Hanoi satisfies the same recurrence as the number of moves used by our recursive solution.

2.3.12   Prove by induction that the recursive program given in the text makes exactly F_n recursive calls to F(1) when computing F(n).

2.3.13 Prove that the second argument to gcd() decreases by at least a factor of two for every second recursive call, and then prove that gcd(p, q) uses at most $\log_2 N$ recursive calls where N is the larger of p and q.

2.3.14 Modify Htree (PROGRAM 2.3.4) to animate the drawing of the H-tree.

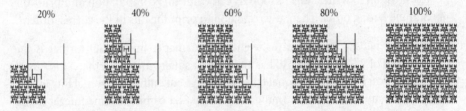

Next, rearrange the order of the recursive calls (and the base case), view the resulting animation, and explain each outcome.

Creative Exercises

2.3.15 *Binary representation.* Write a program that takes a positive integer N (in decimal) from the command line and prints out its binary representation. Recall, in PROGRAM 1.3.7, that we used the method of subtracting out powers of 2. Instead, use the following simpler method: repeatedly divide 2 into N and read the remainders backwards. First, write a while loop to carry out this computation and print the bits in the wrong order. Then, use recursion to print the bits in the correct order.

2.3.16 *A4 paper.* The width-to-height ratio of paper in the ISO format is the square root of 2 to 1. Format A0 has an area of 1 square meter. Format A1 is A0 cut with a vertical line into two equal halves, A2 is A1 cut with a horizontal line into in two halves, and so on. Write a program that takes a command-line integer n and uses StdDraw to show how to cut a sheet of A0 paper into 2^n pieces.

2.3.17 *Permutations.* Write a program Permutations that takes a command-line argument n and prints out all $n!$ permutations of the n letters starting at a (assume that n is no greater than 26). A permutation of n elements is one of the $n!$ possible orderings of the elements. As an example, when $n = 3$ you should get the following output. Do not worry about the order in which you enumerate them.

    bca cba cab acb bac abc

2.3.18 *Permutations of size k.* Modify Permutations so that it takes two command-line arguments n and k, and prints out all $P(n,k) = n! / (n-k)!$ permutations that contain exactly k of the n elements. Below is the desired output when $k = 2$ and $n = 4$. You need not print them out in any particular order.

    ab ac ad ba bc bd ca cb cd da db dc

2.3.19 *Combinations.* Write a program Combinations that takes one command-line argument n and prints out all 2^n combinations of any size. A combination is a subset of the n elements, independent of order. As an example, when $n = 3$ you should get the following output.

    a ab abc ac b bc c

Note that your program needs to print the empty string (subset of size 0).

2.3.20 *Combinations of size k.* Modify `Combinations` so that it takes two command-line arguments *n* and *k*, and prints out all $C(n, k) = n! / (k!(n-k)!)$ combinations of size *k*. For example, when *n* = 5 and *k* = 3, you should get the following output:

    abc abd abe acd ace ade bcd bce bde cde

2.3.21 *Hamming distance.* The Hamming distance between two bit strings of length *n* is equal to the number of bits in which the two strings differ. Write a program that reads in an integer k and a bit string s from the command line, and prints out all bit strings that have Hamming distance at most k from s. For example if k is 2 and s is 0000, then your program should print

    0011 0101 0110 1001 1010 1100

Hint: Choose k of the *n* bits in s to flip.

2.3.22 *Recursive squares.* Write a program to produce each of the following recursive patterns. The ratio of the sizes of the squares is 2.2:1. To draw a shaded square, draw a filled gray square, then an unfilled black square.

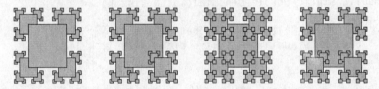

2.3.23 *Pancake flipping.* You have a stack of *n* pancakes of varying sizes on a griddle. Your goal is to rearrange the stack in descending order so that the largest pancake is on the bottom and the smallest one is on top. You are only permitted to flip the top *k* pancakes, thereby reversing their order. Devise a recursive scheme to arrange the pancakes in the proper order that uses at most 2*n* − 3 flips.

2.3.24 *Gray code.* Modify `Beckett` (PROGRAM 2.3.3) to print out the Gray code (not just the sequence of bit positions that change).

2.3.25 *Towers of Hanoi variant.* Consider the following variant of the towers of Hanoi problem. There are 2n discs of increasing size stored on three poles. Initially all of the discs with odd size (1, 3, ..., 2n-1) are piled on the left pole from top to bottom in increasing order of size; all of the discs with even size (2, 4, ..., 2n) are piled on the right pole. Write a program to provide instructions for moving the odd discs to the right pole and the even discs to the left pole, obeying the same rules as for towers of Hanoi.

order 1

2.3.26 *Animated towers of Hanoi.* Use StdDraw to animate a solution to the towers of Hanoi problem, moving the discs at a rate of approximately 1 per second.

order 2

2.3.27 *Sierpinski triangles.* Write a recursive program to draw Sierpinski triangles (see PROGRAM 2.2.3). As with Htree, use a command-line argument to control the depth of the recursion.

order 3

2.3.28 *Binomial distribution.* Estimate the number of recursive calls that would be used by the code

```
public static double binomial(int N, int k)
{
    if ((N == 0) || (k < 0)) return 1.0;
    return (binomial(N-1, k) + binomial(N-1, k-1))/2.0;
}
```

Sierpinski triangles

to compute binomial(100, 50). Develop a better implementation that is based on memoization. *Hint*: See EXERCISE 1.4.37.

2.3.29 *Collatz function.* Consider the following recursive function, which is related to a famous unsolved problem in number theory, known as the *Collatz problem*, or the *3n+1 problem*:

```
public static void collatz(int n)
{
    StdOut.print(n + " ");
    if (n == 1) return;
    if (n % 2 == 0) collatz(n / 2);
    else            collatz(3*n + 1);
}
```

For example, a call to `collatz(7)` prints the sequence

```
7 22 11 34 17 52 26 13 40 20 10 5 16 8 4 2 1
```

as a consequence of 17 recursive calls. Write a program that takes a command-line argument N and returns the value of n < N for which the number of recursive calls for `collatz(n)` is maximized. The unsolved problem is that no one knows whether the function terminates for all positive values of n (mathematical induction is no help, because one of the recursive calls is for a larger value of the argument).

2.3.30 *Brownian island.* B. Mandelbrot asked the famous question *How long is the coast of Britain?* Modify `Brownian` to get a program `BrownianIsland` that plots Brownian islands, whose coastlines resemble that of Great Britain. The modifications are simple: first, change `curve()` to add a Gaussian to the x-coordinate as well as to the y-coordinate; second, change `main()` to draw a curve from the point at the center of the canvas back to itself. Experiment with various values of the parameters to get your program to produce islands with a realistic look.

Brownian islands with Hurst exponent of .76

2.3.31 *Plasma clouds.* Write a recursive program to draw plasma clouds, using the method suggested in the text.

2.3.32 *A strange function.* Consider McCarthy's 91 function:

```
public static int mcCarthy(int n)
{
    if (n > 100) return n - 10;
    return mcCarthy(mcCarthy(n+11));
}
```

Determine the value of mcCarthy(50) without using a computer. Give the number of recursive calls used by mcCarthy() to compute this result. Prove that the base case is reached for all positive integers n or give a value of n for which this function goes into a recursive loop.

2.3.30 *Recursive tree.* Write a program Tree that takes a command-line argument N and produces the following recursive patterns for N equal to 1, 2, 3, 4, and 8.

2.4 Case Study: Percolation

THE PROGRAMMING TOOLS THAT WE HAVE considered to this point allow us to attack all manner of important problems. We conclude our study of functions and modules by considering a case study of developing a program to solve an interesting scientific problem. Our purpose in doing so is to review the basic elements that we have covered, in the context of the various challenges that you might face in solving a specific problem, and to illustrate a programming style that you can apply broadly.

Our example applies a computing technique to a simple model that has been extremely useful in helping scientists and engineers in numerous contexts. We consider a widely applicable technique known as *Monte Carlo simulation* to study a natural model known as *percolation*. This is not just of direct importance in materials science and geology, but also explains many other natural phenomena.

The term "Monte Carlo simulation" is broadly used to encompass any technique that employs randomness to generate approximate solutions to quantitative problems. We have used it in several other contexts already—for example, in the gambler's ruin and coupon collector problems. Rather than develop a complete mathematical model or measure all possible outcomes of an experiment, we rely on the laws of probability.

We will learn quite a bit about percolation in this case study, but our focus is on the process of developing modular programs to address computational tasks. We identify subtasks that can be independently addressed, striving to identify the key underlying abstractions and asking ourselves questions such as the following: Is there some specific subtask that would help solve this problem? What are the essential characteristics of this specific subtask? Might a solution that addresses these essential characteristics be useful in solving other problems? Asking such questions pays significant dividend, because they lead us to develop software that is easier to create, debug, and reuse, so that we can more quickly address the main problem of interest.

Percolation   It is not unusual for local interactions in a system to imply global properties. For example, an electrical engineer might be interested in composite systems comprised of randomly distributed insulating and metallic materials: what fraction of the materials need to be metallic so that the composite system is an electrical conductor? As another example, a geologist might be interested in a porous landscape with water on the surface (or oil below). Under what conditions will the water be able to drain through to the bottom (or the oil to gush through to the surface)? Scientists have defined an abstract process known as *percolation* to model such situations. It has been studied widely, and shown to be an accurate model in a dizzying variety of applications, beyond insulating materials and porous substances to the spread of forest fires and disease epidemics to evolution to the study of the internet.

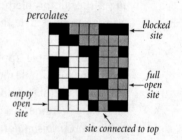

For simplicity, we begin by working in two dimensions and model the system as an *N*-by-*N* grid of *sites*. Each site is either *blocked* or *open*; open sites are initially *empty*. A *full* site is an open site that can be connected to an open site in the top row via a chain of neighboring (left, right, up, down) open sites. If there is a full site in the bottom row, then we say that the system *percolates*. In other words, a system percolates if we fill all open sites connected to the top row and that process fills some open site on the bottom row. For the insulating/metallic materials example, the open sites correspond to metallic materials, so that a system that percolates has a metallic path from top to bottom, with full sites conducting. For the porous substance example, the open sites correspond to empty space through which water might flow, so that a system that percolates lets water fill open sites, flowing from top to bottom.

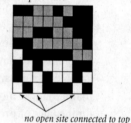

Percolation examples

In a famous scientific problem that has been heavily studied for decades, researchers are interested in the following question: if sites are independently set to be open with *vacancy probability p* (and therefore blocked with probability $1-p$), what is the probability that the system percolates? No mathematical solution to this problem has yet been derived. Our task is to write computer programs to help study the problem.

Basic scaffolding   To address percolation with a Java program, we face numerous decisions and challenges, and we certainly will end up with much more code than in the short programs that we have considered so far in this book. Our goal is to illustrate an incremental style of programming where we independently develop modules that address parts of the problem, building confidence with a small computational infrastructure of our own design and construction as we proceed.

percolation system

blocked sites
```
1 1 0 0 0 1 1 1
0 1 1 0 0 0 0 0
0 0 0 1 1 0 0 1
1 1 0 0 1 0 0 0
1 0 0 0 1 0 0 1
1 0 1 1 1 1 0 0
0 1 0 1 0 0 0 0
0 0 0 0 1 0 1 1
```

open sites
```
0 0 1 1 1 0 0 0
1 0 0 1 1 1 1 1
1 1 1 0 0 1 1 0
0 0 1 1 0 1 1 1
0 1 1 1 0 1 1 0
0 1 0 0 0 0 1 1
1 0 1 0 1 1 1 1
1 1 1 1 0 1 0 0
```

full sites
```
0 0 1 1 1 0 0 0
0 0 0 1 1 1 1 1
0 0 0 0 0 1 1 0
0 0 0 0 0 1 1 1
0 0 0 0 0 1 1 0
0 0 0 0 0 0 1 1
0 0 0 0 1 1 1 1
0 0 0 0 0 1 0 0
```

Percolation representations

The first step is to pick a representation of the data. This decision can have substantial impact on the kind of code that we write later, so it is not to be taken lightly. Indeed, it is often the case that we learn something while working with a chosen representation that causes us to scrap it and start all over using a new one.

For percolation, the path to an effective representation is clear: use two-dimensional arrays. What type of data should we use for each entry? One possibility is to use integers, with a code such as 0 to indicate an empty site, 1 to indicate a blocked site, and 2 to indicate a full site. Alternatively, note that we typically describe sites in terms of questions: Is the site open or blocked? Is the site full or empty? This characteristic of the entries suggests that we might use *boolean* matrices, where all entries are true or false.

Boolean matrices are fundamental mathematical objects with many applications. Java itself does not provide direct support for operations on boolean matrices, but we can use the methods in StdArrayIO (see PROGRAM 2.2.2) to read and write them. This choice illustrates a basic principle that often comes up in programming: *the effort required to build a more general tool usually pays dividends*. Using a natural abstraction such as boolean matrices is preferable to using a specialized representation. In the present context, it turns out that using boolean instead of int matrices also leads to code that is easier to understand. Eventually, we will want to work with random data, but we also want to be able to read and write to files because debugging programs with random inputs can be counterproductive. With random data, you get different input each time that you run the program; after fixing a bug, what you want to see is the *same* input that you just used, to check that the fix was effective. Accordingly, it is best to start with some specific cases that we understand, kept in files formatted to be read by StdArrayIO.readBoolean2D() (dimensions followed by 0 and 1 values in row-major order).

When you start working on a new problem that involves several files, it is usually worthwhile to create a new folder (directory) to isolate those files from others that you may be working on. For example, we might start with stdlib.jar in a folder named percolation, so that we have access to the methods in our libraries StdArrayIO.java, StdIn.java, StdOut.java, StdDraw.java, StdRandom.java, and StdStats.java. We can then implement and debug the basic code for reading and writing percolation systems, create test files, check that the files are compatible with the code, and so forth, before really worrying about percolation at all. This type of code, sometimes called *scaffolding*, is straightforward to implement, but making sure that it is solid at the outset will save us from distraction when approaching the main problem.

Now we can turn to the code for testing whether a boolean matrix represents a system that percolates. Referring to the helpful interpretation in which we can think of the task as simulating what would happen if the top were flooded with water (does it flow to the bottom or not?), our first design decision is that we will want to have a flow() method that takes as an argument a two-dimensional boolean array open[][] that specifies which sites are open and returns another two-dimensional boolean array full[][] that specifies which sites are full. For the moment, we will not worry at all about how to implement this method; we are just deciding how to organize the computation. It is also clear that we will want client code to be able to use a percolates() method that checks whether the array returned by flow() has any full sites on the bottom.

Percolation (Program 2.4.1) summarizes these decisions. It does not perform any interesting computation, but, after running and debugging this code we can start thinking about actually solving the problem. A method that performs no computation, such as flow(), is sometimes called a *stub*. Having this stub allows us to test and debug percolates() and main() in the context in which we will need them. We refer to code like Program 2.4.1 as *scaffolding*. As with scaffolding that construction workers use when erecting a building, this kind of code provides the support that we need to develop a program. By fully implementing and debugging this code (much, if not all, of which we need, anyway) at the outset, we provide a sound basis for building code to solve the problem at hand. Often, we carry the analogy one step further and remove the scaffolding (or replace it with something better) after the implementation is complete.

Program 2.4.1 *Percolation scaffolding*

```
public class Percolation
{
   public static boolean[][] flow(boolean[][] open)
   {
      int N = open.length;
      boolean[][] full = new boolean[N][N];
      // Percolation flow computation goes here.
      return full;
   }

   public static boolean percolates(boolean[][] open)
   {
      boolean[][] full = flow(open);
      int N = full.length;
      for (int j = 0; j < N; j++)
         if (full[N-1][j]) return true;
      return false;
   }

   public static void main(String[] args)
   {
      boolean[][] open = StdArrayIO.readBoolean2D();
      StdArrayIO.print(flow(open));
      StdOut.println(percolates(open));
   }
}
```

N	system size (N-by-N)
full[][]	full sites
open[][]	open sites

To get started with percolation, we implement and debug this code, which handles all the straightforward tasks surrounding the computation. The primary function flow() returns an array giving the full sites (none, in the placeholder code here). The helper function perco-lates() checks the bottom row of the returned array to decide whether the system percolates. The test client main() reads a boolean matrix from standard input and then prints the result of calling flow() and percolates() for that matrix.

```
% more testEZ.txt
5 5
0 1 1 0 1
0 0 1 1 1
1 1 0 1 1
1 0 0 0 1
0 1 1 1 1
```

```
% java Percolation < testEZ.txt
5 5
0 0 0 0 0
0 0 0 0 0
0 0 0 0 0
0 0 0 0 0
0 0 0 0 0
false
```

Vertical percolation Given a boolean matrix that represents the open sites, how do we figure out whether it represents a system that percolates? As we will see at the end of this section, this computation turns out to be directly related to a fundamental question in computer science. For the moment, we will consider a much simpler version of the problem that we call *vertical percolation*.

vertically percolates

*site connected to top
with a vertical path*

does not vertically percolate

The simplification is to restrict attention to vertical connection paths. If such a path connects top to bottom in a system, we say that the system *vertically percolates* along the path (and that the system itself vertically percolates). This restriction is perhaps intuitive if we are talking about sand traveling through cement, but not if we are talking about water traveling through cement or about electrical conductivity. Simple as it is, vertical percolation is a problem that is interesting in its own right because it suggests various mathematical questions. Does the restriction make a significant difference? How many vertical percolation paths do we expect?

*no open site connected to
top with a vertical path*

Vertical percolation

Determining the sites that are filled by some path that is connected vertically to the top is a simple calculation. We initialize the top row of our result array from the top row of the percolation system, with full sites corresponding to open ones. Then, moving from top to bottom, we fill in each row of the array by checking the corresponding row of the percolation system. Proceeding from top to bottom, we fill in the rows of full[][] to mark as true all entries that correspond to sites in open[][] that are vertically connected to a full site on the previous row. PROGRAM 2.4.2 is an implementation of flow() for Percolation that returns a boolean array of full sites (true if connected to the top via a vertical path, false otherwise).

Testing After we become convinced that our code is behaving as planned, we want to run it on a broader variety of test cases and address some of our scientific questions. At this point, our initial scaffolding becomes less useful, as representing large boolean matrices with 0s and 1s on standard input and standard output and maintaining large numbers

*connected to top via a
vertical path of filled sites*

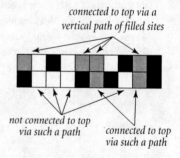

*not connected to top
via such a path*

*connected to top
via such a path*

Vertical percolation calculation

Program 2.4.2   *Vertical percolation detection*

```
public static boolean[][] flow(boolean[][] open)
{  // Compute full sites for vertical percolation.
   int N = open.length;
   boolean[][] full = new boolean[N][N];
   for (int j = 0; j < N; j++)
       full[0][j] = open[0][j];
   for (int i = 1; i < N; i++)
       for (int j = 0; j < N; j++)
           full[i][j] = open[i][j] && full[i-1][j];
   return full;
}
```

N	*system size (N-by-N)*
full[][]	*full sites*
open[][]	*open sites*

Substituting this method for the stub in Program 2.4.2 gives a solution to the vertical-only percolation problem that solves our test case as expected (see text).

```
% more test5.txt
5 5
0 1 1 0 1
0 0 1 1 1
1 1 0 1 1
1 0 0 0 1
0 1 1 1 1
```

```
% java Percolation < test5.txt
5 5
0 1 1 0 1
0 0 1 0 1
0 0 0 0 1
0 0 0 0 1
0 0 0 0 1
true
```

of test cases quickly becomes uninformative and unwieldy. Instead, we want to automatically generate test cases and observe the operation of our code on them, to be sure that it is operating as we expect. Specifically, to gain confidence in our code and to develop a better understanding of percolation, our next goals are to:

• Test our code for large random inputs.

• Estimate the probability that a system percolates for a given *p*.

To accomplish these goals, we need new clients that are slightly more sophisticated than the scaffolding we used to get the program up and running. Our modular programming style is to develop such clients in independent classes *without modifying our percolation code at all*.

Data visualization. We can work with much bigger problem instances if we use StdDraw for output. The following static method for Percolation allows us to visualize the contents of boolean matrices as a subdivision of the StdDraw canvas into squares, one for each site.

```
public static void show(boolean[][] a, boolean which)
{
    int N = a.length;
    StdDraw.setXscale(-1, N);
    StdDraw.setYscale(-1, N);
    for (int i = 0; i < N; i++)
        for (int j = 0; j < N; j++)
            if (a[i][j] == which)
                StdDraw.filledSquare(j, N-i-1, .5);
}
```

The second argument which specifies whether we want to display the entries corresponding to true or to false. This method is a bit of a diversion from the calculation, but pays dividends in its ability to help us visualize large problem instances. Using show() to draw our arrays representing blocked and full sites in different colors gives a compelling visual representation of percolation.

Monte Carlo simulation. We want our code to work properly for *any* boolean matrix. Moreover, the scientific question of interest involves random matrices. To this end, we add another static method to Percolation:

```
public static boolean[][] random(int N, double p)
{
    boolean[][] a = new boolean[N][N];
    for (int i = 0; i < N; i++)
        for (int j = 0; j < N; j++)
            a[i][j] = StdRandom.bernoulli(p);
    return a;
}
```

This method generates a random N-by-N matrix of any given size, each entry true with probability p. Having debugged our code on a few specific test cases, we are ready to test it on random systems. It is possible that such cases may uncover a few more bugs, so some care is in order to check results. However, having debugged our code for a small system, we can proceed with some confidence. It is easier to focus on new bugs after eliminating the obvious bugs.

WITH THESE TOOLS, À CLIENT FOR testing our percolation code on a much larger set of trials is straightforward. Visualize (PROGRAM 2.4.3) consists of just a main() method that takes N and p from the command line, generates T trials (taking this number from the command line), and displays the result of the percolation flow calculation for each case, pausing for a brief time between cases.

This kind of client is typical. Our eventual goal is to compute an accurate estimate of percolation probabilities, perhaps by running a large number of trials, but this simple tool gives us the opportunity to gain more familiarity with the problem by studying some large cases (while at the same time gaining confidence that our code is working properly). Before reading further, you are encouraged to download and run this code from the booksite to study the percolation process. When you run Visualize for moderate size N (50 to 100, say) and various p, you will immediately be drawn into using this program to try to answer some questions about percolation. Clearly, the system never percolates when p is low and always percolates when p is very high. How does it behave for intermediate values of p? How does the behavior change as N increases?

Estimating probabilities   The next step in our program development process is to write code to estimate the probability that a random system (of size N with site vacancy probability p) percolates. We refer to this quantity as the *percolation probability*. To estimate its value, we simply run a number of experiments. The situation is no different than our study of coin flipping (see PROGRAM 2.2.6), but instead of flipping a coin, we generate a random system and check whether or not it percolates.

Estimate (PROGRAM 2.4.4) encapsulates this computation in a method eval() that returns an estimate of the probability that an N-by-N system with site vacancy probability p percolates, obtained by generating T random systems and calculating the fraction of them that percolate. The method takes three arguments: N, p, and T.

How many trials do we need to obtain an accurate estimate? This question is addressed by basic methods in probability and statistics, which are beyond the scope of this book, but we can get a feeling for the problem with computational experience. With just a few runs of Estimate, you can learn that the site vacancy probability is close to 0 or very close to 1, then we do not need many trials, but that there are values for which we need as many as 10,000 trials to be able to estimate it within two decimal places. To study the situation in more detail, we might

Program 2.4.3   Visualization client

```java
public class Visualize
{
    public static void main(String[] args)
    {
        int N     = Integer.parseInt(args[0]);
        double p = Double.parseDouble(args[1]);
        int T     = Integer.parseInt(args[2]);
        for (int t = 0; t < T; t++)
        {
            boolean[][] open = Percolation.random(N, p);
            StdDraw.clear();
            StdDraw.setPenColor(StdDraw.BLACK);
            Percolation.show(open, false);
            StdDraw.setPenColor(StdDraw.BLUE);
            boolean[][] full = Percolation.flow(open);
            Percolation.show(full, true);
            StdDraw.show(1000);
        }
    }
}
```

N	system size (N-by-N)
p	site vacancy probability
T	number of trials
open[][]	open sites
full[][]	full sites

This client generates N-by-N random instances with site vacancy probability p, computes the directed percolation flow, and draws the result on StdDraw. Such drawings increase confidence that our code is operating properly and help develop an intuitive understanding of percolation.

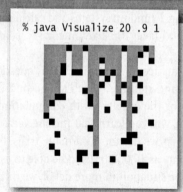

% java Visualize 20 .9 1

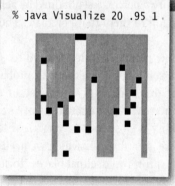

% java Visualize 20 .95 1

modify `Estimate` to produce output like `Bernoulli` (PROGRAM 2.2.6), plotting a histogram of the data points so that we can see the distribution of values (see EXERCISE 2.4.10).

Using `Estimate.eval()` represents a giant leap in the amount of computation that we are doing. All of a sudden, it makes sense to run thousands of trials. It would be unwise to try to do so without first having thoroughly debugged our percolation methods. Also, we need to begin to take the time required to complete the computation into account. The basic methodology for doing so is the topic of SECTION 4.1, but the structure of these programs is sufficiently simple that we can do a quick calculation, which we can verify by running the program. We are doing T trials, each of which involve N^2 sites, so the total running time of `Estimate.eval()` is proportional to N^2T. If we increase T by a factor of 10 (to gain more precision), the running time increases by about a factor of 10. If we increase N by a factor of 10 (to study percolation for larger systems), the running time increases by about a factor of 100.

Can we run this program to determine percolation probabilities for a system with billions of sites with several digits of precision? No computer is fast enough to use `Estimate.eval()` for this purpose. Moreover, in a scientific experiment on percolation, the value of N is likely to be much higher. We can hope to formulate a hypothesis from our simulation that can be tested experimentally on a much larger system, but not to precisely simulate a system that corresponds atom-for-atom with the real world. Simplification of this sort is essential in science.

You are encouraged to download `Estimate` from the booksite to get a feel for both the percolation probabilities and the amount of time required to compute them. When you do so, you are not just learning more about percolation, but also you are testing the hypothesis that the models we have just described apply to the running times of our simulations of the percolation process.

What is the probability that a system with site vacancy probability p vertically percolates? Vertical percolation is sufficiently simple that elementary probabilistic models can yield an exact formula for this quantity, which we can validate experimentally with `Estimate`. Since our only reason for studying vertical percolation was an easy starting point around which we could develop supporting software for studying percolation methods, we leave further study of vertical percolation for an exercise (see EXERCISE 2.4.11) and turn to the main problem.

Program 2.4.4   *Percolation probability estimate*

```java
public class Estimate
{
   public static double eval(int N, double p, int T)
   {  // Generate T random networks, return empirical
      // percolation probability estimate.
      int cnt = 0;
      for (int t = 0; t < T; t++)
      {  // Generate one random network.
         boolean[][] open = Percolation.random(N, p);
         if (Percolation.percolates(open)) cnt++;
      }
      return (double) cnt / T;
   }
   public static void main(String[] args)
   {
      int N    = Integer.parseInt(args[0]);
      double p = Double.parseDouble(args[1]);
      int T    = Integer.parseInt(args[2]);
      double q = eval(N, p, T);
      StdOut.println(q);
   }
}
```

N	*system size (N-by-N)*
p	*site vacancy probability*
T	*number of trials*
open[][]	*open sites*
q	*percolation probability*

To estimate the probability that a network percolates, we generate random networks and compute the fraction of them that percolate. This is a Bernoulli process, no different than coin flipping (see Program 2.2.6). Increasing the number of trials increases the accuracy of the estimate. If the site vacancy probability is close to 0 or to 1, not many trials are needed.

```
% java Estimate 20 .5 10
0.0
% java Estimate 20 .75 10
0.0
% java Estimate 20 .95 10
1.0
% java Estimate 20 .85 10
0.7
% java Estimate 20 .85 1000
0.564
% java Estimate 20 .85 1000
0.561
% java Estimate 40 .85 100
0.1
```

Recursive solution for percolation

How do we test whether a system percolates in the general case when *any* path starting at the top and ending at the bottom (not just a vertical one) will do the job?

Remarkably, we can solve this problem with a compact program, based on a classic recursive scheme known as *depth-first search*. PROGRAM 2.4.5 is an implementation of flow() that computes the flow array, based on a recursive four-argument version of flow() that takes as arguments the site vacancy array open[][], the flow array full[] [], and a site position specified by a row index i and a column index j. The base case is a recursive call that just returns (we refer to such a call as a *null call*), for one of the following reasons:

- Either i or j are outside the array bounds.
- The site is blocked (open[i][j] is false).
- We have already marked the site as full (full[i][j] is true).

The reduction case is to mark the site as filled and issue recursive calls for the site's four neighbors: open[i+1][j], open[i][j+1], open[i][j-1], and open[i-1][j]. To implement flow(), we call the recursive method for every site on the top row. The recursion always terminates because each recursive call either is null or marks a new site as full. We can show by an induction-based argument (as usual for recursive programs) that a site is marked as full if and only if it is connected to one of the sites on the top row.

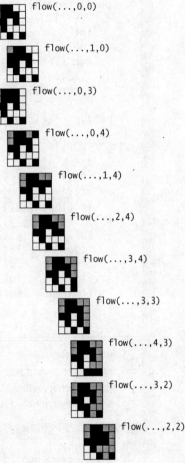

Recursive percolation (null calls omitted)

Tracing the operation of flow() on a tiny test case is an instructive exercise in examining the dynamics of the process. The function calls itself for every site that can be reached via a path of open sites from the top. This example illustrates that simple recursive programs can mask computations that otherwise are quite sophisticated. This method is a special case of the classic depth-first search algorithm, which has many important applications.

Program 2.4.5   *Percolation detection*

```
public static boolean[][] flow(boolean[][] open)
{  // Fill every site reachable from the top row.
   int N = open.length;
   boolean[][] full = new boolean[N][N];
   for (int j = 0; j < N; j++)
      flow(open, full, 0, j);
   return full;
}
public static void flow(boolean[][] open,
                        boolean[][] full, int i, int j)
{  // Fill every site reachable from (i, j).
   int N = full.length;
   if (i < 0 || i >= N) return;
   if (j < 0 || j >= N) return;
   if (!open[i][j]) return;
   if (full[i][j]) return;
   full[i][j] = true;
   flow(open, full, i+1, j);   // Down.
   flow(open, full, i, j+1);   // Right.
   flow(open, full, i, j-1);   // Left.
   flow(open, full, i-1, j);   // Up.
}
```

N	system size (N-by-N)
open[][]	open sites
full[][]	full sites
i, j	current site row, column

Substituting these methods for the stub in Program 2.4.1 gives a depth-first-search-based solution to the percolation problem. The recursive flow() *fills sites by setting to* true *the entry in* full[][] *corresponding to any site that can be reached from* open[i][j] *via a path of open sites. The one-argument* flow() *calls the recursive method for every site on the top row.*

```
% more test8.txt
8 8
0 0 1 1 1 0 0 0
1 0 0 1 1 1 1 1
1 1 1 0 0 1 1 0
0 0 1 1 0 1 1 1
0 1 1 1 0 1 1 0
0 1 0 0 0 0 1 1
1 0 1 0 1 1 1 1
1 1 1 1 0 1 0 0
```

```
% java Percolation < test8.txt
8 8
0 0 1 1 1 0 0 0
0 0 0 1 1 1 1 1
0 0 0 0 0 1 1 0
0 0 0 0 0 1 1 1
0 0 0 0 0 1 1 0
0 0 0 0 0 0 1 1
0 0 0 0 1 1 1 1
0 0 0 0 0 1 0 0
true
```

To avoid conflict with our solution for vertical percolation (PROGRAM 2.4.2), we might rename that class `PercolationEZ`, making another copy of `Percolation` (PROGRAM 2.4.1) and substituting the two `flow()` methods in PROGRAM 2.4.5 for the placeholder `flow()`. Then, we can visualize and perform experiments with this algorithm with the `Visualize` and `Experiment` tools that we have developed. If you do so, and try various values for *N* and *p*, you will quickly get a feeling for the situation: the systems always percolate when *p* is high and never percolate when *p* is low, and (particularly as *N* increases) there is a value of *p* above which the systems (almost) always percolate and below which they (almost) never percolate.

% java Visualize 20 .65 1   % java Visualize 20 .60 1   % java Visualize 20 .55 1

Percolation is less probable as the site vacancy probability decreases

Having debugged `Visualize` and `Experiment` on the simple vertical percolation process, we can use them with more confidence to study percolation, and turn quickly to study the scientific problem of interest. Note that if we want to experiment with vertical percolation again, we would need to edit `Visualize` and `Experiment` to refer to `PercolationEZ` instead of `Percolation`, or write other clients of both `PercolationEZ` and `Percolation` that run methods in both classes to compare them.

Adaptive plot   To gain more insight into percolation, the next step in program development is to write a program that plots the percolation probability as a function of the site vacancy probability *p* for a given value of *N*. Perhaps the best way to produce such a plot is to first derive a mathematical equation for the function, and then use that equation to make the plot. For percolation, however, no one has been able to derive such an equation, so the next option is to use the Monte Carlo method: run simulations and plot the results.

Immediately, we are faced with numerous decisions. For how many values of p should we compute an estimate of the percolation probability? Which values of p should we choose? How much precision should we aim for in these calculations? These decisions constitute an experimental design problem. Much as we might like to instantly produce an accurate rendition of the curve for any given N, the computation cost can be prohibitive. For example, the first thing that comes to mind is to plot, say, 100 to 1,000 equally spaced points, using StdStats (PROGRAM 2.2.5). But, as you learned from using Estimate, computing a sufficiently precise value of the percolation probability for each point might take several seconds or longer, so the whole plot might take minutes or hours or even longer. Moreover, it is clear that a lot of this computation time is completely wasted, because we know that values for small p are 0 and values for large p are 1. We might prefer to spend that time on more precise computations for intermediate p. How should we proceed?

PercPlot (PROGRAM 2.4.6) implements a recursive approach with the same structure as Brownian (PROGRAM 2.3.5) that is widely applicable to similar problems. The basic idea is simple: we choose the minimum distance that we want between values of the x-coordinate (which we refer to as the *gap* tolerance), the minimum known error that we wish to tolerate in the y-coordinate (which we refer to as the *error* tolerance), and the number of trials T per point that we wish to perform. The recursive method draws the plot within a given interval $[x_0, x_1]$, from (x_0, y_0) to (x_1, y_1). For

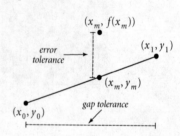

Adaptive plot tolerances

our problem, the plot is from $(0, 0)$ to $(1, 1)$. The base case (if the distance between x_0 and x_1 is less than the gap tolerance, or the distance between the line connecting the two endpoints and the value of the function at the midpoint is less than the error tolerance) is to simply draw a line from (x_0, y_0) to (x_1, y_1). The reduction step is to (recursively) plot the two halves of the curve, from (x_0, y_0) to (x_m, y_m) and from (x_m, y_m) to (x_1, y_1).

The code in PercPlot is relatively simple and produces a good-looking curve at relatively low cost. We can use it to study the shape of the curve for various values of N or choose smaller tolerances to be more confident that the curve is close to the actual values. Precise mathematical statements about quality of approximation can, in principle, be derived, but it is perhaps not appropriate to go into too much detail while exploring and experimenting, since our goal is simply to develop a hypothesis about percolation that can be tested by scientific experimentation.

Program 2.4.6   Adaptive plot client

```java
public class PercPlot
{
    public static void curve(int N,
                             double x0, double y0,
                             double x1, double y1)
    { // Perform experiments and plot results.
        double gap = .005;
        double err = .05;
        int T      = 10000;
        double xm  = (x0 + x1)/2;
        double ym  = (y0 + y1)/2;
        double fxm = Estimate.eval(N, xm, T);
        if (x1 - x0 < gap && Math.abs(ym - fxm) < err)
        {
            StdDraw.line(x0, y0, x1, y1);
            return;
        }
        curve(N, x0, y0, xm, fxm);
        StdDraw.filledCircle(xm, fxm, .005);
        curve(N, xm, fxm, x1, y1);
    }

    public static void main(String[] args)
    { // Plot experimental curve for N-by-N percolation system.
        int N = Integer.parseInt(args[0]);
        curve(N, 0.0, 0.0, 1.0, 1.0);
    }
}
```

N	system size
x0, y0	left endpoint
x1, y1	right endpoint
xm, ym	midpoint
fxm	value at midpoint
gap	gap tolerance
err	error tolerance
T	number of trials

This recursive program draws a plot of the percolation probability (experimental observations) against the site vacancy probability (control variable).

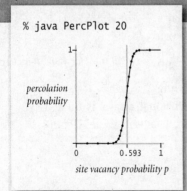

% java PercPlot 20

percolation probability

0   0.593   1

site vacancy probability p

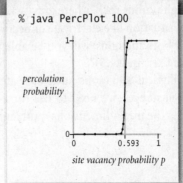

% java PercPlot 100

percolation probability

0   0.593   1

site vacancy probability p

Indeed, the curves produced by PercPlot immediately confirm the hypothesis that there is a *threshold* value (about .593): if p is greater than the threshold, then the system almost certainly percolates; if p is less than the threshold, then the system almost certainly does not percolate. As N increases, the curve approaches a step function that changes value from 0 to 1 at the threshold. This phenomenon, known as a *phase transition,* is found in many physical systems.

The simple form of the output of PROGRAM 2.4.6 masks the huge amount of computation behind it. For example, the curve drawn for $N = 100$ has 18 points, each the result of 10,000 trials, each trial involving N^2 sites. Generating and testing each site involves a few lines of code, so this plot comes at the cost of executing *billions* of statements. There are two lessons to be learned from this observation: First, we need to have confidence in any line of code that might be executed billions of times, so our care in developing and debugging code incrementally is justified. Second, although we might be interested in systems that are much larger, we need further study in computer science to be to handle larger cases: to develop faster algorithms and a framework for knowing their performance characteristics.

With this reuse of all of our software, we can study all sorts of variants on the percolation problem, just by implementing different flow() methods. For example, if you leave out the last recursive call in the recursive flow() method in PROGRAM 2.4.6, it tests for a type of percolation known as *directed percolation,* where paths that go up are not considered. This model might be important for a situation like a liquid percolating through porous rock, where gravity might play a role, but not for a situation like electrical connectivity. If you run PercPlot for both methods, will you be able to discern the difference (see EXERCISE 2.4.5)?

To model physical situations such as water flowing through porous substances, we need to use three-dimensional arrays. Is there a similar threshold in the three-dimensional problem? If so, what is its value? Depth-

```
PercPlot.curve()
  Estimate.eval()
    Percolation.random()
      StdRandom.bernoulli()
      ⋮ N² times
      StdRandom.bernoulli()
    return
    Percolation.percolates()
      flow()
    return
  return
  ⋮ T times
    Percolation.random()
      StdRandom.bernoulli()
      ⋮ N² times
      StdRandom.bernoulli()
    return
    Percolation.percolates()
      flow()
    return
  return
  return
  ⋮ once for each point
  Estimate.eval()
    Percolation.random()
      StdRandom.bernoulli()
      ⋮ N² times
      StdRandom.bernoulli()
    return
    Percolation.percolates()
      flow()
    return
  return
  ⋮ T times
    Percolation.random()
      StdRandom.bernoulli()
      ⋮ N² times
      StdRandom.bernoulli()
    return
    Percolation.percolates()
      flow()
    return
  return
  return
return
```

Call trace for java PercPlot

first search is effective for studying this question, though the addition of another dimension requires that we pay even more attention to the computational cost of determining whether a system percolates (see EXERCISE 2.4.19). Scientists also study more complex lattice structures that are not well-modeled by multidimensional arrays—we will see how to model such structures in SECTION 4.5.

percolates (path never goes up)

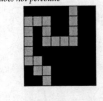

does not percolate

Percolation is interesting to study via *in silico* experimentation because no one has been able to derive the threshold value mathematically for several natural models. The only way that scientists know the value is by using simulations like Percolation. A scientist needs to do experiments to see whether the percolation model reflects what is observed in nature, perhaps through refining the model (for example, using a different lattice structure). Percolation is an example of an increasing number of problems where computer science of the kind described here is an essential part of the scientific process.

Directed percolation

Lessons We might have approached the problem of studying percolation by sitting down to design and implement a single program, which probably would run to hundreds of lines, to produce the kind of plots that are drawn by PROGRAM 2.4.6. In the early days of computing, programmers had little choice but to work with such programs, and would spend enormous amounts of time isolating bugs and correcting design decisions. With modern programming tools like Java, we can do better, using the incremental modular style of programming presented in this chapter and keeping in mind some of the lessons that we have learned.

Expect bugs. Every interesting piece of code that you write is going to have at least one or two bugs, if not many more. By running small pieces of code on small test cases that you understand, you can more easily isolate any bugs and then more easily fix them when you find them. Once debugged, you can depend on using a library as a building block for any client.

Keep modules small. You can focus attention on at most a few dozen lines of code at a time, so you may as well break your code into small modules as you write it. Some classes that contain libraries of related methods may eventually grow to contain hundreds of lines of code; otherwise, we work with small files.

Limit interactions. In a well-designed modular program, most modules should depend on just a few others. In particular, a module that *calls* a large number of other modules needs to be divided into smaller pieces. Modules that *are called by* a large number of other modules (you should have only a few) need special attention, because if you do need to make changes in a module's API, you have to reflect those changes in all its clients.

Develop code incrementally. You should run and debug each small module as you implement it. That way, you are never working with more than a few dozen lines of unreliable code at any given time. If you put all your code in one big module, it is difficult to be confident that *any* of it is safe from bugs. Running code early also forces you to think sooner rather than later about I/O formats, the nature of problem instances, and other issues. Experience gained when thinking about such issues and debugging related code makes the code that you develop later in the process more effective.

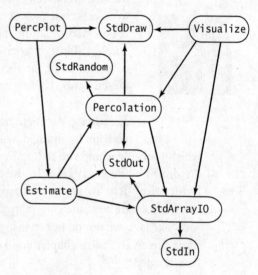

Case study dependencies (not including system calls)

Solve an easier problem. Some working solution is better than no solution, so it is typical to begin by putting together the simplest code that you can craft that solves a given problem, as we did with vertical-only percolation. This implementation is the first step in a process of continual refinements and improvements as we develop a more complete understanding of the problem by examining a broader variety of test cases and developing support software such as our Visualize and Experiment classes.

Consider a recursive solution. Recursion is an indispensable tool in modern programming that you should learn to trust. If you are not already convinced of this fact by the simplicity and elegance of PercPlot and Percolation, you might wish to try to develop a nonrecursive program for testing whether a system percolates and then reconsider the issue.

Build tools when appropriate. Our visualization method show() and random boolean matrix generation method random() are certainly useful for many other applications, as is the adaptive plotting method of PercPlot. Incorporating these methods into appropriate libraries would be simple. It is no more difficult (indeed, perhaps easier) to implement general-purpose methods like these than it would be to implement special-purpose methods for percolation.

Reuse software when possible. Our StdIn, StdRandom, and StdDraw libraries all simplified the process of developing the code in this section, and we were also immediately able to reuse programs such as PercPlot, Estimate, and Visualize for percolation after developing them for vertical percolation. After you have written a few programs of this kind, you might find yourself developing versions of these programs that you can reuse for other Monte Carlo simulations or other experimental data analysis problems.

THE PRIMARY PURPOSE OF THIS CASE study is to convince you that modular programming will take you much further than you could get without it. Although no approach to programming is a panacea, the tools and approach that we have discussed in this section will allow you to attack complex programming tasks that might otherwise be far beyond your reach.

The success of modular programming is only a start. Modern programming systems have a vastly more flexible programming model than the class-as-a-library-of-functions model that we have been considering. In the next two chapters, we develop this model, along with many examples that illustrate its utility.

Q. Editing `Visualize` and `Estimate` to rename `Percolation` to `PercolationEZ` or whatever method we want to study seems to be a bother. Is there a way to avoid doing so?

A. Yes, this is a key issue to be revisited in CHAPTER 3. In the meantime, you can keep the implementations in separate subdirectories and use the classpath, but that can get confusing. Advanced Java language mechanisms are also helpful, but they also have their own problems.

Q. That recursive `flow()` method makes me nervous. How can I better understand what it's doing?

A. Run it for small examples of your own making, instrumented with instructions to print a function call trace. After a few runs, you will gain confidence that it always fills the sites connected to the start point.

Q. Is there a simple nonrecursive approach?

A. There are several methods that perform the same basic computation. We will revisit the problem at the end of the book, in SECTION 4.5. In the meantime, working on developing a nonrecursive implementation of `flow()` is certain to be an instructive exercise, if you are interested.

Q. `PrecPlot` (PROGRAM 2.4.6) seems to involve a huge amount of calculation to get a simple function graph. Is there some better way?

A. Well, the best would be a mathematical proof of the threshold value, but that derivation has eluded scientists.

Exercises

2.4.1   Write a program that takes N from the command line and creates an N-by-N matrix with the entry in row i and column j set to true if i and j are relatively prime, then shows the matrix on the standard drawing (see EXERCISE 1.4.13). Then, write a similar program to draw the Hadamard matrix of order N (see EXERCISE 1.4.25) and the matrix such with the entry in row N and column j set to true if the coefficient of x^k in $(1+x)^N$ (binomial coefficient) is odd (see EXERCISE 1.4.33). You may be surprised at the pattern formed by the latter.

2.4.2   Implement a `print()` method for `Percolation` that prints 1 for blocked sites, 0 for open sites, and * for full sites.

2.4.3   Give the recursive calls for `Percolation` given the following input:

```
3 3
1 0 1
0 0 0
1 1 0
```

2.4.4   Write a client of `Percolation` like `Visualize` that does a series of experiments for a value of N taken from the command line where the site vacancy probability p increases from 0 to 1 by a given increment (also taken from the command line).

2.4.5   Create a program `PercolationDirected` that tests for *directed* percolation (by leaving off the last recursive call in the recursive `show()` method in PROGRAM 2.4.5, as described in the text), then use `PercPlot` to draw a plot of the directed percolation probability as a function of the site vacancy probability.

2.4.5   Write a client of `Percolation` and `PercolationDirected` that takes a site vacancy probability p from the command line and prints an estimate of the probability that a system percolates but does not percolate down. Use enough experiments to get an estimate that is accurate to three decimal places.

2.4.6   Describe the order in which the sites are marked when `Percolation` is used on a system with no blocked sites. Which is the last site marked? What is the depth of the recursion?

2.4.7   Experiment with using `PercPlot` to plot various mathematical functions (just by replacing the call on `Estimate.eval()` with an expression that evaluates the function). Try the function `sin(x) + cos(10*x)` to see how the plot adapts to an oscillating curve, and come up with interesting plots for three or four functions of your own choosing.

2.4.8   Modify `Percolation` to animate the flow computation, showing the sites filling one by one. Check your answer to the previous exercise.

2.4.9   Modify `Percolation` to compute that maximum depth of the recursion used in the flow calculation. Plot the expected value of that quantity as a function of the site vacancy probability p. How does your answer change if the order of the recursive calls is reversed?

2.4.10   Modify `Estimate` to produce output like that produced by `Bernoulli` (PROGRAM 2.2.6). *Extra credit*: Use your program to validate the hypothesis that the data obeys the Gaussian (normal) distribution.

Creative Exercises

2.4.11 *Vertical percolation.* Show that a system with site vacancy probability p vertically percolates with probability $1 - (1 - p^N)^N$, and use `Estimate` to validate your analysis for various values of N.

2.4.12 *Rectangular percolation systems.* Modify the code in this section to allow you to study percolation in rectangular systems. Compare the percolation probability plots of systems whose ratio of width to height is 2 to 1 with those whose ratio is 1 to 2.

2.4.13 *Adaptive plotting.* Modify `PercPlot` to take its control parameters (gap tolerance, error tolerance, and number of trials) from the command line. Experiment with various values of the parameters to learn their effect on the quality of the curve and the cost of computing it. Briefly describe your findings.

2.4.14 *Percolation threshold.* Write a `Percolation` client that uses binary search to estimate the threshold value (see Exercise 2.1.29).

2.4.15 *Nonrecursive directed percolation.* Write a nonrecursive program that tests for directed percolation by moving from top to bottom as in our vertical percolation code. Base your solution on the following computation: if any site in a contiguous subrow of open sites in the current row is connected to some full site on the previous row, then all of the sites in the subrow become full.

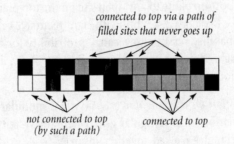

connected to top via a path of filled sites that never goes up

not connected to top (by such a path)   *connected to top*

Directed percolation calculation

2.4.16 *Fast percolation test.* Modify the recursive `flow()` method in Program 2.4.5 so that it returns as soon as it finds a site on the bottom row (and fills no more sites). *Hint*: Use an argument done that is `true` if the bottom has been hit, `false` otherwise. Give a rough estimate of the performance improvement factor for this change when running `PercPlot`. Use values of N for which the programs run at least a few seconds but not more than a few minutes. Note that the improvement is ineffective unless the first recursive call in `flow()` is for the site below the current site.

2.4.17 *Bond percolation.* Write a modular program for studying percolation under the assumption that the edges of the grid provide connectivity. That is, an edge can be either empty or full, and a system percolates if there is a path consisting of full edges that goes from top to bottom. *Note*: This problem has been solved analytically, so your simulations should validate the hypothesis that the percolation threshold approaches 1/2 as N gets large.

percolates

does not

2.4.19 *Percolation in three dimensions.* Implement a class `Percolation3D` and a class `BooleanMatrix3D` (for I/O and random generation) to study percolation in three-dimensional cubes, generalizing the two-dimensional case studied in this chapter. A percolation system is an N-by-N-by-N cube of sites that are unit cubes, each open with probability p and blocked with probability $1-p$. Paths can connect an open cube with any open cube that shares a common face (one of six neighbors, except on the boundary). The system percolates if there exists a path connecting any open site on the bottom plane to any open site on the top plane. Use a recursive version of `flow()` like Program 2.4.5, but with eight recursive calls instead of four. Plot percolation probability versus site vacancy probability for as large a value of N as you can. Be sure to develop your solution incrementally, as emphasized throughout this section.

percolates

2.4.18 *Bond percolation on a triangular grid.* Write a modular program for studying bond percolation on a triangular grid, where the system is composed of $2N^2$ equilateral triangles packed together in an N-by-N grid of rhombus shapes. Each interior point has six bonds; each point on the edge has four; and each corner point has two.

does not

2.4.20 *Game of life.* Implement a class Life that simulates Conway's *game of life.* Consider a boolean matrix corresponding to a system of cells that we refer to as being either live or dead. The game consists of checking and perhaps updating the value of each cell, depending on the values of its neighbors (the adjacent cells in every direction, including diagonals). Live cells remain live and dead cells remain dead, with the following exceptions:

• A dead cell with exactly three live neighbors becomes live.
• A live cell with exactly one live neighbor becomes dead.
• A live cell with more than three live neighbors becomes dead.

Initialize with a random matrix, or use one of the starting patterns on the booksite. This game has been heavily studied, and relates to foundations of computer science (see the booksite for more information).

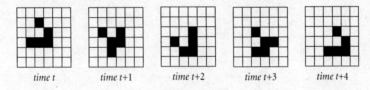

| time t | time t+1 | time t+2 | time t+3 | time t+4 |

Five generations of a glider

Chapter Three

Object-Oriented Programming

YOUR NEXT STEP TO PROGRAMMING EFFECTIVELY is conceptually simple. Now that you know how to use primitive types of data, you will learn in this chapter how to *use*, *create*, and *design* higher-level data types.

An *abstraction* is a simplified description of something that captures its essential elements while suppressing all other details. In science, engineering, and programming, we are always striving to understand complex systems through abstraction. In Java programming, we do so with *object-oriented programming*, where we break a large and potentially complex program into a set of interacting elements, or *objects*. The idea originates from modeling (in software) real-world entities such as electrons, people, buildings, or solar systems and readily extends to modeling abstract entities such as bits, numbers, colors, images, or programs.

A data type is a set of values and a set of operations defined on those values. The values and operations for primitive types such as int and double are built into the Java language. In object-oriented programming, we write Java code to create new data types. An *object* is an entity that can take on a data-type value. An object's value can be returned to a client or changed by one of its data type's operations.

This ability to define new data types and to manipulate objects holding data-type values is also known as *data abstraction*, and leads us to a style of modular programming that naturally extends the *function abstraction* style for primitive types that was the basis for CHAPTER 2. A data type allows us to isolate *data* as well as functions. Our mantra for this chapter is this: *Whenever you can clearly separate data and associated tasks within a computation, you should do so.*

3.1 Data Types

ORGANIZING DATA FOR PROCESSING IS AN essential step in the development of a computer program. Programming in Java is largely based on doing so with data types known as *reference* types that are designed to support object-oriented programming, a style of programming that facilitates organizing and processing data.

The eight primitive data types (`bool-ean`, `byte`, `char`, `double`, `float`, `int`, `long`, and `short`) that you have been using are supplemented in Java by extensive libraries of *reference types* that are tailored for a large variety of applications. `String` is one example of such a type that you have used. You will learn more about the `String` data type in this section, as well as how to use several other reference types for image processing and input/output. Some of them are built into Java (`String` and `Color`), and some were developed for this book (`In`, `Out`, `Draw`, and `Picture`) and are useful as general resources, like the `Std*` static method libraries that we introduced in SECTION 1.5.

You certainly noticed in the first two chapters of this book that our programs were largely confined to operations on numbers. Of course, the reason is that Java's primitive types represent numbers; however, with reference types you can write programs that operate on strings, pictures, sounds, or any of hundreds of other abstractions that are available in Java's standard libraries or on the booksite.

Even more significant than this large library of predefined data types is the idea that the range of data types that are available to you in Java programming is open-ended, because *you can define your own data types* to implement any abstraction whatsoever. This ability is crucial in modern programming. No library can meet the needs of all possible applications, so programmers routinely build data types to meet their own needs. You will learn how to do so in SECTION 3.2.

In this section, we focus on client programs that use data types, to give you some concrete reference points for understanding these new concepts and to illustrate their broad reach. We will consider programs that manipulate colors, images, strings, files, and web pages—quite a leap from the primitive types of CHAPTER 1.

Basic definitions. A *data type* is a set of values and a set of operations defined on those values. This statement is one of several mantras that we repeat often because of its importance. In CHAPTER 1, we discussed in detail Java's *primitive* data types: for example, the values of the primitive data type int are integers between -2^{31} and $2^{31} - 1$; the operations of int are the basic arithmetic and comparison operations, including +, *, %, <, and >. You also have been using a data type that is not primitive—the String data type. Your experience with using String demonstrates that *you do not need to know how a data type is implemented in order to be able to use it* (yet another mantra). You know that values of String are sequences of characters and that you can perform the operation of concatenating two String values to produce a String result. You will learn in this section that there are dozens of other operations available for processing strings, such as finding a string's length or extracting a substring. Every data type is defined by its set of values and the operations defined on them, but when we *use* the data type, we focus on the *operations*, not the values. When you write programs that use int or String values, you are not concerning yourself with *how* they are represented (we never did spell out the details), and the same holds true when you write programs that use reference types such as Color and Picture.

Example. As a running example of how to use a data type, we will consider a data type Charge for charged particles. In particular, we are interested in a two-dimensional model that uses *Coulomb's law*, which tells us that the electric potential at a point due to a given charged particle is represented by $V = kq/r$, where q is the charge value, r is the distance from the point to the charge, and $k = 8.99 \times 10^9$ N m^2/C^2 is the electrostatic constant. For consistency, we use SI (Système International d'Unités): in this formula, N designates Newtons (force), m designates meters (distance), and C represent coulombs (electric charge). When there are multiple charged particles, the electric potential at any point is the sum of the potentials due to each charge. Our interest is computing the potential at various points in the plane due to a given set of charged particles. To do so, we will write programs that define, create, and manipulate variables of type Charge. In SECTION 3.2, you will learn how to implement the data type, but *you do not need to know how a data type is implemented in order to be able to use it.*

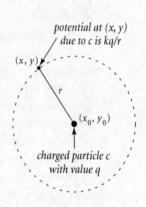

Coulomb's law for a
charged particle in the plane

API. The Java *class* provides a mechanism for defining data types. In a class, we specify the data-type values and implement the data-type operations. In order to fulfill our promise that *you do not need to know how a data type is implemented in order to be able to use it,* we specify the behavior of classes for clients by listing their methods in an *API* (*applications programming interface*), in the same manner as we have been doing for libraries of static methods. The purpose of an API is to provide the information that you need to write programs using the data type. (In SECTION 3.2, you will see that the same information specifies the operations that you need to implement it.) For example, this API specifies our class `Charge` for writing programs that process charged particles:

```
public class Charge
```

```
        Charge(double x0, double y0, double q0)

 double potentialAt(double x, double y)    electric potential at (x, y) due to charge

 String toString()                          string representation
```

API for charged particles

The first entry, with the same name as the class and no return type, defines a special method known as a *constructor*. The other entries define *instance methods* that can take arguments and return values in the same manner as the static methods that we have been using, but they are *not* static methods: they implement operations for the data type. `Charge` has two instance methods: The first is `potentialAt()`, which computes and returns the potential due to the charge at the given point (x, y). The second is `toString()`, which returns a string that represents the charged particle.

Using a data type. As with libraries of static methods, the code that implements each class resides in a file that has the same name as the class but with a `.java` extension. To write a client program that uses `Charge`, you need access to the file `Charge.java`, either by having a copy in the current directory or by using Java's classpath mechanism (described in the booksite). With this understood, you will next learn how to use a data type in your own client code. To do so, you need to be able to *declare variables*, *create objects* to hold data-type values, and *invoke methods* to manipulate these values. These processes are different than the corresponding processes for primitive types, though you will notice many similarities.

Declaring variables. You declare variables of a reference type in precisely the same way that you declare variables of a primitive type, using a statement consisting of the data type name followed by a variable name. For example, the declaration

```
Charge c;
```

declares a variable c of type Charge. This statement does not *create* anything; it just says that we will use the name c to refer to a Charge object.

Creating objects. In Java, each data type value is stored in an *object*. When a client invokes a constructor, the Java system creates (or *instantiates*) an individual object. To invoke a constructor, use the keyword new; followed by the class name; followed by the constructor's arguments, enclosed in parentheses and separated by commas, in the same manner as a static method call. For example, new Charge(x0, y0, q0) creates a new Charge object with position (x_0, y_0) and charge q_0. Typically, client code invokes a constructor to create an object and assigns it to a variable in the same line of code as the declaration:

```
Charge c = new Charge(0.51, 0.63, 21.3);
```

You can create any number of objects from the same class; each object has its own identity and may or may not store the same value as another object of the same type. For example, the code

```
Charge c1 = new Charge(0.51, 0.63, 21.3);
Charge c2 = new Charge(0.13, 0.94, 85.9);
Charge c3 = new Charge(0.51, 0.63, 21.3);
```

creates three different Charge objects. In particular, c1 and c3 refer to different objects, even though the objects store the same value.

Invoking methods. The most important difference between a variable of a reference type and a variable of a primitive type is that you can use reference type variables to invoke the methods that implement data type operations (in contrast to the built-in syntax involving operators such as + and * that we used for primitive types). Such methods are known as *instance methods*. Invoking an instance method is similar to invoking a static method in another class, except that an instance method is associated not just with a class, but also with an individual object. Accordingly, we use an *object* name (variable of the given type) instead of the *class* name to identify the method. For example, if c is a variable of type Charge, then

Program 3.1.1   Charged particles

```
public class ChargeClient
{
   public static void main(String[] args)
   { // Print total potential at (x, y).
      double x = Double.parseDouble(args[0]);
      double y = Double.parseDouble(args[1]);
      Charge c1 = new Charge(.51, .63, 21.3);
      Charge c2 = new Charge(.13, .94, 81.9);
      double v1 = c1.potentialAt(x, y);
      double v2 = c2.potentialAt(x, y);
      StdOut.printf("%.1e\n", v1+v2);
   }
}
```

x, y	*query point*
c1	*first charge*
v1	*potential due to c1*
c2	*second charge*
v2	*potential due to c2*

This object-oriented client takes a query point (x, y) as command-line argument, creates two charges c1 and c2 with fixed position and electric charge, and uses the potentialAt() instance method in Charge to compute the potential at (x, y) due to the two charges.

```
% java ChargeClient .2 .5
2.2e+12
% java ChargeClient .51 .94
2.5e+12
```

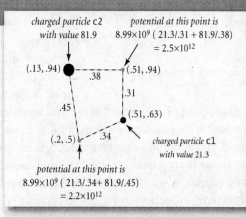

c.potentialAt(x, y) returns a double value that represents the potential at (x, y) due to the charge q_0 at (x_0, y_0). The values x and y belong to the *client*; the values x_0, y_0, and q_0 belong to the *object*. For example, ChargeClient (PROGRAM 3.1.1) creates two Charge objects and computes the total potential at a query point taken from the command line due to the two charges. This code clearly exhibits the idea of developing an abstract model and separating the code that implements the abstraction from the code that uses it. This ability characterizes object-oriented programming and is a turning point in this book: we have not yet seen any code of this nature, but virtually all of the code that we write from this point forward will be based on defining and invoking methods that implement data types operations.

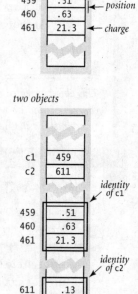

one object

References. A constructor creates an object and returns to the client a *reference* to the object, not the object itself (hence the name *reference type*). What is a reference? Nothing more than a mechanism for accessing an object. There are several different ways for Java to implement references, but we do not need to know the details in order to use them. Still, it is worthwhile to have a mental model of one common implementation. One approach is for new to assign memory space to hold the object's current data type value and return a *pointer* (machine address) to that space. We refer to the memory space associated with the object as the object's *identity*. Why not just process the object itself? For small objects, it might make sense to do so, but for large objects, cost becomes an issue: data-type values can be complicated and consume large amounts of memory. It does not make sense to copy or move all of its data every time that we pass an object as an argument to a method. If this reasoning seems familiar to you, it is because we have used precisely the same reasoning before, when talking about passing arrays as arguments to static methods in SECTION 2.1. Indeed, arrays *are* objects, as we will see later in this section. By contrast, primitive types have values that are natural to represent directly in memory and operations that translate directly to machine operations, so that it does not make sense to use a reference to access each value. We will discuss references in more detail after you have seen several examples of client code that uses reference types. Your Java system might use something more complicated than machine addresses to implement references, but this model captures the essential difference between primitive and reference types.

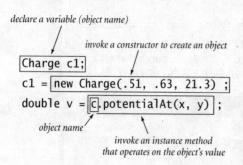

Using a reference data type

two objects

Object representation

Using objects. A declaration give us a variable name for an object that we can use in code in much the same way as we use a variable name for an integer or floating-point number:
  • As an argument or return value for a method
  • In an assignment statement
  • In an array
We have been using String objects in this way ever since HelloWorld: most of our programs call StdOut.println() with a String argument, and all of our programs have a main() method that takes an argument that is an array of String objects. As we have already seen, there is one critically important addition to this list for variables that refer to objects:
  • To invoke an instance method defined on it
This usage is not available for variables of a primitive type, where all operations are built into the language and invoked using operators such as +, -, *, and /.

Type conversion. If you want to convert an object from one type to another, you have to write code to do it. Often, there is no issue, because values for different data types are so different that no conversion is contemplated. For instance, what would it mean to convert a Charge to a Color? But you have already seen one case where conversion is worthwhile: all Java reference types have a method toString() that returns a String. Moreover, Java automatically calls this method for any object when a String is expected. One consequence of this convention is that it enables you to write StdOut.println(x) for any variable x. For example, adding the call StdOut.println(c1); to ChargeClient would add charge 21.3 at (0.51, 0.63) to the output. The nature of the conversion is completely up to the implementation, but usually the string encodes the object's value.

Uninitialized variables. When you declare a variable of a reference type but do not assign a value to it, the variable is *uninitialized*, which leads to the same behavior as for primitive types when you try to use the variable. For example, the code

```
Charge bad;
double v = bad.potentialAt(.5, .5);
```

will not compile, because it is trying to use an uninitialized variable, which leads to the error variable bad might not have been initialized.

Distinction between instance methods and static methods. Finally, you are ready to appreciate the meaning of the keyword `static` that we have been using since PROGRAM 1.1, one of the last mysterious details in the Java programs that you have been writing. The primary purpose of static methods is to implement functions; the primary purpose of non-static (instance) methods is to implement data-type operations. You can distinguish between the uses of the two types of methods in our client code, because a static method call always starts with a *class* name (uppercase, by convention) and a non-static method call always starts with an *object* name (lowercase, by convention). These differences are summarized in the following table, but after you have written some client code yourself, you will be able to quickly recognize the difference.

	instance method	static method
sample call	`c1.potentialAt(x, y)`	`Math.sqrt(2.0)`
invoked with	object name	class name
parameters	reference to object and argument(s)	argument(s)
primary purpose	manipulate object value	compute return value

Instance methods vs. static methods

THE BASIC CONCEPTS THAT WE HAVE just covered are the starting point for object-oriented programming, so it is worthwhile to briefly summarize them: A *data type* is a set of values and a set of operations defined on those values. We implement data types in independent modules and write client programs that use them. An *object* is an *instance* of a data type. Objects are characterized by three essential properties: *state*, *behavior*, and *identity*. The *state* of an object is a value from its data type. The *behavior* of an object is defined by the data type's operations. The *identity* of an object is the place where it is stored in memory. In object-oriented programming, we invoke constructors to create objects and then modify their state by invoking their instance methods.

To demonstrate the power of object orientation, we next consider several more examples. First, we consider the familiar world of image processing, where we process `Color` and `Picture` objects. Then, we consider the operations associated with `String` objects and their importance in a scientific application.

Color. *Color* is a sensation in the eye from electromagnetic radiation. Since we want to view and manipulate color images on our computers, color is a widely used abstraction in computer graphics, and Java provides a `Color` data type. In professional publishing in print and on the web, working with color is a complex task. For example, the appearance of a color image depends in a significant way on the medium used to present it. The `Color` data type separates the creative designer's problem of specifying a desired color from the system's problem of faithfully reproducing it.

Java has hundreds of data types in its libraries, so we need to explicitly list which Java libraries we are using in our program to avoid naming conflicts. Specifically, we include the statement

```
import java.awt.Color;
```

at the beginning of any program that uses `Color`. (Until now, we have been using standard Java libraries or our own, so there has been no need to import them.)

To represent color values, `Color` uses the *RGB system* where a color is defined by three integers (each between 0 and 255) that represent the intensity of the red, green, and blue (respectively) components of the color. Other color values are obtained by mixing the red, green, and blue components. That is, the data type values of `Color` are three 8-bit integers. We do not need to know whether the implementation uses `int`, `short`, or `char` values to represent these integers. With

red	green	blue	
255	0	0	*red*
0	255	0	*green*
0	0	255	*blue*
0	0	0	*black*
100	100	100	*dark gray*
255	255	255	*white*
255	255	0	*yellow*
255	0	255	*magenta*
9	90	166	*this color*

Some color values

this convention, Java is using 24 bits to represent each color and can represent $256^3 = 2^{24} \approx 16.7$ million possible colors. Scientists estimate that the human eye can distinguish only about 10 million distinct colors.

`Color` has a constructor that takes three integer arguments, so that you can write, for example

```
Color red     = new Color(255,  0,   0);
Color bookBlue = new Color( 9,  90, 166);
```

to create objects whose values represent red and the blue used to print this book, respectively. We have been using colors in `StdDraw` since SECTION 1.5, but have been limited to a set of predefined colors, such as `StdDraw.BLACK`, `StdDraw.RED`, and `StdDraw.PINK`. Now you have millions of available colors. `AlbersSquares` (PROGRAM 3.1.2) is a `StdDraw` client that allows you to experiment with them.

Program 3.1.2   *Albers squares*

```java
import java.awt.Color;

public class AlbersSquares
{
    public static void main(String[] args)
    { // Display Albers squares for the two RGB
      // colors entered on the command line.
        int r1 = Integer.parseInt(args[0]);
        int g1 = Integer.parseInt(args[1]);
        int b1 = Integer.parseInt(args[2]);
        Color c1 = new Color(r1, g1, b1);

        int r2 = Integer.parseInt(args[3]);
        int g2 = Integer.parseInt(args[4]);
        int b2 = Integer.parseInt(args[5]);
        Color c2 = new Color(r2, g2, b2);

        StdDraw.setPenColor(c1);
        StdDraw.filledSquare(.25, .5, .2);
        StdDraw.setPenColor(c2);
        StdDraw.filledSquare(.25, .5, .1);
        StdDraw.setPenColor(c2);
        StdDraw.filledSquare(.75, .5, .2);
        StdDraw.setPenColor(c1);
        StdDraw.filledSquare(.75, .5, .1);
    }

}
```

r1, g1, b1	*RGB values*
c1	*first color*
r2, g2, b2	*RGB values*
c2	*second color*

This program displays the two colors entered in RGB representation on the command line in the familiar format developed in the 1960s by the color theorist Josef Albers that revolutionized the way that people think about color.

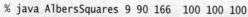

% java AlbersSquares 9 90 166   100 100 100

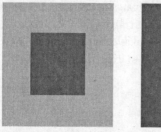

As usual, when we address a new abstraction, we are introducing you to `Color` by describing the essential elements of Java's color model, not all of the details. The API for `Color` contains several constructors and over 20 methods; the ones that we will use are briefly summarized next.

`public class java.awt.Color`

	`Color(int r, int g, int b)`	
`int`	`getRed()`	*red intensity*
`int`	`getGreen()`	*green intensity*
`int`	`getBlue()`	*blue intensity*
`Color`	`brighter()`	*brighter version of this color*
`Color`	`darker()`	*darker version of this color*
`String`	`toString()`	*string representation of this color*
`boolean`	`equals(Color c)`	*is this color's value the same as c's?*

See online documentation and booksite for other available methods.

Excerpts from the API for Java's Color data type

Our primary purpose is to use `Color` as an example to illustrate object-oriented programming, while at the same time developing a few useful tools that we can use to write programs that process colors. Accordingly, we choose one color property as an example to convince you that writing object-oriented code to process abstract concepts like color is a convenient and useful approach

Luminance. The quality of the images on modern displays such as LCD monitors, plasma TVs, and cellphone screens depends on an understanding of a color property known as *monochrome luminance,* or effective brightness. A standard formula for luminance is derived from the eye's sensitivity to red, green, and blue. It is a linear combination of the three intensities: if a color's red, green, and blue values are r, g, and b, respectively, then its luminance is defined by this equation:

$$Y = 0.299r + 0.587g + 0.114b$$

Since the coefficients are positive and sum to 1 and the intensities are all integers between 0 and 255, the luminance is a real number between 0 and 255.

Grayscale. The RGB system has the property that when all three color intensities are the same, the resulting color is on a grayscale that ranges from black (all 0s) to white (all 255s). To print a color photograph in a black-and-white newspaper (or a book), we need a static method to convert from color to grayscale. A simple way to convert a color to grayscale is to replace the color with a new one whose red, green, and blue values equal its monochrome luminance.

Color compatibility. The luminance value is also crucial in determining whether two colors are compatible, in the sense that printing text in one of the colors on a background in the other color will be readable. A widely used rule of thumb is that the difference between the luminance of the foreground and background colors should be at least 128. For example, black text on a white background has a luminance difference of 255, but black text on a (book) blue background has a luminance difference of only 74. This rule is important in the design of advertising, road signs, websites, and many other applications. Luminance (PROGRAM 3.1.3) is a static method library that we can use to convert a color to grayscale and to test whether two colors are compatible, for example, when we use colors in StdDraw applications. The methods in Luminance illustrate the utility of using data types to organize information. Using the Color reference type and passing objects as arguments makes these implementations substantially simpler than the alternative of having to pass around the three intensity values. Returning multiple values from a function also would be problematic without reference types.

red	green	blue		
9	90	166	*this color*	■
74	74	74	*grayscale version*	■
0	0	0	*black*	■

$0.299 * 9 + 0.587 * 90 + 0.114 * 166 = 74.445$

Grayscale example

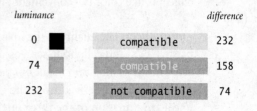

Compatibility example

HAVING AN ABSTRACTION FOR COLOR IS important not just for direct use, but also in building higher-level data types that have Color values. Next, we illustrate this point by building on the color abstraction to develop a data type that allows us to write programs to process digital images.

Program 3.1.3   Luminance library

```
import java.awt.Color;

public class Luminance
{
    public static double lum(Color color)
    {  // Compute luminance of color.
        int r = color.getRed();
        int g = color.getGreen();
        int b = color.getBlue();
        return .299*r + .587*g + .114*b;
    }

    public static Color toGray(Color color)
    {  // Use luminance to convert to grayscale.
        int y = (int) Math.round(lum(color));
        Color gray = new Color(y, y, y);
        return gray;
    }

    public static boolean compatible(Color a, Color b)
    {  // Print true if colors are compatible, false otherwise.
        return Math.abs(lum(a) - lum(b)) >= 128;

    }

    public static void main(String[] args)
    {  // Are the two given RGB colors compatible?
        int[] a = new int[6];
        for (int i = 0; i < 6; i++)
            a[i] = Integer.parseInt(args[i]);
        Color c1 = new Color(a[0], a[1], a[2]);
        Color c2 = new Color(a[3], a[4], a[5]);
        StdOut.println(compatible(c1, c2));
    }
}
```

r, g, b	*RGB values*

y	*luminance of arg color*

a[]	int *values of args*
c1	*first color*
c2	*second color*

This library comprises three important functions for manipulating color: luminance, conversion to gray, and background/foreground compatibility.

```
% java Luminance 232 232 232    0   0   0
true
% java Luminance   9  90 166  232 232 232
true
% java Luminance   9  90 166    0   0   0
false
```

Digital image processing You are familiar with the concept of a *photograph*. Technically, we might define a photograph as a two-dimensional image created by collecting and focusing visible wavelengths of electromagnetic radiation that constitutes a representation of a scene at a point in time. That technical definition is beyond our scope, except to note that the history of photography is a history of technological development. During the last century, photography was based on chemical processes, but its future is now based in computation. Your camera and your cellphone are computers with lenses and light-sensitive devices capable of capturing images in digital form, and your computer has photo-editing software that allows you to process those images. You can crop them, enlarge and reduce them, adjust the contrast, brighten or darken them, remove red-eye, or perform scores of other operations. Many such operations are remarkably easy to implement, given a simple basic data type that captures the idea of a digital image, as you will now see.

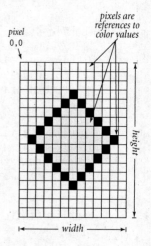

Anatomy of a digital image

Digital images. We have been using StdDraw to plot geometric objects (points, lines, circles, squares) in a window on the computer screen. Which set of values do we need to process digital images, and which operations do we need to perform on those values? The basic abstraction for computer displays is the same one that is used for digital photographs and is very simple: A *digital image* is a rectangular grid of *pixels* (picture elements), where the color of each pixel is individually defined. Digital images are sometimes referred to as *raster* or *bitmapped* images, in contrast to the types of images we produce with StdDraw, which are referred to as *vector* images.

Our class Picture is a data type for digital images whose definition follows immediately from the digital image abstraction. The set of values is nothing more than a two-dimensional matrix of Color values, and the operations are what you might expect: create an image (either a blank one with a given width and height or one initialized from a picture file), set the value of a pixel to a given color, return the color of a given pixel, return the width or the height, show the image in a window on your computer screen, and save the image to a file. In this description, we intentionally use the word *matrix* instead of *array* to emphasize that we are referring to an abstraction (a matrix of pixels), not a specific implementation (a Java two-dimensional array of Color objects). *You do not need to know how a class is implemented in order to be able to use it.* Indeed, typical images have so many pixels that implementations are likely to use a more efficient representation than an array of `Color` values (see Exercise 3.1.29). Such considerations are interesting, but can be dealt with independent of client code. To write client programs that manipulate images, you just need to know this API:

`public class Picture`

	`Picture(String filename)`	*create a picture from a file*
	`Picture(int w, int h)`	*create a blank w-by-h picture*
`int`	`width()`	*return the width of the picture*
`int`	`height()`	*return the height of the picture*
`Color`	`get(int i, int j)`	*return the color of pixel (i, j)*
`void`	`set(int i, int j, Color c)`	*set the color of pixel (i, j) to c*
`void`	`show()`	*display the image in a window*
`void`	`save(String filename)`	*save the image to a file*

API for our data type for image processing

By convention, $(0, 0)$ is the upper leftmost pixel, so the image is laid as in the customary order for arrays (by contrast, the convention for `StdDraw` is to have the point $(0,0)$ at the lower left corner, so that drawings are oriented as in the customary manner for Cartesian coordinates). Most image processing programs are filters that scan through the pixels in a source image as they would a two-dimensional array and then perform some computation to determine the color of each pixel in a target image. The supported file formats for the first constructor and the `save()` method are the widely used `.png` and `.jpg` formats, so that you can write programs to process your own photographs and add the results to an album or a website. The `show()` window also has an interactive option for saving to a file. These methods, together with Java's `Color` data type, open the door to image processing.

Grayscale. You will find many examples of color images on the booksite, and all of the methods that we describe are effective for full-color images, but all our example images in the text will be grayscale. Accordingly, our first task is to write a program that can convert images from color to grayscale. This task is a prototypical image-

Program 3.1.4   *Converting color to grayscale*

```java
import java.awt.Color;
public class Grayscale
{
   public static void main(String[] args)
   { // Show image in grayscale.
     Picture pic = new Picture(args[0]);
     for (int i = 0; i < pic.width(); i++)
     {
        for (int j = 0; j < pic.height(); j++)
        {
           Color color = pic.get(i, j);
           Color gray  = Luminance.toGray(color);
           pic.set(i, j, gray);
        }
     }
     pic.show();
   }
}
```

pic	*image from file*
i, j	*pixel coordinates*
color	*pixel color*
gray	*pixel grayscale*

This program illustrates a simple image processing client. First, it creates a Picture *object initialized with an image file named by the command-line argument. Then it converts each pixel in the image to grayscale by creating a grayscale version of each pixel's color and resetting the pixel to that color. Finally, it shows the image. You can perceive individual pixels in the image on the right, which was upscaled from a low-resolution image (see "Scaling" on the next page).*

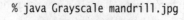

% java Grayscale mandrill.jpg

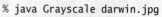

% java Grayscale darwin.jpg

processing task: for each pixel in the source, we have a pixel in the target with a different color. Grayscale (PROGRAM 3.1.4) is a filter that takes a file name from the command line and produces a grayscale version of that image. It creates a new Picture object initialized with the color image, then sets the color of each pixel to a new Color having a grayscale value computed by applying the toGray() method in Luminance (PROGRAM 3.1.3) to the color of the corresponding pixel in the source.

downscaling

source

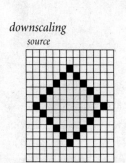

target

upscaling

source

target

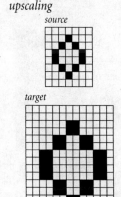

Scaling a digital image

Scaling. One of the most common image-processing tasks is to make an image smaller or larger. Examples of this basic operation, known as *scaling*, include making small thumbnail photos for use in a chat room or a cellphone, changing the size of a high-resolution photo to make it fit into a specific space in a printed publication or on a web page, or zooming in on a satellite photograph or an image produced by a microscope. In optical systems, we can just move a lens to achieve a desired scale, but in digital imagery, we have to do more work.

In some cases, the strategy is clear. For example, if the target image is to be half the size (in each dimension) of the source image, we simply choose half the pixels, say, by deleting half the rows and half the columns. This technique is known as *sampling*. If the target image is to be double the size (in each dimension) of the source image, we can replace each source pixel by four target pixels of the same color. Note that we can lose information when we downscale, so halving an image and then doubling it generally does not give back the same image.

A single strategy is effective for both downscaling and upscaling. Our goal is to produce the target image, so we proceed through the pixels in the target, one by one, scaling each pixel's coordinates to identify a pixel in the source whose color can be assigned to the target. If the width and height of the source are w_s and h_s (respectively) and the width and height of the target are w_t and h_t (respectively), then we scale the row index by w_s/w_t and the column index by h_s/h_t. That is, we get the color of the pixel in row i and column j of the target from row $i \times w_s/w_t$ and column $j \times h_s/h_t$ in the source. For example, if we are halving the size of a picture, the scale factors are 2, so the pixel in row 2 and column 3 of the target

Program 3.1.5 *Image scaling*

```
public class Scale
{
   public static void main(String[] args)
   {
      int w = Integer.parseInt(args[1]);
      int h = Integer.parseInt(args[2]);
      Picture source = new Picture(args[0]);
      Picture target = new Picture(w, h);
      for (int ti = 0; ti < w; ti++)
      {
         for (int tj = 0; tj < h; tj++)
         {
            int si = ti * source.width()  / w;
            int sj = tj * source.height() / h;
            target.set(ti, tj, source.get(si, sj));
         }
      }
      source.show();
      target.show();
   }
}
```

w, h	target dimensions
source	source image
target	target image
ti, tj	target pixel coords
si, sj	source pixel coords

This program takes the name of a picture file and two integers (width w and height h) as command-line arguments and scales the image to w-by-h.

java Scale mandrill.jpg 800 800

600 300

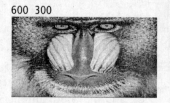

200 400

200 200

gets the color of the pixel in row 4 and column 6 of the source; if we are doubling the size of the picture, the scale factors are 1/2, so the pixel in row 6 and column 4 of the target gets the color of the pixel in row 3 and column 2 of the source. Scale (PROGRAM 3.1.5) is an implementation of this strategy. More sophisticated strategies can be effective for low-resolution images of the sort that you might find on old web pages or from old cameras. For example, we might downscale to half size by averaging the values of four pixels in the source to make one pixel in the target. For the high-resolution images that are common in most applications today, the simple approach used in Scale is effective.

`java Fade mandrill.jpg Darwin.jpg 9`

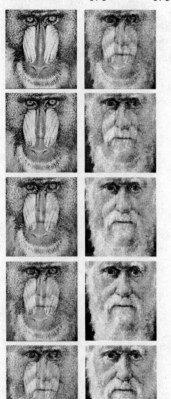

The same basic idea of computing the color value of each target pixel as a function of the color values of specific source pixels is effective for all sorts of image-processing tasks. Next, we consider two more examples, and you will find numerous other examples in the exercises and on the booksite.

Fade effect. Our next image-processing example is an entertaining computation where we transform one image to another in a series of discrete steps. Such a transformation is sometimes known as a *fade effect*. Fade (PROGRAM 3.1.6) is a Picture and Color client that uses a *linear interpolation* strategy to implement this effect. It computes $M-1$ intermediate images, with each pixel in the tth image a weighted average of the corresponding pixels in the source and target. The static method blend() implements the interpolation: the source color is weighted by a factor of $1 - t / M$ and the target color by a factor of t / M (when t is 0, we have the source color, and when t is M, we have the target color). This simple computation can produce striking results. When you run Fade on your computer, the change appears to happen dynamically. Try running it on some images from your photo library. Note that Fade assumes that the images have the same width and height; if you have images for which this is not the case, you can use Scale to created a scaled version of one or both of them for Fade.

Program 3.1.6   Fade effect

```java
import java.awt.Color;

public class Fade
{
   public static Color blend(Color c, Color d, double alpha)
   {  // Compute blend of c and d, weighted by x.
      double r = (1-alpha)*c.getRed()   + alpha*d.getRed();
      double g = (1-alpha)*c.getGreen() + alpha*d.getGreen();
      double b = (1-alpha)*c.getBlue()  + alpha*d.getBlue();
      return new Color((int) r, (int) g, (int) b);
   }
   public static void main(String[] args)
   {  // Show M-image fade sequence from source to target.
      Picture source = new Picture(args[0]);
      Picture target = new Picture(args[1]);
      int M = Integer.parseInt(args[2]);
      int width  = source.width();
      int height = source.height();
      Picture pic = new Picture(width, height);
      for (int t = 0; t <= M; t++)
      {
         for (int i = 0; i < width; i++)
         {
            for (int j = 0; j < height; j++)
            {
               Color c0 = source.get(i, j);
               Color cM = target.get(i, j);
               Color c = blend(c0, cM, (double) t / M);
               pic.set(i, j, c);
            }
         }
         pic.show();
      }
   }
}
```

M	number of images
pic	current image
t	image counter
c0	source color
c1	target color
c	blended color

To fade from one image into another in M steps, we set each pixel in the tth image to a weighted average of the corresponding pixel in the source and the destination, with the source getting weight 1-t/M and the destination getting weight t/M. An example transformation is shown on the facing page.

Potential value visualization. Image processing is also helpful in scientific visualization. As an example, we consider a `Picture` client for visualizing properties of the `Charge` data type that we introduced at the beginning of this chapter. `Potential` (PROGRAM 3.1.7) visualizes the potential values created by a set of charged particles. First, `Potential` creates an array of particles, with values taken from standard input. Next, it creates a `Picture` object and sets each pixel in the picture to a shade of gray that is proportional to the potential value at the corresponding point. The calculation at the heart of the method is very simple: for each pixel, we compute corresponding (x, y) values in the unit square, then call `potentialAt()` to find the potential at that point due to all of the charges, summing the values returned. With appropriate assignment of potential values to grayscale values (scaling them to fall between 0 and 255), we get a striking visual representation of the electric potential that is an excellent aid to understanding interactions among such particles. We could produce a similar image using `filledSquare()` in `StdDraw`, but `Picture` provides us with more accurate control over the color of each pixel on the screen. The same basic method is useful in many other settings—you can find several examples on the booksite.

```
% more charges.txt
9
.51 .63 -100
.50 .50   40
.50 .72   10
.33 .33    5
.20 .20  -10
.70 .70   10
.82 .72   20
.85 .23   30
.90 .12  -50
% java Potential < charges.txt
```

Potential value visualization for a set of charges

IT IS WORTHWHILE TO REFLECT BRIEFLY on the code in `Potential`, because it exemplifies data abstraction and object-oriented programming. We want to produce an image that shows interactions among charged particles, and our code reflects precisely the process of creating that image, using a `Picture` object for the image (which is manipulated via `Color` objects) and `Charge` objects for the particles. When we want information about a `Charge`, we invoke the appropriate method directly for that `Charge`; when we want to create a `Color`, we use a `Color` constructor; when we want to set a pixel, we directly involve the appropriate method for the `Picture`. These data types are independently developed, but their use together in a single client is easy and natural. We next consider several more examples, to illustrate the broad reach of data abstraction while at the same time adding a number of useful data types to our basic programming model.

Program 3.1.7 *Visualizing electric potential*

```java
import java.awt.Color;
public class Potential
{
   public static void main(String[] args)
   {  // Read charges from StdIn into a[].
      int N = StdIn.readInt();
      Charge[] a = new Charge[N];
      for (int k = 0; k < N; k++)
      {
         double x0 = StdIn.readDouble();
         double y0 = StdIn.readDouble();
         double q0 = StdIn.readDouble();
         a[k] = new Charge(x0, y0, q0);
      }

      // Create and show image depicting potential values.
      int size = 512;
      Picture pic = new Picture(size, size);
      for (int i = 0; i < size; i++)
      {
         for (int j = 0; j < size; j++)
         {  // Compute pixel color.
            double x = (double) i / size;
            double y = (double) j / size;
            double V = 0.0;
            for (int k = 0; k < N; k++)
               V += a[k].potentialAt(x, y);
            int g = 128 + (int) (V / 2.0e10);
            if (g < 0)   g = 0;
            if (g > 255) g = 255;
            Color c = new Color(g, g, g);
            pic.set(i, size-1-j, c);
         }

      }
      pic.show();
   }
}
```

N	number of charges
a[]	array of charges
x0, y0	charge position
q0	charge value

i, j	pixel position
x, y	point in unit square
g	scaled potential value
c	pixel color

This program reads values from standard input to create an array of charged particles, sets each pixel color in an image to a grayscale value proportional to the total of the potentials due to the particles at corresponding points, and shows the resulting image.

String processing   You have been using strings since your first Java program.
Java's String data type includes a long list of other operations on strings. It is one
of Java's most important data types because string processing is critical to many
computational applications. Strings lie at the heart of our ability to compile and
run Java programs and to perform many other core computations; they are the
basis of the information-processing systems that are critical to most business systems; people use them every day when typing into email, blog, or chat applications
or preparing documents for publication; and they have proven to be critical ingredients in scientific progress in several fields, particularly molecular biology.

A String value is an indexed sequence of char values. We summarize here
the methods from the Java API that we use most often. Several of the methods use
integers to refer to a character's index within a string; as with arrays, these indices
start at 0. As indicated in the note at the bottom, this list is a small subset of the
String API; the full API has over 60 methods!

`public class String` (Java string data type)

	String(String s)	*create a string with the same value as* s
int	length()	*string length*
char	charAt(int i)	*i th character*
String	substring(int i, int j)	*i th through (j-1)st characters*
boolean	contains(String sub)	*does string contain* sub *as a substring?*
boolean	startsWith(String pre)	*does string start with* pre?
boolean	endsWith(String post)	*does string end with* post?
int	indexOf(String p)	*index of first occurrence of* p
int	indexOf(String p, int i)	*index of first occurrence of* p *after* i
String	concat(String t)	*this string with* t *appended*
int	compareTo(String t)	*string comparison*
String	replaceAll(String a, String b)	*result of changing* a*s to* b*s*
String[]	split(String delim)	*strings between occurrences of* delim
boolean	equals(String t)	*is this string's value the same as* t*'s?*

See online documentation and booksite for many other available methods.

Excerpts from the API for Java's String *data type*

Java provides special language support for manipulating strings. Instead of initializing a string with a constructor, we can use a string literal, and instead of invoking the method concat(), we can use the + operator:

shorthand	`String s = "abc";`	`String t = r + s;`	
longhand	`String s = new String("abc");`	`String t = r.concat(s);`	

These notations are shorthand for standard data-type mechanisms.

`String` values are not the same as arrays of characters, but the two are similar, and novice Java programmers sometimes confuse them. For example, the differences are evident in one of the most common code idioms for both strings and arrays: for loops to process each element (for arrays) or character (for strings):

```
for (int i = 0; i < a.length; i++)        for (int i = 0; i < s.length(); i++)
{  ...  a[i]  ...  }                       {  ...  s.charAt(i)  ...  }
```
           array   *string*

For arrays, we have direct language support: brackets for indexed access and .length (with no parentheses) for length. For strings, both indexed access and length are just `String` methods.

The split() method in the `String` API is powerful because many options, known as *regular expressions*, are available for delim. For example, "\\s+" means "one or more whitespace characters." Using this delimiter with split() transforms a string of words delimited by whitespace into an array of words.

Why not just use arrays of characters instead of `String` values? When we process strings, we want to write client code that operates on strings, not arrays. The methods in Java's `String` data type implement natural operations on `String` values and also simplify client code, as you will see. We have been working with programs that use a few short strings for output, but it is not unusual for *strings*, not numbers, to be the primary data type of interest in an application, and to have programs that process huge strings or huge numbers of strings. Next, we consider in detail such an application.

```
String a = "now is ";
String b = "the time ";
String c = "to"
```

call	value
`a.length()`	`7`
`a.charAt(4)`	`i`
`a.substring(2, 5)`	`"w i"`
`b.startsWith("the")`	`true`
`a.indexOf("is")`	`4`
`a.concat(c)`	`"now is to"`
`b.replace('t','T')`	`"The Time "`
`a.split(" ")[0]`	`"now"`
`a.split(" ")[1]`	`"is"`
`b.equals(c)`	`false`

Examples of string operations

| *is the string a palindrome?* | ```java
public static boolean isPalindrome(String s)
{
    int N = s.length();
    for (int i = 0; i < N/2; i++)
        if (s.charAt(i) != s.charAt(N-1-i))
            return false;
    return true;
}
``` |
| *extract file name and extension from a command-line argument* | ```java
String s = args[0];
int dot = s.indexOf(".");
String base      = s.substring(0, dot);
String extension = s.substring(dot + 1, s.length());
``` |
| *print all lines in standard input that contain a string specified on the command line* | ```java
String query = args[0];
while (!StdIn.isEmpty())
{
    String s = StdIn.readLine();
    if (s.contains(query)) StdOut.println(s);
}
``` |
| *create an array of the strings on* StdIn *delimited by whitespace* | ```java
String input = StdIn.readAll();
String[] words = input.split("\\s+");
``` |
| *check whether an array of strings is in alphabetical order* | ```java
public boolean isSorted(String[] a)
{
    for (int i = 1; i < a.length; i++)
    {
        if (a[i-1].compareTo(a[i]) > 0)
            return false;
    }
    return true;
}
``` |
| *print all the hyperlinks (to educational institutions) in the text file on standard input* | ```java
while (!StdIn.isEmpty())
{
    String s = StdIn.readString();
    if (s.startsWith("http://") && s.endsWith(".edu"))
        StdOut.println(s);
}
``` |

Typical string-processing code

String-processing application: genomics   To give you more experience with string processing, we will give a very brief overview of the field of *genomics* and consider a Java program that solves a basic problem known as *gene finding*. Genomics is a quintessential string-processing application.

Biologists use a simple model to represent the building blocks of life: The letters A, C, T, and G represent the four nucleotides in the DNA of living organisms. In each living organism, these basic building blocks appear in a set of long sequences (one for each chromosome) known as a *genome*. Scientists know that understanding properties of the genome is a key to understanding the processes that manifest themselves in living organisms. The genomic sequences for many living things are known, including a human genome, which is a sequence of about three billion characters. You can find these sequences in many places on the web. (We have collected several on the booksite: for instance, the file genomeVirus.txt, which is the 6252-character genome of a simple virus.) Knowing the sequences, scientists are now writing computer programs to study the structure of these sequences. String processing is now one of the most important methodologies—experimental or computational—in molecular biology for elucidating biological function.

Gene finding. A *gene* is a substring of a genome that represents a functional unit of critical importance in understanding life processes. Genes are substrings of the genome of varying length, and there are varying numbers of them within a genome. A gene is a sequence of *codons*, each of which is a nucleotide triplet that represents one amino acid. The *start codon* ATG marks the beginning of a gene, and any of the *stop codons* TAG, TAA, or TGA mark the end of a gene (and there are no occurrences of any of the codons ATG, TAA, TAG, or TGA within the gene). One of the first steps in analyzing a genome is to identify its genes, which, as you certainly now realize, is a string-processing problem that Java's String data type equips us to solve. GeneFind (PROGRAM 3.1.8) is a Java program that can do the job. To understand how it works, we will consider a tiny example that does not represent a real genome. Take a moment to identify the genes marked by the start codon ATG and the end codon TAG in the following string:

ATAGATGCATAGCGCATAGCTAGATGTGCTAGC

There are several occurrences of both ATG and TAG, and they overlap in various ways, so you have to do a bit of work to identify the genes. GeneFind accomplishes the task in one left-to-right scan through the genome, as shown next.

Program 3.1.8   *Finding genes in a genome*

```
public class GeneFind
{
    public static void main(String[] args)
    { // Use start and stop to find genes in genome.
        String start  = args[0];
        String stop   = args[1];
        String genome = StdIn.readAll();
        int beg = -1;
        for (int i = 0; i < genome.length() - 2; i++)
        { // Check next codon for start or stop.
            String codon = genome.substring(i, i+3);
            if (codon.equals(start)) beg = i;
            if ((codon.equals(stop)) && beg != -1)
            { // Check putative gene alignment.
                String gene;
                gene = genome.substring(beg+3, i);
                if (gene.length() % 3 == 0)
                { // Print and restart.
                    StdOut.println(gene);
                    beg = -1;
                }
            }
        }
    }
}
```

start	start *codon*
stop	stop *codon*
genome	*full genome*
beg	*putative gene start position*
i	*character index*
codon	*next codon*
gene	*discovered gene*

This program prints all the genes in the genome on standard input defined by the start and stop codes on the command line. To find a gene in a genome, we scan for the start codon, remember its index, and then scan to the next stop codon. If the length of the intervening sequence is a multiple of 3, we have found a gene.

```
% more genomeTiny.txt
ATAGATGCATAGCGCATAGCTAGATGTGCTAGC

% java GeneFind ATG TAG < genomeTiny.txt
CATAGCGCA
TGC

% java GeneFind ATG TAG < genomeVirus.txt
CGCCTGCGTCTGTAC
TCGAGCGGATCGCTCACAACCAGTCGG
...
AGATTATCAAAAAGGATCTTCACC
```

| i | codon | | beg | gene | *remaining portion of input string* |
	start	stop			
0			-1		ATAGATGCATAGCGCATAGCTAGATGTGCTAGC
1		TAG	-1		ATAGATGCATAGCGCATAGCTAGATGTGCTAGC
4	ATG		4		ATAGATGCATAGCGCATAGCTAGATGTGCTAGC
9		TAG	4		ATAGATGCATAGCGCATAGCTAGATGTGCTAGC
16		TAG	4	CATAGCGCA	ATAGATGCATAGCGCATAGCTAGATGTGCTAGC
20		TAG	-1		ATAGATGCATAGCGCATAGCTAGATGTGCTAGC
23	ATG		23		ATAGATGCATAGCGCATAGCTAGATGTGCTAGC
29		TAG	23	TGC	ATAGATGCATAGCGCATAGCTAGATGTGCTAGC

The variable beg holds the index of the most recently encountered ATG start codon: the value -1 indicates that the current portion of the genome could not be a gene, either because no ATG has been seen (at the beginning) or because no ATG has been seen since the last gene was found. If we encounter a TAG stop codon when beg is -1, we ignore it; otherwise, we have found a gene. This trace illustrates the cases of interest: we ignore the TAG codons at 1 and 20 because beg is -1, indicating that we have not seen an ATG; we set beg to the current index each time that we encounter an ATG; we ignore the TAG at 9 because it marks the putative gene CA whose length is not a multiple of 3, so it could not be a sequence of codons; and we output genes at 16 and 29 because we have valid start and stop codons with no intervening stop codons and a gene length that is a multiple of 3.

GeneFind is simple but subtle, typical of string processing programs. In practice, the rules that define genes are more complicated than those we have sketched: other codons may be prohibited, there may be bounds on the length, some genes have to be spliced from multiple pieces, and genes satisfying various other criteria may be of interest. GeneFind is intended to exemplify how a basic knowledge of Java programming can enable a scientist to make appropriate tools to study these sequences. Actual genomes are similar to our test case, just much longer. You can experiment with GeneFind to look for genes in genomeVirus.txt and several other genomes on the booksite. The quick leap from examining a toy programming example that illustrates the basic Java String data type to studying scientific questions on actual data is a remarkable characteristic of modern genomics. As we will see, some of the very same algorithms that were developed by computer scientists that underly basic computational mechanisms and have proven important in commercial applications are also now playing a critical role in genomic research.

Input and output revisited In SECTION 1.5 you learned how to read and write numbers and text using StdIn and StdOut and to make drawings with StdDraw. You have certainly come to appreciate the utility of these mechanism in getting information into and out of your programs. One reason that they are convenient is that the "standard" conventions make them accessible from anywhere within a program. One disadvantage of these conventions is that they leave us dependent upon the operating system's piping and redirection mechanism for access to files, and they restrict us to working with just one input file, one output file, and one drawing for any given program. With object-oriented programming, we can define mechanisms that are similar to StdIn, StdOut, and StdDraw but allow us to work with *multiple* input streams, output streams, and drawings within one program.

Specifically, we define in this section the data types In, Out, and Draw for input streams, output streams, and drawings (respectively). As usual, you can download the files In.java, Out.java, and Draw.java from the booksite to use these data types.

These data types give us the flexibility that we need to address many common data-processing

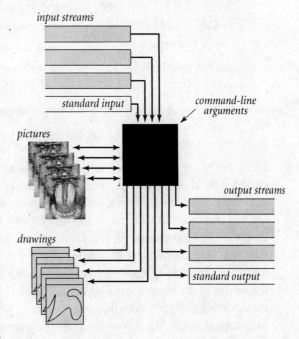

A bird's-eye view of a Java program (revisited again)

tasks within our Java programs. Rather than being restricted to just one input stream, one output stream, and one drawing, we can easily define multiple objects of each type, connecting the streams to various sources and destinations. We also get the flexibility to assign such objects to variables, pass them as arguments or return values from methods, and to create arrays of them, manipulating them just as we manipulate objects of any type. We will consider several examples of their use after we have presented the APIs.

Input stream data type. The data type In is a more general version of StdIn that supports reading numbers and text from files and websites as well as the standard input stream. It implements the *input stream* data type, with the following API:

```
public class In
```

	In()	*create an input stream from standard input*
	In(String name)	*create an input stream from a file or website*
boolean	isEmpty()	true *if no more input,* false *otherwise*
int	readInt()	*read a value of type* int
double	readDouble()	*read a value of type* double
	...	

Note: All operations supported by StdIn *are also supported for* In *objects.*

API for our data type for input streams

Instead of being restricted to one abstract input stream (standard input), you now also have the ability to directly specify the source of an input stream. Moreover, that source can be either a *file* or a *website*. When invoked with a constructor having a String argument, In will first try to find a file in the current directory of your local computer that has that name. If it cannot do so, it will assume the argument to be a website name and will try to connect to that website. (If no such website exists, it will issue a runtime exception.) In either case, the specified file or website becomes the source of the input for the input stream object thus created, and the read*() methods will provide values from that stream. This arrangement makes it possible to process multiple files within the same program. Moreover, the ability to directly access the web opens up the whole web as potential input for your programs. For example, it allows you to process data that is provided and maintained by someone else. You can find such files all over the web. Scientists now regularly post data files with measurements or results of experiments, ranging from genome and protein sequences to satellite photographs to astronomical observations; financial services companies, such as stock exchanges, regularly publish on the web detailed information about the performance of stock and other financial instruments; governments publish election results; and so forth. Now you can write Java programs that read these kinds of files directly. In gives you a great deal of flexibility to take advantage of the multitude of data sources that are now available.

Output stream data type. Similarly, our data type Out is a more general version of StdOut that supports writing text to a variety of output streams, including standard output and files. Again, the API specifies the same methods as its StdOut counterpart. You specify the file that you want to use for output by using the one-argument constructor with the file's name as argument. Out interprets this string as the name of a new file on your local computer, and sends its output there. If you use the no-argument constructor, then you obtain standard output.

```
public class Out
```

	Out()	*create an output stream to standard output*
	Out(String name)	*create an output stream to a file*
void	print(String s)	*print s to the output stream*
void	println(String s)	*print s and a newline to the output stream*
void	println()	*print a newline to the output stream*
void	printf(String f, ...)	*formatted print to the output steam*

API for our data type for output streams

File concatenation and filtering. PROGRAM 3.1.9 is a sample client of In and Out that uses multiple input streams to concatenate several input files into a single output file. Some operating systems have a command known as cat that implements this function. However, a Java program that does the same thing is perhaps more useful, because we can tailor it to *filter* the input files in various ways: we might wish to ignore irrelevant information, change the format, or select only some of the data, to name just a few examples. We now consider one example of such processing, and you can find several others in the exercises.

Screen scraping. The combination of In (which allows us to create an input stream from any page on the web) and String (which provides powerful tools for processing text strings) opens up the entire web to direct access by our Java programs, without any direct dependence on the operating system or the browser. One paradigm is known as *screen scraping*: the goal is to extract some information from a web page with a program rather than having to browse to find it. To do so, we take

Program 3.1.9 Concatenating files

```
public class Cat
{
    public static void main(String[] args)
    { // Copy input files to out (last argument).
        Out out = new Out(args[args.length-1]);
        for (int i = 0; i < args.length - 1; i++)
        { // Copy input file named on ith arg to out.
            In in = new In(args[i]);
            String s = in.readAll();
            out.println(s);
        }
    }
}
```

out	*output stream*
i	*argument index*
in	*current input stream*
s	*contents of* in

This program creates an output file whose name is given by the last argument and whose contents are copies of the input files whose names are given as the other arguments.

```
% more in1.txt
This is

% more in2.txt
a tiny
test.
```

```
% java Cat in1.txt in2.txt out.txt

% more out.txt
This is
a tiny
test.
```

advantage of the fact that many web pages are defined with text files in a highly structured format (because they are created by computer programs!). Your browser has a mechanism that allows you to examine the source code that produces the web page that you are viewing, and by examining that source you can often figure out what to do. For example, suppose that we want to take a stock trading symbol as a command-line argument and print out its current trading price. Such information is published on the web by financial service companies and internet service providers. For example, you can find the stock price of a company whose symbol is goog by browsing to http://finance.yahoo.com/q?s=goog. Like many web pages, the name encodes an argument (goog), and we could substitute any other ticker symbol to get a web page with financial information for any other company. Also, like many other files on the web, the referenced file is a text file, written in a formatting language known as HTML. (See the CONTEXT section at the end of this book for some details about this language.) From the point of view of a Java program, it is just a String value accessible through an In input stream. You can use your browser to download the source of that file, or you could use

```
java Cat "http://finance.yahoo.com/q?s=goog" mycopy.txt
```

to put the source into a local file mycopy.txt on your computer (though there is no real need to do so). Now, suppose that goog is trading at $475.11 at the moment. If you search for the string "475.11" in the source of that page, you will find the stock price buried within some HTML code. Without having to know details of HTML, you can figure out something about the context in which the price appears. In this case, you can see that the stock price is enclosed between the tags "" and "", a bit after the string "Last Trade:". With the String data type methods indexOf() and substring() you can easily grab this information, as illustrated in StockQuote (PROGRAM 3.1.10). This program depends on the web page format of http://finance.yahoo. com; if this format changes, StockQuote not work. Still, making appropriate changes is not likely to be difficult. You can entertain yourself by embellishing StockQuote in all kinds of interesting ways. For example, you could grab the stock price on a periodic basis and plot it, compute a moving average, or save the results to a file for later analysis. Of course, the same technique works for sources of data found all over the web. You can find many examples in the exercises at the end of this section and on the booksite.

```
...
<tr>
<td class="yfnc_tablehead1"
width="48%">
Last Trade:
</td>
<td class="yfnc_tabledata1">
<big><b>475.11</b></big>
</td></tr>
<tr>
<td class="yfnc_tablehead1"
width="48%">
Trade Time:
</td>
<td class="yfnc_tabledata1">
11:13AM ET
...
```

HTML code from the web

Extracting data. The ability to maintain multiple input and output streams gives us a great deal of flexibility in meeting the challenges of processing large amounts of data coming from a variety of sources. We consider one more example: Suppose that a scientist or a financial analyst has a large amount of data within a spreadsheet program. Typically such spreadsheets are tables with a relatively large number of rows and a relatively small number of columns. You are not likely to be interested

Program 3.1.10   *Screen scraping for stock quotes*

```
public class StockQuote
{
   public static double price(String symbol)
   {  // Return current stock price for symbol.
      In page = new In("http://finance.yahoo.com/q?s=" + symbol);
      String in = page.readAll();
      int trade = in.indexOf("Last Trade:", 0);
      int from =  in.indexOf("<b>", trade);
      int to =    in.indexOf("</b>", from);
      String price = in.substring(from + 3, to);
      return Double.parseDouble(price);
   }

   public static void main(String[] args)
   {  StdOut.println(price(args[0]));  }
}
```

page	*input stream*
in	*contents of* page
trade	Last... *index*
from	<b> *index*
to	</b> *index*
price	*current price*

This program takes the ticker symbol of a stock as a command-line argument, reads a web page containing the stock price, finds the stock price using the String method indexOf()*, extracts it using the method* substring()*, and prints the price out to standard output.*

```
% java StockQuote goog
475.11
% java StockQuote adbe
41.125
```

in all the data in the spreadsheet, but you may be interested in a few of the columns. You can do some calculations within the spreadsheet program (this is its purpose, after all), but you certainly do not have the flexibility that you have with Java programming. One way to address this situation is to have the spreadsheet *export* the data to a text file, using some special character to delimit the columns, and then write a Java program that reads that file from an input stream. One standard practice is to use commas as delimiters: print one line per column, with commas separating row entries. Such files are known as *comma-separated-value* or .csv files. With the split() method in Java's String data type, we can read the file line-by-

Program 3.1.11 Splitting a file

```
public class Split
{
    public static void main(String[] args)
    { // Split file by column into M+1 files.
        String name = args[0];
        int N = Integer.parseInt(args[1]);
        String delim = ",";

        // Create output streams.
        Out[] out = new Out[N];
        for (int i = 0; i < N; i++)
            out[i] = new Out(name + i + ".txt");

        In in = new In(name + ".csv");
        while (!in.isEmpty())
        { // Read a line and write fields to output streams.
            String line = in.readLine();
            String[] fields = line.split(delim);
            for (int i = 0; i < N; i++)
                out[i].println(fields[i]);
        }
    }
}
```

name	*base file name*
N	*argument index*
delim	*delimiter (comma)*
in	*input stream*
out[]	*output streams*
line	*current line*
fields[]	*values in current line*

This program uses multiple output streams to split a .csv *file into separate files, one for each comma-delimited field. The name of the output file corresponding to the* i *th field is formed by concatenating* i *and then* .txt *to the end of the original file name.*

```
% more DJIA.csv
...
31-Oct-29,264.97,7150000,273.51
30-Oct-29,230.98,10730000,258.47
29-Oct-29,252.38,16410000,230.07
28-Oct-29,295.18,9210000,260.64
25-Oct-29,299.47,5920000,301.22
24-Oct-29,305.85,12900000,299.47
23-Oct-29,326.51,6370000,305.85
22-Oct-29,322.03,4130000,326.51
21-Oct-29,323.87,6090000,320.91
...
```

```
% java Split DJIA 3

% more DJIA2.txt
...
7150000
10730000
16410000
9210000
5920000
12900000
6370000
4130000
6090000
...
```

line and isolate the data that we want. We will see several examples of this approach later in the book. Split (PROGRAM 3.1.11) is an In and Out client that goes one step further: it creates multiple output streams and makes one file for each column.

THESE EXAMPLES ARE CONVINCING ILLUSTRATIONS OF the utility of working with text files, with multiple input and output streams, and with direct access to web pages. Web pages are written in HTML precisely so that they are accessible to any program that can read strings. People use text formats such as .csv files rather than data formats that are beholden to particular applications precisely in order to allow as many people as possible to access the data with simple programs like Split.

Drawing data type. When using the Picture data type that we considered earlier in this section, we could write programs that manipulated multiple pictures, arrays of pictures, and so forth, precisely because the data type provides us with the capability for computing with Picture objects. Naturally, we would like the same capability for computing with the kinds of objects that we create with StdDraw. Accordingly, we have a Draw data type with the following API:

```
public class Draw
```
```
        Draw()
  void  line(double x0, double y0, double x1, double y1)
  void  point(double x, double y)

        . . .
```

Note: All operations supported by StdDraw *are also supported for* Draw *objects.*

As for any data type, you can create a new drawing by using new to create a Draw object, assign it to a variable, and use that variable name to call the methods that create the graphics. For example, the code

```
Draw d = new Draw();
d.circle(.5, .5, .2);
```

draws a circle in the center of a window on your screen. As with Picture, each drawing has its own window, so that you can address applications that call for multiple different drawings.

Properties of reference types Now that you have seen several examples of reference types (Charge, Color, Picture, String, In, Out, and Draw) and client programs that use them, we discuss in more detail some of their essential properties. To a large extent, Java protects novice programmers from having to know these details. Experienced programmers know that a firm understanding of these properties is helpful in writing correct, effective, and efficient object-oriented programs.

A reference captures the distinction between a thing and its name. This distinction is a familiar one, as illustrated in these examples:

type	typical object	typical name
website	our booksite	www.cs.princeton.edu/IntroProgramming
person	father of computer science	Alan Turing
planet	third rock from the sun	Earth
building	our office	35 Olden Street
ship	superliner that sank in 1912	RMS Titanic
number	circumference/diameter in a circle	π
Picture	new Picture("mandrill.jpg")	pic

A given object may have multiple names, but each object has its own identity. We can create a new name for an object without changing the object's value (via an assignment statement), but when we change an object's value (by invoking an instance method), all of the object's names refer to the changed object.

The following analogy may help you keep this crucial distinction clear in your mind. Suppose that you want to have your house painted, so you write the street address of your house in pencil on a piece of paper and give it to a few house painters. Now, if you hire one of the painters to paint the house, it becomes a different color. No changes have been made to any of the pieces of paper, but the house that they all refer to has changed. One of the painters might erase what you've written and write the address of another house, but changing what is written on one piece of paper does not change what is written on another piece of paper. Java references are like the pieces of paper: they hold names of objects. Changing a reference does not change the object, but changing an object makes the change apparent to everyone having a reference to it.

The famous Belgian artist René Magritte captured this same concept in a painting where he created an image of a pipe along with the caption *ceci n'est pas une pipe* (*this is not a pipe*) below it. We might interpret the caption as saying that the image is not actually a pipe, just an image of a pipe. Or perhaps Magritte meant that the caption is neither a pipe nor an image of a pipe, just a caption! In the present context, this image reinforces the idea that a reference to an object is nothing more than a reference; it is not the object itself.

Ceci n'est pas une pipe.

This is a picture of a pipe

Aliasing. An assignment statement with a reference type creates a second copy of the reference. The assignment statement *does not create a new object*, just another reference to an existing object. This situation is known as *aliasing*: both variables refer to the same object. The effect of aliasing is a bit unexpected, because it is different than for variables holding values of a primitive type. *Be sure that you understand the difference.* If x and y are variables of a primitive type, then the assignment statement x = y copies the value of y to x. For reference types, the reference is copied (not the value). Aliasing is a common source of bugs in Java programs, as illustrated by the following example:

```
Color a =
   new Color(160, 82, 45);
Color b = a;
```

```
a   811          references to
b   811          same object
```

```
811   160
812    82  ◄── sienna
813    45
```

Aliasing

```
Picture a = new Picture("mandrill.jpg");
Picture b = a;
a.set(i, j, color1);   // a is updated
b.set(i, j, color2);   // a is updated again
```

After the assignment statement, the variables a and b both refer to the same Picture. Changing the state of an object impacts *all* code involving aliased variables referencing that object. We are used to thinking of two different variables of primitive types as being independent, but that intuition does not carry over to reference objects. For example, if the code above is assuming that a and b refer to different Picture objects, then it will produce the wrong result. Such *aliasing bugs* are common in programs written by people without much experience in using reference objects (that's you, so pay attention here!).

Immutable types. For this very reason, it is common to define data types whose values cannot change. A data type that has no methods that can change an object's value is said to be *immutable* (as are objects of that type). For example, Java's Color and String objects are immutable (there are no operations available to clients that change a color's value), but Picture objects are mutable (we can change pixel colors). We will consider immutability in detail in SECTION 3.3.

Comparing objects. When applied to references, the == operator checks whether the two *references* have the same identity (that is, whether they point to the same object). That is not the same as checking whether the *objects* have the same value. For example, consider the following code:

```
Color a = new Color(142, 213, 87);
Color b = new Color(142, 213, 87);
Color c = b;
```

Now (a == b) is false and (b == c) is true, but when you are thinking about equality testing for Color, you probably are thinking that you want to test whether their *values* are the same—you might want all three of these to test as equal. Java does not have an automatic mechanism for testing equality of object values, which leaves programmers with the opportunity (and responsibility) to define it for themselves by defining for any class a customized method named equals(), as described in SECTION 3.3. For example, Color has such a method, and a.equals(c) is true in our example. String also contains an implementation of equals() because we often want to test that two String objects have the same value.

Pass by value. When we call a method with arguments, the effect in Java is as if each argument value were to appear on the right-hand side of an assignment statement with the corresponding argument name on the left. That is, Java passes a *copy* of the argument value from the calling program to the method. This arrangement is known as *pass by value*. One important consequence is that the method cannot change the value of a caller's variable. For primitive types, this policy is what we expect (the two variables are independent), but each time that we use a reference type as a method argument, we create an alias, so we must be cautious. In other words, the convention is to pass the *reference* by value (make a copy of it) but to pass the *object* by reference. For example, if we pass a reference to an object of type Picture, the method cannot change the original reference (make it point to a different Picture), but it *can* change the value of the object, for example by invoking the method set() to change a pixel's color.

Arrays are objects. In Java, every value of any nonprimitive type is an object. In particular, arrays are objects. As with strings, there is special language support for certain operations on arrays: declarations, initialization, and indexing. As with any other object, when we pass an array to a method or use an array variable on the right hand side of an assignment statement, we are making a copy of the array reference, not a copy of the array. Arrays are mutable objects: This convention is appropriate for the typical case where we expect the method to be able to modify the array by rearranging its entries, as in, for example, the exch() and shuffle() methods that we considered in SECTION 2.1.

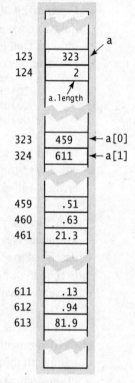

Arrays of objects. Array entries can be of any type, as we have already seen on several occasions, from args[] (an array of strings) in our main() implementations, to the array of Charge objects in PROGRAM 3.1.7. When we create an array of objects, we do so in two steps:
- Create the array, using the bracket syntax for array constructors
- Create each object in the array, using a standard constructor

For example, we would use the following code to create an array of two Charge objects:

```
Charge[] a = new Charge[2];
a[0] = new Charge(.51, .63, 21.3);
a[1] = new Charge(.13, .94, 85.9);
```

Naturally, an array of objects in Java is an array of *references*, not the objects themselves. If the objects are large, then we gain efficiency by not having to move them around, just their references. If they are small, we lose efficiency by having to follow a reference each time we need to get to some information.

An array of objects

Safe pointers. To provide the capability to manipulate memory addresses that refer to data, many programming languages include the *pointer* (which is like the Java reference) as a primitive data type. Programming with pointers is notoriously error prone, so operations provided for pointers need to be carefully designed to help programmers avoid errors. Java takes this point of view to an extreme (that is favored by many modern programming-language designers). In Java, there is only *one* way to create a reference (new) and only *one* way to change a reference (with an assignment statement). That is, the only things that a programmer can do with references is to create them and copy them. In programming-language jargon, Java references are known as *safe pointers*, because Java can guarantee that each reference points to an object of the specified type. Programmers used to writing code that directly manipulates pointers think of Java as having no pointers at all, but people still debate whether it is really desirable to have unsafe pointers. In short, when you program in Java, you will not be directly accessing pointer values, but if you find yourself doing so in some other language in the future, be careful!

```
Color a =
   new Color(160, 82, 45);
Color b =
   new Color(255, 255, 0);
Color b = a;
```

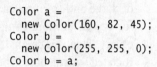

Orphaned objects. The ability to assign a new value to a reference variable creates the possibility that a program may have created an object that it can no longer reference. For example, consider the three assignment statements in the figure at right. After the third assignment statement, not only do a and b refer to the same Color object (the one whose RGB values are 160, 82, and 45), but also there is no longer a reference to the Color object that was created and used to initialize b. The only reference to that object was in the variable b, and this reference was overwritten by the assignment, so there is no way to refer to the object again. Such an object is said to be *orphaned*. Objects are also orphaned when they go out of scope. Java programmers pay little attention to orphaned objects because the system automatically reuses the memory that they occupy, as we discuss next.

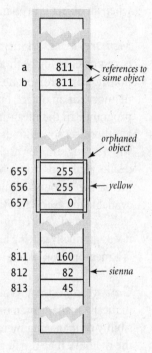

An orphaned object

Memory management. Programs tend to create huge numbers of objects (and primitive-type variables) but only have a need for a small number of them at any given point in time. Accordingly, programming languages and systems need mechanisms to *allocate* memory for data type values during the time they are needed and to *free* the memory when they are no longer needed (for an object, sometime after it is orphaned). Memory management is easier for primitive types because all of the information needed for memory allocation is known at compile time. Java (and most other systems) take care of reserving space for variables when they are declared and freeing that space when they go out of scope. Memory management for objects is more complicated: the compiler knows to allocate memory for an object when it is created, but cannot know precisely when to free the memory associated with an object, because the dynamics of a program in execution determine when an object is orphaned.

Memory leaks. In many languages (such as C and C++) the programmer is responsible for both allocating and freeing memory. Doing so is tedious and notoriously error-prone. For example, suppose that a program deallocates the memory for an object, but then continues to refer to it (perhaps much later in the program). In the meantime, the system may have allocated the same memory for another use, so all kinds of havoc can result. Another insidious problem occurs when a programmer neglects to ensure that the memory for an orphaned object is deallocated. This bug is known as a *memory leak* because it can result in a steadily increasing amount of memory devoted to orphaned objects (and therefore not available for use). The effect is that performance degrades, just as if memory were leaking out of your computer. Have you ever had to reboot your computer because it was gradually getting less and less responsive? A common cause of such behavior is a memory leak in one of your applications.

Garbage collection. One of Java's most significant features is its ability to automatically manage memory. The idea is to free the programmers from the responsibility of managing memory by keeping track of orphaned objects and returning the memory they use to a pool of free memory. Reclaiming memory in this way is known as *garbage collection*, and Java's safe pointer policy enables it to do this efficiently and automatically. Garbage collection is an old idea, but people still debate whether the overhead of automatic garbage collection justifies the convenience of not having to worry about memory management. The same conclusion that we drew for pointers holds: when you program in Java, you will not be writing code to allocate and free memory, but if you find yourself doing so in some other language in the future, be careful!

FOR REFERENCE, WE SUMMARIZE THE EXAMPLES that we have considered in this section in the table below. These examples are chosen to help you understand the essential properties of data types and object-oriented programming.

A data type is a set of values and a set of operations defined on those values. With primitive data types, we worked with a small and simple set of values. Colors, pictures, strings, and input-output streams are high-level data types that indicate the breadth of applicability of data abstraction. *You do not need to know how a data type is implemented in order to be able to use it.* Each data type (there are hundreds in the Java libraries, and you will soon learn to create your own) is characterized by an API (applications programming interface) that provides the information that you need in order to use it. A client program creates objects that hold data type values and invokes instance methods to manipulate those values. We write client programs with the basic statements and control constructs that you learned in CHAPTERS 1 and 2, but now have the capability to work with a vast variety of data types, not just the primitive ones to which you have grown accustomed. With experience, you will find that this ability opens up for you new horizons in programming.

API	description
Charge	electrical charges
Color	colors
Picture	digital images
String	character strings
In	input streams
Out	output streams
Draw	drawings

Summary of data types in this section

Our Charge example indicates that you can tailor one or more data types to the needs of your application. The ability to do so is profound, and also is the subject of the next section. When properly designed and implemented, data types lead to client programs that are clearer, easier to develop, and easier to maintain than equivalent programs that do not take advantage of data abstraction. The client programs in this section are testimony to this claim. Moreover, as you will see in the next section, implementing a data type is a straightforward application of the basic programming skills that you have already learned. In particular, addressing a large and complex application becomes a process of understanding its data and the operations to be performed on it, then writing programs that directly reflect this understanding. Once you have learned to do so, you might wonder how programmers *ever* developed large programs without using data abstraction.

Q. Why the distinction between primitive and reference types?

A. Performance. Java provides the *wrapper* reference types Integer, Double, and so forth that correspond to primitive types and can be used by programmers who prefer to ignore the distinction. Primitive types are closer to the types of data that are supported by computer hardware, so programs that use them usually run faster than programs that use corresponding reference types.

Q. What happens if I forget to use new when creating an object?

A. To Java, it looks as though you want to call a static method with a return value of the object type. Since you have not defined such a method, the error message is the same as when you refer to an undefined symbol. If you compile the code

```
Charge c = Charge(.51, .63, 21.3);
```

you get this error message:

```
cannot find symbol
symbol  : method Charge(double,double,double)
```

Constructors do not provide return values (their signature has no return value type)—they can only follow new. You get the same kind of error message if you provide the wrong number of arguments to a constructor or method.

Q. Why don't we write StdOut.println(x.toString()) to print objects that are not strings?

A. Good question. That code works fine, but Java saves us the trouble of writing it by automatically invoking toString() for us anytime a String type is needed. This policy implies that every data type must have a toString() method. We will discuss in Section 3.3. Java's mechanism for ensuring that this is the case.

Q. What is the difference between =, ==, and equals()?

A. The single equals sign (=) is the basis of the assignment statement—you certainly are familiar with that. The double equals sign (==) is a binary operator for checking whether its two operands are identical. If the operands are of a primitive

type, the result is `true` if they have the same value, and `false` otherwise. If the operands are references, the result is `true` if they refer to the same object, and `false` otherwise. That is, we use `==` to test object identity equality. The data-type method `equals()` is included in every Java type so that the implementation can provide the capability for clients to test whether two objects have the same *value*. Note that (a `==` b) implies a.`equals`(b), but not the other way around.

Q. How can I arrange to pass an array to a function in such a way that the function cannot change the array?

A. There is no direct way to do so—arrays are mutable. In SECTION 3.3, you will see how to achieve the same effect by building a wrapper data type and passing a value of that type instead (`Vector`, in PROGRAM 3.3.3).

Q. What happens if I forget to use `new` when creating an array of objects?

A. You need to use `new` for each object that you create, so when you create an array of *N* objects, you need to use `new` *N*+1 times: once for the array and once for each of the *N* objects. If you forget to create the array:

```
Charge[] a;
a[0] = new Charge(0.51, 0.63, 21.3);
```

you get the same error message that you would get when trying to assign a value to any uninitialized variable:

```
variable a might not have been initialized
        a[0] = new Charge(0.51, 0.63, 21.3);
        ^
```

but if you forget to use `new` when creating an object within the array and then try to use it to invoke a method:

```
Charge[] a = new Charge[2];
double x = a[0].potentialAt(.5, .5);
```

you get a `NullPointerException`. As usual, the best way to answer such questions is to write and compile such code yourself, then try to interpret Java's error message. Doing so might help you more quickly recognize mistakes later.

Q. Where can I find more details on how Java implements references and garbage collection?

A. One Java system might differ completely from another. For example, one natural scheme is to use a pointer (machine address); another is to use a handle (a pointer to a pointer). The former gives faster access to data; the latter provides for better garbage collection.

Q. Why red, green, and blue instead of red, *yellow*, and blue?

A. In theory, any three colors that contain some amount of each primary would work, but two different schemes have evolved: one (RGB) that has proven to produce good colors on television screens, computer monitors, and digital cameras, and the other (CMYK) that is typically used for the printed page (see Exercise 1.2.21). CMYK does include yellow (cyan, magenta, yellow, and black). Two different schemes are appropriate because printed inks *absorb* color, so where there are two different inks there are more colors absorbed and *fewer* reflected; but video displays *emit* color, so where there are two different colored pixels there are *more* colors emitted.

Q. What exactly does it mean to `import` a name?

A. Not much: it just saves some typing. You could type `java.awt.Color` everywhere in your code instead of using the `import` statement.

Q. Is there anything wrong with allocating and deallocating thousands of `Color` objects, as in `Grayscale` (Program 3.1.4)?

A. All programming-language constructs come at some cost. In this case the cost is reasonable, since the time for these allocations is tiny compared to the time to actually draw the picture.

Q. Why does the `String` method call `s.substring(i, j)` return the substring of `s` starting at index `i` and ending at `j-1` (and not `j`)?

A. Why do the indices of an array `a[]` go from 0 to `a.length-1` instead of from 1 to `length`? Programming-language designers make choices; we live with them.

Exercises

3.1.1   Write a program that takes a double value w from the command line, creates four Charge objects with charge value 1.0 that are each distance w in each of the four cardinal directions from (.5, .5), and prints the potential at (.25, .5).

3.1.2   Write a program that takes from the command line three integers between 0 and 255 that represent red, green, and blue values of a color and then creates and shows a 256-by-256 Picture of that color.

3.1.3   Modify AlbersSquares (PROGRAM 3.1.2) to take *nine* command-line arguments that specify *three* colors and then draws the six squares showing all the Albers squares with the large square in each color and the small square in each different color.

3.1.4   Write a program that takes the name of a grayscale picture file as a command-line argument and uses StdDraw to plot a histogram of the frequency of occurrence of each of the 256 grayscale intensities.

3.1.5   Write a program that takes the name of a picture file as a command-line argument and flips the image horizontally.

3.1.6   Write a program that takes the name of an picture file as a command-line input, and creates three images, one that contains only the red components, one for green, and one for blue.

3.1.7   Write a program that takes the name of an picture file as a command-line argument and prints the pixel coordinates of the lower left corner and the upper right corner of the smallest bounding box (rectangle parallel to the x- and y-axes) that contains all of the non-white pixels.

3.1.8   Write a program that takes as command line arguments the name of an image file and the pixel coordinates of a rectangle within the image; reads from standard input a list of Color values (represented as triples of int values); and serves as a filter, printing out those color values for which all pixels in the rectangle are background/foreground compatible. (Such a filter can be used to pick a color for text to label an image.)

3.1.9 Write a function `isValidDNA()` that takes a string as input and returns `true` if and only if it is comprised entirely of the characters A, C, T, and G.

3.1.10 Write a function `complementWC()` that takes a DNA string as its inputs and returns its *Watson-Crick complement*: replace A with T, C with G, and vice versa.

3.1.11 Write a function `palindromeWC()` that takes a DNA string as its input and returns `true` if the string is a Watson-Crick complemented palindrome, and `false` otherwise. A *Watson-Crick complemented palindrome* is a DNA string that is equal to the reverse of its Watson-Crick complement.

3.1.12 Write a program to check whether an ISBN number is valid (see EXERCISE 1.3.33), taking into account that an ISBN number can have hyphens inserted at arbitrary places.

3.1.13 What does the following code fragment print?

```
String string1 = "hello";
String string2 = string1;
string1 = "world";
StdOut.println(string1);
StdOut.println(string2);
```

3.1.14 What does the following code fragment print?

```
String s = "Hello World";
s.toUpperCase();
s.substring(6, 11);
StdOut.println(s);
```

Answer: `"Hello World"`. `String` objects are immutable—string methods each return a new `String` object with the appropriate value (but they do not change the value of the object that was used to invoke them). This code ignores the objects returned and just prints the original string. To print `"WORLD"`, use `s = s.toUpperCase()` and `s = s.substring(6, 11)`.

3.1.15 A string s is a *circular shift* of a string t if it matches when the characters are circularly shifted by any number of positions. For example, ACTGACG is a circular shift of TGACGAC, and vice versa. Detecting this condition is important in the study of genomic sequences. Write a program that checks whether two given strings s and t are circular shifts of one another. *Hint*: The solution is a one-liner with indexOf() and string concatenation.

3.1.16 Given a string site that represents a website, write a code fragment to determine its domain type. For example, the domain type for the string http://www.cs.princeton.edu/IntroProgramming is edu.

3.1.17 Write a static method that takes a domain name as argument and returns the reverse domain (reverse the order of the strings between periods). For example, the reverse domain of cs.princeton.edu is edu.princeton.cs. This computation is useful for web log analysis. (See EXERCISE 4.2.35.)

3.1.18 What does the following recursive function return?

```
public static String mystery(String s)
{
    int N = s.length();
    if (N <= 1) return s;
    String a = s.substring(0, N/2);
    String b = s.substring(N/2, N);
    return mystery(b) + mystery(a);
}
```

3.1.19 Modify GeneFind to handle all three stop codes (instead of handling them one at a time through the command line). Also add command-line arguments to allow the user to specify lower and upper bounds on the length of the gene sought.

3.1.20 Write a version of GeneFind based on using the indexOf() method in String to find patterns.

3.1.21 Write a program that takes a start string and a stop string as command-line arguments and prints all substrings of a given string that start with the first, end with the second, and otherwise contain neither. *Note*: Be especially careful of overlaps!

3.1.22 Write a filter that reads text from an input stream and prints it to an output stream, removing any lines that consist only of whitespace.

3.1.23 Modify `Potential` (PROGRAM 3.1.7) to take an integer N from the command line and generate N random `Charge` objects in the unit square, with potential values drawn randomly from a Gaussian distribution with mean 50 and standard deviation 10.

3.1.24 Modify `StockQuote` (PROGRAM 3.1.10) to take multiple symbols on the command line.

3.1.25 The example file `data` used for `Split` (PROGRAM 3.1.11) lists the date, high price, volume, and low price of the Dow Jones stock market average for every day since records have been kept. Download this file from the booksite and write a program that creates two `Draw` objects, one for the prices and one for the volumes, and plots them at a rate taken from the command line.

3.1.26 Write a program `Merge` that takes a delimiter string followed by an arbitrary number of file names as command line arguments, concatenates the corresponding lines of each file, separated by the delimiter, and then writes the result to standard output, thus performing the opposite operation from `Split` (PROGRAM 3.1.11).

3.1.27 Find a website that publishes the current temperature in your area, and write a screen-scraper program `Weather` so that typing `java Weather` followed by your zip code will give you a weather forecast.

3.1.28 Suppose that `a[]` and `b[]` are each integer arrays consisting of millions of integers. What does the following code do, and how long does it take?

```
int[] t = a; a = b; b = t;
```

Answer. It swaps them, but it does so by copying references, so that it is not necessary to copy millions of elements.

Creative Exercises

3.1.29 *Picture filtering.* Write a library RawPicture with read() and write() methods for use with standard input and standard output. The write() method takes a Picture as argument and writes the picture to standard output, using the following format: if the picture is *w*-by-*h*, write *w*, then *h*, then *wh* triples of integers representing the pixel color values, in row major order. The read() method takes no arguments and returns a Picture, which it creates by reading a picture from standard input, in the format just described. *Note*: Be aware that this will use up much more disk space than the picture—the standard formats *compress* this information so that it will not take up so much space.

3.1.30 *Sound visualization.* Write a program that uses StdAudio and Picture to create an interesting two-dimensional color visualization of a sound file while it is playing. Be creative!

3.1.31 *Kama Sutra cipher.* Write a filter KamaSutra that takes two strings as command-line argument (the *key* strings), then reads standard input, substitutes for each letter as specified by the key strings, and writes the result to standard output. This operation is the basis for one of the earliest known cryptographic systems. The condition on the key strings is that they must be of equal length and that any letter in standard input must be in one of them. For example, if input is all capital letters and the keys are THEQUICKBROWN and FXJMPSVRLZYDG, then we make the table.

```
T H E Q U I C K B R O W N
F X J M P S V L A Z Y D G
```

which tells us that we should substitute F for T, T for F, H for X, X for H, and so forth when copying the input to the output. The message is encoded by replacing each letter with its pair. For example, the message MEET AT ELEVEN is encoded as QJJF BF JKJCJG. Someone receiving the message can use the same keys to get the message back.

3.1.32 *Safe password verification.* Write a static method that takes a string as argument and returns true if it meets the following conditions, false otherwise:
- At least eight characters long
- Contains at least one digit (0-9)
- Contains at least one upper-case letter

• Contains at least one lower-case letter
• Contains at least one character that is neither a letter nor a number

Such checks are commonly used for passwords on the web.

3.1.33 *Color study.* Write a program that displays the color study shown at right, which gives Albers squares corresponding to each of the 256 levels of blue and gray that were used to print this book.

3.1.34 *Entropy.* The *Shannon entropy* measures the information content of an input string and plays a cornerstone role in information theory and data compression. Given a string of N characters, let f_c be the frequency of occurrence of character c The quantity $p_c = f_c/N$ is an estimate of the probability that c would be in the string if it were a random string, and the entropy is defined to be the sum of the quantity $-p_c \log_2 p_c$, over all characters that appear in the string. The entropy is said to measure the *information content* of a string: if each character appears the same number times, the entropy is at its minimum value. Write a program that computes and prints the entropy of the string on standard input. Run your program on a web page that you read regularly, a recent paper that you wrote, and on the fruit fly genome found on the website.

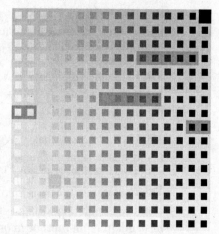

A color study

3.1.35 *Minimize potential.* Write a function that takes an array of Charge objects with positive potential as its argument and finds a point such that the potential at that point is within 1% of the minimum potential anywhere in the unit square. Use a Charge object to return this information. Add a call to this function and print out the point coordinates and charge value for the data given in the text and for the random charges described in Exercise 3.1.23.

3.1.36 *Slide show.* Write a program that takes the names of several image files as command-line arguments and displays them in a slide show (one every two seconds), using a fade effect to black and a fade from black between pictures

.3.1.37 *Tile.* Write a program that takes the name of an image file and two integers M and N as command-line arguments and creates an M-by-N tiling of the picture.

3.1.38 *Rotation filter.* Write a program that takes two command-line arguments (the name of an image file and a real number theta) and rotates the image θ degrees counterclockwise. To rotate, copy the color of each pixel (s_i, s_j) in the source image to a target pixel (t_i, t_j) whose coordinates are given by the following formulas:

rotate 30 degrees

$$t_i = -(s_i - c_i)\cos\theta + (s_j - c_j)\sin\theta$$
$$t_j = -(s_i - c_i)\sin\theta + (s_j - c_j)\cos\theta$$

where (c_i, c_j) is the center of the image.

swirl filter

3.1.39 *Swirl filter.* Creating a swirl effect is similar to rotation, except that the angle changes as a function of distance to the center. Use the same formulas as in the previous exercise, but compute θ as a function of (s_i, s_j), specifically π/256 times the distance to the center.

3.1.40 *Wave filter.* Write a filter like those in the previous two exercises that creates a wave effect, by copying the color of each pixel (s_i, s_j) in the source image to a target pixel (t_i, t_j), where $t_i = s_i$ and $t_j = s_j + 20\sin(2\pi s_j/128)$. Add code to take the amplitude (20 in the accompanying figure) and the frequency (128 in the accompanying figure) as command-line arguments. Experiment with various values of these parameters.

wave filter

3.1.41 *Glass filter.* Write a program that takes the name of an image file as a command-line argument and applies a *glass filter*: set each pixel p to the color of a random neighboring pixel (whose pixel coordinates both differ from p's coordinates by at most 5).

glass filter

Exercises in filtering

3.1.42 *Morph.* The example images in the text for Fade do not quite line up in the vertical direction (the mandrill's mouth is much lower than Darwin's). Modify Fade to add a transformation in the vertical dimension that makes a smoother transition.

`java Zoom pup.jpg 1 .5 .5`

3.1.43 *Digital zoom.* Write a program Zoom that takes the name of an image file and three numbers s, x, and y as command-line arguments and shows an output image that zooms in on a portion of the input image. The numbers are all between 0 and 1, with s to be interpreted as a scale factor and (x, y) as the relative coordinates of the point that is to be at the center of the output image. Use this program to zoom in on your dog or a friend in some digital image on your computer. (If your image came from a cell phone or an old camera, you may not be able to zoom in too close without having visible artifacts from scaling.)

`java Zoom pup.jpg .3 .40 .45`

3.1.43 *Clusters.* Write a program that take a Picture file name from the command line and produces a Draw object with filled circles that cover compatible areas. First, scan the image to determine the background color (a dominant color that is found in more than half the pixels). Use depth-first search (see PROGRAM 2.4.5) to find contiguous sets of pixels that are foreground-compatible with the background. A scientist might use a program to study natural scenarios such as birds in flight or particles in motion. Take a photo of balls on a billiards table and try to get your program to identify the balls and positions.

`java Zoom pup.jpg .1 .39 .47`

Digital zoom

3.2 Creating Data Types

IN PRINCIPLE, WE COULD WRITE ALL of our programs using only the eight built-in primitive types, but, as we saw in the last section, it is much more convenient to write programs at a higher level of abstraction. Thus, a variety of data types are built into the Java language and libraries. Still, we certainly cannot expect Java to contain every conceivable data type that we might ever wish to use, so we need to be able to *define* our own. The purpose of this section is to explain how to build data types with the familiar Java `class`.

Implementing a data type as a Java class is not very different from implementing a function library as a set of static methods. The primary difference is that we associate *data* with the method implementations. The API specifies the methods that we need to implement, but we are free to choose any convenient representation. To cement the basic concepts, we begin by considering the implementation of the data type for charged

particles that we introduced at the beginning of SECTION 3.1. Next, we illustrate the process of creating data types by considering a range of examples, from complex numbers to stock accounts, including a number of software tools that we will use later in the book. Useful client code is testimony to the value of any data type, so we also consider a number of clients, including one that depicts the famous and fascinating *Mandelbrot set.*

The process of defining a data type is known as *data abstraction* (as opposed to the *function abstraction* style that is the basis of CHAPTER 2). We focus on the data and implement operations on that data. *Whenever you can clearly separate data and associated operations within a program, you should do so.* Modeling physical objects or familiar mathematical abstractions is straightforward and extremely useful, but the true power of data abstraction is that it allows us to model *anything* that we can precisely specify. Once you gain experience with this style of programming, you will see that it naturally helps us address programming challenges of arbitrary complexity.

Basic elements of a data type   To illustrate the process of implementing a data type in a Java `class`, we discuss in detail an implementation of the `Charge` data type of SECTION 3.1. We have already considered client programs that demonstrate the utility of having such a data type (in PROGRAMS 3.1.1 and 3.1.7)—now we focus on the *implementation* details. Every data-type implementation that you will develop has the same basic ingredients as this simple example.

API. The applications programming interface is the contract with all clients and, therefore, the starting point for any implementation. To emphasize that APIs are critical for implementations, we repeat here our example `Charge` API:

```
public class Charge
```

```
         Charge(double x0, double y0, double q0)

    double potentialAt(double x, double y)    electric potential at (x, y) due to charge

    String toString()                         string representation
```

API for charged particles (see PROGRAM 3.2.1)

To implement `Charge`, we need to define the data type values, implement the constructor that creates objects having specified values, and implement two methods that manipulate those values. When faced with the problem of creating a completely new class for some application, the first step is to develop an API. This step is a design activity that we will address in SECTION 3.3. We need to design APIs with care because after we implement classes and write client programs that use them, we *do not change the API*, because that would imply changing all clients.

Class. The data-type implementation is a Java `class`. As with the libraries of static methods that we have been using, we put the code for a data type in a file with the same name as the class, followed by the `.java` extension. We have been implementing Java classes, but the classes that we have been implementing do not have the key features of data types: *instance variables*, *constructors*, and *instance methods*. Instance variables are similar to the variables that we have been using in our program, and constructors and methods are similar to functions, but their effect is quite different. Each of these building blocks is also qualified by an *access* (or *visibility*) *modifier*. We next consider these four concepts, with examples.

Access modifiers. The keywords `public`, `private`, and `final` that sometimes precede class and variable names are known as *access modifiers*. The `public` and `private` modifiers control access from client code: we designate every instance variable and method within a class as either `public` (this entity is accessible by clients) or `private` (this entity is not accessible by clients). The `final` modifier indicates that the value of the variable will not change once it is initialized—its access is read-only. Our convention is to use `public` for the constructors and methods in the API (since we are promising to provide them to clients) and `private` for everything else. Typically, our private methods are helper methods used to simplify code in other methods in the class. Java is not so restrictive on its usage of modifiers—we defer to SECTION 3.3 a discussion of our reasons for these conventions.

Instance variables. To write code for the methods that manipulate data type values, the first thing that we need is to declare variables that we can use to refer to these values in code. These variables can be any type of data. We declare the types and names of these *instance variables* in the same way as we declare local variables: for `Charge`, we use three `double` values, two to describe the charge's position in the plane and one to describe the amount of charge. These declarations appear as the first statements in the class, not inside `main()` or any other method. There is a critical distinction between instance variables and the local variables within a static method or a block that you are accustomed to: there is just *one* value corresponding to each local variable at a given time, but there are *numerous* values corresponding to each instance variable (one for each object that is an instance of the data type). There is no ambiguity with this arrangement, because each time that we invoke an instance method, we do so with an object name—that object is the one whose value we are manipulating.

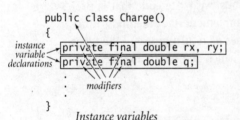

Instance variables

Constructors. A constructor creates an object and provides a reference to that object. Java automatically invokes a constructor when a client program uses the keyword `new`. Java does most of the work: our code only needs to initialize the instance variables to meaningful values. Constructors always share the same name as the class, but we can overload the name and have multiple constructors with different signatures, just as with static methods. To the client, the combination of

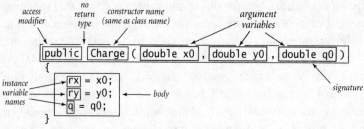

Anatomy of a constructor

new followed by a constructor name (with argument values enclosed within paren-
theses) is the same as a function call that returns a value of the corresponding type.
A constructor signature has no return type, because constructors always return
a reference to an object of its data type (the name of the type, the class, and the
constructor are all the same). Each time that a client invokes a constructor, Java
automatically:
  • Allocates memory space for the object
  • Invokes the constructor code to initialize the instance variables
  • Returns a reference to the object
The constructor in Charge is typical: it initializes the instance variables with the
values provided by the client as arguments.

Instance methods. To implement instance methods, we write code that is precisely like the code that we learned in CHAPTER 2 to implement static methods (functions). Each method has a signature (which specifies its return type and the types
and names of its argument variables) and a body (which consists of a sequence of

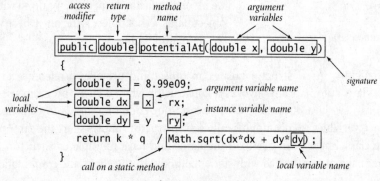

Anatomy of an instance method

statements, including a return statement that provides a value of the return type back to the client). When a client invokes a method, the system initializes the argument variables with client values; executes statements until reaching a `return` statement; and returns the computed value to the client, with the same effect as if the method invocation in the client were replaced with that return value. All of this action is the same as for static methods, but there is one critical distinction for instance methods: *they can perform operations on instance variables.*

Variables within methods. Accordingly, the Java code that we write to implement instance methods uses *three* kinds of variables:
• Argument variables
• Local variables
• *Instance variables*

The first two are the same as for static methods: argument variables are specified in the method signature and initialized with client values when the method is called, and local variables are declared and initialized within the method body. The scope of argument variables is the entire method; the scope of local variables is the following statements in the block where they are defined. Instance variables are completely different: they hold data-type values for objects in a class, and their scope is the entire class. How do we specify which object's value we want to use? If you think for a moment about this question, you will recall the answer. Each object in the class has a value: the code in a class method refers to the value *for the object that was used to invoke the method.* When we say `c1.potentialAt(x, y)`, the code in `potentialAt()` is referring to the instance variables for `c1`. The code in `potentialAt()` uses all three kinds of variable names, as summarized in this table:

variable	purpose	example	scope
instance	specify data-type value	`rx, ry`	class
argument	pass value from client to method	`x, y`	method
local	temporary use within method	`dx, dy`	block

Variables within instance methods

Be sure that you understand the distinctions among these three kinds of variables. These differences are a key to object-oriented programming.

Program 3.2.1   *Charged-particle implementation*

```java
public class Charge
{
    private final double rx, ry;
    private final double q;

    public Charge(double x0, double y0, double q0)
    {   rx = x0; ry = y0; q = q0;   }

    public double potentialAt(double x, double y)
    {
        double k = 8.99e09;
        double dx = x - rx;
        double dy = y - ry;
        return k * q / Math.sqrt(dx*dx + dy*dy);
    }

    public String toString()
    {
        return q + " at " + "(" + rx + ", " + ry + ")";
    }

    public static void main(String[] args)
    {
        double x = Double.parseDouble(args[0]);
        double y = Double.parseDouble(args[1]);
        Charge c1 = new Charge(.51, .63, 21.3);
        Charge c2 = new Charge(.13, .94, 81.9);
        double v1 = c1.potentialAt(x, y);
        double v2 = c2.potentialAt(x, y);
        StdOut.printf("%.1e\n", v1 + v2);
    }
}
```

rx, ry	*query point*
q	*charge*

k	*electrostatic constant*
dx, dy	*delta distances to query point*

x, y	*query point*
c1	*first charge*
v1	*potential due to c1*
c2	*second charge*
v2	*potential due to c2*

This implementation of our data type for charged particles contains the basic elements found in every data type: instance variables rx, ry, and q; a constructor Charge(); instance methods potentialAt() and toString(); and a test client main() (see also Program 3.1.1).

```
% java Charge .2 .5
2.2e+12
% java Charge .51 .94
2.5e+12
```

THESE ARE THE BASIC COMPONENTS THAT you need to understand to be able to build data types in Java. Every data-type implementation (Java class) that we will consider has instance variables, constructors, instance methods, and a test client. In each data type that we develop, we go through the same steps. Rather than thinking about what action we need to take next to accomplish a computational goal (as we did when first learning to program), we think about the needs of a client, then accommodate them in a data type.

The first step in creating a data type is to specify an API. The purpose of the API is to *separate clients from implementations*, to enable modular programming. We have two goals when specifying an API. First, we want to enable clear and correct client code. Indeed, it is a good idea to write some client code before finalizing the API to gain confidence that the specified data-type operations are the ones that clients need. Second, we want to be able to implement the operations. There is no point specifying operations that we have no idea how to implement.

The second step in creating a data type is to implement a Java class that meets the API specifications. First, we choose the instance variables, then we write the code that manipulates the instance variables to implement the specified methods.

The third step in creating a data type is to write test clients, to validate the design decisions made in the first two steps.

In this section, we start each example with an API, and then consider implementations, then clients. You will find many exercises at the end of this section intended to give you experience with data-type creation. SECTION 3.3 is an overview of the design process and related language mechanisms.

What are the values that define the type, and what operations do clients need to perform on those values? With these basic decisions made, you can create new data types and write clients that use the data types that you have defined in the same way as you have been using built-in types.

```
public class Charge                                     class
{                                                       name

private final double rx, ry;
private final double q;

public Charge(double x0, double y0, double q0)
{  rx = x0;  ry = y0;  q = q0;  }

public double potentialAt(double x, double y)
{                                                       instance
                                                        variable
    double k = 8.99e09;                                 names
    double dx = x - rx;
    double dy = y - ry;
    return k * q / Math.sqrt(dx*dx+dy*dy);
}

public String toString()
{  return q +" at " + "("+ rx + ", " + ry +")";  }

public static void main(String[] args)
{
    double x = Double.parseDouble(args[0]);
    double y = Double.parseDouble(args[1]);
    Charge c1 = new Charge(.51, .63, 21.3);
    Charge c2 = new Charge(.13, .94, 81.9);
    double v1 = c1.potentialAt(x, y);
    double v2 = c2.potentialAt(x, y);                   invoke
    StdOut.printf("%.1e\n", v1+v2);                     constructor
}

}
```

instance
variables

constructor

instance
methods

test client

create
and
initialize
object

object
name

invoke
method

Anatomy of a class

Stopwatch   One of the hallmarks of object-oriented programming is the idea of easily modeling real-world objects by creating abstract programming objects. As a simple example, consider Stopwatch (PROGRAM 3.3.2), which implements the following API:

`public class Stopwatch`

	Stopwatch()	*create a new stopwatch and start it running*
`double`	`elapsedTime()`	*return the elapsed time since creation, in seconds*

API for stopwatches (see PROGRAM 3.2.2)

In other words, a Stopwatch is a stripped-down version of an old-fashioned stopwatch. When you create one, it starts running, and you can ask it how long it has been running by invoking the method elapsedTime(). You might imagine adding all sorts of bells and whistles to Stopwatch, limited only by your imagination. Do you want to be able to reset the stopwatch? Start and stop it? Include a lap timer? These sorts of things are easy to add (see EXERCISE 3.2.11).

The implementation in PROGRAM 3.2.2 uses the Java system method System. currentTimeMillis(), which (as well-described by its name) returns a long value giving the current time in milliseconds (the number of milliseconds since midnight on January 1, 1970 UTC). The data-type implementation could hardly be simpler. A Stopwatch saves its creation time in an instance variable, then returns the difference between that time and the current time whenever a client invokes its elapsedTime() method. A Stopwatch itself does not actually tick (an internal system clock on your computer does all the ticking for all Stopwatch objects and many other data types); it just creates the illusion that it does for clients. Why not just use System.currentTimeMillis() in clients? We could do so, but using the higher-level Stopwatch abstraction leads to client code that is easier to understand and maintain.

The test client is typical. It creates two Stopwatch objects, uses them to measure the running time of two different computations, then prints the ratio of the running times. The question of whether one approach to solving a problem is better than another has been lurking since the first few programs that you have run, and plays an essential role in program development. In SECTION 4.1, we will develop a scientific approach to understanding the cost of computation. Stopwatch is a useful tool in that approach.

Program 3.2.2   Stopwatch

```
public class Stopwatch
{
    private final long start;

    public Stopwatch()
    {   start = System.currentTimeMillis();   }

    public double elapsedTime()
    {
        long now = System.currentTimeMillis();
        return (now - start) / 1000.0;
    }

    public static void main(String[] args)
    {
        int N = Integer.parseInt(args[0]);

        double totalMath = 0.0;
        Stopwatch swMath = new Stopwatch();
        for (int i = 0; i < N; i++)
            totalMath += Math.sqrt(i);
        double timeMath = swMath.elapsedTime();

        double totalNewton = 0.0;
        Stopwatch swNewton = new Stopwatch();
        for (int i = 0; i < N; i++)
            totalNewton += Newton.sqrt(i);
        double timeNewton = swNewton.elapsedTime();

        StdOut.println(totalNewton/totalMath);
        StdOut.println(timeNewton/timeMath);
    }
}
```

| start | creation time |

This class implements a simple data type that we can use to compare running times of performance-critical methods (see Section 4.1). The test client compares the method for computing square roots in Java's Math *library with our implementation from Program 2.1.1 that uses Newton's method for the task of computing the sum of the square roots of the numbers from 0 to N-1. For this quick test, the Java implementation* Math.sqrt() *is about 20 times faster than our* Newton.sqrt() *(as it should be!).*

```
% java Stopwatch 1000000
1.0
19.961538461538463
```

Histogram   Data-type instance variables can be arrays. As an illustration, consider `Histogram` (PROGRAM 3.2.3), which maintains an array of the frequency of occurrence of integer values in a given interval $[0, N)$ and uses `StdStats.plotBars()` to display a histogram of the values, controlled by this API:

```
public class Histogram
```

	`Histogram(int N)`	*create a dynamic histogram for the N int values in [0, N)*
`double`	`addDataPoint(int i)`	*add an occurrence of the value i*
`void`	`draw()`	*draw the histogram using standard draw*

API for histograms (see PROGRAM 3.2.3)

By creating a simple class such as `Histogram`, we reap the benefits of modular programming (reusable code, independent development of small programs, and so forth) that we discussed in CHAPTER 2, with the additional benefit that we also separate the *data*. A histogram client need not maintain the data (or know anything about its representation); it just creates a histogram and calls `addDataPoint()`.

When studying this code and the next several examples, it is best to carefully consider the client code. Each class that we implement essentially extends the Java language, allowing us to declare variables of the new data type, instantiate them with values, and perform operations on them. All client programs are conceptually the same as the first programs that you learned that use primitive types and built-in operations. Now you have the ability to define whatever types and operations you need in your client code! In this case, using `Histogram` actually *enhances* readability of the client code, as the `addDataPoint()` call focuses attention on the data being studied. Without `Histogram`, we would have to mix the code for creating the histogram with the code for the computation of interest, resulting in a program much more difficult to understand and maintain than the two separate programs. *Whenever you can clearly separate data and associated operations within a program, you should do so.*

Once you understand how a data type will be used in client code, you can consider the implementation. An implementation is characterized by its instance variables (data type values). `Histogram` maintains an array with the frequency of each point and a `double` value `max` that stores the height of the tallest bar (for scaling). Its private `draw()` method scales the drawing and then plots the frequencies.

Program 3.2.3   Histogram

```java
public class Histogram
{
    private final double[] freq;
    private double max;

    public Histogram(int N)
    { // Create a new histogram.
        freq = new double[N];
    }

    public void addDataPoint(int i)
    { // Add one occurrence of the value i.
        freq[i]++;
        if (freq[i] > max) max = freq[i];
    }

    private void draw()
    { // Draw (and scale) the histogram.
        StdDraw.setYscale(0, max);
        StdStats.plotBars(freq);
    }

    public static void main(String[] args)
    { // See Program 2.2.6.
        int N = Integer.parseInt(args[0]);
        int T = Integer.parseInt(args[1]);
        Histogram histogram = new Histogram(N+1);
        for (int t = 0; t < T; t++)
            histogram.addDataPoint(Bernoulli.binomial(N));
        StdDraw.setCanvasSize(500, 100);
        histogram.draw();
    }
}
```

freq[]	*frequency counts*
max	*maximum frequency*

% java Histogram 50 1000000

This data type supports simple client code to create dynamic histograms of the frequency of occurrence of values in [0, N). The frequencies are kept in an instance-variable array, and an instance variable max *tracks the maximum frequency (for scaling). To make a dynamically changing histogram, add a call to* StdDraw.clear() *before and a call to* StdDraw.show(20) *after the call to* histogram.draw() *in the client code..*

Turtle graphics *Whenever you can clearly separate tasks within a program, you should do so.* In object-oriented programming, we extend that mantra to include *state* with the tasks. A small amount of state can be immensely valuable in simplifying a computation. Next, we consider *turtle graphics*, which is based on the data type defined by this API:

```
public class Turtle
```

Turtle(double x0, double y0, double a0)	*create a new turtle at (x_0, y_0) facing a_0 degrees counterclockwise from the x-axis*
void turnLeft(double delta)	*rotate* delta *degrees counterclockwise*
void goForward(double step)	*move distance* step, *drawing a line*

API for turtle graphics (see PROGRAM 3.2.4)

Imagine a turtle that lives in the unit square and draws lines as it moves. It can move a specified distance in a straight line, or it can rotate left (counterclockwise) a specified number of degrees. According to the API, when we create a turtle, we place it at a specified point, facing a specified direction. Then, we create drawings by giving the turtle a sequence of goForward() and turnLeft() commands.

```
double x0 = 0.5;
double y0 = 0.0;
double a0 = 60.0;
double step = Math.sqrt(3)/2;
Turtle t  = new Turtle(x0, y0, a0);
t.goForward(step);
```

For example, to draw a triangle we create a Turtle at (0, .5) facing at an angle of 60 degrees counterclockwise from the origin, then direct it to take a step forward, then rotate 120 degrees counterclockwise, then take another step forward, then rotate another 120 degrees counterclockwise, and then take a third step forward to complete the triangle. Indeed, all of the turtle clients that we will examine simply create a turtle, then give it an alternating series of step and rotate commands, varying the step size and the amount of rotation. As you will see in the next several pages, this simple model

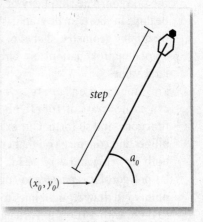

A turtle's first step

allows us to create arbitrarily complex drawings, with many important applications.

Turtle (PROGRAM 3.2.4) is an implementation of this API that uses StdDraw. It maintains three instance variables: the coordinates of the turtle's position and the current direction it is facing, measured in degrees counterclockwise from the x-axis. Implementing the two methods requires *updating* the values of these variables, so they are not final. The necessary updates are straightforward: turnLeft(delta) adds delta to the current angle, and goForward(step) adds the step size times the sine of its argument to the current x-coordinate and the step size times the cosine of its argument to the current y-coordinate.

Turtle trigonometry

The test client in Turtle takes an integer N as command-line argument and draws a regular polygon with N sides. If you are interested in elementary analytic geometry, you might enjoy verifying that fact. Whether or not you choose to do so, think about what you would need to do to compute the coordinates of all the points in the polygon. The simplicity of the turtle's approach is very appealing. In short, turtle graphics serves as a useful abstraction for describing geometric shapes of all sorts. For example, we obtain a good approximation to a circle by taking N to a sufficiently large value.

You can use a Turtle as you use any other object. Programs can create arrays of Turtle objects, pass them as arguments to functions, and so forth. Our examples will illustrate these capabilities and convince you that creating a data type like Turtle is both very easy and very useful. For each of them, as with regular polygons, it is *possible* to compute the coordinates of all the points and draw straight lines to get the drawings, but it is *easier* to do so with a Turtle. Turtle graphics exemplifies the value of data abstraction.

t.goForward(step);

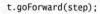

t.turnLeft(120.0);

t.goForward(step);

t.turnLeft(120.0);

t.goForward(step);

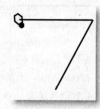

Your first turtle graphics drawing

Program 3.2.4   *Turtle graphics*

```
public class Turtle
{
    private double x, y;
    private double angle;

    public Turtle(double x0, double y0, double a0)
    {   x = x0; y = y0; angle = a0;   }

    public void turnLeft(double delta)
    {   angle += delta;   }

    public void goForward(double step)
    {   // Compute new position, move and draw line to it.
        double oldx = x, oldy = y;
        x += step * Math.cos(Math.toRadians(angle));
        y += step * Math.sin(Math.toRadians(angle));
        StdDraw.line(oldx, oldy, x, y);
    }

    public static void main(String[] args)
    {   // Draw an N-gon.
        int N = Integer.parseInt(args[0]);
        double angle = 360.0 / N;
        double step = Math.sin(Math.toRadians(angle/2));
        Turtle turtle = new Turtle(.5, .0, angle/2);
        for (int i = 0; i < N; i++)
        {
            turtle.goForward(step);
            turtle.turnLeft(angle);
        }
    }
}
```

| x, y | position (in unit square) |
| angle | direction of motion (degrees, counterclockwise from x axis) |

This data type supports turtle graphics, which often simplifies the creation of drawings.

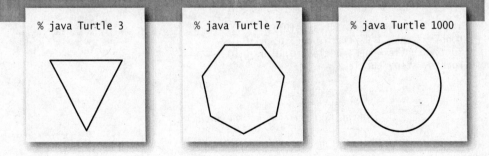

```
% java Turtle 3        % java Turtle 7        % java Turtle 1000
```

Recursive graphics. A *Koch curve* of order 0 is a straight line. To form a Koch curve of order n, draw a Koch curve of order $n-1$, turn left 60 degrees, draw a second Koch curve of order $n-1$, turn right 60 degrees (left -120 degrees), draw a third Koch curve of order $n-1$, turn left 60 degrees, and draw a fourth Koch curve of order $n-1$. These recursive instructions lead immediately to turtle client code. With appropriate modifications, recursive schemes like this have proven useful in modeling self-similar patterns found in nature, such as snowflakes.

The client code below is straightforward, except for the value of the step size sz. If you carefully examine the first few examples, you will see (and be able to prove by induction) that the width of the curve of order n is 3^n times the step size, so setting the step size to $1/3^n$ produces a curve of width 1. Similarly, the number of steps in a curve of order n is 4^n, so Koch will not finish if you invoke it for large n.

You can find many examples of recursive patterns of this sort that have been studied and developed by mathematicians, scientists, and artists from many cultures in many contexts. Here, our interest in them is that the turtle graphics abstraction greatly simplifies client code that draws them.

```
public class Koch                                              0
{
   public static void koch(int n, double step, Turtle turtle)
   {                                                    ─────────────
      if (n == 0)
      {                                                          1
         turtle.goForward(step);
         return;
      }
      koch(n-1, step, turtle);
      turtle.turnLeft(60.0);                                     2
      koch(n-1, step, turtle);
      turtle.turnLeft(-120.0);
      koch(n-1, step, turtle);
      turtle.turnLeft(60.0);
      koch(n-1, step, turtle);                                   3
   }

   public static void main(String[] args)
   {                                                             4
      int n = Integer.parseInt(args[0]);
      double step = 1.0 / Math.pow(3.0, n);
      Turtle turtle = new Turtle(0.0, 0.0, 0.0);
      koch(n, step, turtle);
   }
}
```

Drawing Koch curves with turtle graphics

Spira mirabilis. Perhaps the turtle is a bit tired after taking 4^n steps to draw a Koch curve. Accordingly, imagine that the turtle's step size decays by a tiny constant factor each time that it takes a step. What happens to our drawings? Remarkably, modifying the polygon-drawing test client in PROGRAM 3.2.4 to answer this question leads to an image known as a *logarithmic spiral*, a curve that is found in many contexts in nature.

Spiral (PROGRAM 3.2.5) is an implementation of this curve. It takes N and the decay factor as command-line arguments and instructs the turtle to alternately step and turn until it has wound around itself 10 times. As you can see from the four examples given with the program, the path spirals into the center of the drawing. The argument N controls the shape of the spiral. You are encouraged to experiment with Spiral yourself in order to develop an understanding of the way in which the parameters control the behavior of the spiral.

The logarithmic spiral was first described by René Descartes in 1638. Jacob Bernoulli was so amazed by its mathematical properties that he named it the *spira mirabilis* (miraculous spiral) and even asked to have it engraved on his tombstone. Many people also consider it to be "miraculous" that this precise curve is clearly present in a broad variety of natural phenomena. Three examples are depicted below: the chambers of a nautilus shell, the arms of a spiral galaxy, and the cloud formation in a tropical storm. Scientists have also observed it as the path followed by a hawk approaching its prey and the path followed by a charged particle moving perpendicular to a uniform magnetic field.

One of the goals of scientific enquiry is to provide simple but accurate models of complex natural phenomena. Our tired turtle certainly passes that test!

nautilus shell

galaxy

storm

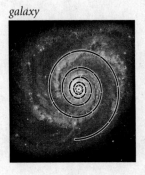

Examples of the spira mirabilis in nature

Program 3.2.5   *Spira mirabilis*

```
public class Spiral
{
   public static void main(String[] args)
   {
      int N        = Integer.parseInt(args[0]);
      double decay = Double.parseDouble(args[1]);
      double angle = 360.0 / N;
      double step  = Math.sin(Math.toRadians(angle/2));
      Turtle turtle = new Turtle(0.5, 0, angle/2);

      for (int i = 0; i < 10 * 360 / angle; i++)
      {
         step /= decay;
         turtle.goForward(step);
         turtle.turnLeft(angle);
      }
   }
}
```

step	*step size*
decay	*decay factor*
angle	*rotation amount*
turtle	*tired turtle*

This code is a modification of the test client in Program 3.2.4 that decreases the step size at each step and cycles around 10 times. The angle controls the shape; the decay controls the nature of the spiral.

% java Spiral 3 1.0

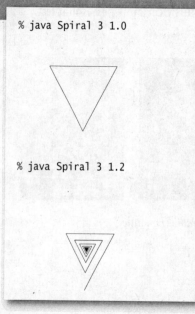

% java Spiral 3 1.2

% java Spiral 1440 1.00004

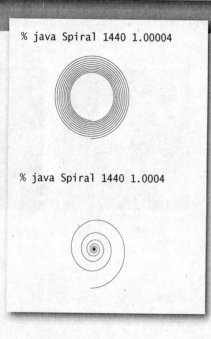

% java Spiral 1440 1.0004

Brownian motion. Or, perhaps the turtle has had one too many. Accordingly, imagine that the disoriented turtle (again following its standard alternating turn and step regimen) turns in a *random* direction before each step. Again, it is easy to plot the path followed by such a turtle for millions of steps, and again, such paths are found in nature in many contexts. In 1827, the botanist Robert Brown observed through a microscope that pollen grains immersed in water seemed to move about in just such a random fashion, which later became known as *Brownian motion* and led to Albert Einstein's insights into the atomic nature of matter.

Or perhaps our turtle has friends, all of whom have had one too many. After they have wandered around for a sufficiently long time, their paths merge together and become indistinguishable from a single path. Astrophysicists today are using this model to understand observed properties of distant galaxies.

TURTLE GRAPHICS WAS ORIGINALLY DEVELOPED BY Seymour Papert at MIT in the 1960s as part of an educational programming language, LOGO, that is still used today in toys. But turtle graphics is no toy, as we have just seen in numerous scientific examples. Turtle graphics also has numerous commercial applications. For example, it is the basis for POSTSCRIPT, a programming language for creating printed pages that is used for most newspapers, magazines, and books. In the present context, Turtle is a quintessential object-oriented programming example, showing that a small amount of saved state (data abstraction using objects, not just functions) can vastly simplify a computation.

10000 .01

```
public class DrunkenTurtle
{
    public static void main(String[] args)
    {
        int T = Integer.parseInt(args[0]);
        double step = Double.parseDouble(args[1]);
        Turtle turtle = new Turtle(0.5, 0.5, 0.0);
        for (int t = 0; t < T; t++)
        {
            turtle.turnLeft(360.0 * Math.random());
            turtle.goForward(step);
        }
    }
}
```

Brownian motion of a drunken turtle (moving a fixed distance in a random direction)

```
public class DrunkenTurtles
{
    public static void main(String[] args)
    {
        int N = Integer.parseInt(args[0]);         // number of turtles
        int T = Integer.parseInt(args[1]);         // number of steps
        double step = Double.parseDouble(args[2]);  // step size
        Turtle[] turtles = new Turtle[N];
        for (int i = 0; i < N; i++)
            turtles[i] = new Turtle(Math.random(), Math.random(), 0.0);
        for (int t = 0; t < T; t++)
        { // All turtles take one step.
            for (int i = 0; i < N; i++)
            { // Turtle i takes one step in a random direction.
                turtles[i].turnLeft(360.0 * Math.random());
                turtles[i].goForward(step);
            }
        }
    }
}
```

20 500 .005

20 5000 .005

20 1000 .005

Brownian motion of a bale of drunken turtles

Complex numbers A *complex number* is a number of the form $x + iy$, where x and y are real numbers and i is the square root of -1. The number x is known as the *real* part of the complex number, and the number y is known as the *imaginary* part. This terminology stems from the idea that the square root of -1 has to be an imaginary number, because no real number can have this value. Complex numbers are a quintessential mathematical abstraction: whether or not one believes that it makes sense physically to take the square root of -1, complex numbers help us understand the natural world. They are used extensively in applied mathematics and play an essential role in many branches of science and engineering. They are used to model physical systems of all sorts, from circuits to sound waves to electromagnetic fields. These models typically require extensive computations involving manipulating complex numbers according to well-defined arithmetic operations, so we want to write computer programs to do the computations. In short, we need a new data type.

Developing a data type for complex numbers is a prototypical example of object-oriented programming. No programming language can provide implementations of every mathematical abstraction that we might need, but the ability to implement data types give us not just the ability to write programs to easily manipulate abstractions such as complex numbers, polynomials, vectors, matrices, but also the freedom to think in terms of new abstractions.

The operations on complex numbers that are needed for basic computations are to add and multiply them by applying the commutative, associative, and distributive laws of algebra (along with the identity $i^2 = -1$); to compute the magnitude; and to extract the real and imaginary parts, according to the following equations:

- *Addition*: $(x+iy) + (v+iw) = (x+v) + i(y+w)$
- *Multiplication*: $(x + iy) * (v + iw) = (xv - yw) + i(yv + xw)$
- *Magnitude*: $|x + iy| = \sqrt{x^2 + y^2}$
- *Real part*: $\mathrm{Re}(x + iy) = x$
- *Imaginary part*: $\mathrm{Im}(x + iy) = y$

For example, if $a = 3 + 4i$ and $b = -2 + 3i$, then $a + b = 1 + 7i$, $a * b = -18 + i$, $\mathrm{Re}(a) = 3$, $\mathrm{Im}(a) = 4$, and $|a| = 5$.

With these basic definitions, the path to implementing a data type for complex numbers is clear. As usual, we start with an API that specifies the data-type operations:

```
public class Complex
```
Complex(double real, double imag)	
Complex plus(Complex b)	*sum of this number and* b
Complex times(Complex b)	*product of this number and* b
double abs()	*magnitude*
double re()	*real part*
double im()	*imaginary part*
String toString()	*string representation*

API for complex numbers (see Program 3.2.6)

For simplicity, we concentrate in the text on just the basic operations in this API, but EXERCISE 3.2.19 asks you to consider several other useful operations that might be included in such an API.

Complex (PROGRAM 3.2.2) is a class that implements this API. It has all of the same components as did Charge (and every Java data type implementation): instance variables (re and im), a constructor, instance methods (plus(), times(), abs(), re(), im(), and toString()), and a test client. The test client first sets z_0 to $1 + i$, then sets z to z_0, and then evaluate:

$$z = z^2 + z_0 = (1 + i)^2 + (1 + i) = (1 + 2i - 1) + (1 + i) = 1 + 3i$$
$$z = z^2 + z_0 = (1 + 3i)^2 + (1 + i) = (1 + 6i - 9) + (1 + i) = -7 + 7i$$

This code is straightforward and similar to code that you have seen earlier in this chapter, with one exception: the code that implements the arithmetic methods makes use of a new mechanism for accessing object values.

Accessing instance variables in objects of this type. Both plus() and times() need to access values in two objects: the object passed as an argument and the object used to invoke the method. If we call the method with a.plus(b), we can access the instance variables of a using the names re and im, as usual, but to access the instance variables of of b we use the code b.re and b.im. Keeping the instance variables private means that *client code cannot access directly instance variables in another class* (but code in the same class can access any object's instance variables directly).

Chaining. Observe the manner in which `main()` *chains* two method calls into one compact expression: the expression `z.times(z).plus(z0)` evaluates to $z^2 + z_0$. This usage is convenient because we do not have to invent a variable name for the intermediate value. If you study the expression, you can see that there is no ambiguity: moving from left to right, each method returns a reference to a `Complex` object, which is used to invoke the next method. If desired, we can use parentheses to override the default precedence order (for example, `z.times(z.plus(z0))` evaluates to $z(z + z_0)$).

Creating and returning new objects. Observe the manner in which `plus()` and `times()` provide return values to clients: they need to return a `Complex` value, so they each compute the requisite real and imaginary parts, use them to create a new object, and then return a reference to that object. This arrangement allow clients to manipulate complex numbers by manipulating local variables of type `Complex`.

Final values. The two instance variables in `Complex` are `final`, meaning that their values are set for each `Complex` object when it is created and do not change during the lifetime of an object. Again, we discuss the reasons behind this design decision in SECTION 3.3.

COMPLEX NUMBERS ARE THE BASIS FOR sophisticated calculations from applied mathematics that have many applications. Some programming languages have complex numbers built in as a primitive type, and provide special language support for use of operators such as * and + to perform addition, multiplication, and other operations, in the same way as for integers or floating-point numbers. *Java does not support overloading for built-in operators.* Java's support for data types is much more general, allowing us to compute with abstractions of all description. `Complex` is but one example.

To give you a feeling for the nature of calculations involving complex numbers and the utility of the complex number abstraction, we next consider a famous example of a `Complex` client.

Program 3.2.6   *Complex numbers*

```java
public class Complex
{
   private final double re;
   private final double im;

   public Complex(double real, double imag)
   {  re = real; im = imag;  }

   public Complex plus(Complex b)
   {  // Return the sum of this number and b.
      double real = re + b.re;
      double imag = im + b.im;
      return new Complex(real, imag);
   }

   public Complex times(Complex b)
   {  // Return the product of this number and b.
      double real = re * b.re - im * b.im;
      double imag = re * b.im + im * b.re;
      return new Complex(real, imag);
   }

   public double abs()
   {  return Math.sqrt(re*re + im*im);  }

   public double re()  { return re; }
   public double im()  { return im; }

   public String toString()
   {  return re + " + " + im + "i";  }

   public static void main(String[] args)
   {
      Complex z0 = new Complex(1.0, 1.0);
      Complex z = z0;
      z = z.times(z).plus(z0);
      z = z.times(z).plus(z0);
      StdOut.println(z);
   }
}
```

re	real part
im	imaginary part

This data type is the basis for writing Java programs that manipulate complex numbers.

```
% java Complex
-7.0 + 7.0i
```

Mandelbrot set The *Mandelbrot set* is a specific set of complex numbers discovered by Benoit Mandelbrot. It has many fascinating properties. It is a fractal pattern that is related to the Barnsley fern, the Sierpinski triangle, the Brownian bridge, the Koch curve, the drunken turtle, and other recursive (self-similar) patterns and programs that we have seen in this book. Patterns of this kind are found in natural phenomena of all sorts, and these models and programs are very important in modern science.

The set of points in the Mandelbrot set cannot be described by a single mathematical equation. Instead, it is defined by an *algorithm*, and therefore a perfect candidate for a `Complex` client: we study the set by writing programs to plot it.

The rule for determining whether a complex number z_0 is in the Mandelbrot set is simple: Consider the sequence of complex numbers $z_0, z_1, z_2, \ldots, z_t, \ldots$, where $z_{t+1} = (z_t)^2 + z_0$. For example, this table shows the first few entries in the sequence corresponding to $z_0 = 1 + i$:

t	z_t	$(z_t)^2$	$(z_t)^2 + z_0$
0	$1 + i$	$1 + 2i + i^2 = 2i$	$2i + (1 + i) = 1 + 3i$
1	$1 + 3i$	$1 + 6i + 9i^2 = -8 + 6i$	$-8 + 6i + (1 + i) = -7 + 7i$
2	$-7 + 7i$	$49 - 98i + 49i^2 = -98i$	$-98i + (1 + i) = 1 - 97i$

Mandelbrot sequence computation

Now, if the sequence $|z_t|$ diverges to infinity, then z_0 is *not* in the Mandelbrot set; if the sequence is bounded, then z_0 is in the Mandelbrot set. For many points, the test is simple; for many other points, the test requires more computation, as indicated by the examples in this table:

t	$0 + 0i$	$2 + 0i$	$1 + i$	$-.5 + 0i$	$.10 - .64i$
0	$0 + 0i$	$2 + 0i$	$1 + i$	$-.5 + 0i$	$.10 - .64i$
1	$0 + 0i$	$6 + 0i$	$1 + 3i$	$-.25 + 0i$	$-.30 - .77i$
2	$0 + 0i$	$36 + 0i$	$-7 + 7i$	$-.44 + 0i$	$-.40 - .18i$
3	$0 + 0i$	$1446 + 0i$	$1 - 97i$	$-.31 + 0i$	$.23 - .50i$
4	$0 + 0i$	$2090918 + 0i$	$-9407 - 193i$	$-.40 + 0i$	$-.09 - .87i$
in the set?	yes	no	no	yes	yes

Mandelbrot sequence for several starting points

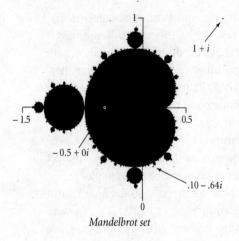

Mandelbrot set

For brevity, the numbers in the rightmost two columns of this table are given to just two decimal places. In some cases, we can prove whether numbers are in the set: for example, $0 + 0i$ is certainly in the set (since the magnitude of all the numbers in its sequence is 0), and $2 + 0i$ is certainly not in the set (since its sequence dominates the powers of 2, which diverges). In some other cases, the growth is readily apparent: for example, $1 + i$ does not seem to be in the set. Other sequences exhibit a periodic behavior: for example, i maps to $-1 + i$ to $-i$ to $-1 + i$ to $-i$ .... And some sequences go on for a very long time before the magnitude of the numbers begins to get large.

.1015 -.633 1.0

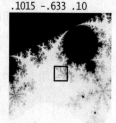

.1015 -.633 .10

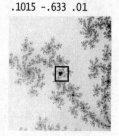

.1015 -.633 .01

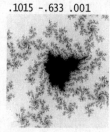

.1015 -.633 .001

To visualize the Mandelbrot set, we sample *complex* points, just as we sample real-valued points to plot a real-valued function. Each complex number $x + iy$ corresponds to a point (x, y) in the plane, so we can plot the results as follows: for a specified resolution N, we define a regularly spaced N-by-N pixel grid within a specified square and draw a black pixel if the corresponding point is in the Mandelbrot set and a white pixel if it is not. This plot is a strange and wondrous pattern, with all the black dots connected and falling roughly within the 2-by-2 square centered on the point $-1/2 + 0i$. Large values of N will produce higher-resolution images, at the cost of more computation. Looking closer reveals self-similarities throughout the plot. For example, the same bulbous pattern with self-similar appendages appears all around the contour of the main black cardioid region, of sizes that resemble the simple ruler function of PROGRAM 1.2.1. When we zoom in near the edge of the cardioid, tiny self-similar cardioids appear!

But how, precisely, do we produce such plots? Actually, no one knows for sure, because there is no simple test that would enable us to

Zooming in on the set

conclude that a point is surely in the set. Given a complex point, we can compute the terms at the beginning of its sequence, but may not be able to know for sure that the sequence remains bounded. There *is* a test that tells us for sure that a point is *not* in the set: if the magnitude of any number in the sequence ever gets to be greater than 2 (such as $2 + 0i$), then the sequence surely will diverge.

Mandelbrot (PROGRAM 3.2.7) uses this test to plot a visual representation of the Mandelbrot set. Since our knowledge of the set is not quite black-and-white, we use grayscale in our visual representation. It is based on the function mand() (a Complex client), which takes a Complex argument z0 and an int argument max and computes the Mandelbrot iteration sequence starting at z0, returning the number of iterations for which the magnitude stays less than 2, up to the limit max.

For each pixel, the method main() in Mandelbrot computes the point z0 corresponding to the pixel and then computes 255 - mand(z0, 255) to create a grayscale color for the pixel. Any pixel that is not black corresponds to a point that we know to be not in the Mandelbrot set because the magnitude of the numbers in its sequence grew past 2 (and therefore will go to infinity). The black pixels (grayscale value 0) correspond to points that we assume to be in the set because the magnitude stayed less than 2 for 255 iterations, but we do not necessarily know for sure.

The complexity of the images that this simple program produces is remarkable, even when we zoom in on a tiny portion of the plane. For even more dramatic pictures, we can use use color (see EXERCISE 3.2.34). And the Mandelbrot set is derived from iterating just one function ($z^2 + z_0$): we have a great deal to learn from studying the properties of other functions, as well.

The simplicity of the code masks a substantial amount of computation. There are about one-quarter million pixels in a 512-by-512 image, and all of the black ones require 255 iterations, so producing an image with Mandelbrot requires hundreds of millions of operations on Complex values.

Fascinating as it is to study, our primary interest in Mandelbrot is as an example client of Complex, to illustrate that computing with a type of data that is not built into Java (complex numbers) is a natural and useful programming activity. Mandelbrot is a simple and natural expression of the computation, made so by the design and implementation of Complex. You could implement Mandelbrot without using Complex, but the code would essentially have to merge together the code in PROGRAMS 3.2.6 and 3.2.7 and therefore would be much more difficult to understand. *Whenever you can clearly separate tasks within a program, you should do so.*

Program 3.2.7 *Mandelbrot set*

```java
import java.awt.Color;

public class Mandelbrot
{
   private static int mand(Complex z0, int max)
   {
      Complex z = z0;
      for (int t = 0; t < max; t++)
      {
         if (z.abs() > 2.0) return t;
         z = z.times(z).plus(z0);
      }
      return max;
   }

   public static void main(String[] args)
   {
      double xc   = Double.parseDouble(args[0]);
      double yc   = Double.parseDouble(args[1]);
      double size = Double.parseDouble(args[2]);
      int N = 512;
      Picture pic = new Picture(N, N);
      for (int i = 0; i < N; i++)
         for (int j = 0; j < N; j++)
         {
            double x0 = xc - size/2 + size*i/N;
            double y0 = yc - size/2 + size*j/N;
            Complex z0 = new Complex(x0, y0);
            int t = 512 - mand(z0, 512);
            Color c = new Color(t, t, t);
            pic.set(i, N-1-j, c);
         }
      pic.show();
   }
}
```

x0, y0	*point in square*
z0	$x_0 + i\, y_0$
max	*iteration limit*
xc, yc	*center of square*
size	*square is size-by-size*
N	*grid is N-by-N pixels*
pic	*image for output*
c	*pixel color for output*

-.5 0 2

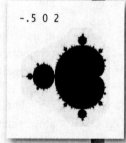

-.1015 -.633 .01

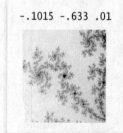

This program takes three command-line arguments that specify the center and size of a square region of interest, and makes a digital image showing the result of sampling the Mandelbrot set in that region at a 512*512 grid of equally spaced pixels. It colors each pixel with a grayscale value that is determined by counting the number of iterations before the Mandelbrot sequence for the corresponding complex number grows past 2.0, up to 255.

Commercial data processing   One of the driving forces behind the development of object-oriented programming has been the need for an extensive amount of reliable software for commercial data processing. As an illustration, we consider next an example of a data type that might be used by a financial institution to keep track of customer information.

Suppose that a stock broker needs to maintain customer accounts containing shares of various stocks. That is, the set of values the broker needs to process includes the customer's name, numbers of different stocks held, amount of shares and ticker symbols for each, and perhaps the total value of the stocks in the account. To process an account, the broker needs at least the operations defined in this API:

```
public class StockAccount
```

	StockAccount(In in)	*create a new account from information in input stream*
double	value()	*total value in dollars*
void	buy(int amount, String symbol)	*add shares of stock to account*
double	sell(int amount, String symbol)	*subtract shares of stock from account*
void	write(Out out)	*save account to an output stream*
void	printReport()	*print a detailed report of stocks and values*

API for processing stock accounts (see PROGRAM 3.2.8)

The broker certainly needs to buy, sell, and provide reports to the customer, but the first key to understanding this kind of data processing is to consider the StockAccount() constructor and the write() method in this API. The customer information has a long lifetime and needs to be saved in a *file* or *database*. To process an account, a client program needs to read information from the corresponding file; process the information as appropriate; and, if the information changes, write it back to the file, saving it for later. To enable this kind of processing, we need a *file format* and an *internal representation*, or a *data structure*, for the account information. The situation is analogous to what we saw for matrix processing in CHAPTER 1, where we defined a file format (numbers of rows and columns followed by entries in row-major order) and an internal representation (Java two-dimensional arrays) to enable us to write programs for the random surfer and other applications.

As a (whimsical) running example, we imagine that a broker is maintaining a small portfolio of stock in leading software companies for Alan Turing, the father of computing. *As an aside*: Turing's life story is a fascinating one that is worth pursuing. Among many other things, he worked on computational cryptography that helped to bring about the end of the Second World War, he developed the basis for modern theoretical computer science, he designed and built one of the first computers, and he was a pioneer in artificial intelligence research. It is perhaps safe to assume that Turing, whatever his financial situation as an academic researcher in the middle of the last century, would be sufficiently optimistic about the potential impact of computing software in today's world that he would make some small investments.

File format. Modern systems normally use text files, even for data, to minimize dependence on formats defined by any one program. For simplicity, we use a direct representation where we list the account holder's name (a string), cash balance (a floating-point number), and number of stocks held (an integer), followed by a line for each stock giving the number of shares and the ticker symbol. It is also wise to use *tags* such as <Name> and <Number of shares> and so forth to label all the information, to further minimize dependencies on any one program, but we omit tags here for brevity.

```
% more Turing.txt
Turing, Alan
10.24
5
100 ADBE
 25 GOOG
 97 IBM
250 MSFT
200 YHOO
```

File format

Data structure. To represent information for processing by Java programs, we use *object instance variables.* They specify the type of information and provide the structure that we need in order to clearly refer to it in code. For our example, we clearly need the following:
- A String value for the account name
- A double value for the cash balance
- An int value for the number of stocks
- An array of String values for stock symbols
- An array of int values for numbers of shares

We directly reflect these choices in the instance variable declarations in StockAccount (PROGRAM 3.2.8). The arrays stocks[] and shares[] are known as *parallel arrays.* Given an index i, stocks[i] gives a stock symbol and shares[i] give the number of shares of that

```
public class StockAccount
{
    private final String name;
    private double cash;
    private int N;
    private int[] shares;
    private String[] stocks;
    ...
}
```

Data structure blueprint

stock in the account. An alternative design would be to define a separate data type for stocks to manipulate this information for each stock and maintain an array of objects of that type in StockAccount.

StockAccount includes a constructor, which reads a file and builds an account with this internal representation, and the method implementation for value(), which uses StockQuote (PROGRAM 3.1.10) to get each stock's price from the web. For example, our broker needs to provide a periodic detailed report to customers, perhaps using the following code for printReport() in StockAccount:

```
public void printReport()
{
    StdOut.printf("%s\n", name);
    StdOut.printf("                    Cash: $%9.2f\n", cash);
    double total = cash;
    for (int i = 0; i < N; i++)
    {
        int amount = shares[i];
        double p = StockQuote.price(stocks[i]);
        StdOut.printf("%4d  %4s ", amount, stocks[i]);
        StdOut.printf(" $%6.2f    $%9.2f\n", p, amount * p);
        total += amount * p;
    }
    StdOut.printf("                 Total: $%9.2f\n", total);
}
```

On the one hand, this client illustrates the kind of computing that was one of the primary drivers in the evolution of computing in the 1950s. Banks and other companies bought early computers precisely because of the need to do such financial reporting. For example, formatted printing was developed precisely for such applications. On the other hand, this client exemplifies modern web-centric computing, as it gets information directly from the web, without using a browser.

The implementations of buy() and sell() require the use of basic mechanisms introduced in SECTION 4.4, so we defer them to that section. Beyond these basic methods, an actual application of these ideas would likely use a number of other clients. For example, a broker might want to build an array of all accounts, then process a list of transactions that both modify the information in those accounts and actually carry out the transactions through the web. Of course, such code needs to be developed with great care!

Program 3.2.8   *Stock account*

```java
public class StockAccount
{
    private final String name;
    private double cash;
    private int N;
    private int[] shares;
    private String[] stocks;

    public StockAccount(In in)
    { // Build data structure from input stream.
        name = in.readLine();
        cash = in.readDouble();
        N = in.readInt();
        shares = new int[N];
        stocks = new String[N];
        for (int i = 0; i < N; i++)
        { // Process one stock.
            shares[i] = in.readInt();
            stocks[i] = in.readString();
        }
    }

    public void printReport()
    { /* See text. */  }

    public static void main(String[] args)
    {
        In in = new In(args[0]);
        StockAccount acct = new StockAccount(in);
        acct.printReport();
    }
}
```

name	customer name
cash	cash balance
N	number of stocks
shares[]	share counts
stocks[]	stock symbols

in	input stream

This class for processing stock accounts illustrates typical usage of object-oriented programming for commercial data processing.

```
% more Turing.txt
Turing, Alan
10.24
5
100 ADBE
 25 GOOG
 97 IBM
250 MSFT
200 YHOO
```

```
% java StockAccount Turing.txt
Turing, Alan
                  Cash: $    10.24
100  ADBE  $ 42.23  $  4222.91
 25  GOOG  $473.25  $ 11831.25
 97  IBM   $104.40  $ 10126.80
250  MSFT  $ 30.25  $  7562.50
200  YHOO  $ 28.39  $  5678.00
               Total: $ 39431.70
```

WHEN YOU LEARNED HOW TO DEFINE functions that can be used in multiple places in a program (or in other programs) in CHAPTER 2, you moved from a world where programs are simply lists of statements in a single file to the world of modular programming, summarized in our mantra: *whenever you can clearly separate subtasks within a program, you should do so.* The analogous capability for data, introduced in this chapter, moves you from a world where data has to be one of a few elementary types of data to a world where you can define your own types of data. This profound new capability vastly extends the scope of your programming. As with the concept of a function, once you have learned to implement and use data types, you will marvel at the primitive nature of programs that do not use them.

But object-oriented programming is much more than structuring data. It enables us to associate the data relevant to a subtask with the operations that manipulate that data and to keep both separate in an independent module. With object-oriented programming, our mantra is this: *whenever you can clearly separate data and associated operations for subtasks within a computation, you should do so.*

The examples that we have considered are persuasive evidence that object-oriented programming can play a useful role in a broad range of activities. Whether we are trying to design and build a physical artifact, develop a software system, understand the natural world, or process information, a key first step is to define an appropriate abstraction, such as a geometric description of the physical artifact, a modular design of the software system, a mathematical model of the natural world, or a data structure for the information. When we want to write programs to manipulate instances of a well-defined abstraction, we can just implement it as a data type in a Java class and write Java programs to create and manipulate objects of that type.

Each time that we develop a class that makes use of other classes by creating and manipulating objects of the type defined by the class, we are programming at a higher layer of abstraction. In the next section, we discuss some of the design challenges inherent in this kind of programming.

Q. Do instance variables have initial values that we can depend upon?

A Yes. They are automatically set to 0 for numeric types, `false` for the `boolean` type, and the special value `null` for all reference types. These values are consistent with the way array entries are initialized. This automatic initialization ensures that every instance variable always stores a legal (but not necessarily meaningful) value. Writing code that depends on these values is controversial: some experienced programmers embrace the idea because the resulting code can be very compact; others avoid it because the code is opaque to someone who does not know the rules.

Q. What is `null`?

A It is a literal value that refers to no object. Invoking a method using the `null` reference is meaningless and results in a `NullPointerException`. If you get this error message, check to make sure that your constructor properly initializes all of its instance variables.

Q. Can we initialize instance variables to other values when declaring them?

A. Yes, you can initialize instance variables using the same conventions as you have been using for initializing local variables. Each time a client creates an object with new, Java initializes its instance variables with those values, and then calls the constructor.

Q. Must every class have a constructor?

A. Yes, but if you do not specify a constructor, Java provides a default (no-argument) constructor automatically. When the client invokes that constructor with new, the instance variables are auto-initialized as usual. If you *do* specify a constructor, the default no-argument constructor disappears.

Q. Suppose I do not include a `toString()` method. What happens if I try to print an object of that type with `StdOut.println()`?

A. The printed output is an integer that is unlikely to be of much use to you.

Q. Can I have a static method in a class that implements a data type?

A. Of course. For example, all of our classes have `main()`. But it is easy to get confused when static methods and instance methods are mixed up in the same code. For example, it is natural to consider using static methods for operations that involve multiple objects where none of them naturally suggests itself as the one that should invoke the method. For example, we say `z.abs()` to get $|z|$, but saying `a.plus(b)` to get the sum is perhaps not so natural. Why not `b.plus(a)`? An alternative is to define a static method like the following within `Complex`:

```
public static Complex plus(Complex a, Complex b)
{
    return new Complex(a.re + b.re, a.im + b.im);
}
```

We generally avoid such usage and live with expressions that do not mix static and instance methods to avoid having to write code like this:

```
z = Complex.plus(Complex.times(z, z), z0)
```

Instead, we would write:

```
z = z.times(z).plus(z0)
```

Q. These computations with `plus()` and `times()` seem rather clumsy. Is there some way to use symbols like + and * in expressions involving objects where they make sense, like `Complex` and `Vector`, so that we could write expressions like `z = z * z + z0` instead?

A. Some languages (notably C++) support this feature, which is known as *operator overloading*, but Java does not do so (except that there is language support for overloading + with string concatenation). As usual, this is a decision of the language designers that we just live with, but many Java programmers do not consider this to be much of a loss. Operator overloading makes sense only for types that represent numeric or algebraic abstractions, a small fraction of the total, and many programs are easier to understand when operations have descriptive names such as `plus` and `times`. The APL programming language of the 1970s took this issue to the opposite extreme by insisting that *every* operation be represented by a single symbol (including Greek letters).

Q. Are there other kinds of variables besides argument, local, and instance variables in a class?

A. If you include the keyword `static` in a variable declaration (outside of any method), it creates a completely different type of variable, known as a *static variable* or *class variable*. Like instance variables, static variables are accessible to every method in the class; however, they are not associated with any object—there is one variable per class. In older programming languages, such variables are known as *global variables* because of their global scope. In modern programming, we focus on limiting scope and therefore rarely use such variables.

Q. `Mandelbrot` creates hundreds of millions of `Complex` objects. Doesn't all that object-creation overhead slow things down?

A. Yes, but not so much that we cannot generate our plots. Our goal is to make our programs readable and easy to maintain—limiting scope via the complex number abstraction helps us achieve that goal. You certainly could speed up `Mandelbrot` by bypassing the complex number abstraction or by using a different implementation of `Complex`. We will revisit this issue in the next section.

Exercises

3.2.1 Consider the following data-type implementation for (axis-aligned) rectangles, which represents each rectangle with the coordinates of its center point and its width and height:

```
public class Rectangle
{
    private final double x
    private final double y;

    private final double width
    private final double height;

    public Rectangle(double x0, double y0, double w, double h)
    {
        x = x0;
        y = y0;
        width = w;
        height = h;
    }
    public double area()
    {   return width * height;  }

    public double perimeter()
    {   /* Compute perimeter. */  }

    public boolean intersects(Rectangle b)
    {   /* Does this rectangle intersect b? */  }

    public boolean contains(Rectangle b)
    {   /* Is b inside this rectangle? */  }

    public void show(Rectangle b)
    {   /* Draw rectangle on StdDraw. */  }

}
```

Write an API for this class, and fill in the code for `perimeter()`, `intersects()`, and `contains()`. *Note*: Treat coincident lines as intersecting, so that, for example, `a.intersects(a)` is `true` and `a.contains(a)` is `false`.

3.2.2 Write a test client for `Rectangle` that takes three command-line arguments N, min, and max; generates N random rectangles whose width and height are uni-

formly distributed between min and max in the unit square; draws them on Std-Draw; and prints their average area and average perimeter to standard output.

3.2.3   Add code to your test client from the previous exercise code to compute the average number of pairs of rectangles that intersect and are contained in one another.

3.2.4   Develop an implementation of your Rectangle API from Exercise 3.2.1 that represents rectangles with the coordinates of their lower left and upper right corners. Do *not* change the API.

3.2.5   What is wrong with the following code?

```
public class Charge
{
    private double rx, ry;     // position
    private double q;          // charge

    public Charge(double x0, double y0, double q0)
    {
        double rx = x0;
        double ry = y0;
        double q = q0;
    }
    ...
}
```

Answer.   The assignment statements in the constructor are also *declarations* that create new local variables rx, ry, and q, which are assigned values from the arguments but are never used. The instance variables rx, ry, and q remain at their default value of 0. *Note*: A local variable with the same name as an instance variable is said to *shadow* the instance variable—we discuss in the next section a way to refer to shadowed instance variables, which are best avoided by beginners.

3.2.6   Create a data type Location that represents a location on Earth using latitudes and longitudes. Include a method distanceTo() that computes distances using the great-circle distance (see Exercise 1.2.33).

3.2.7 Implement a data type `Rational` for rational numbers that supports addition, subtraction, multiplication, and division.

```
public class Rational
```
―――
```
             Rational(int numerator, int denominator)
```
Rational	plus(Rational b)	*sum of this number and b*
Rational	minus(Rational b)	*difference of this number and b*
Rational	times(Rational b)	*product of this number and b*
Rational	over(Rational b)	*quotient of this number and b*
String	toString()	*string representation*

Use `Euclid.gcd()` (PROGRAM 2.3.1) to ensure that the numerator and denominator never have any common factors. Include a test client that exercises all of your methods. Do not worry about testing for overflow (see EXERCISE 3.3.24).

3.2.8 Write a data type `Interval` that implements the following API:

```
public class Interval
```
―――
```
             Interval(double left, double right)
```
boolean	contains(double x)	*is x in this interval?*
boolean	intersects(Interval b)	*does this interval and b intersect?*
String	toString()	*string representation*

An interval is defined to be the set of all points on the line greater than or equal to `left` and less than or equal to `right`. In particular, an interval with `right` less than `left` is empty. Write a client that is a filter that takes a `double` value x from the command line and prints all of the intervals on standard input (each defined by a pair of `double` values) that contain x.

3.2.9 Write a client for your `Interval` class from the previous exercise that takes an `int` value N as command-line argument, reads N intervals (each defined by a

pair of `double` values) from standard input, and prints all pairs that intersect.

3.2.10 Develop an implementation of your `Rectangle` API from EXERCISE 3.2.1 that takes advantage of `Interval` to simplify and clarify the code.

3.2.11 Write a data type `Point` that implements the following API:

```
public class Point
```

`Point(double x, double y)`	
`double` `distanceTo(Point q)`	*Euclidean distance between this point and* q
`String` `toString()`	*string representation*

3.2.12 Add methods to `Stopwatch` that allow clients to stop and restart the stopwatch.

3.2.13 Use a `Stopwatch` to compare the cost of computing Harmonic numbers with a for loop (see PROGRAM 1.3.5) as opposed to using the recursive method given in SECTION 2.3.

3.2.14 Develop a version of `Histogram` that uses `Draw`, so that a client can create multiple histograms. Add to the display a red vertical line showing the sample mean and blue vertical lines at a distance of two standard deviations from the mean. Use a test client that creates histograms for flipping coins (Bernoulli trials) with a biased coin that is heads with probability p, for $p = .2, .4, .6.$ and $.8$, taking the number of flips and the number of trials from the command line, as in PROGRAM 3.2.3.

3.2.15 Modify the test client in `Turtle` to produce stars with N points for odd N.

3.2.16 Modify the `toString()` method in `Complex` (PROGRAM 3.2.2) so that it prints complex numbers in the traditional format. For example, it should print the value $3 - i$ as `3 - i` instead of `3.0 + -1.0i`, the value 3 as `3` instead of `3.0 + 0.0i`, and the value $3i$ as `3i` instead of `0.0 + 3.0i`.

3.2.17 Write a `Complex` client that takes three `double` values a, b, and c as command-line arguments and prints out the complex roots of $ax^2 + bx + c$.

3.2.18 Write a `Complex` client `Roots` that takes two `double` values a and b and an integer N from the command line and prints the Nth roots of $a + bi$. *Note*: skip this exercise if you are not familiar with the operation of taking roots of complex numbers.

3.2.19 Implement the following additions to the `Complex` API:

`double  theta()`	*phase (angle) of this number*
`Complex  minus(Complex b)`	*difference of this number and b*
`Complex  conjugate()`	*conjugate of this number*
`Complex  divides(Complex b)`	*result of dividing this number by b*
`Complex  power(int b)`	*result of raising this number to the bth power*

Write a test client that exercises all of your methods.

3.2.20 Suppose you want to add a constructor to `Complex` that takes a `double` value as argument and creates a `Complex` number with that value as the real part (and no imaginary part). You write the following code:

```
public void Complex(double real)
{
    re = real;
    im = 0.0;
}
```

But then `Complex c = new Complex(1.0)` does not compile. Why?

Answer: Constructors do not have return types, not even `void`. The code above defines a method named `Complex`, not a constructor. Remove the keyword `void`.

3.2.21 Find a `Complex` value for which `mand()` returns a number greater than 100, and then zoom in on that value, as in the example in the text.

3.2.22 Implement the `write()` method for `StockAccount` (PROGRAM 3.2.8).

3.2.23 *Mutable charges.* Modify `Charge` so that the charge q is not `final`, and add a method `increaseCharge()` that takes a `double` argument and adds the given value to the charge. Then, write a client that initializes an array with:

−5

```
Charge[] a = new Charge[3];
a[0] = new Charge(.4, .6, 50);
a[1] = new Charge(.5, .5, -5);
a[2] = new Charge(.6, .6, 50);
```

and then displays the result of slowly decreasing the charge value of `a[i]` by wrapping the code that computes the picture in a loop like the following:

−55

```
for (int t = 0; t < 100; t++)
{
    // compute the picture
    pic.show();
    a[1].change(-2);
}
```

3.2.24 *Complex timing.* Write a `Stopwatch` client that compares the cost of using `Complex` to the cost of writing code that directly manipulates two double values, for the task of doing the calculations in `Mandelbrot`. Specifically, create a version of `Mandelbrot` that just does the calculations (remove the code that refers to `Picture`), then create a version of that program that does not use `Complex`, and then compute the ratio of the running times.

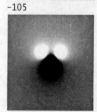

−105

−155

3.2.25 *Quaternions.* In 1843, Sir William Hamilton discovered an extension to complex numbers called quaternions. A quaternion is a vector $a = (a_0, a_1, a_2, a_3)$ with the following operations:
- *Magnitude:* $|a| = \sqrt{a_0^2 + a_1^2 + a_2^2 + a_3^2}$.
- *Conjugate:* the conjugate of a is $(a_0, -a_1, -a_2, -a_3)$.
- *Inverse:* $a^{-1} = (a_0/|a|, -a_1/|a|, -a_2/|a|, -a_3/|a|)$.
- *Sum:* $a + b = (a_0 + b_0, a_1 + b_1, a_2 + b_2, a_3 + b_3)$.
- *Product:* $a * b = (a_0 b_0 - a_1 b_1 - a_2 b_2 - a_3 b_3, a_0 b_1 - a_1 b_0 + a_2 b_3 - a_3 b_2,$
$a_0 b_2 - a_1 b_3 + a_2 b_0 + a_3 b_1, a_0 b_3 + a_1 b_2 - a_2 b_1 + a_3 b_0)$.
- *Quotient:* $a/b = ab^{-1}$.

−205

Mutating a charge

Create a data type for quaternions and a test client that exercises all of your code. Quaternions extend the concept of rotation in three dimensions to four dimensions. They are used in computer graphics, control theory, signal processing, and orbital mechanics.

3.2.26 *Dragon curves.* Write a recursive `Turtle` client `Dragon` that draws dragon curves (see EXERCISES 1.2.35 and 1.5.9).

% java Dragon 15

Answer: These curves, originally discovered by three NASA physicists, were popularized in the 1960s by Martin Gardner and later used by Michael Crichton in the book and movie *Jurassic Park*. This exercise can be solved with remarkably compact code, based on a pair of mutually interacting recursive functions derived directly from the definition in EXERCISE 1.2.35. One of them, `dragon()`, should draw the curve as you expect; the other, `nogard()`, should draw the curve in *reverse* order. See the booksite for details.

3.2.27 *Hilbert curves.* A space-filling curve is a continuous curve in the unit square that passes through every point. Write a recursive `Turtle` client that produces these recursive patterns, which approach a space-filling curve that was defined by the mathematician David Hilbert at the end of the 19th century.

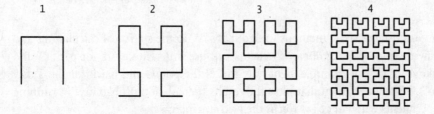

Partial answer See the previous exercise. You need a pair of methods: `hilbert()`, which traverses a Hilbert curve, and `treblih()`, which traverses a Hilbert curve *in reverse order*. See the booksite for details.

3.2.28 *Gosper island.* Write a recursive `Turtle` client that produces these recursive patterns.

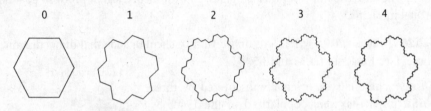

3.2.29 *Data analysis.* Write a data type for use in running experiments where the control variable is an integer in the range $[0, N)$ and the dependent variable is a `double` value. (For example, studying the running time of a program that takes an integer argument would involve such experiments.) Implement the following API.

```
public class Data
```

`Data(int N, int max)`	*create a new data analysis object for the N int values in [0, N)*
`double  addDataPoint(int i, double x)`	*add a data point (i, x)*
`void  plot()`	*plot all the data points*
`void  TukeyPlot()`	*draw a Tukey plot (see Exercise 2.2.18)*

You can use the static methods in `StdStats` to do the statistical calculations and draw the plots. Use `StdDraw` so clients can use different colors for `plot()` and `TukeyPlot()` (for example, light gray for all the points and black for the Tukey plot). Write a test client that plots the results (percolation probability) of running experiments with `Percolation` as the grid size increases.

3.2.30 *Elements.* Create a data type `Element` for entries in the *Periodic Table of Elements*. Include data type values for element, atomic number, symbol, and atomic weight and accessor methods for each of these values. Then, create a data type

PeriodicTable that reads values from a file to create an array of Element objects (you can find the file and a description of its format on the booksite) and responds to queries on standard input so that a user can type a molecular equation like H2O and the program responds by printing the molecular weight. Develop APIs and implementations for each data type.

3.2.31 *Stock prices.* The file DJIA.txt on the booksite contains all closing stock prices in the history of the Dow Jones Industrial Average, in the comma-separated-value format. Create a data type Entry that can hold one entry in the table, with values for date, opening price, daily high, daily low, closing price, and so forth. Then, create a data type Table that reads the file to build an array of Entry objects and supports methods for computing averages over various periods of time. Finally, create interesting Table clients to produce plots of the data. Be creative: this path is well-trodden.

3.2.32 *Chaos with Newton's method.* The polynomial $f(z) = z^4 - 1$ has four roots: at 1, -1, i, and $-i$. We can find the roots using Newton's method in the complex plane: $z_{k+1} = z_k - f(z_k)/f'(z_k)$. Here, $f(z) = z^4 - 1$ and $f'(z) = 4z^3$. The method converges to one of the four roots, depending on the starting point z_0. Write a Complex client Newton that takes a command-line argument N and colors pixels in an N-by-N Picture white, red, green, or blue by mapping the pixels complex points in a regularly spaced grid in the square of size 2 centered at the origin and coloring each pixel according to which of the four roots the corresponding point converges (black if no convergence after 100 iterations).

`if (g != 255) g = g * 17 % 256;`

3.2.33 *Equipotential surfaces.* An equipotential surface is the set of all points that have the same electric potential V. Given a group of point charges, it is useful to visualize the electric potential by plotting equipotential surfaces (also known as a *contour plot*). Write a program Equipotential that draws a line every $5V$ by computing the potential at each pixel and checking whether the potential at the corresponding point

is within 1 pixel of a multiple of 5V. *Note*: A *very easy* approximate solution to this exercise is obtained from PROGRAM 3.1.7 by scrambling the color values assigned to each pixel, rather than having them be proportional to the grayscale value. For example, the accompanying figure is created by inserting the code above it before creating the Color. Explain why it works, and experiment with your own version.

3.2.34 *Color Mandelbrot plot.* Create a file of 256 integer triples that represent interesting Color values, and then use those colors instead of grayscale values to plot each pixel in Mandelbrot: Read the values to create an array of 256 Color values, then index into that array with the return value of mand(). By experimenting with various color choices at various places in the set, you can produce astonishing images. See mandel.txt on the booksite for an example.

3.2.35 *Julia sets.* The *Julia set* for a given complex number c is a set of points related to the Mandelbrot function. Instead of fixing z and varying c, we fix c and vary z. Those points z for which the modified Mandelbrot function stays bounded are in the *Julia set*; those for which the sequence diverges to infinity are not in the set. All points z of interest lie in the 4-by-4 box centered at the origin. The Julia set for c is connected if and only if c is in the Mandelbrot set! Write a program Color-Julia that takes two command line arguments a and b, and plots a color version of the Julia set for $c = a + bi$, using the color-table method described in the previous exercise.

3.2.36 *Biggest winner and biggest loser.* Write a StockAccount client that builds an array of StockAccount objects, computes the total value of each account, and prints a report for the accounts with the largest value and the account with the smallest value. Assume that the information in the accounts are kept in a single file that contains the information for the accounts, one after the other, in the format given in the text.

3.3 Designing Data Types

THE ABILITY TO CREATE DATA TYPES turns every programmer into a language designer. You do not have to settle for the types of data and associated operations that are built into the language, because you can easily create your own types of data and then write client programs that use them. Java does not have complex numbers built in, but you can define `Complex` and write programs such as `Mandelbrot`. Java does not have a built-in facility for turtle graphics, but you can define `Turtle` and write client programs that take immedi-

ate advantage of this abstraction. Even when Java does have a particular facility, we can use a data type to tailor it to our needs, as we do when we use our `Std*` libraries instead the more extensive ones provided by Java for software developers.

Now, the first thing that we strive for when creating a program is an understanding of the types of data that we will need. Developing this understanding is a *design* activity. In this section, we focus on developing APIs as a critical step in the development of any program. We need to consider various alternatives, understand their impact on both client programs and implementations, and refine the design to strike an appropriate balance between the needs of clients and the possible implementation strategies.

If you take a course in systems programming, you will learn that this design activity is critical when building large systems, and that Java and similar languages have powerful high-level mechanisms that support code reuse when writing large programs. Many of these mechanisms are intended for use by experts building large systems, but the general approach is worthwhile for every programmer, and some of these mechanisms are useful when writing small programs.

In this section we discuss *encapsulation*, *immutability*, and *inheritance*, with particular attention to the use of these mechanisms in data-type design to enable modular programming, facilitate debugging, and write clear and correct code.

At the end of the section, we discuss Java's mechanisms for use in checking design assumptions against actual conditions at runtime. Such tools are invaluable aids in developing reliable software.

Designing APIs.   In Section 3.1, we wrote client programs that *use* APIs; in Section 3.2, we *implemented* APIs. Now we consider the challenge of *designing* APIs. Treating these topics in this order and with this focus is appropriate because most of the time that you spend programming will be writing client programs.

Often the most important and most challenging steps in building software is designing the APIs. This task takes practice, careful deliberation, and many iterations. However, any time spent designing a good API is certain to be repaid in time saved during debugging or with code reuse.

Articulating an API might seem to be overkill when writing a small program, but you should consider writing every program as though you will need to reuse the code someday—not because you know that you will reuse that code, but because you are quite likely to want to reuse *some* of your code and you cannot know *which* code you will need.

client

```
Charge c1 = new Charge(.51, .63, 21.3);


      c1.potentialAt(x, y)
```

*creates objects
and invokes methods*

API

```
public class Charge

        Charge(double x0, double y0, double q0)

double potentialAt(double x, double y)    potential at (x, y)
                                                due to charge
String toString()                               string
                                            representation
```

*defines signatures
and describes methods*

Standards. It is easy to understand why writing to an API is so important by considering other domains. From railroad tracks, to threaded nuts and bolts, to fax machines, to radio frequencies, to DVD standards, we know that using a common standard interface enables the broadest usage of a technology. Java itself is another example: your Java programs are clients of the *Java virtual machine*, which is a standard interface that is implemented on a wide variety of hardware and software platforms. By using APIs to separate clients from implementations, we reap the benefits of standard interfaces for every program that we write.

implementation

```
public class Charge
  private final double rx, ry;
  private final double q;

  public Charge(double x0, double y0, double q0)
  { ... }

  public double potentialAt(double x, double y)
  { ... }

  public String toString()
  { ... }
```

*defines instance variables
and implements methods*

Object-oriented library abstraction

Specification problem. Our APIs are lists of methods, along with brief English-language descriptions of what the methods are supposed to do. Ideally, an API would clearly articulate behavior for all possible inputs, including side effects, and then we would have software to check that implementations meet the specification. Unfortunately, a fundamental result from theoretical computer science, known as the *specification problem*, says that this goal is actually *impossible* to achieve. Briefly, such a specification would have to be written in a formal language like a programming language, and the problem of determining whether two programs perform the same computation is known, mathematically, to be *unsolvable*. (If you are interested in this idea, you can learn much more about the nature of unsolvable problems and their role in our understanding of the nature of computation in a course in theoretical computer science.) Therefore, we resort to informal descriptions with examples, such as those in the text surrounding our APIs.

Wide interfaces. A *wide interface* is one that has an excessive number of methods. An important principle to follow in designing an API is to *avoid wide interfaces*. The size of an API naturally tends to grow over time because it is easy to add methods to an existing API, whereas it is difficult to remove methods without breaking existing clients. In certain situations, wide interfaces are justified—for example, in widely used systems libraries such as String. Various techniques are helpful in reducing the effective width of an interface. For example, we considered in CHAPTER 2 several libraries that use overloading to provide implementations of basic methods for all types of data. Another approach is to include methods that are orthogonal in functionality. For example, Java's Math library includes methods for sin(), cos(), and tan(), but not sec().

Start with client code. One of the primary purposes of developing a data type is to simplify client code. Therefore, it makes sense to pay attention to client code form the start when designing an API. Very often, doing so is no problem at all, because a typical reason to develop a data type in the first place is to simplify client code that is becoming cumbersome. When you find yourself with some client code that you are not proud of, one way to proceed is to write a fanciful simplified version of the code that expresses the computation the way you are thinking about it, at some higher level that does not involve the details of the code. If you have done a good job of writing succinct comments to describe your computation, one possible starting point is to think about opportunities to convert the comments into code.

Remember the basic mantra for data types: *whenever you can clearly separate data and associated operations within a program, you should do so.* Whatever the source, it is normally wise to write client code (and develop the API) *before* working on an implementation. Writing two clients is even better. Starting with client code is one way of ensuring that developing an implementation will be worth the effort.

Avoid dependence on representation. Usually when developing an API, we have a representation in mind. After all, a data type is a set of values and a set of operations on those values, and it does not make much sense to talk about the operations without knowing the values. But that is different from knowing the representation of the values. One purpose of the data type is to simplify client code by allowing it to avoid details of and dependence on a particular representation. For example, our client programs for `Picture` and `StdAudio` work with simple abstract representations of pictures and sound, respectively. The primary value of the APIs for these abstraction is that they allow client code to ignore a substantial amount of detail that is found in the standard representations of those abstractions.

Pitfalls in API design. An API may be *too hard to implement*, implying implementations that are difficult or impossible to develop; or *too hard to use*, creating client code that is more complicated than without the API. An API might be *too narrow*, omitting methods that clients need; or *too wide*, including a large number of methods not needed by any client. An API may be *too general*, providing no useful abstractions; or *too specific*, providing abstractions so detailed or so diffuse as to be useless. These considerations are sometimes summarized in yet another motto: *provide to clients the methods they need and no others.*

WHEN YOU FIRST STARTED PROGRAMMING, YOU typed in `HelloWorld.java` without understanding much about it except the effect that it produced. From that starting point, you learned to program by mimicking the code in the book and eventually developing your own code to solve various problems. You are at a similar point with API design. There are many APIs available in the book, on the booksite, and in online Java documentation that you can study and use, to gain confidence in designing and developing APIs of your own.

Encapsulation.   The process of separating clients from implementations by hiding information is known as *encapsulation*. Details of the implementation are kept hidden from clients, and implementations have no way of knowing details of client code, which may even be created in the future.

As you may have surmised, we have been practicing encapsulation in our data type implementations. In SECTION 3.1, we started with the mantra *you do not need to know how a data type is implemented in order to use it*. This statement describes one of the prime benefits of encapsulation. We consider it to be so important that we have not described to you any other way of building a data type. Now, we describe our three primary reasons for doing so in more detail. We use encapsulation:
  • To enable modular programming
  • To facilitate debugging
  • To clarify program code
These reasons are tied together (well-designed modular code is easier to debug and understand than code based entirely on primitive types in long programs).

Modular programming.   The programming style that we have been developing since learning functions in CHAPTER 2 has been predicated on the idea of breaking large programs into small modules that can be developed and debugged independently. This approach improves the resiliency of our software by limiting and localizing the effects of making changes, and it promotes code reuse by making it possible to substitute new implementations of a data type to improve performance, accuracy, or memory footprint. The same idea works in many settings. We often reap the benefits of encapsulation when we use system libraries. New versions of the Java system often include new implementations of various data types or static method libraries, but *the APIs do not change*. There is strong and constant motivation to improve data-type implementations because *all* clients can potentially benefit from an improved implementation. The key to success in modular programming is to maintain *independence* among modules. We do so by insisting on the API being the *only* point of dependence between client and implementation. *You do not need to know how a data type is implemented in order to use it.* The flip side of this mantra is that a data-type implementation code can assume that the client knows nothing but the API.

Example.   For example, consider Complex (PROGRAM 3.3.1). It has the same name and API as PROGRAM 3.2.6, but uses a different representation for the complex num-

Program 3.3.1   *Complex numbers (alternate)*

```java
public class Complex
{
    private final double r;
    private final double theta;

    public Complex(double re, double im)
    {
        r = Math.sqrt(re*re + im*im);
        theta = Math.atan2(im, re);
    }

    public Complex plus(Complex b)
    {  // Return the sum of this number and b.
        double real = re() + b.re();
        double imag = im() + b.im();
        return new Complex(real, imag);
    }

    public Complex times(Complex b)
    {  // Return the product of this number and b.
        double radius = r * b.r;
        double angle  = theta + b.theta;
        // See Q & A.
    }

    public double abs()
    {  return r;  }

    public double re()  { return r * Math.cos(theta); }
    public double im()  { return r * Math.sin(theta); }

    public String toString()
    {  return re() + " + " + im() + "i";  }

    public static void main(String[] args)
    {
        Complex z0 = new Complex(1.0, 1.0);
        Complex z = z0;
        z = z.times(z).plus(z0);
        z = z.times(z).plus(z0);
        StdOut.println(z);
    }
}
```

r	radius
theta	angle

Polar representation

This data type implements the same API as Program 3.2.5. It uses the same instance methods but different instance variables. Since the instance variables are private, *this program might be used in place of Program 3.2.5 without changing any client code.*

```
% java Complex
-7.0 + 7.0i
```

bers. PROGRAM 3.2.6 uses the *Cartesian* representation, where instance variables x and y represent a complex number $x + iy$. PROGRAM 3.3.1 uses the *polar* representation, where instance variables r and theta represent a complex number in the form $r(\cos \theta + i \sin \theta)$. The polar representation is of interest because certain operations on complex number are easier to perform in the polar representation. Addition and subtraction are easier in the Cartesian representation; multiplication and division are easier in the polar representation. As you will learn in SECTION 4.1, it is often the case that performance differences are dramatic. The idea of encapsulation is that we can substitute one of these programs for the other (for whatever reason) *without changing client code*. The

Polar coordinates

choice between the two implementations depends on the client. Indeed, in principle, the *only* difference to the client should be in different performance properties. This capability is of critical importance for many reasons. One of the most important is that it allows us to improve software constantly: when we develop a better way to implement a data type, all of its clients can benefit. You take advantage of this property every time you install a new version of a software system, including Java itself.

Private. Java's language support for enforcing encapsulation is the private visibility modifier. When you declare a variable to be private, you are making it impossible for any client (code in another module) to directly access the instance variable (or method) that is the subject of the modifier. Clients can only access the API through the public methods and constructors (the API). Accordingly, you can modify the implementation of private methods (or use different private instance variables) with certain knowledge that no client will be directly affected. Java does not *require* that all instance variables be private, but we insist on this convention in the programs in this book. For example, if the instance variable re and im in Complex (PROGRAM 3.2.6) were public, then a client could write code that directly accesses them. If z refers to a Complex object, z.re and z.im refer to those values. But any client code that does so becomes completely dependent on that implementation, violating a basic precept of encapsulation. A switch to a different implementation, such as the one in PROGRAM 3.3.1, would render that code useless. To protect ourselves against such situations, we always make instance variables private; there is no good reason to make them public. Next, we examine some ramifications of this convention.

Planning for the future. There have been numerous examples of important applications where significant expense can be directly traced to programmers not encapsulating their data types.

- *Zip codes.* In 1963, The United States Postal Service (USPS) began using a five-digit zip code to improve the sorting and delivery of mail. Programmers wrote software that assumed that these codes would remain at five digits forever, and represented them in their programs using a single 32-bit integer. In 1983, the USPS introduced an expanded zip code called ZIP+4, which consists of the original five-digit zip code plus four extra digits.

- *IPv4 vs. IPv6.* The Internet Protocol (IP) is a standard used by electronic devices to exchange data over the internet. Each device is assigned a unique integer or address. IPv4 uses 32-bit addresses and supports about 4.3 billion addresses. Due to explosive growth of the internet, a new version, IPv6, uses 128-bit addresses and supports 2^{128} addresses.

- *Vehicle identification numbers.* The 17-character naming scheme for vehicles known as the Vehicle Identification Number (VIN) that was established in 1981 describes the make, model, year, and other attributes of cars, trucks, buses, and other vehicles in the United States. But automakers expect to run out of numbers by 2010. Either the length of the VIN must be increased, or existing VINs must be reused.

In each of these cases, a necessary change to the internal representation means that a large amount of client code that depends on a current standard (because the data type is not encapsulated) will simply not function as intended. The estimated costs for the changes in each of these cases runs to hundreds of millions of dollars! That is a huge cost for failing to encapsulate a single number. These predicaments might seem distant to you, but you can be sure that every individual programmer (that's you) who does not take advantage of the protection available through encapsulation risks losing significant amounts of time and effort fixing broken code when conventions change. Our convention to define *all* of our instance variables with the private access modifier provides some protection against such problems. If you adopt this convention when implementing a data type for a zip code, IP address, VIN, or whatever, you can change the representation without affecting clients. The *data-type implementation* knows the data representation, and the *object* holds the data; the *client* holds only a reference to the object and does not know the details.

Limiting the potential for error. Encapsulation also helps programmers ensure that their code operates as intended. As an example, we consider yet another horror story: In the 2000 presidential election, Al Gore received *negative* 16,022 votes on an electronic voting machine in Volusia County, Florida. The counter variable was not properly encapsulated in the voting machine software! To understand the problem, consider Counter (PROGRAM 3.3.2), which implements a simple counter according to the following API:

```
public class Counter
```

	Counter(String id, int max)	*create a counter, initialized to* 0
void	increment()	*increment the counter unless its value is* max
int	value()	*return the value of the counter*
String	toString()	*string representation*

API for a counter (*see* PROGRAM 3.3.2)

This abstraction is useful in many contexts, including, for example, an electronic voting machine. It encapsulates a single integer and ensures that the only operation that can be performed on the integer is *increment by one*. Therefore, it can never go negative. The goal of data abstraction is to *restrict* the operations on the data. It also *isolates* operations on the data. For example, we could add a new implementation with a logging capability so that increment() saves a timestamp for each vote or some other information that can be used for consistency checks. But without the private modifier, there could be client code like the following somewhere in the voting machine:

```
Counter c = new Counter("Volusia", VOTERS_IN_VOLUSIA_COUNTY);
c.count = -16022;
```

With private, code like this will not compile; without it, Gore's vote count was negative. Using encapsulation is far from a complete solution to the voting security problem, but it is a good start.

Code clarity. Precisely specifying a data type is good design also because it leads to client code that can more clearly express its computation. You have seen many examples of such client code in SECTIONS 3.1 and 3.2, and we already mentioned this issue in our discussion of Histogram (PROGRAM 3.2.3). Clients of that program are

Program 3.3.2   Counter

```java
public class Counter
{
   private final String name;
   private final int maxCount;
   private int count;

   public Counter(String id, int max)
   {  name = id;  maxCount = max;  }

   public void increment()
   {  if (count < maxCount) count++;  }

   public int value()
   {  return count;  }

   public String toString()
   {  return name + ": " + count;  }

   public static void main(String[] args)
   {
     int N = Integer.parseInt(args[0]);
     int T = Integer.parseInt(args[1]);
     Counter[] hits = new Counter[N];
     for (int i = 0; i < N; i++)
        hits[i] = new Counter(i + "", T);

     for (int t = 0; t < T; t++)
        hits[StdRandom.uniform(N)].increment();
     for (int i = 0; i < N; i++)
        StdOut.println(hits[i]);
   }
}
```

name	counter name
maxCount	maximum value
count	value

This class encapsulates a simple integer counter, assigning it a string name and initializing it to 0 (Java's default initialization), incrementing it each time the client calls increment(), reporting the value when the client calls value(), and creating a string with its name and value in toString().

```
% java Counter 6 600000
0: 100684
1: 99258
2: 100119
3: 100054
4: 99844
5: 100037
```

more clear than without it because calls on the instance method addDataPoint() clearly identify points of interest in the client. One key to good design is to observe that code written with the proper abstractions can be nearly self-documenting. Some aficionados of object-oriented programming might argue that Histogram itself would be easier to understand if it were to use Counter (see EXERCISE 3.3.5), but that point is perhaps debatable.

WE HAVE STRESSED THE BENEFITS OF encapsulation throughout this book. We summarize them again here, in the context of designing data types. Encapsulation enables modular programming, allowing us to:

- Independently develop of client and implementation code
- Substitute improved implementations without affecting clients
- Support programs not yet written (any client can write to the API)

Encapsulation also isolates data-type operations, which leads to the possibility of:

- Adding consistency checks and other debugging tools in implementations
- Clarifying client code

A properly implemented data type (encapsulated) extends the Java language, allowing any client program to make use of it.

Immutability.   An *immutable* data type, such as a Java `String`, has the property that the value of an object never changes once constructed. By contrast, a *mutable* data type, such as a Java array, manipulates object values that are intended to change. Of the data types considered in this chapter, `Charge`, `Color`, `Stopwatch`, and `Complex` are all immutable, and `Picture`, `Histogram`, `Turtle`, `StockAccount`, and `Counter` are all mutable. Whether to make a data type immutable is an important design decision and depends on the application at hand.

Immutable types.   The purpose of many data types is to encapsulate values that do not change so that they behave in the same way as primitive types. For example, a programmer implementing a `Complex` client might reasonably expect to write the code $z = z0$ for two `Complex` variables, in the same way as for `double` or `int` values. But if `Complex` were mutable and the value of z were

to change *after* the assignment $z = z0$, then the value of $z0$ would *also* change (they are both references to the same object)! This unexpected result, known as an *aliasing* bug, comes as a surprise to many newcomers to object-oriented programming. One very important reason to implement immutable types is that we can use immutable objects in assignment statements and as arguments and return values from functions without having to worry about their values changing.

mutable	immutable
Picture	Charge
Histogram	Color
Turtle	Stopwatch
StockAccount	Complex
Counter	String
Java arrays	primitive types

Mutable types.   For many data types, the very purpose of the abstraction is to encapsulate values as they change. `Turtle` (PROGRAM 3.2.4) is a prime example. Our reason for using `Turtle` is to relieve client programs of the responsibility of tracking the changing values. Similarly, `Picture`, `Histogram`, `StockAccount`, `Counter`, and Java arrays are all types where we expect values to change. When we pass a `Turtle` as an argument to a method, as in Koch, we expect the values of the instance variables to change.

Arrays and strings.   You have already encountered this distinction as a client programmer, when using Java arrays (mutable) and Java's `String` data type (immutable). When you pass a `String` to a method, you do not need to worry about that method changing the sequence of characters in the `String`, but when you pass an array to a method, the method is free to change the elements of the array. `String` objects are immutable because we generally do *not* want `String` values to change, and Java arrays are mutable because we generally *do* want array values to change. There are also situations where we want to have mutable strings (that is the purpose of Java's `StringBuilder` class) and where we want to have immutable arrays (that is the purpose of the `Vector` class that we consider later in this section).

Advantages of immutability. Generally, immutable types are easier to use and harder to misuse because the scope of code that can change their values is far smaller than for mutable types. It is easier to debug code that uses immutable types because it is easier to guarantee that variables in the client code that uses them remain in a consistent state. When using mutable types, you must always be concerned about where and when their values change.

```
Complex z0;
z0 = new Complex(1.0, 1.0);
Complex z = z0;
z = z.times(z).plus(z0);
```

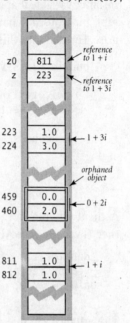

Cost of immutability. The downside of immutability is that *a new object must be created for every value.* For example, the expression `z = z.times(z).plus(z0)` involves creating a new object (the return value of `z.times(z)`, then using that object to invoke `plus()`, but never saving a reference to it. A program such as `Mandelbrot` (PROGRAM 3.2.7) might create a large number of such intermediate orphans. However, this expense is normally manageable because Java garbage collectors are typically optimized for such situations. Also, as in the case of `Mandelbrot`, when the point of the calculation is to create a large number of values, we expect to pay the cost of representing them. `Mandelbrot` also creates a large number of (immutable) `Color` objects.

An intermediate orphan

Final. Java's language support for helping to enforce immutability is the `final` modifier. When you declare a variable to be `final`, you are promising to assign it a value only once, either in an initializer or in the constructor. Code that could modify the value of a `final` variable leads to a compile-time error. In our code, we always use the modifier `final` with instance variables whose values never change. This policy serves as documentation that the value does not change, prevents accidental changes, and makes programs easier to debug. For example, you do not have to include a `final` value in a trace, since you know that its value never changes.

Reference types. Unfortunately, `final` guarantees immutability only when instance variables are primitive types, not reference types. If an instance variable of a reference type has the `final` modifier, the value of that instance variable (the reference to an object) will never change—it will always refer to the same object. However, the value of the object itself *can* change. For example, if you have a `final` instance variable that is an array, you cannot change the array (to change its length, say), but you *can* change the individual array elements. Thus, aliasing bugs can arise. For example, this code does *not* implement an immutable type:

```
public class Vector
{
    private final double[] coords;
    public Vector(double[] a)
    {
        coords = a;
    }
    ...
}
```

A client program could create a `Vector` by specifying the entries in an array, and then (bypassing the API) change the elements of the `Vector` after construction:

```
double[] a = { 3.0, 4.0 };
Vector vector = new Vector(a);
a[0] = 17.0;  // Bypasses the public API.
```

The instance variable `coords[]` is `private` and `final`, but `Vector` is mutable because the *client* holds the data, not the *implementation*. To ensure immutability of a data type that includes an instance variable of a mutable type, we need to make a local copy, known as a *defensive copy*. Next, we consider such an implementation.

IMMUTABILITY NEEDS TO BE TAKEN INTO account in any data-type design. Ideally, whether a data type is immutable should be specified in the API, so that clients know that object values will not change. Implementing an immutable type can be a burden in the presence of reference types. For complex types, making the copy is one challenge; ensuring that none of the instance methods change values is another.

Example: spatial vectors   To illustrate these ideas in the context of a useful mathematical abstraction, we now consider a *vector* data type. Like complex numbers, the basic definition of the vector abstraction is familiar because it has played a central role in applied mathematics for over 100 years. The field of mathematics known as *linear algebra* is concerned with properties of vectors. Linear algebra is a rich and successful theory with numerous applications, and plays an important role in all fields of social and natural science. Full treatment of linear algebra is certainly beyond the scope of this book, but several important applications are based upon elementary and familiar calculations, so we touch upon vectors and linear algebra throughout the book (for example, the random surfer example in SECTION 1.6 is based on linear algebra). Accordingly, it is worthwhile to encapsulate such an abstraction in a data type.

A *spatial vector* is an abstract entity that has a *magnitude* and a *direction*. Spatial vectors provide a natural way to describe properties of the physical world, such as force, velocity, momentum, or acceleration. One standard way to specify a vector is as an arrow from the origin to a point in a Cartesian coordinate system: the direction is the ray from the origin to the point and the magnitude is the length of the arrow (distance from the origin to the point). To specify the vector it suffices to specify the point.

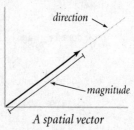

A spatial vector

This concept extends to any number of dimensions: an ordered list of N real numbers (the coordinates of an N-dimensional point) suffices to specify a vector in N-dimensional space. By convention, we use a boldface letter to refer to a vector and numbers or indexed variable names (the same letter in italics) separated by commas within square brackets to denote its value. For example, we might use $\mathbf{x}$ to denote $(x_0, x_1, \ldots, x_{N-1})$ and $\mathbf{y}$ to denote $(y_0, y_1, \ldots, y_{N-1})$.

API.   The basic operations on vectors are to add two vectors, multiply a vector by a scalar (real number), compute the dot product of two vectors, and compute the magnitude and direction, as follows:

- *Addition*: $\mathbf{x} + \mathbf{y} = (x_0 + y_0, x_1 + y_1, \ldots, x_{N-1} + y_{N-1})$
- *Scalar product*: $t\mathbf{x} = (tx_0, tx_1, \ldots, tx_{N-1})$
- *Dot product*: $\mathbf{x} \cdot \mathbf{y} = x_0 y_0 + x_1 y_1 + \ldots + x_{N-1} y_{N-1}$
- *Magnitude*: $|\mathbf{x}| = (x_0{}^2 + x_1{}^2 + \ldots + x_{N-1}{}^2)^{1/2}$
- *Direction*: $\mathbf{x} / |\mathbf{x}| = (x_0 / |\mathbf{x}|, x_1 / |\mathbf{x}|, \ldots, x_{N-1} / |\mathbf{x}|)$

The result of addition, scalar product, and the direction are vectors, but the magnitude and the dot product are scalar quantities (`double` values). For example, if $\mathbf{x} = (0, 3, 4, 0)$, and $\mathbf{y} = (0, -3, 1, -4)$, then $\mathbf{x} + \mathbf{y} = (0, 0, 5, -4)$, $3\mathbf{x} = (0, 9, 12, 0)$, $\mathbf{x} \cdot \mathbf{y} = -5$, $|\mathbf{x}| = 5$, and $\mathbf{x} / |\mathbf{x}| = (0, .6, .8, 0)$. The direction vector is a *unit vector*: its magnitude is 1. These definitions lead immediately to an API:

`public class Vector`

	`Vector(double[] a)`	*create a vector with the given Cartesian coordinates*
`Vector`	`plus(Vector b)`	*sum of this vector and* b
`Vector`	`minus(Vector b)`	*difference of this vector and* b
`Vector`	`times(double t)`	*scalar product of this vector and* t
`double`	`dot(Vector b)`	*dot product of this vector and* b
`double`	`magnitude()`	*magnitude of this vector*
`Vector`	`direction()`	*unit vector with same direction as this vector*
`double`	`cartesian(int i)`	i*th cartesian coordinate of this vector*
`String`	`toString()`	*string representation*

API for a spatial vector (see PROGRAM 3.3.3)

As with `Complex`, this API does not explicitly specify that this type is immutable, knowing that client programmers (who are likely to be thinking in terms of the mathematical abstraction) certainly expect that, and perhaps we would rather not explain to them that we are going to protect them from aliasing bugs!

Representation. As usual, our first choice in developing an implementation is to choose a representation for the data. Using an array to hold the Cartesian coordinates provided in the constructor is a clear choice, but not the only reasonable choice. Indeed, one of the basic tenets of linear algebra is that other sets of N vectors can be used as the basis for a coordinate system: any vector can be expressed as a linear combination of a set of N vectors, satisfying a certain condition known as *linear independence*. This ability to change coordinate systems aligns nicely with encapsulation. Most clients do not need to know about the representation at all and can work with `Vector` objects and operations. If warranted, the implementation can change the coordinate system without affecting client code.

Program 3.3.3 *Spatial vectors*

```
public class Vector
{
    private final double[] coords;          coords[] | Cartesian coordinates

    public Vector(double[] a)
    {   // Make a defensive copy to ensure immutability.
        coords = new double[a.length];
        for (int i = 0; i < a.length; i++)
            coords[i] = a[i];
    }

    public Vector plus(Vector b)
    {   // Sum of this vector and b.
        double[] c = new double[coords.length];
        for (int i = 0; i < coords.length; i++)
            c[i] = coords[i] + b.coords[i];
        return new Vector(c);
    }

    public Vector times(double t)
    {   // Product of this vector and b.
        double[] c = new double[coords.length];
        for (int i = 0; i < coords.length; i++)
            c[i] = t * coords[i];
        return new Vector(c);
    }

    public double dot(Vector b)
    {   // Dot product of this vector and b.
        double sum = 0.0;
        for (int i = 0; i < coords.length; i++)
            sum = sum + (coords[i] * b.coords[i]);
        return sum;
    }

    public double magnitude()
    {   return Math.sqrt(this.dot(this));  }

    public Vector direction()
    {   return this.times(1/this.magnitude());  }

    public double cartesian(int i)
    {   return coords[i];  }
}
```

This implementation encapsulates the mathematical spatial-vector abstraction. in an immutable Java data type. Document *(Program 3.3.4) and* Body *(Program 3.4.2) are typical clients.*

Implementation. Given the representation, the code that implements all of these operations (Vector, in PROGRAM 3.3.3) is straightforward. Two of the methods (minus() and toString()) are left for exercises, as is the test client. The constructor makes a defensive copy of the client array and none of the methods assign values to the copy, so that Vector objects are immutable. The cartesian() method is easy to implement in our Cartesian coordinate representation: return the ith coordinate in the array. It actually implements a mathematical function that is defined for any Vector representation: the geometric projection onto the ith Cartesian axis.

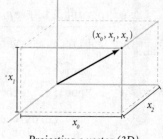

Projecting a vector (3D)

The this reference. The magnitude() and direction() methods in Vector make use of the name this. Java provides the this keyword to give us a way to refer within the code of an instance method to the object whose name was used to invoke this method. You can use this in code in the same way you use any other name. Some Java programmers *always* use this to refer to instance variables. Their scope is the whole class, and this policy is easy to defend because it documents references to instance variables. However, it does result in a surfeit of this keywords, so we take the opposite tack and use this sparingly in our code.

WHY GO TO THE TROUBLE OF using a Vector data type when all of the operations are so easily implemented with arrays? By now the answer to this question should be obvious to you: to enable modular programming, facilitate debugging, and clarify code. The array is a low-level Java mechanism that admits all kinds of operations. By restricting ourselves to just the operations in the Vector API (which are the only ones that we need, for many clients), we simplify the process of designing, implementing, and maintaining our programs. Because the type is immutable, we can use it as we use primitive types. For example, when we pass a Vector to a method, we are assured its value will not change, but we do not have that assurance with an array. After you have seen several more examples of object-oriented programming, we will discuss some more nuances in support of the assertion that it simplifies design, implementation, and maintenance. In the case of Vector, writing programs that use Vector and well-defined Vector operations is an easy and natural way to take advantage of the extensive amount of mathematical knowledge that has been developed around this abstract concept.

Inheritance Java provides language support for defining relationships among objects, known as *inheritance*. Software developers use these mechanisms widely, so you will study them in detail if you take a course in software engineering. Generally, effective use of such mechanisms is beyond the scope of this book, but we briefly describe them here because there are a few situations where you may encounter them.

Interfaces. Interfaces provide a mechanism for specifying a relationship between otherwise unrelated classes, by specifying a set of common methods that each implementing class must contain. We refer to this arrangement as *interface inheritance* because an implementing class *inherits* methods that are not otherwise in its API through the interface. This arrangement allows us to write client programs that can manipulate objects of varying types, by invoking methods in the interface. As with most new programming concepts, it is a bit confusing at first, but will make sense to you after you have seen a few examples.

Comparable. One interface that you are likely to encounter is Java's `Comparable` interface. The interface associates a *natural order* for values within a data type, using a method named `compareTo()`, as described in the following API:

```
public interface Comparable<Key>
```

    `int compareTo(Key b)`   *compare this object with* b *for order*

API for Java's Comparable interface

The `<Key>` notation, which we will introduce in SECTION 4.3, ensures that the two objects being compared have the same type. Assuming a and b are objects of the same type, `a.compareTo(b)` must return:
- A negative integer if a is *less than* b
- A positive integer if if a *greater than* b
- Zero if a is *equal to* b

Additionally, the `compareTo()` method must be consistent: for example, if a is less than b, then b must be greater than a. A class that implements the `Comparable` interface—such as `String`, `Integer`, or `Double`—promises to include a `compareTo()` method according to these rules. As expected, the natural order for strings is alphabetical and for integers is ascending.

To illustrate the utility of having such an interface, we start by considering a sort filter for String objects. The following code takes an integer N from the command-line, reads in N strings from standard input, sorts them, and prints the strings on standard output in alphabetical order.

```java
import java.util.Arrays;

public class SortClient
{
    public static void main(String[] args)
    {
        int N = Integer.parseInt(args[0]);
        String[] names = new String[N];
        for (int i = 0; i < N; i++)
            names[i] = StdIn.readString();
        Arrays.sort(names);
        for (int i = 0; i < N; i++)
            StdOut.println(names[i]);
    }
}
```

We will examine sorting in detail in SECTION 4.2, so for the moment, we use a static method Arrays.sort() from Java's java.util library. Now, if we replace the array input with the three lines

```java
Integer[] names = new Integer[N];
for (int i = 0; i < N; i++)
    names[i] = StdIn.readInt();
```

SortClient sorts Integer values from standard input. You might speculate that Arrays.sort() has overloaded implementations, one for String and one for Integer. But this is *not* the case because Arrays.sort() must be able to sort an array of *any* type that implements the Comparable interface (even a data type not contemplated when writing the sorting method). To do so, the code in Arrays. sort() declares variables of type Comparable—such variables may store values of type String, Integer, Double, or of *any* type that implements the Comparable interface. When you invoke the compareTo() method of such a variable, Java knows which compareTo() method to call, because it knows the type of the invoking object. This powerful programming mechanism is known as *polymorphism* or *dynamic dispatch*.

To make a class implement the Comparable interface, include the phrase imple-ments Comparable after the class definition, and then add a compareTo() method. For example, modify Counter (PROGRAM 3.3.2) as follows:

```
public Counter implements Comparable<Counter>
{
  ...
   public int compareTo(Counter b)
   {
     if      (count < b.count) return -1;
     else if (count > b.count) return +1;
     else                      return  0;
   }
  ...
}
```

Since you are implementing compareTo(), you have the flexibility to specify any sort order whatever. For example, you might create a version of Counter to allow clients to sort Counter values in *decreasing* order (perhaps for a voting application), by changing the compareTo() method as follows:

```
public int compareTo(Counter b)
{
  if      (count < b.count) return +1;
  else if (count > b.count) return -1;
  else                      return  0;
}
```

For another example, if you were to modify StockAccount as follows:

```
public class StockAccount implements Comparable<StockAccount>
{
  ...
   public int compareTo(StockAccount b)
   {
      return name.compareTo(b.name);
   }
  ...
}
```

you could then sort an array of StockAccount values by account name with Ar-rays.sort(). (Note that this compareTo() implementation for StockAccount uses Java's `compareTo()` method for `String`.) This ability to arrange to write a client to sort any type of data is a persuasive example of interface inheritance.

Computing with functions. Often, particularly in scientific computing, we want to compute with *functions*: we want to compute integrals and derivatives, find roots, and so forth. In some programming languages, known as *functional programming languages*, this desire aligns with the underlying design of the language, which uses computing with functions to substantially simplify client code. Unfortunately, *methods are not first-class objects in Java.* As an example, consider the problem of estimating the integral of a positive function (area under the curve) in an interval (a, b).

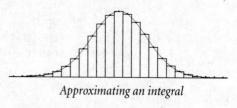

Approximating an integral

This computation is known as *quadrature* or *numerical integration*. One simple method for estimating the integral is the *rectangle rule*: compute the total area of N equally-spaced rectangles under the curve. To implement this rule, we might try to write the following code to approximate the value of an integral by:

```java
public double integrate(double f(double x),
                                double a, double b, int N)
{
    double delta = (a - b) / N;
    double sum = 0.0;
    for (int i = 0; i < N; i++)
        sum += delta * f(a + delta * (i + 0.5));
}
```

Such a method would enable client code such as this:

```java
integrate(Gaussian.phi(), a, b, N)
```

Unfortunately, *this code is not legal in Java.* You cannot pass methods as arguments. We can get around this restriction by defining an interface for functions and using that interface to implement `integrate()`. You can find that solution on the book-site, along with many examples of methods and classes that involve computing with functions in Java, which will be of interest if you plan to take future courses in scientific computing.

Event-based programming. Another powerful example of the value of interface inheritance is its use in *event-based programming*. In a familiar setting, consider the problem of extending Draw to respond to user input such as mouse clicks and keystrokes. One way to do so is to define an interface to specify which methods the draw package should call when user input happens. The descriptive term *callback* is sometimes used to describe a call from a method in one class to a method in another class through an interface. You can find on the booksite an example interface DrawListener and information on how to write code to respond to user mouse clicks and keystrokes within Draw.java. You will find it easy to write code that creates a Draw object and includes a method that the Draw method can invoke (*callback* your code) to tell your method the character typed on a user keystroke event or the mouse position on a mouse click. Writing interactive code is fun but challenging because you have to plan for all possible user input actions.

Subtyping. Another approach to enabling code reuse is known as *subtyping*. It is a powerful technique that enables a programmer to change the behavior of a class and add functionality without rewriting the entire class from scratch. The idea is to define a new class (*subclass*, or *derived class*) that *inherits* instance variables and instance methods from another class (*superclass*, or *base class*). The subclass contains more methods than the superclass. Subtyping is widely used by systems programmers to build so-called *extensible* libraries. The idea is that one programmer (even you) can add methods to a library built by another programmer (or, perhaps, a team of systems programmers), effectively reusing the code in a potentially huge library. This approach is widely used, particularly in the development of user interfaces, so that the large amount of code required to provide all the facilities that users expect (drop-down menus, cut-and-paste, access to files, and so forth) can be reused. The use of subtyping is controversial among systems programmers (its advantages over interface inheritance are debatable), and we do not use it in this book, because it generally works against encapsulation. Subtyping makes modular programming more difficult for two reasons. First, any change in the superclass affects all subclasses. The subclass cannot be developed *independently* of the superclass; indeed, it is *completely dependent* on the superclass. This problem is known as the *fragile base class* problem. Second, the subclass code, having access to instance variables, can subvert the intention of the superclass code. For example, the designer of a class such as Vector may have taken great care to make the Vector immutable, but a subclass, with full access to the instance variables, can just change them. However, certain vestiges of the approach are built into Java and therefore unavoidable. Specifically, every class is a subtype of Java's Object class. This structure enables implementation of the "convention" that every class includes an implementations of toString(), equals(), hashCode() (a method that we will encounter later in this section and in CHAPTER 4), and several other methods. Every class inherits these methods from Object through subtyping.

Application: data mining   To illustrate some of the concepts discussed in this section in the context of an application, we next consider a software technology that is proving important in addressing the daunting challenges of *data mining*, a term that is widely used to describe the process of searching through the massive amounts of information now accessible to every user on the web (not to mention our own computers). This technology can serve as the basis for dramatic improvements in the quality of web search results, for multimedia information retrieval, for biomedical databases, for plagiarism detection, for research in genomics, for improved scholarship in many fields, for innovation in commercial applications, for learning the plans of evildoers, and for many other purposes. Accordingly, there is intense interest and extensive ongoing research on data mining.

You have direct access to thousands of files on your computer and indirect access to billions of files on the web. As you know, these files are remarkably diverse: there are commercial web pages, music and video, email, program code, and all sorts of other information. For simplicity, we will restrict attention to *text* documents (though the method we will consider applies to pictures, music, and all sorts of other files as well). Even with this restriction, there is remarkable diversity in the types of documents. For reference, you can find these documents on the booksite: Our interest is in finding efficient ways to search through the files using their *content* to characterize documents. One fruitful approach to this problem is to as-

file name	description	sample text
Constitution.txt	*legal document*	... of both Houses shall be determined by ...
TomSawyer.txt	*American novel*	..."Say, Tom, let ME whitewash a little." ...
HuckFinn.txt	*American novel*	...was feeling pretty good after breakfast...
Prejudice.txt	*English novel*	... dared not even mention that gentleman....
Picture.java	*Java code*	...String suffix = filename.substring(file...
DJIA.csv	*financial data*	...01-Oct-28,239.43,242.46,3500000,240.01 ...
Amazon.html	*web page source*	...<table width="100%" border="0" cellspac...
ACTG.txt	*virus genome*	...GTATGGAGCAGCAGACGCGCTACTTCGAGCGGAGGCATA...

Some text documents

sociate with each document a vector known as a *profile*, which is a function of its content. The basic idea is that the profile should characterize a document, so that documents that are different have profiles that are different and documents that are similar have profiles that are similar. You probably are not surprised to learn that this approach can enable us to distinguish among a novel, a Java program, and a genome, but you might be surprised to learn that content searches can tell the difference between novels written by different authors and can be effective as the basis for many other subtle search criteria.

To start, we need an abstraction for documents. What is a document? What operations do we want to perform on documents? The answers to these questions inform our design and therefore, ultimately, the code that we write. For the purposes of data mining, it is clear that the answer to the first question is that a document is defined by an input stream. The answer to the second question is that we need to be able to compute a number (for example, a `double` value) to measure the similarity between a document and any other document. These considerations lead to the following API.

```
public class Document
```

	Document(String name, int k, int d)	
double	simTo(Document doc)	*similarity measure between this document and* doc
String	name()	*name of this document*

API for documents (see PROGRAM *3.3.4)*

The arguments of the constructor are a file or website name (for use by `In`) and two integers that control the quality of the search. Clients can use `simTo()` to determine the extent of similarity between this `Document` and any other `Document` on a scale of 0 (not similar) to 1 (similar). This simple data type provides a good separation between implementing a similarity measure and implementing clients that use the measure to search among documents.

Computing profiles Computing the profile is the first challenge. Our first choice is to use `Vector` to represent a document's profile. But what information should go into computing the profile and how do we compute the value of the `Vector` profile of a `Document` (in the constructor)? Many different approaches have been studied, and researchers are still actively seeking efficient and effective algorithms for this

Program 3.3.4   Document

```
public class Document
{
    private final String id;
    private final Vector profile;

    public Document(String name, int k, int d)
    {
        id = name;
        String s = (new In(name)).readAll();
        int N = s.length();
        double[] freq = new double[d];
        for (int i = 0; i < N-k; i++)
        {
            int h = s.substring(i, i+k).hashCode();
            freq[Math.abs(h % d)] += 1;
        }
        profile = (new Vector(freq)).direction();
    }

    public double simTo(Document doc)
    {  return profile.dot(doc.profile);  }

    public String name()
    {  return id;  }

    public static void main(String[] args)
    {
        String name = args[0];
        int k = Integer.parseInt(args[1]);
        int d = Integer.parseInt(args[2]);
        Document doc = new Document(name, k, d);
        StdOut.println(doc.profile);
    }
}
```

id	*file name or URL*
profile	*unit vector*

name	*document name*
k	*length of gram*
d	*dimension*
s	*entire document*
N	*document length*
freq[]	*hash frequencies*
h	*hash for k-gram*

This Vector *client creates a unit vector from a document's k-grams that clients can use to measure its similarity with other documents (see text).*

```
% more genomeA.txt
ATAGATGCATAGCGCATAGC
% java Document genomeA.txt 2 16
[ 0 0 0.51 0.39 0.39 0 0 0 .13 0.39 0 0 0.13 0.13 0.51 0 0 ]
```

task. Our implementation Document (PROGRAM 3.3.4) uses a simple *frequency count* approach. The constructor has two arguments, an integer k and a vector dimension d. It scans the document and examines all of the k-*grams* in the document: the substrings of length k starting at each position. In its simplest form, the profile is a vector that gives the relative frequency of occurrence of the k-grams in the string: an entry for each possible k-gram giving the number of k-grams in the content that have that value. For example, suppose that we use $k = 2$ in genomic data, with $d = 16$ (there are 4 possible character values and therefore 16 possible 2-grams). The 2-gram AT occurs 4 times in the string ATAGATGCATAGCGCATAGC, so, for example, the vector entry corresponding to AT would be 4. To build the frequency vector, we need to be able to convert each of the k-grams into an integer between 0 and 15 (this integer function of a string is known as a *hash* value). For genomic data, this is an easy exercise (see EXERCISE 3.3.26). Then, we can compute an array to build the frequency vector in one scan through the text, incrementing the array entry corresponding to each k-gram encountered. It would seem that we lose information by disregarding the order of the k-grams, but the remarkable fact is that the information content of that order is lower than that of their frequency. A Markov model paradigm not dissimilar from the one that we studied for the random surfer in SECTION 1.6 can be used to take order into account— such models are effective, but much more work to implement. Encapsulating the computation in Document gives us the flexibility to experiment with various designs without needing to rewrite Document clients.

```
CTTTCGGTTT
GGAACCGAAG
CCGCGCGTCT
ATAGATGCAT TGTCTGCTGC
AGCGCATAGC AGCATCGTTC
```

2-gram	hash	count	unit	count	unit
AA	0	0	0	2	.137
AC	1	0	0	1	.069
AG	2	4	.508	1	.069
AT	3	3	.381	2	.137
CA	4	3	.381	3	.206
CC	5	0	0	2	.137
CG	6	0	0	4	.275
CT	7	1	.127	6	.412
GA	8	3	.381	0	0
GC	9	0	0	5	.343
GG	10	0	0	6	.412
GT	11	1	.127	4	.275
TA	12	1	.127	2	.137
TC	13	4	.508	6	.412
TG	14	0	0	4	.275
TT	15	0	0	2	.137

Profiling genomic data

Hashing. For ASCII text strings there are 128 different possible char values for each character, so there are 128^k possible k-grams, and the dimension d would have to be 128^k for the simple scheme just described. This number is prohibitively large even for moderately large k. For Unicode, with 65,536 characters, even 2-grams lead to huge vector profiles. To ameliorate this problem, we use *hashing*, a fundamental operation related to search algorithms that we consider in SECTION 4.4. Indeed, the problem of converting a string to an integer index is so important that it is built into Java. As just mentioned in our discussion of inheritance, all objects inherit from `Object` a method `hashCode()` that returns an `int` value. Given any string s, we compute `Math.abs(s.hashcode() % d)`. This value is an integer between 0 and $d-1$ that we can use as an index into an array to compute frequencies. The profile that we use is the *direction* of the vector defined by frequencies of these values for all k-grams in the document (the unit vector with the same direction).

Comparing profiles. The second challenge is to compute a similarity measure between two profiles. Again, there are many different ways to compare two vectors. Perhaps the simplest is to compute the Euclidean distance between them. Given vectors **x** and **y**, this distance is defined by:

$$|\mathbf{x} - \mathbf{y}| = ((x_0 - y_0)^2 + (x_1 - y_1)^2 + \ldots + (x_{d-1} - y_{d-1})^2)^{1/2}$$

You are familiar with this formula for $d = 2$ or $d = 3$. With `Vector`, the distance is easy to compute. If x and y are two `Vector` values, then `x.minus(y).magnitude()` is the Euclidean distance between them. If documents are similar, we expect their profiles to be similar and the distance between them to be low. Another widely used similarity measure, known as the *cosine similarity measure*, is even simpler: since our profiles are unit vectors with nonnegative coordinates, their *dot product*

```
% more docs.txt
Consititution.txt
TomSawyer.txt
HuckFinn.txt
Prejudice.txt
Picture.java
DJIA.csv
Amazon.html
ACTG.txt
```

$$\mathbf{x} \cdot \mathbf{y} = x_0 y_0 + x_1 y_1 + \ldots + x_{d-1} y_{d-1}$$

is a number between 0 and 1. Geometrically, this quantity is the cosine of the angle formed by the two vectors (see EXERCISE 3.3.12). The more similar the documents, the closer we expect this measure to be to 1.

Comparing all pairs. `CompareAll` (PROGRAM 3.3.5) is a simple and useful Document client that provides the information needed to solve the following problem: given a set of documents, find the two that are most similar. Since this specification is a bit subjective, `CompareAll` prints out the cosine similarity measure for all pairs of documents on an input list. For moderate-size k and d, the profiles do a remarkably good job of characterizing our sample set of documents. The results say not only that genomic data, financial data, Java code, and web source code are quite different from legal documents and novels, but also that *Tom Sawyer* and *Huckleberry*

Program 3.3.5   *Similarity detection*

```
public class CompareAll
{
  public static void main(String[] args)
  {
    int k = Integer.parseInt(args[0]);
    int d = Integer.parseInt(args[1]);
    int N = StdIn.readInt();
    Document[] a = new Document[N];
    for (int i = 0; i < N; i++)
      a[i] = new Document(StdIn.readString(), k, d);
    StdOut.print("     ");
    for (int j = 0; j < N; j++)
      StdOut.printf("    %.4s", a[j].name());
    StdOut.println();
    for (int i = 0; i < N; i++)
    {
      StdOut.printf("%.4s", a[i].name());
      for (int j = 0; j < N; j++)
        StdOut.printf("%8.2f", a[i].simTo(a[j]));
      StdOut.println();
    }
  }
}
```

k	length of gram
d	dimension
N	number of documents
a[]	all documents

This `Document` *client reads a document list from standard input, computes profiles based on k-gram frequencies for all the documents, and prints a matrix of similarity measures between all pairs of documents. It takes two arguments from the command line: the value of* k *and the dimension* d *of the profiles.*

```
% java CompareAll 5 10000 < docs.txt
       Cons   TomS   Huck   Prej   Pict   DJIA   Amaz   ACTG
Cons   1.00   0.66   0.60   0.64   0.17   0.18   0.21   0.11
TomS   0.66   1.00   0.93   0.88   0.10   0.24   0.18   0.14
Huck   0.60   0.93   1.00   0.82   0.07   0.23   0.16   0.12
Prej   0.64   0.88   0.82   1.00   0.10   0.25   0.19   0.15
Pict   0.17   0.10   0.07   0.10   1.00   0.05   0.37   0.03
DJIA   0.18   0.24   0.23   0.25   0.05   1.00   0.16   0.11
Amaz   0.21   0.18   0.16   0.19   0.37   0.16   1.00   0.07
ACTG   0.11   0.14   0.12   0.15   0.03   0.11   0.07   1.00
```

Finn are much more similar to each other than to *Pride and Prejudice*. A researcher in comparative literature could use this program to discover relationships between texts; a teacher could also use this program to detect plagiarism in a set of student submissions (indeed, many teachers *do* use such programs on a regular basis); or a biologist could use this program to discover relationships among genomes. You can find many documents on the booksite (or gather your own collection) to test the effectiveness of CompareAll for various parameter settings.

Searching for similar documents. Another natural Document client is one that uses profiles to search among a large number of documents to identify those that are similar to a given document. For example, web search engines uses clients of this type to present you with pages that are similar to those you have previously visited, online book merchants use clients of this type to recommend books that are similar to ones you have purchased, and social networking websites use clients of this type to identify people whose personal interests are similar to yours. Since In can take web addresses instead of file names, it is feasible to write a program that can surf the web, compute profiles, and return links to pages that have profiles that are similar to the one sought. We leave this client for a challenging exercise.

THIS SOLUTION IS JUST A SKETCH. Many sophisticated algorithms for efficiently computing profiles and comparing them are still being invented and studied by computer scientists. Our purpose here is to introduce you to this fundamental problem domain while at the same time illustrating the power of abstraction in addressing a computational challenge. Vectors are an essential mathematical abstraction, and we can build search solutions by developing *layers of abstraction*: Vector is built with the Java array, Document is built with Vector, and client code uses Document. As usual, we have spared you from a lengthy account of our many attempts to develop these APIs, but you can see that the data types are designed in response to the needs of the problem, with an eye toward the requirements of implementations. Identifying and implementing appropriate abstractions is the key to effective object-oriented programming. The power of abstraction—in mathematics, physical models, and in computer programs—pervades these examples. As you become fluent in developing data types to address your own computational challenges, your appreciation for this power will surely grow.

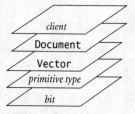

Layers of abstraction

Design-by-contract. To conclude, we briefly discuss Java language mechanisms that enable you to verify assumptions about your program *as it is running*. For example, if you have a data type that represents a particle, you might assert that its mass is positive and its speed is less than the speed of light. Or if you have a method to add two vectors of the same length, you might assert that the length of the resulting vector also has the same length.

Exceptions. An exception is a disruptive event that occurs while a program is running, often to signal an error. The action taken is known as *throwing an exception*. We have already encountered exceptions thrown by Java system methods in the course of learning to program: `StackOverflowException`, `DivideByZeroException`, `NullPointerException`, and `ArrayOutOfBoundsException` are typical examples. You can also create your own exceptions. The simplest kind is a `RuntimeException` that terminates execution of the program and prints out an error message.

```
throw new RuntimeException("Error message here.");
```

It is good practice to use exceptions when they can be helpful to the user. For example, in `Vector` (PROGRAM 3.3.3), we should throw an exception in `plus()` if the two `Vector`s to be added have different dimensions. To do so, we insert the following statement at the beginning of `plus()`:

```
if (coords.length != b.coords.length)
    throw new RuntimeException("Vector dimensions disagree.");
```

This leads to a more informative error message than the `ArrayOutOfBoundsException` than the client would otherwise receive.

Assertions. An *assertion* is a boolean expression that you are affirming is `true` at that point in the program. If the expression is `false`, the program will terminate and report an error message. Assertions are widely used by programmers to detect bugs and gain confidence in the correctness of programs. They also serve to document the programmer's intent. For example, in `Counter` (PROGRAM 3.3.2), we might check that the counter is never negative by adding the following assertion as the last statement in `increment()`:

```
assert count >= 0;
```

which would identify a negative count. You can also add an optional detail message, such as

```
assert count >= 0 : "Negative count detected in increment()";
```

to help you locate the bug. By default, assertions are disabled, but you can enable them from the command line by using the -enableassertions flag (-ea for short). Assertions are for debugging only: your program should not rely on assertions for normal operation since they may be disabled. When you take a course in systems programming, you will learn to use assertions to ensure that your code *never* terminates in a system error or goes into an infinite loop. One model, known as the *design-by-contract* model of programming, expresses the idea. The designer of a data type expresses a *precondition* (the condition that the client promises to satisfy when calling a method), a *postcondition* (the condition that the implementation promises to achieve when returning from a method), *invariants* (any condition that the implementation promises to satisfy while the method is executing), and *side effects* (any other change in state that the method could cause). During development, these conditions can be tested with assertions. Many programmers use assertions liberally to aid in debugging.

THE LANGUAGE MECHANISMS DISCUSSED THROUGHOUT THIS section illustrate that effective data-type design takes us into deep water in programming-language design. Experts are still debating the best ways to support some of the design ideas that we are discussing. Why does Java not allow functions as arguments? Why does MATLAB not support mutable data types? As mentioned early in CHAPTER 1, it is a slippery slope from complaining about features in a programming language to becoming a programming-language designer. If you do not plan to do so, your best strategy is to use widely available languages. Most systems have extensive libraries that you certainly should use when appropriate, but you often can simplify your client code and protect yourself by building abstractions that can easily transport to other languages. Your main goal is to develop data types so that most of your work is done at a level of abstraction that is appropriate to the problem at hand.

Q. What happens if I try to access a `private` instance variable or method from another file?

A. You get a compile-time error that says the given instance variable or method has private access in the given class.

Q. The instance variables in `Complex` are `private`, but when I am executing the method `times()` for a `Complex` object `a`, I can access object b's instance variables. Shouldn't they be inaccessible?

A. The granularity of private access is at the class level, not the instance level. Declaring an instance variable as private means that it is not directly accessible from any other class. Methods within the `Complex` class can access (read or write) the instance variables of any instance in that class. It might be nice to have a more restrictive access modifier, say, `superprivate`—that would make the granularity at the instance level so that only the invoking object can access its instance variables, but Java does not have such a facility.

Q I see the problem with the `times()` method in `Complex`. It needs a constructor that takes polar coordinates as arguments. How can we add such a constructor?

A. That is a problem since we already have one constructor that takes two real arguments. A better design would be to have two methods `createRect(x, y)` and `createPolar(r, theta)` in the API that create and return new objects. This design is better because it would provide the *client* with the capability to switch to polar coordinates. This example demonstrates that it is a good idea to think about more than one implementation when developing a data type.

Q. Is there a relationship between the `Vector` in this section and the `Vector` class in the Java library?

A. No. We use the name because the term *vector* properly belongs to linear algebra and vector calculus.

Q. What is a deprecated method?

A. A method that is no longer fully supported, but kept in an API to maintain

compatibility. For example, Java once included a method Character.isSpace(), and programmers wrote programs that relied on using that method's behavior. When the designers of Java later wanted to support additional Unicode whitespace characters, they could not change the behavior of isSpace() without breaking client programs. So, instead, they added a new method Character.isWhiteSpace() and *deprecated* the old method. As time wears on, this practice certainly complicates APIs.

Q. I am interested in the methods that all objects inherit from Object. We have been using toString() and the use of hashCode() in Document is interesting, but what about equals()? Isn't it important for me to know how about that?

A. Well, yes, in principle, but you would be very surprised at how difficult it is to properly implement equals(), even for simple objects. For example, the following is an implementation of equals() for Counter:

```
public boolean equals(Object y)
{
    if (y == this) return true;
    if (y == null) return false;
    if (y.getClass() != this.getClass()) return false;
    Counter b = (Counter) y;
    return (count == b.count);
}
```

Exercises

3.3.1 Represent a point in time by using an `int` to store the number of seconds since January 1, 1970. When will programs that use this representation face a time bomb? How should you proceed when that happens?

3.3.2 Create a data type `Location` for dealing with locations on Earth using spherical coordinates (latitude/longitude). Include methods to generate a random location on the surface of the Earth, parse a location "25.344 N, 63.5532 W", and compute the great circle distance between two locations.

3.3.3 Create a data type for a three-dimensional particle with position (r_x, r_y, r_z), mass (m), and velocity (v_x, v_y, v_z). Include a method to return its kinetic energy, which equals $1/2\ m\ (v_x^2 + v_y^2 + v_z^2)$. Use `Vector`.

3.3.4 If you know your physics, develop an alternate implementation for you data type of the previous exercise based on using the *momentum* (p_x, p_y, p_z) as an instance variable.

3.3.5 Develop an implementation of `Histogram` (Program 3.2.3) that uses Counter (Program 3.3.2).

3.3.6 Give an implementation of `minus()` for `Vector` solely in terms of the other `Vector` methods, such as `direction()` and `magnitude()`.

Answer:
```
public Vector minus(Vector b)
{
    return this.plus(b.times(-1.0));
}
```

The advantage of such implementations is that they limit the amount of detailed code to check; the disadvantage is that they can be inefficient. In this case, `plus()` and `times()` both create new `Vector` objects, so copying the code for `plus()` and replacing the minus sign with a plus sign is probably a better implementation.

3.3.7 Implement the method `toString()` for `Vector`.

3.3.8   Add the code necessary to make `Vector` implement `Comparable` (using the value of the magnitude to determine the sort order) and write a test client that takes k and N as command-line arguments, reads N k-dimensional vectors from standard input, sorts them with `Arrays.sort()`, and prints the sorted result on standard output.

3.3.10   Implement a data type `Vector2D` for two-dimensional vectors that has the same API as `Vector`, except that the constructor takes two `double` values as arguments. Use two `double` values (instead of an array) for instance variables.

3.3.11   Implement the `Vector2D` data type of the previous exercise using one `Complex` value as the only instance variable.

3.3.12   Prove that the dot product of two two-dimensional unit-vectors is the cosine of the angle between them.

3.3.13   Implement a data type `Vector3D` for three-dimensional vectors that has the same API as `Vector`, except that the constructor takes three `double` values as arguments. Also, add a *cross product* method: the cross product of two vectors is another vector, defined by the equation

$$\mathbf{a} \times \mathbf{b} = \mathbf{c} \, |\mathbf{a}| \, |\mathbf{b}| \, \sin\theta$$

where $\mathbf{c}$ is the unit normal vector perpendicular to both $\mathbf{a}$ and $\mathbf{b}$, and θ is the angle between $\mathbf{a}$ and $\mathbf{b}$. In Cartesian coordinates, the following equation defines the cross product:

$$(a_0, a_1, a_2) \times (b_0, b_1, b_2) = (a_1 b_2 - a_2 b_1, a_2 b_0 - a_0 b_2, a_0 b_1 - a_1 b_0)$$

The cross product arises in the definition of torque, angular momentum, and vector operator curl. Also, $|\mathbf{a} \times \mathbf{b}|$ is the area of the parallelogram with sides $\mathbf{a}$ and $\mathbf{b}$.

3.3.14   Use assertions and exceptions to develop an implementation of `Rational` (see EXERCISE 3.2.7) that is immune to overflow.

3.3.15   Add code to `Counter` to throw a `RuntimeException` if the client tries to construct a `Counter` object using a negative value for `max`.

Data-type Design Exercises

This list of exercises is intended to give you experience in developing data types. For each problem, design one or more APIs with API implementations, testing your design decisions by implementing typical client code. Some of the exercises require either knowledge of a particular domain or a search for information about it on the web.

3.3.16 *Statistics.* Develop a data type for maintaining statistics of a set of `double` values. Provide a method to add data points and methods that return the number of points, the mean, the standard deviation, and the variance. Develop two implementations: one whose instance values are the number of points, the sum of the values, and the sum of the squares of the values, and another that keeps an array containing all the points. For simplicity, you may take the maximum number of points in the constructor. Your first implementation is likely to be faster and use substantially less space, but is also likely to be susceptible to roundoff error. See the booksite for a well-engineered alternative.

3.3.17 *Genome.* Develop a data type to store the genome of an organism. Biologists often abstract the genome to a sequence of nucleotides (A, C, G, or T). The data type should support the methods `addCodon(char c)` and `nucleotideAt(int i)`, as well as `findGene()` (see PROGRAM 3.1.8). Develop three implementations. First, use one instance variable of type `String`, implementing `addCodon()` with string concatenation. Each method call takes time proportional to the size of the current genome. Second, use an array of characters, doubling the size of the array each time it fills up. Third, use a `boolean` array, using two bits to encode each codon.

3.3.18 *Time.* Develop a data type for the time of day. Provide client methods that return the current hour, minute, and second, as well as `toString()` and `compareTo()` methods. Develop two implementations: one that keeps the time as a single `int` value (number of seconds since midnight) and another that keeps three `int` values, one each for seconds, minutes, and hours.

3.3.19 *Vector fields.* Develop a data type for force vectors in two dimensions. Provide a constructor, a method to add two vectors, and an interesting test client.

3.3.20 *VIN number.* Develop a data type for VIN numbers that can report back all relevant information.

3.3.21 *Generating random numbers.* Develop a data type for random numbers. (Convert StdRandom to a data type). Instead of using Math.random(), base your data type on a linear congruential random number generator. This method traces to the earliest days of computing and is also a quintessential example of the value of maintaining state in a computation (implementing a data type). To generate random int values, maintain an int value x (the value of the last "random" number returned). Each time the client asks for a new value, return a*x + b for suitably chosen values of a and b (ignoring overflow). Use arithmetic to convert these values to "random" values of other types of data. As suggested by D. E. Knuth, use the values 3141592621 for a and 2718281829 for b, or check the booksite for other suggestions. Provide a constructor allowing the client to start with an int value known as a seed (the initial value of x). This ability makes it clear that the numbers are not at all random (even though they may have many of the properties of random numbers) but that fact can be used to aid in debugging, since clients can arrange to see the same numbers each time.

Creative Exercises

3.3.22 *Encapsulation.* Is the following class immutable?

```java
import java.util.Date;
public class Appointment
{
    private Date date;
    private String contact;

    public Appointment(Date date)
    {
        // Code to check for a conflict.
        this.date = date;
        this.contact = contact;
    }
    public Date getDate()
    {  return date;  }
}
```

Answer: No. Java's Date class is mutable. The method setDate(seconds) changes the value of the invoking date to the number of milliseconds since January 1, 1970, 00:00:00 GMT. This has the unfortunate consequence that when a client gets a date with d = getDate(), the client program can then invoke d.setDate() and change the date in an Appointment object type, perhaps creating a conflict. In a data type, we cannot let references to mutable objects escape because the caller can then modify its state. One solution is to create a defensive copy of the Date before returning it using new Date(date.getTime()); and a defensive copy when storing it via this.date = new Date(date.getTime()). Many programmers regard the mutability of Date as a Java design flaw. (GregorianCalendar is a more modern Java library for storing dates, but it is mutable, too.)

3.3.23 *Date.* Develop an implementation of Java's Date API that is immutable and therefore corrects the defects of the previous exercise.

3.3.24 *Calendar.* Develop Appointment and Calendar APIs that can be used to keep track of appointments (by day) in a calendar year. Your goal is to enable clients to schedule appointments that do not conflict and to report current appointments to clients.

3.3.25 *Vector field.* A vector field associates a vector with every point in a Euclidean space. Write a version of `Potential` (PROGRAM 3.1.7) that takes as input a grid size N, computes the `Vector` value of the potential due to the point charges at each point in an N-by-N grid of equally spaced points, and draws the unit vector in the direction of the accumulated field at each point. (Modify `Charge` to return a `Vector`.)

3.3.26 *Genome profiling.* Write a function `hash()` that takes as argument a k-gram (string of length k) whose characters are all A, C, G, or T and returns an `int` value between 0 and 4^k that corresponds to treating the string as base-4 numbers with {A, C, G, T} replaced by {0, 1, 2, 3}, respectively, as suggested by the table in the text. Next, write a function `unhash()` that reverses the transformation. Use your methods to create a class `Genome` that is like `Document`, but is based on exact counting of k-grams in genomes. Finally, write a version of `CompareAll` for `Genome` objects and use it to look for similarities among the set of genome files on the booksite.

3.3.27 *Profiling.* Pick an interesting set of documents from the booksite (or use a collection of your own) and run `CompareAll` with various values of the two parameters, to learn about their effect on the computation.

3.3.28 *Multimedia search.* Develop profiling strategies for sound and pictures, and use them to discover interesting similarities among songs in the music library and photos in the photo album on your computer.

3.3.29 *Data mining.* Write a recursive program that surfs the web, starting at a page given as the first command-line argument, looking for pages that are similar to the page given as the second command-line argument, as follows: to process a name, open an input stream, do a `readAll()`, profile it, and print the name if its distance to the target page is greater than the threshold value given as the third command-line argument. Then scan the page for all strings that contain the substring `http://` and (recursively) process pages with those names. *Note*: This program could read a very large number of pages!

3.4   Case Study: *N*-body Simulation

SEVERAL OF THE EXAMPLES THAT WE considered in CHAPTERS 1 AND 2 are better expressed as object-oriented programs. For example, BouncingBall (PROGRAM 1.5.6) is naturally implemented as a data type whose values are the position and the velocity of the ball and a client that calls instance methods to move and draw the ball. Such a data type enables, for example, clients that can simulate the motion of several balls at once (see EXERCISE 3.4.1). Similarly, our case study for Percolation in

SECTION 2.4 certainly makes an interesting exercise in object-oriented programming, as does our random surfer case study in SECTION 1.6. We leave the former for an exercise (see EXERCISE 3.4.2) and will revisit the latter in SECTION 4.5. In this section, we consider a new example that exemplifies object-oriented programming.

Our task is to write a program that dynamically simulates the motion of *N* bodies under the influence of mutual gravitational attraction. This problem was first formulated by Newton over 350 years ago, and it is still studied intensely today.

What is the set of values, and what are the operations on those values? One reason that this problem is an amusing and compelling example of object-oriented programming is that it presents a direct and natural correspondence between physical objects in the real world and the abstract objects that we use in programming. The shift from solving problems by putting together sequences of statements to be executed to beginning with data type design is a difficult one for many novices. As you gain more experience, you will appreciate the value in this approach to computational problem-solving.

We recall a few basic concepts and equations that you learned in high school physics. Understanding those equations fully is not required to appreciate the code—because of *encapsulation*, these equations are restricted to a few methods, and because of *data abstraction*, most of the code is intuitive and will make sense to you. In a sense, this is the ultimate object-oriented program.

N-body simulation   The bouncing ball simulation of SECTION 1.5 is based on *Newton's first law of motion*: a body in motion remains in motion at the same velocity unless acted on by an outside force. Embellishing that example to include Newton's *second* law of motion (which explains how outside forces affect velocity) leads us to a basic problem that has fascinated scientists for ages. Given a system of N bodies, mutually affected by gravitational forces, the problem is to describe their motion. The same basic model applies to problems ranging in scale from astrophysics to molecular dynamics.

In 1687, Isaac Newton formulated the principles governing the motion of two bodies under the influence of their mutual gravitational attraction, in his famous *Principia*. However, Newton was unable to develop a mathematical description of the motion of *three* bodies. It has since been shown that not only is there no such description in terms of elementary functions, but also that chaotic behavior is possible, depending on initial values. To study such problems, scientists have no recourse but to develop an accurate simulation. In this section, we develop an object-oriented program that implements such a simulation. Scientists are interested in studying such problems at a high degree of accuracy for huge numbers of bodies, so our solution is only an introduction to the subject, but you are likely to be surprised at the ease with which we can develop realistic images depicting the complexity of the motion.

Body data type. In `BouncingBall` (PROGRAM 1.5.6), we keep the displacement from the origin in the `double` values `rx` and `ry` and the velocity in the `double` values `vx` and `vy`, and displace the ball the amount it moves in one time unit with the statements:

```
rx = rx + vx;
ry = ry + vy;
```

With `Vector` (PROGRAM 3.3.3), we can keep the position in the `Vector` value `r` and the velocity in the `Vector` value `v`, and then displace the body the amount it moves in `dt` time units with a single statement:

```
r = r.plus(v.times(dt));
```

In N-body simulation, we have several operations of this kind, so our first design decision is to work with `Vector` values instead of individual component values. This decision

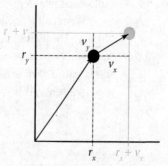

Adding vectors to move a ball

leads to code that is clearer, more compact, and more flexible than the alternative of working with individual components. Body (PROGRAM 3.4.1) is a Java class that uses Vector to implement a data type for moving bodies. The values of the data type are Vector values that carry the body's position and velocity, as well as a double value that carries the mass. The data-type operations allow clients to move and to draw the body (and to compute the force vector due to gravitational attraction of another body), as defined by the following API:

---

public class Body

	Body(Vector r, Vector v, double mass)	
void	move(Vector f, double dt)	*apply force* f, *move body for* dt *seconds*
void	draw()	*draw the ball*
Vector	forceFrom(Body b)	*force vector between this body and* b

API for bodies moving under Newton's laws (see PROGRAM 3.4.1)

Technically, the body's position (displacement from the origin) is not a vector (it is a point in space, not a direction and a magnitude), but it is convenient to represent it as a Vector because Vector's operations lead to compact code for the transformation that we need to move the body, as just discussed. When we move a Body, we need to change not just its position, but also its velocity.

Force and motion. *Newton's second law of motion* says that the force on a body (a vector) is equal to the scalar product of its mass and its acceleration (also a vector): $\mathbf{f} = m\mathbf{a}$. In other words, to compute the acceleration of a body, we compute the

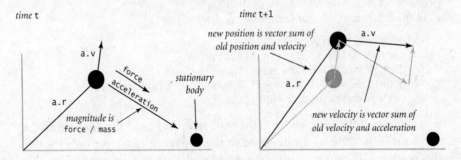

Motion near a stationary body

force, then divide by its mass. In Body, the force is a Vector argument f to move(), so that we can first compute the acceleration vector just by dividing by the mass (a scalar value that is kept as a double value in an instance variable) and then compute the change in velocity by adding to it the amount this vector changes over the time interval (in the same way as we used the velocity to change the position). This law immediately translates to the following code for updating the position and velocity of a body due to a given force vector f and amount of time dt:

```
Vector a = f.times(1/mass);
v = v.plus(a.times(dt));
r = r.plus(v.times(dt));
```

This code appears in the move() instance method in Body, to adjust its values to reflect the consequences of that force being applied for that amount of time: the body moves and its velocity changes. This calculation assumes that the acceleration is constant during the time interval.

Forces among bodies. The computation of the force imposed by one body on another is encapsulated in the instance method forceFrom() in Body, which takes a Body object as argument and returns a Vector. *Newton's law of universal gravitation* is the basis for the calculation: it says that the magnitude of the gravitational force between two bodies is given by the product of their masses divided by the square of the distance between them (scaled by the gravitational constant G, which is 6.67×10^{-11} N m^2 / kg^2) and that the direction of the force is the line between the two particles. This law translates to the following code for computing a.forceFrom(b):

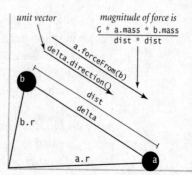

Force from one body to another

```
double G = 6.67e-11;
Vector delta = a.r.minus(b.r);
double dist = delta.magnitude();
double F = (G * a.mass * b.mass) / (dist * dist);
return delta.direction().times(F);
```

The *magnitude* of the force vector is the double value F, and the *direction* of the force vector is the same as the direction of the difference vector between the two body's positions. The force vector is the product of magnitude and direction.

Program 3.4.1 Gravitational body

```
public class Body
{
   private Vector r;
   private Vector v;
   private final double mass;

   public Body(Vector r0, Vector v0, double m0)
   {  r = r0;  v = v0;  mass = m0;  }

   public void move(Vector f, double dt)
   {  // Update position and velocity.
      Vector a = f.times(1/mass);
      v = v.plus(a.times(dt));
      r = r.plus(v.times(dt));
   }

   public Vector forceFrom(Body b)
   {  // Compute force on this body from b.
      Body a = this;
      double G = 6.67e-11;
      Vector delta = a.r.minus(b.r);
      double dist = delta.magnitude();
      double F = (G * a.mass * b.mass)
                           / (dist * dist);
      return delta.direction().times(F);
   }

   public void draw()
   {
       StdDraw.setPenRadius(0.025);
       StdDraw.point(r.cartesian(0), r.cartesian(1));
   }
}
```

r	*position*
v	*velocity*
mass	*mass*

f	*force on this body*
dt	*time increment*
a	*acceleration*

a	*this body*
b	*another body*
G	*gravitational constant*
delta	*vector from b to a*
dist	*distance from b to a*
F	*magnitude of force*

This data type provides the operations that we need to simulate the motion of physical bodies such as planets or atomic particles. It is a mutable type whose instance variables are the position and velocity of the body, which change in the move() *method in response to external forces (the body's mass is not mutable). The* forceFrom() *method returns a force vector.*

Universe data type. `Universe` (PROGRAM 3.4.2) is a data type that implements the following API:

```
public class Universe
─────────────────────────────────────────────
         Universe()
   void  increaseTime(double dt)      simulate the passing of dt seconds
   void  draw()                       draw the universe
```

API for a universe (see PROGRAM 3.4.2)

Its data-type values define a universe (its size, number of bodies, and an array of bodies) and two data-type operations: `increaseTime()`, which adjusts the positions (and velocities) of all of the bodies, and `draw()`, which draws all of the bodies. The key to the N-body simulation is the implementation of `increaseTime()` in `Universe`. The first part of the computation is a double loop that computes the force vector that describes the gravitational force of each body on each other body. It applies the *principle of superposition*, which says that we can add together the force vectors affecting a body to get a single vector representing all the forces. After it has computed all of the forces, it calls the `move()` operation for each body to apply the computed force for a fixed time quantum.

```
% more 2body.txt
2
5.0e10
0.0e00   4.5e10   1.0e04 0.0e00 1.5e30
0.0e00  -4.5e10  -1.0e04 0.0e00 1.5e30
```

```
% more 3body.txt
3
1.25e11
0.0e00   0.0e00 0.05e04 0.0e00 5.97e24
0.0e00   4.5e10  3.0e04 0.0e00 1.989e30
0.0e00  -4.5e10 -3.0e04 0.0e00 1.989e30
```

File format. As usual, we use a data-driven design with input taken from standard input. The constructor reads the universe parameters and body descriptions from a file that contains the following information:
- The radius of the universe
- The number of bodies
- The position, velocity, and mass of each body

As usual, for consistency, all measurements are in standard SI units (recall also that the gravitational constant G appears in our code). With this defined file format, the code for our `Universe` constructor is straightforward.

```
% more 4body.txt
 4  ←── N                        velocity      mass
 5.0e10  ←── radius
-3.5e10 0.0e00 0.0e00  1.4e03   3.0e28
-1.0e10 0.0e00  0.0e00   1.4e04  3.0e28
 1.0e10 0.0e00 0.0e00 -1.4e04   3.0e28
 3.5e10 0.0e00 0.0e00 -1.4e03   3.0e28
        ↑
     position
```

Universe file format examples

```
public Universe()
{
   N = StdIn.readInt();
   radius = StdIn.readDouble();
   StdDraw.setXscale(-radius, +radius);
   StdDraw.setYscale(-radius, +radius);
   orbs = new Body[N];
   for (int i = 0; i < N; i++)
   {
      double rx = StdIn.readDouble();
      double ry = StdIn.readDouble();
      double[] position = { rx, ry };
      double vx = StdIn.readDouble();
      double vy = StdIn.readDouble();
      double[] velocity = { vx, vy };
      double mass = StdIn.readDouble();
      Vector r = new Vector(position);
      Vector v = new Vector(velocity);
      orbs[i] = new Body(r, v, mass);
   }
}
```

Each Body is described by five double values: the *x* and *y* coordinates of its position, the *x* and *y* components of its initial velocity, and its mass.

TO SUMMARIZE, WE HAVE IN THE test client main() in Universe a data-driven program that simulates the motion of *N* bodies mutually attracted by gravity. The constructor creates an array of *N* Body objects, reading each body's initial position, initial velocity, and mass from standard input. The increaseTime() method calculates the mutual force on the bodies and uses that information to update the acceleration, velocity, and position of each body after a time quantum dt. The main() test client invokes the constructor, then stays in a loop calling increaseTime() and draw() to simulate motion.

You will find on the booksite a variety of files that define "universes" of all sorts, and you are encouraged to run Universe and observe their motion. When you view the motion for even a small number of bodies, you will understand why Newton had trouble deriving the equations that define their paths. The images on the chapter openings for CHAPTERS 2, 3, and 4 of this book show the result of running Universe for the 2-body, 3-body, and 4-body examples in the data files shown here. The 2-body example is a mutually orbiting pair, the 3-body example is a cha-

Program 3.4.2 N-body simulation

```java
public class Universe
{
    private final double radius;
    private final int N;
    private final Body[] orbs;

    public Universe()
    { /* See text. */ }

    public void increaseTime(double dt)
    {
        Vector[] f = new Vector[N];
        for (int i = 0; i < N; i++)
            f[i] = new Vector(new double[2]);
        for (int i = 0; i < N; i++)
            for (int j = 0; j < N; j++)
                if (i != j)
                    f[i] = f[i].plus(orbs[i].forceFrom(orbs[j]));
        for (int i = 0; i < N; i++)
            orbs[i].move(f[i], dt);
    }

    public void draw()
    {
        for (int i = 0; i < N; i++)
            orbs[i].draw();
    }

    public static void main(String[] args)
    {
        Universe newton = new Universe();
        double dt = Double.parseDouble(args[0]);
        while (true)
        {
            StdDraw.clear();
            newton.increaseTime(dt);
            newton.draw();
            StdDraw.show(10);
        }
    }
}
```

radius	radius of universe
N	number of bodies
orbs[]	array of bodies

% java Universe 20000 < 3body.txt

880 steps

This data-driven program simulates motion in the universe defined by the standard input stream, increasing time at the rate specified on the command line.

otic situation with a moon jumping between two orbiting planets, and the 4-body example is a relatively simple situation where two pairs of mutually orbiting bodies are slowly rotating. The static images on these pages are made by modifying Universe and Body to draw the bodies in white, and then black on a gray background, as in BouncingBall (PROGRAM 1.5.6): the dynamic images that you get when you run Universe as it stands give a realistic feeling of the bodies orbiting one another, which is difficult to discern in the fixed pictures. When you run Universe on an example with a large number of bodies, you can appreciate why simulation is such an important tool for scientists trying to understand a complex problem. The *N*-body simulation model is remarkably versatile, as you will see if you experiment with some of these files.

planetary scale

```
% more 2body.txt
2
5.0e10
0.0e00   4.5e10   1.0e04 0.0e00 1.5e30
0.0e00  -4.5e10  -1.0e04 0.0e00 1.5e30
```

subatomic scale

```
% more 2bodyTiny.txt
2
5.0e-10
0.0e00   4.5e-10   1.0e-16 0.0e00 1.5e-30
0.0e00  -4.5e-10  -1.0e-16 0.0e00 1.5e-30
```

You will certainly be tempted to design your own universe (see EXERCISE 3.4.7). The biggest challenge in creating a data file is appropriately scaling the numbers so that the radius of the universe, time scale, and the mass and velocity of the bodies lead to interesting behavior. You can study the motion of planets rotating around a sun or subatomic particles interacting with one another, but you will have no luck studying the interaction of a planet with a subatomic particle. When you work with your own data, you are likely to have some bodies that will fly off to infinity and some others that will be sucked into others, but enjoy!

Our purpose in presenting this example is to illustrate the utility of data types, not present simulation code for production use. There are many issues that scientists have to deal with when using this approach to study natural phenomena. The first is *accuracy*: it is common for inaccuracies in the calculations to accumulate to present dramatic effects in the simulation that would not be observed in nature. For example, our code takes no special action when bodies collide. The second is *efficiency*: the move() method in Universe takes time proportional to N^2 and is therefore not usable for huge numbers of bodies. As with genomics, addressing scientific problems related to the *N*-body problem now involves not just knowledge of the original problem domain, but also understanding core issues that computer scientists have been studying since the early days of computation.

For simplicity, we are working with a *two-dimensional* universe, which is realistic only when we are considering bodies in motion on a plane. But an important implication of basing the implementation of Body on Vector is that a client could use *three-dimensional* vectors to simulate the motion of moving balls in three dimensions (actually, any number of dimensions) without changing the code at all! The draw() method projects the position onto the plane defined by the first two dimensions.

The test client in Universe is just one possibility: we can use the same basic model in all sorts of other situations (for example, involving different kinds of interactions among the bodies). One such possibility is to observe and measure the current motion of some existing bodies and then run the simulation backwards! That is one method that astrophysicists use to try to understand the origins of the universe. In science, we try to understand the past and to predict the future; with a good simulation, we can do both.

```
% java Universe 25000 < 4body.txt
```

100 steps

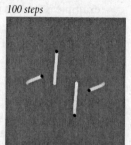

500 steps

1000 steps

3000 steps

Simulating a 4-body universe

Q. The Universe API is certainly small. Why not just implement that code in a main() test client for Body?

A. Well, our design is an expression of what most people believe about the universe: it was created, and then time moves on. It clarifies the code and allows for maximum flexibility in simulating what goes on in the universe.

Q. Why is forceFrom() an instance method? Wouldn't it be better for it to be a static method that takes two Body objects as arguments?

A. Yes, implementing forceFrom() as an instance method is one of several possible alternatives, and having a static method that takes two Body objects as arguments is certainly a reasonable choice. Some programmers prefer to completely avoid static methods in data-type implementations; another option is to maintain the force acting on each Body as an instance variable. Our choice is a compromise between these two.

Exercises

3.4.1   Write an object-oriented version of BouncingBall (PROGRAM 1.5.6). Include a constructor that starts each ball moving a random direction at a random velocity (within reasonable limits) and a test client that takes an integer N from the command line and simulates the motion of N bouncing balls.

3.4.2   Write an object-oriented version of Percolation (PROGRAM 2.4.5). Think carefully about the design before you begin, and be prepared to defend your design decisions.

3.4.3   What happens in a universe where Newton's second law does not apply? This situation would correspond to forceTo() in Body always returning the zero vector.

3.4.4   Create a data type Universe3D to model three-dimensional universes. Develop a data file to simulate the motion of the planets in our solar system around the sun.

3.4.5   Modify Universe so that its constructor takes an In object and a Draw object as arguments. Write a test client that simulates the motion of two different universes (defined by two different files and appearing in two different Draw windows). You also need to modify the draw() method in Body.

3.4.6   Implement a class RandomBody that initializes its instance variables with (carefully chosen) random values instead of using a constructor and a client RandomUniverse that takes a single argument N from the command line and simulates motion in a random universe with N bodies.

Creative Exercise

3.4.7 *New universe.* Design a new universe with interesting properties and simulate its motion with `Universe`. This exercise is truly an opportunity to be creative!

Index

476